Lecture Notes in Computer Science 1107

Edited by G. Goos, J. Hartmanis and J. van Leeuwen

Advisory Board: W. Brauer   D. Gries   J. Stoer

Springer

Berlin
Heidelberg
New York
Barcelona
Budapest
Hong Kong
London
Milan
Paris
Santa Clara
Singapore
Tokyo

Jean-Pierre Briot   Jean-Marc Geib
Akinori Yonezawa (Eds.)

Object-Based
Parallel and Distributed
Computation

France-Japan Workshop, OBPDC '95
Tokyo, Japan, June 21-23, 1995
Selected Papers

 Springer

Series Editors

Gerhard Goos, Karlsruhe University, Germany

Juris Hartmanis, Cornell University, NY, USA

Jan van Leeuwen, Utrecht University, The Netherlands

Volume Editors

Jean-Pierre Briot
LAFORIA, IBP - Case 169, 4 place Jussieu
F-75252 Paris Cedex 05, France

Jean-Marc Geib
LIFL - University of Lille 1, Bat. M3
F-59655 Villeneuve d'Ascq Cedex, France

Akinori Yonezawa
University of Tokyo, Department of Information Science
7-3-1 Hongo, Bunkyo-ku, Tokyo 113, Japan

Cataloging-in-Publication data applied for

Die Deutsche Bibliothek - CIP-Einheitsaufnahme

Object based parallel and distributed computation : France-
Japan workshop ; selected papers / OBPDC '95, Tokyo, Japan,
June 21 - 23, 1995. Jean-Pierre Briot ... (ed.). - Berlin ;
Heidelberg ; New York ; Barcelona ; Budapest ; Hong Kong ;
London ; Milan ; Paris ; Santa Clara ; Singapore ; Tokyo :
Springer, 1996
  (Lecture notes in computer science ; Vol. 1107)
  ISBN 3-540-61487-7
NE: Briot, Jean-Pierre [Hrsg.]; OBPDC <1995, Tōkyō>; GT

CR Subject Classification (1991): F.1.2, D.1.5, D.1.3, D.2, D.4.1-3, C.2.4

ISSN 0302-9743
ISBN 3-540-61487-7 Springer-Verlag Berlin Heidelberg New York

© Springer-Verlag Berlin Heidelberg 1996
Printed in Germany

Typesetting: Camera-ready by author
SPIN 10512449   06/3142 – 5 4 3 2 1 0   Printed on acid-free paper

Preface

It is now well accepted that the notion of object provides good foundations for new challenges of parallel, distributed, and open computing. The notions of objects and message passing help in structuring and encapsulation of software modules. At the same time these notions are flexible enough to match various granularities of software and hardware architectures.

A workshop, named "France-Japan Workshop on Object-Based Parallel and Distributed Computation" (OBPDC'95), was held in Tokyo, June 21-23, 1995. It provided a forum for researchers from conceptual, theoretical, implementational, and applicational backgrounds, to discuss, and compare their respective proposals and experiences, for developing next-generation (object-based) parallel and distributed computing systems.

Contribution of the Book

This volume represents the formal proceedings of this workshop. After the workshop, the participants were requested to submit full papers and a standard review process was taken for the submissions. The 18 selected papers compose a representative and balanced set of timely research contributions to the growing field of object-based parallel and distributed computation. They reflect various aspects, from programming language and operating system design, to application-oriented development, without forgetting the needs for formal foundations for specifying and proving properties of programs. They are organized into groups, according to their subjects:

- Massively parallel programming languages
- Distributed programming languages
- Formalisms
- Distributed operating systems
- Dependable distributed computing
- Software management

Organization of the Workshop

The OBPDC'95 workshop took place for three full days from June 21 to June 23, 1995, in the brand new building of the Maison Franco-Japonaise (Nichi Futsu Kaikan) in Tokyo. The participation was on an invitation basis. As well as providing a forum for discussing common research issues, this meeting was also intended to promote cooperations between French and Japanese research teams.

Twenty-one talks were scheduled during the workshop and over 40 participants attended. Each session, composed of two or three papers, included extensive time devoted for discussions. One conclusive panel was held at the end of the workshop.

We were fortunate to have Pr. Hiroyuki Yoshikawa, President of University of Tokyo, as the key person to formally open the workshop. His speech reminds us of the importance, in parallel to the development of computer technology, of developing a full scientific methodology. The transcript of his talk is included in the annex of this preface.

The organizers of the workshop were: Jean-Pierre Briot (University of Tokyo & CNRS) as the general coordinator, Jean-Marc Geib (LIFL-CNRS, University of Lille), François-Xavier Testard-Vaillant (Sc. & Tech. Dept., French Embassy in Japan), and Akinori Yonezawa (University of Tokyo).

This workshop was primarily sponsored by the Science and Technology Department of the French Embassy in Japan. Additional support was also provided by the Engineering Sciences (Sciences pour l'Ingénieur) Department of the Centre National de la Recherche Scientifique (CNRS), and by Yonezawa's Research Group, Department of Information Science, University of Tokyo.

Acknowledgements

We would like to express our appreciation to François-Xavier Testard-Vaillant, Science and Technology Attaché of the French Embassy in Japan, for his invaluable contribution in organizing the workshop. We would also like to thank: Jean-François Stuyck-Taillandier, Counselor for Science and Technology of the French Embassy in Japan, and Jean-Jacques Gagnepain, Director of the Engineering Sciences Department of CNRS, for their support, Olivier Ansart, Director of the Maison Franco-Japonaise in Tokyo, for welcoming the workshop in the impressive new settings of the institution, and Hiroyuki Yoshikawa, President of University of Tokyo, for giving us a nice and challenging opening address.

Last but not the least, we would like to thank the authors of the included papers for their invaluable contributions to the book and for their cooperation during the editing process.

Jean-Pierre Briot

Paris and Tokyo, April 1996 Jean-Marc Geib

Akinori Yonezawa

Opening Address

Hiroyuki Yoshikawa, President
The University of Tokyo
7-3-1 Hongo, Bunkyo-ku, Tokyo 113, Japan

Ladies and gentlemen, distinguished guests! On behalf of the University of Tokyo, I should like to take the oportunity of the opening of a new Maison Franco-Japonaise to praise the successful organization of the Workshop on Object-Based Parallel and Distributed Computation. I am very impressed by the design of this building, built to strengthen the linkage between France and Japan. The participants of this workshop are fortunate to be able to work here.

I am not an expert in the field to be discussed at this workshop: computer programming languages, parallel computation, etc. However, I know that the research subjects you deal with are complex.

It is my impression that every scientific field has its own degree of maturity. If we consider physics, this may have been started by Sir Isaac Newton almost 300 years ago. The method of research was established back in the 17th century, i.e., defining the object of research first, then establishing some axioms or laws, and then deriving various theorems by deduction. By proving the appropriateness of these theorems through experiments, the whole system of the theory is verified. This method can be traced back to Hellenism.

By utilizing this method, physics, chemistry, and other natural sciences have become well developed, and we now understand so many things, such as properties of matter, even of elementary particles and biological entities. Moreover, we have started to understand the history of the universe.

However, if we consider information science, no such universal method of research has been established. Let us take language, for example. Language exists in this world without doubt. However, it is difficult to establish a few fundamental axioms of a language that can derive several theorems of language, including spoken language. Human beings can make correct sentences without any difficulty, but a set of axioms cannot. Even if it is possible to establish some axioms, it is almost impossible to verify them by experiments.

On the other hand, we may be able to create an artificial language system. Is it easy to fabricate a new artificial atom? The answer is no. This means that the object of research in information science is much more liberated from the existing real world, than is the case in physical science.

I feel strongly that it is necessary to develop a more productive method for research in information science. If we fail to develop one, some imbalances in the speed of development between physical science and information science will occur and that will cause some problems in our society. These might be: a gap between physical technology and information technology; insufficient skill of utilization of physical entities; the generation of useless wastes; etc.

I know that the distinguished participants of this workshop are friends and share research methodologies, perhaps implicitly. I hope that you will have a chance to discuss your shared research methodologies explicitly and spread your ideas throughout the community to stimulate other research areas that suffer from a lack of research methodology. It can be said that the common problem of the various research fields of information science, at present, is this: the shortage of explicit research methodology.

The expected product of this workshop is, of course, anything but such methodology. However, I would like to ask you (from my heart) to consider the methodology as a by-product in order to raise the level of information science in general. Thank you.

Table of Contents

Massively Parallel Programming Languages

Data Parallel Programming in the Parallel Object-Oriented
Language OCore 1
Hiroki Konaka, Takashi Tomokiyo, Munenori Maeda,
Yutaka Ishikawa, and Atsushi Hori

Polymorphic Matrices in Paladin 18
Frédéric Guidec and Jean-Marc Jézéquel

Programming and Debugging for Massive Parallelism: The
Case for a Parallel Object-Oriented Language A-NETL 38
Takanobu Baba, Tsutomu Yoshinaga, and Takahiro Furuta

Schematic: A Concurrent Object-Oriented Extension to
Scheme 59
Kenjiro Taura and Akinori Yonezawa

Distributed Programming Languages

(Thread and Object)-Oriented Distributed Programming 83
Jean-Marc Geib, Christophe Gransart, Chrystel Grenot, and
Philippe Merle

Distributed and Object Oriented Symbolic Programming in
April 104
Keith L. Clark and Frank G. McCabe

Reactive Programming in Eiffel// 125
Denis Caromel and Yves Roudier

Formalisms

Proofs, Concurrent Objects, and Computations in a FILL
Framework 148
Didier Galmiche and Eric Boudinet

Modular Description and Verification of Concurrent
Objects 168
Jean-Paul Bahsoun, Stephan Merz, and Corinne Servières

Distributed Operating Systems

CHORUS/COOL: CHORUS Object Oriented Technology 187
Christian Jacquemot, Peter Strarup Jensen, and Stéphane Carrez

Adaptive Operating System Design using Reflection 205
Rodger Lea, Yasuhiko Yokote, and Jun-ichiro Itoh

Isatis: A Customizable Distributed Object-Based Runtime
System 219
*Michel Banâtre, Yasmina Belhamissi, Valérie Issarny,
Isabelle Puaut, and Jean-Paul Routeau*

Dependable Distributed Computing

Lessons from Designing and Implementing GARF 238
Rachid Guerraoui, Benoît Garbinato, and Karim Mazouni

Design and Implementation of DROL Runtime
Environment on Real-Time Mach Kernel 257
Kazunori Takashio, Hidehisa Shitomi, and Mario Tokoro

ActNet: The Actor Model Applied to Mobile Robotic
Environments 273
Philippe Darche, Pierre-Guillaume Raverdy, and Eric Commelin

Software Management

Component-Based Programming and Application
Management with Olan 290
Luc Bellissard, Slim Ben Atallah, Alain Kerbrat, and Michel Riveill

The Version Management Architecture of an Object-
Oriented Distributed Systems Environment: OZ++ 310
*Michiharu Tsukamoto, Yoichi Hamazaki, Toshihiro Nishioka, and
Hideyuki Otokawa*

Formal Semantics of Agent Evolution in Language Flage 329
*Yasuyuki Tahara, Fumihiro Kumeno, Akihiko Ohsuga, and
Shinichi Honiden*

Author Index 349

Data Parallel Programming in the Parallel Object-Oriented Language *OCore*

Hiroki Konaka, Takashi Tomokiyo,
Munenori Maeda, Yutaka Ishikawa, Atsushi Hori

Real World Computing Partnership,
1-6-1 Takezono, Tsukuba, Ibaraki 305, JAPAN

Abstract. The parallel object-oriented language *OCore* is designed to generate efficient code especially for multi computers. To support massively parallel computation models, advanced communication models, and optimization techniques, *OCore* introduces the notion of *communities*, a *meta-level architecture*, and a *distributed garbage collection mechanism* on top of a fundamental concurrent object-oriented layer.
A community structures a set of objects and provides an abstraction of parallelism. Communities support data parallel computation as well as multi-access data.
In this paper we show data parallel programming in *OCore*. After giving an overview of *OCore*, we will introduce the notion of communities. Then we will present a molecular dynamics simulation program and a wave equation solver as examples of data parallel programming using communities.

1 Introduction

Although recent advances in VLSI technology have made a variety of multi computers available, it is often difficult to use them to their full advantage because of the insufficient descriptive power of existing parallel programming languages. More parallelism and communication latency increase the complexity of writing efficient parallel programs for such machines.

We propose a parallel programming language *OCore*, especially for multi computers[5]. *OCore* is designed to reduce such complexity and provide programmers with a research vehicle for massively parallel computation models, advanced communication models, and optimization techniques. For these purposes, *OCore* introduces the notion of *communities*, a *meta-level architecture*, and a *distributed garbage collection mechanism* on top of a fundamental concurrent object-oriented layer. A prototype language processing system for the Intel Paragon XP/S[2], the Thinking Machines Corp. CM-5[13] and Sun SPARC stations is currently available[6].

A community structures a set of objects and provides an abstraction of parallelism. Communities can be used for data parallel computations as well as multi-access data. In this paper we will show how to write data parallel programs in *OCore* using communities.

In Sect. 2, after giving an overview of *OCore* and a brief description of its concurrent object-oriented foundation, we introduce the notion of *communities*. Sect. 3 describes programming with communities. We present a molecular dynamics simulation program and a wave equation solver as examples of data parallel programming using communities. After discussing some related work in Sect. 4, we conclude in Sect. 5.

2   *OCore*

2.1   Overview of *OCore*

OCore provides the notion of *communities*, a *meta-level architecture*, and a *distributed garbage collection mechanism*, on top of a fundamental concurrent object-oriented layer, to make it easier to program efficient parallel applications for multi computers.

OCore adopts static typing to make programs more efficient and easier to debug.

In the concurrent object-oriented layer, objects perform a range of operations including message passing. Message passing is either synchronous or asynchronous. Messages are handled sequentially in an object. Since there is no intra-object concurrency, no extra concurrency control within an object is needed. Synchronizing structures[9][11] are supported to enable flexible communication and synchronization.

Communities have been introduced to reduce complexity in writing parallel applications. They are explained in Sect. 2.3.

A meta-level architecture has been introduced to separate algorithmic descriptions from others, such as the descriptions for optimization, resource management, exception handling, and profiling. From an application programmer's point of view, *OCore*'s meta-level architecture is carefully designed so as not to degrade performance or the soundness of statically typed semantics. See [14] for details about the meta-level architecture.

OCore will also provide a garbage collection mechanism to assist modular and reliable programming. For multi computers, we propose a distributed garbage collection algorithm, called the *Gleaner* algorithm[8], which is designed to be efficient, scalable, and incremental.

2.2   Objects

The processing of an object is done either at the base-level or at the meta-level. Messages sent to an object are handled at the base-level.

Class. The behavior of an object is described in a class. A class defines slots, methods, broadcast handlers, local functions, and other meta-level definitions. Broadcast handlers are explained in Sect. 2.3.

Fig. 1 shows simple examples of classes.

```
1 (class Counter
2   (vars (Int count :init 0))
3   (methods
4     ([:add (Int x)] (replies Int)
5       (let ()
6         (set count (+ count x))
7         (reply count)))
8     ([:show] (printf "%d\n" count))
9   ))
10
11 (class Foo
12   (vars (Counter counter :init (new Counter)))
13   (methods
14     ([:foo] (replies Int)
15       (let ((Int val))
16         (set val (send counter [:add 3]))
17         (send counter [:show])
18         (send counter [:add 5] :with-cont)))
19   ))
```

Fig. 1. Simple class examples

The syntax of *OCore* is based upon S-expressions. Some of the control structures are borrowed from Common Lisp (such as **if**, **cond** and **let**).

Class **Counter** has one slot and two methods. The slot **count** is of integer type and is initialized to 0. Each method definition consists of a message pattern enclosed in [ ], a reply type declaration (**replies**) if applicable, and a body expression. A method is synchronous if it has the **replies** declaration, otherwise it is asynchronous. Lines 4 to 7 define a synchronous method that replies with an integer. The operator **reply** performs the reply and completes method processing. Line 8 defines an asynchronous method that does not perform reply.

Classes can be defined using single inheritance and/or parametric types. These improve the reusability of definitions.

Creation of Objects. The operator **new** is used to create an object. The slot **counter** of an object of class **Foo** is initialized with an object of class **Counter** in line 12. Objects can be created remotely with an optional meta-level argument, as follows:

```
(new Counter :on 7)
```

Message Passing. The operator **send** sends a message, enclosed in [ ], to a given object. Message passing is done either synchronously or asynchronously according to the corresponding method. In line 16, a message is sent synchronously and execution is suspended until a reply is received, which will then be the value of the send expression. That is, the invocation of a synchronous method is associated with a continuation. In line 17, however, a message is sent asynchronously, and method processing is continued.

The operator send can be used with the optional meta-argument :with-cont only in a synchronous method as in line 18. In that case it sends a synchronous message with the current continuation of the method to complete method processing. The reply to the message goes directly to the continuation.

2.3 Communities

A community structures a set of objects in a multi-dimensional space. Each member object in a community can handle messages independently. They support multi-access data abstractions as well as data parallel computations.

The implementation of a community depends heavily on whether the set of member objects varies dynamically. Therefore we have two kinds of communities: *static communities* and *dynamic communities*. They have different usage restrictions, which will be discussed later.

Fig. 2 shows the images and descriptions of some operations common to both kinds of communities. They will be explained later.

The behavior of a community is specified by the classes of its member objects and by what we call a *community template*.

Community Templates. A community template defines the logical space of a community and the mapping of the logical space to real processors. The base-level descriptions of a community template include a member class, the dimensions of the logical space where member objects are structured, whether the community is static (this is the default) or dynamic, and what we call *community procedures*. Community procedures are used mainly to describe the logical space of a community. Mapping from the logical space to the processor space can be specified at the meta-level; otherwise default mapping is used.

Community templates can also be defined parametrically. Therefore programmers often need not program templates themselves, but can draw on library templates. Fig. 3 shows the parametric definition of the static community template Comm2D together with its use. (P) in line 1 declares that P is used as a type parameter in the definition. Line 2 declares P as the member class and that the template is for static communities that structure member objects of class P into a two-dimensional space. For dynamic communities, line 3 would be used instead. The template also defines some community procedures that calculate indices according to the logical structure of the community. { } forms a tuple of types or data.

Parametric definitions must be substantiated to be practical. The community template CounterComm with NewCounter as the member class is obtained from Comm2D in line 14.

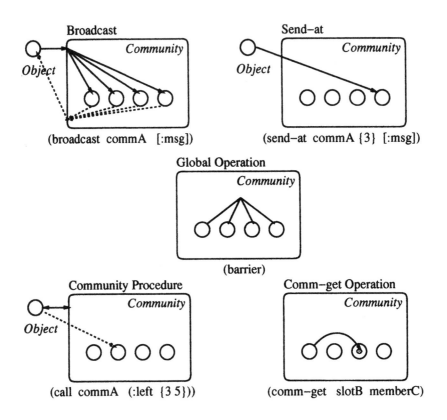

Fig. 2. Operation images related to communities

```
1 (parametric-community Comm2D (P)
2   (consists-of P 2)
3 ;; (consists-of P 2 :dynamic)
4   (procedures
5     (:right (({Int Int} coords)) (returns {Int Int})
6       (let ((Int x y))
7         (set {x y} coords)
8         (set x (mod (+ x 1) (size-of-dim 0)))
9         (return {x y})))
10    (:left (({Int Int} coords)) (returns {Int Int})
11         ...)
12    ...))
13
14 (substantiated-community CounterComm (Comm2D NewCounter))
```

Fig. 3. Definition of a community template

Creation of Communities. The operator new is also used for creating a community instance. The following expression creates a community instance, using the community template CounterComm with a logical space of 50 × 70.

(new CounterComm {50 70})

In the case of a dynamic community, the logical space is created first and only, then may members be added to or removed from the dynamic community.

On the other hand, in the case of a static community, member objects are also created and aligned to the logical space. Member objects cannot be added to or removed from a static community.

Reorganization of Dynamic Communities. To add an object to a dynamic community, the following operators are supported:

(add-member *community object*)
(put-member *community tuple-of-indices object*)

add-member adds an existing object to a community. The object is given unoccupied indices in the logical subspace mapped to the current processor, if possible. With an optional meta-level argument, an object can be put in another logical subspace, which is mapped remotely:

(add-member commA objB :on 7)

put-member puts an existing object in a community at its given indices, if those indices are unoccupied. Note that add-member and put-member do not involve object migration.

For removing member objects from a dynamic community, the following operators are supported.

(remove-member *community tuple-of-indices*)
(remove-any-member *community*)
(remove-all-members *community*)

Member objects are not actually added to or removed from a community until the following operation is invoked.

(reorganize *community*)

This determines a globally consistent set of member objects on which community operations are guaranteed to be performed correctly. Community operations during reorganization cause runtime errors in a dynamic community.

Operations to Communities. Any object that knows a community, whether it is a member of the community or not, can:

1. broadcast a message to all members in the community,
     (broadcast *community message*)

2. send a message to a member object having given indices in the community,

 (send-at *community tuple-of-indices message*)

3. and call a community procedure.

 (call *community* (*procedure argument...*))

The broadcast operation supports data parallel computation, while the send-at operation supports multi-access data. Community procedures make it easy to describe communication according to the logical structure of the community.

Member Object Operations. Each member object may use the pseudo variables comm, indices and dimension to obtain the name of the community instance to which it belongs, the tuple of its indices, and the community dimension, respectively. The size of a community of a given dimension and the name of some other member object with given indices are obtained using the following operators:

 (size-of-dim *dimension*)
 (member *tuple-of-indices*)

These operators are also available in community template definitions.

The following operators perform barrier synchronization or reduction for all members in a community:

 (barrier)
 (reduce (*function expression*))

Any user-defined associative functions as well as built-in associative operators, such as addition, can be used for reduction. Fuzzy global operations are also available. These global operations are realized by local processing on each node and by inter-node communication. Inter-node communication patterns for global operations are set up at creation time in static communities, and during the reorganize operation in dynamic communities. These operations support data parallel computations.

The comm-get operation obtains the value of the slot of another member object in the same community.

 (comm-get *slot-name member-object*)

Broadcast Handlers. After being delivered to each node, a broadcast message is shared among the member objects of a community on each node. It is then handled by a *broadcast handler* rather than by a method at each member object. The broadcasting is also either synchronous or asynchronous depending on whether the corresponding broadcast handler has the replies declaration.

The main difference between a broadcast handler and a method appears in synchronous communication. In synchronous message broadcasting, after synchronizing at the reply operation for all members, one arbitrary member replies to the broadcast message on behalf of all members. Members can also perform reduction and return the result using the following operator:

(reply-reduce (*function expression*))

Restrictions on Communities. Since the two kinds of communities are implemented differently, they have different usage restrictions. Static communities are efficiently implemented assuming the following restrictions:

S1 The set of member objects in a static community is created and fixed at community creation.

S2 The member objects must be *of the same class*.

S3 One or more member objects must reside on each node.

S4 The set of member objects must be mapped one-to-one *onto* the logical space of the community.

S5 A member object cannot belong to multiple communities simultaneously.

S1 leads to inflexibility but simplifies the organization of static communities. The operator **new** creates and initializes not only the logical space but also the member objects in a distributed manner.

To efficiently implement **member** and **send-at** operations, it is desirable that the global address of each member object is obtained without using remote operations. To realize this, member objects with the same local index in a static community are allocated at the same local address on each node. This requires S2 as well as global memory management.

Assuming S3 makes it easy to prepare inter-node communication patterns for global operations. S4 means that the number of member objects is equal to the size of the logical space, which must be larger than that of the processing nodes according to S3. S5 is a natural consequence of S1.

On the other hand, restrictions on using a dynamic community are as follows:

D1 The member objects in a dynamic community must be *of a class or a subclass thereof*.

D2 The set of member objects must be mapped one-to-one *to* the logical space of the community.

D3 Each member object cannot belong to multiple communities simultaneously.

There are no restrictions corresponding to S1 and S3. S4 is relaxed to D2, which means that the number of member objects must be less than or equal to the size of the logical space. Thus dynamic communities can be used for dynamic and/or sparse collections of objects. However, since we cannot assume S3, inter-node communication patterns for global operations must be reconstructed according to the distribution of member objects during **reorganize** operations.

Unlike in a static community, member objects are created first, then added to a dynamic community. Therefore member objects in a dynamic community are managed by a distributed table of global pointers. This requires **member** and **send-at** operations to access the table, which may involve remote memory access; however, S2 is relaxed to D1. Thus dynamic communities can be used for heterogeneous groups as well. A simple example of a heterogeneous group is shown in Sect. 3.2. However D3, same as S5, remains.

Table 1. Basic operation times

Operation	Time (μs)
Switch Context	4.2
Create Local Object	11.5
Create Remote Object	154.7
Asynchronous Send to Local *dormant* Object	5.2
Asynchronous Send to Local *running* Object	2.1
Asynchronous Send to Remote Object	49.0
Synchronous Send to Local Object	12.7
Synchronous Send to Remote Object	156.3
Community Procedure Call	1.3
Local comm-get	0.2
Remote comm-get	142.0

2.4 Performance on the Paragon XP/S

A prototype language processing system for the Intel Paragon XP/S[2], the
Thinking Machines Corp. CM-5[13] and Sun SPARC stations is available[6].
However, part of the meta-level architecture as well as garbage collection have
not yet been implemented.

Here we show the performance of the prototype system measured on a Paragon
XP/S running the operating system OSF/1 R1.2. Table 1 shows some basic operation times.

For community operations, we used three isomorphic communities of 2048
member objects to see performance difference: a static community **SC**, a dynamic community **LDC** where each member object is mapped to the logical
subspace of the same node, and a dynamic community **RDC** where each member object is mapped to the logical subspace of the adjacent node.

Fig. 4 shows times for organizing and reorganizing communities. Organizing a dynamic community consists of community creation, creating and adding
member objects in a distributed way, and the **reorganize** operation. In **LDC**,
reorganizing time is dominated by the time required to hierarchically recon-
struct inter-node communication patterns for global operations, which increases
almost logarithmically to the number of nodes. During the **reorganize** operation
in **RDC**, remotely mapped members are registered on the node they exist, to
avoid the extra overhead to forward messages during the **broadcast** operation.
The communication overhead for registration at each node is inversely propor-
tional to the number of nodes, and dominates reorganization time in **RDC**.

Fig. 5 shows times for synchronous broadcasting and global operations. It
shows that isomorphic static and dynamic communities, even **RDC**, differ little
in the performance of broadcast and global operations. However, these would
take longer in the case of unequally distributed dynamic communities.

As mentioned in the previous section, **send-at** and **member** operations may
require additional overhead due to remote memory access in dynamic communities.

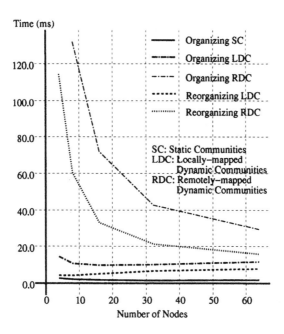

Fig. 4. Times for organizing and reorganizing communities

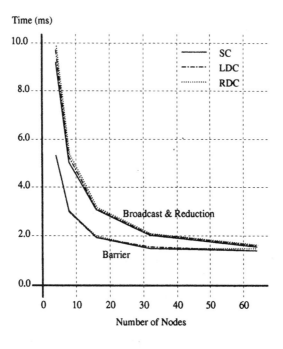

Fig. 5. Times for broadcast and global operations

3   Community Programming

3.1   Communication using Communities

A community may be used as a communication medium where each member object is used to pool data. Objects may access member objects according to their status and other conditions; some objects put data into a member object while others take data out. Data are exchanged between objects accessing the same member object, thus realizing a kind of group communication where grouping may be changed dynamically.

Each member object may propagate data according to the logical structure of the community, or pre-process data using the results of global or local operations. For example, when a community models a physical field, data propagation may simulate physical transmission. For a search problem a community can be used to pool sub-problems. Each member may prune some of the sub-problems according to the globally best value acquired so far, which may be propagated through a broadcast operation, and convey others to assure load balancing. See [7] for details about abstract, distributed, and hierarchical communication models using multi-access communities.

3.2   Data Parallel Programming

We can distribute data to a community and broadcast a message to start data parallel computation. Member objects perform global operations when necessary. Data can be exchanged between member objects by message passing or the comm-get operation.

OCore enables a data parallel computation to be encapsulated in a community. Multiple data parallel computations can run in parallel using multiple communities. A dynamic community allows the size of data to vary at runtime. It also allows member objects to be heterogeneous. These features support data parallel programming in a more structured and flexible manner.

In the following sections, we show two data parallel programming examples. One is a molecular dynamics simulation, which is suitable for static communities. The other is a wave equation solver, which is a simple example of heterogeneous computing.

Molecular dynamics simulation. The molecular dynamics simulation program *Water* was originally in the SPLASH benchmark[12]. It calculates forces and potentials in a system of liquid water molecules in a cubical box with periodic boundary conditions, using Gear's predictor-corrector method. After initialization, it repeatedly i) predicts atomic variable values, ii) calculates intramolecular forces, iii) calculates inter-molecular forces, iv) calculates corrected atomic variable values, v) considers boundary conditions, and vi) calculates the kinetic energy of the system. A spherical cutoff range is used to avoid computing all molecule interactions.

The original program was written using a shared-memory model. In *OCore*, however, a system of water molecules is represented naturally by a static community (Water) of water molecule objects (Mol). Fig. 6 shows the main part of the program in *OCore*.

```
1 (let ((Water water)
2       (Int i)
3       (Double ke))
4   (set water (new Water {NMOL}))
5   (broadcast water [:initial])                      ;; initialize
6   (dotimes (i NSTEP)
7     (broadcast water [:predic-intraf])              ;; i), ii)
8     (broadcast water [:interf FORCES])              ;; iii)
9     (qread done)
10    (set ke (broadcast water [:correc-bndry-kineti])) ;; iv) v) vi)
11  ))
```

Fig. 6. Main part of the Water program

The synchronous broadcast handlers of Mol do the following tasks. :initial does initialization, :predic-intraf does i) and ii), and :correc-bndry-kineti does iv) to vi). These are handled independently in each molecule object.

On the other hand, calculation iii), invoked by the broadcast handler :interf, requires the exchange of molecule data. Since only one of two molecules needs to calculate the force between them, each molecule calculates inter-molecular forces for almost half of the others by obtaining the status of another object, calculating the force, and reporting the result.

Such information exchange in a community can be realized by either (a) reading the slot of another member by using the comm-get operation, (b) sending its status to each partner object, or (c) broadcasting its status to all the molecules, whether it is necessary or not.

(a) leads to a naive program where messages for the comm-get operation on a remote partner go back and forth. And besides, current *OCore* implementation does not allow multiple data to be read in one comm-get operation, so a relatively large number of messages are required.

(b) requires fewer messages but a more complex flow of control than (a). Each molecule object sends its status to almost half of the molecules.

In (c), almost half of the molecules handle a broadcast message in vain. However, even fewer messages are required than in (b), since a broadcast message is shared among the member objects of a community on each node.

Termination detection of iii) is not trivial. Simply performing barrier synchronization at the end of :interf may cause deadlock because, for example, some synchronous messages for reporting may arrive at already suspended ob-

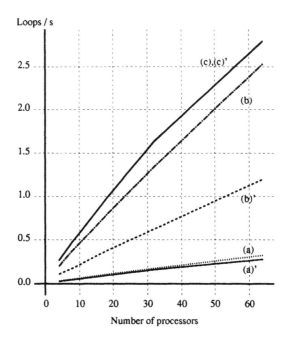

Fig. 7. Performance of the Water programs on a Paragon XP/S

jects. In the above programs, all broadcast handlers and methods used in iii) are defined as asynchronous. Each molecule performs barrier synchronization after handling a predetermined number of messages, and then a representative molecule uses a synchronizing structure to report the termination. Line 9 waits for the termination by reading the synchronizing structure.

Although static communities are adequate, we have also made corresponding programs (a)' to (c)' that use isomorphic dynamic communities similar to **LDC** in Sect. 2.4, to see the performance difference between the two kinds of communities.

Performance of each program for 343 water molecules was also measured on the Paragon XP/S. Fig. 7 gives the numbers of iterations executed per second, for varying numbers of nodes. It reveals that (a) is not so efficient. However, we implemented a tentative mechanism for caching comm-get data, which improved performance. (b) and (c) show good performance but both require a large message buffer. The performance difference between a program using static communities and its correspondent is rather small except between (b) and (b)' where **send-at** operations are used.

Wave equation solver. Dynamic communities can be used for collections of heterogeneous objects. We take a wave equation solver as a simple example of such heterogeneous computing. It solves the two-dimensional wave equation on the domain $0 \leq x \leq L, 0 \leq y \leq L$:

$$\frac{\partial^2 \psi}{\partial t^2} = c^2 \left(\frac{\partial^2 \psi}{\partial x^2} + \frac{\partial^2 \psi}{\partial y^2} \right)$$

with fixed edges and a given initial form of $\psi = \psi(x, y, t)$:

$$\psi(0, y, t) = \psi(L, y, t) = \psi(x, 0, t) = \psi(x, L, t) = 0$$

$$\psi(x, y, 0) = f(x, y)$$

Our program actually solves the following approximate differential equation at $N \times N$ points:

$$\psi_{i,j}(t + \Delta t) = \begin{cases} 2\psi_{i,j}(t) - \psi_{i,j}(t - \Delta t) & \text{(if } 1 \leq i, j \leq N - 2\text{)} \\ \quad + \tau^2 [\psi_{i-1,j}(t) + \psi_{i+1,j}(t) + \psi_{i,j-1}(t) + \psi_{i,j+1}(t) - 4\psi_{i,j}(t)] \\ 0 & \text{(otherwise)} \end{cases}$$

where $\psi_{i,j}(t)$ is the value of ψ at the point $(i\Delta x, j\Delta x)$ at time t, $\tau = c\Delta t / \Delta x$ and $\Delta x = L/(N-1)$.

This can be solved incrementally by a community consisting of $N \times N$ objects. However, the above equation requires the boundary objects and the inner objects to behave in a different manner. Although it is possible to use a static community where each member object behaves according to some boundary flag, it is straightforward to use a dynamic community consisting of two kinds of objects.

Fig. 8 shows part of a wave equation solver that uses such a dynamic community. The abstract class Point and its subclasses IPoint and BPoint, for inner objects and boundary objects respectively, and the community template Plane are defined.

Class Point defines a slot val for value at time t, and declares a broadcast handler :step which is to be defined in its subclasses to calculate values at each point.

In class IPoint, slots oldval,newval are defined for values at time $t-1, t+1$, and north, east, west, south initialized using member operator for the adjacent four member objects. In the broadcast handler :step, the comm-get operation is used for data exchange and barrier is used to prevent comm-get from reading updated values. On the other hand, only barrier is performed in the broadcast handler :step of class BPoint. Thus, the two different behaviors are defined separately.

After initialization, the program simply broadcasts :step messages repeatedly to the dynamic community Plane consisting of IPoint and BPoint objects.

We have also created a corresponding program that uses a static community; however, there is a small performance difference between both programs: Both take nearly 20.0 ms for a single time step simulation of 100×100 points on a Paragon XP/S with 64 nodes. This encourages programmers to use dynamic communities for heterogeneous data parallel computing.

```
1 (community Plane (consists-of Point 2 :dynamic) ...)
2
3 (class Point                        ;; abstract class
4   (belongs-to Plane)
5   (vars (Double val))
6   (broadcast-handlers
7     ([:step (Double tau2)] (replies Void) :abstract)
8     ...))
9
10 (class IPoint                       ;; inner object class
11   (parents Point)
12   (vars (Double oldval newval)
13         (Point north east west south))
14   (broadcast-handlers
15     ([:step (Double tau2)] (replies Void)
16       (let ()
17         (set newval
18             (+ (* 2.0 val) (- oldval)
19                 (* tau2 (+ (comm-get val north) (comm-get val east)
20                           (comm-get val west) (comm-get val south)
21                           (* -4.0 val)))))
22         (barrier)
23         (set oldval val)
24         (set val newval)))
25     ...))
26
27 (class BPoint                       ;; boundary object class
28   (parents Point)
29   (broadcast-handlers
30     ([:step (Double tau2)] (replies Void)
31         (barrier))
32     ...))
```

Fig. 8. Wave equation solver

4 Related Work

Some languages introduce the notion of abstract parallelism. For example, CA (Concurrent Aggregates)[1] introduces the notion of *aggregate*, a set of the same kind of objects, called *representatives*. An object may send a message to an aggregate in the same way as it would to an ordinary object. A message sent to an aggregate is actually sent to an arbitrarily chosen representative. Then, if necessary, the receiver forwards the message to an appropriate representative. This feature enables a programming style where a program can be made more efficient by replacing bottleneck objects with aggregates. However, message forwarding overhead is incurred even if the receiver is known to the sender. CA supports neither broadcast nor global operations in its language specification.

EPEE (Eiffel Parallel Execution Environment)[3] provides a data parallel model on top of the sequential object-oriented language Eiffel by introducing the *Distributed_Aggregate* class, which is used through multiple inheritance. Distributed_Aggregate provides methods to access distributed data, invoke methods on each element, as well as perform reduction and redistribution. A sequential programming point of view is preserved, however, control parallelism is not supported.

Kilian also proposes the notion of *parallel sets* to support data parallelism[4]. Similar to a dynamic community in *OCore*, a parallel set may change in size dynamically. Unlike *OCore*, an object may belong to more than one parallel set concurrently. It is also allowed that a parallel set contain other parallel sets as well as objects. In *OCore*, such nested parallelism is not supported, but it can be realized by using forwarding member objects that forward a broadcast message to other communities. In a parallel set, synchronous broadcast is supported in a limited way. Global operations are not supported. A parallel set is designed with flexibility, but its efficient implementation is not considered.

Communities in *OCore* are unique in that they support both multi-access data abstractions and data parallel computations that can be executed efficiently on multi computers. And besides, member objects in a dynamic community can be heterogeneous, sparse, and changed dynamically, which leads to flexible parallel programming.

5   Conclusions

We have presented an overview of *OCore*, placing special emphasis on two kinds of communities. We have also described community programming, presenting a molecular dynamics simulation program and a wave equation solver as examples of data parallel programming using communities.

Static communities are more efficient and adequate for regular data parallel computing, but dynamic communities provide more flexibility for a wider range of applications. Preliminary evaluation of the examples shows that dynamic communities do not incur significant overhead, unless they are **reorganize**'d too frequently.

Further research includes the refinement of the *OCore* language specification, the exploration of community applications, and implementation on the RWC-1[10] and other multi computers.

References

1. A. A. Chien. *Concurrent Aggregates.* The MIT Press, 1993.
2. Intel Supercomputer Systems Division. *Paragon OSF/1 C System Calls Reference Manual,* 1993.
3. J. Jézéquel, F. André, and F. Bergheul. A parallel execution environment for a sequential object oriented language. In *Proc. International Conf. on Supercomputing '92,* pages 368–376. ACM, 1992.

4. M. F. Killian. Object-oriented programming for massively parallel machines. In *Proc. International Conf. on Parallel Processing*, pages 227–230, 1991.

5. H. Konaka. An Overview of *OCore*: A Massively Parallel Object-based Language. TR-P-93 2, Real World Computing Partnership, 1993.

6. H. Konaka, Y. Ishikawa, M. Maeda, T. Tomokiyo, and A. Hori. An Implementation of the Massively Parallel Object-based Language *OCore* for Multi Computers. *Trans.IPS.Japan*, 36(7):1520–1528, 1995. (in Japanese).

7. H. Konaka, T. Yokota, and K. Seo. Indirect Communication between Objects on a Parallel Machine. *Proc. of SIGPRG, IPS Japan*, 9(3):17–24, 1992. (in Japanese).

8. M. Maeda, H. Konaka, Y. Ishikawa, T. Tomokiyo, A. Hori, and J. Nolte. On-the-fly global garbage collection based on partly mark-sweep. In *Lecture Notes in Computer Science*, volume 986, pages 283–296. Springer-Verlag, Sept. 1995. (Proc. IWMM'95).

9. R. Nikhil and K. Pingali. I–Structure: Data Structures for Parallel Computing. *ACM Trans. on Prog. Lang. and Syst.*, 11(4):598–639, 1989.

10. S. Sakai, H. Matsuoka, K. Okamoto, T. Yokota, H. Hirono, Y. Kodama, and M. Sato. Rwc–1 massively parallel architecture. In *Proc. High Performance Computing Conf. '94*, pages 33–38, 1994.

11. M. Sato, Y. Kodama, S. Sakai, Y. Yamaguchi, and S. Sekiguchi. Distributed Data Structure in Thread-based Programming for a Highly Parallel Dataflow Machine EM–4. *Proc. of ISCA 92 Dataflow Workshop*, 1992.

12. J. P. Singh, W.-D. Weber, and A. Gupta. SPLASH: Stanford parallel applications for shared-memory. Technical Report CSL-TR-92-526, Computer Systems Laboratory, Stanford Univ., 1992.

13. Thinking Machines Corp. *CM5 Technical Summary*.

14. T. Tomokiyo, H. Konaka, Y. Ishikawa, M. Maeda, and A. Hori. Meta-Level Programming in the Massively-Parallel Object-Based Language *OCore*. In *Proc. JSSST 11th Annual Conf.*, 1994. (in Japanese).

Polymorphic Matrices in Paladin

F. Guidec and J.-M. Jézéquel

I.R.I.S.A. Campus de Beaulieu
F-35042 RENNES CEDEX, FRANCE
Tel: +33–99.84.71.92 — Fax: +33–99.84.71.71
E-mail: jezequel@irisa.fr

Abstract. Scientific programmers are eager to take advantage of the computational power offered by Distributed Computing Systems (DCSs), but are generally reluctant to undertake the porting of their application programs onto such machines. The DCS commercially available today are indeed widely believed to be difficult to use, which should not be a surprise since they are traditionally programmed with software tools dating back to the days of punch cards and paper tape. We claim that provided modern object oriented technologies are used, these computers can be programmed easily and efficiently. In EPEE, our Eiffel Parallel Execution Environment, we propose to use a kind of parallelism known as data-parallelism, encapsulated within classes of the Eiffel sequential object-oriented language, using the SPMD (Single Program Multiple Data) programming model. We describe our method for designing with this environment PALADIN, an object-oriented linear algebra library for DCSs. We show how dynamic binding and polymorphism can be used to solve the problems set by the dynamic aspects of the distribution of linear algebra objects such as matrices and vectors.

1 Introduction

Distributed computing systems (DCSs)—also called distributed memory parallel computers or *multiprocessors*—consist of hundreds or thousands of processors and are now commercially available. An example of this kind of DCS is the Intel Paragon supercomputer, a distributed-memory multicomputer with architecture that can accommodate more than a thousand heterogeneous nodes connected in a two-dimensional rectangular mesh (see Figure 1). Its computation nodes are based on Intel i860 processors, and communicate by passing messages over a high-speed internal interconnect network. These kinds of multiprocessors provide orders of magnitude more raw power than traditional supercomputers at lower costs. They enable the development of previously infeasible applications (called *grand challenges*) in various scientific domains, such as materials science (for the aerospace and automobile industries), molecular biology, high-energy physics (Quantic Chromo-Dynamic), and global climate modeling.

Although the physical world they model is inherently parallel, scientific programmers used to rely on sequential techniques and algorithms to solve their problems, because these algorithms *e.g.*, the N-body problem) often present a better computational complexity than possible direct solutions. Their interest in concurrency only results from their desire to improve the performance of sequential algorithms applied

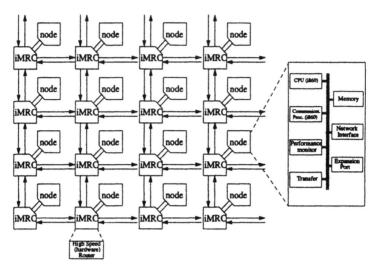

Fig. 1. The architecture of the Intel Paragon XP/S supercomputer

to large-scale numerical computations [12]. Scientific programmers are generally reluctant to cope with the manual porting of their applications on DCSs, because the average user will not move from an environment in which programming is relatively easy to one in which it is relatively hard unless the performance gains are truly remarkable and unachievable by any other method. They soon discovered how tedious it was to write parallel programs in a dialect that made the user responsible for creating and managing distribution and parallel computations and for explicit communication between the processors.

In this paper, we show how a sequential object oriented language such as Eiffel (featuring strong encapsulation, static type checking, multiple inheritance, dynamic binding and genericity) can be used to override these drawbacks. The idea is to build easy-to-use parallel object-oriented libraries permitting an efficient and transparent use of DCSs. We use the EPEE framework [11] to encapsulate the tricky parallel codes in object-oriented software components that can be reused, combined and customized in confidence by application programmers. Section 2 describes the principles underlining our method for designing an object-oriented linear algebra library for DCSs. We illustrate our approach with the example of PALADIN, an object-oriented library devoted to linear algebra computation on DCSs, whose design and implementation is outlined in Section 3. We then investigate the various aspects of dealing with multiple representations of linear algebra objects (Section 4). In the conclusion, we enumerate the advantages of our approach and make a few prospective remarks.

2 Encapsulating Parallelism and Distribution

2.1 A Simple Parallel Programming Model

The kind of parallelism we consider is inspired from Valiant's Block Synchronous Parallel (BSP) model [13]. A computation that fits the BSP model can be seen as a succession of parallel phases separated by synchronizations and sequential phases.

In EPEE, Valiant's model is implemented based on the Single Program Multiple Data (SPMD) programming model. Each process executes the same program, which corresponds to the initial user-defined sequential program. The SPMD model preserves the conceptual simplicity of the sequential instruction flow: a user can write an application program as a purely sequential one. At runtime, though, the distribution of data leads to a parallel execution.

When data parallelism is involved, only a subset of the data is considered on each processor: its own data partition. On the other hand, when control parallelism is involved, each processor runs a subset of the original execution flow (typically some parts of the iteration domain). In both cases, the user still views his program as a sequential one and the parallelism is derived from the data representation. Although EPEE allows the encapsulation of both kinds of parallelism in Eiffel classes, we mainly focused on the encapsulation of data parallelism so far. Yet, some work is now in progress to incorporate control parallelism in EPEE as well [9].

Our method for encapsulating parallelism within a class can be compared with the encapsulation of tricky pointer manipulations within a linked list class that provides the user with the abstraction of a list without any visible pointer handling. Opposite to concurrent OO languages along the line of POOL-T [2], ABCL/1 [14], or more recently pC++ [6], which were designed to tackle problems with explicit parallelism, our goal is to completely hide the parallelism to the application programmer.

A major consequence of this approach is that there exists two levels of programming with EPEE: the class user (or *client*) level and the class designer level. The aim is that, at client level, nothing but performance improvements appear when running an application program on a parallel computer. For a user of a library designed with EPEE, it must be possible to handle distributed objects just like local —*i.e.* non-distributed— ones.

The problem is thus for the designer of the library to implement distributed objects using the general data distribution and/or parallelization rules presented in this paper. While implementing these objects, the designer must notably ensure their portability and efficiency, and preserve a "sequential-like" interface for the sake of the user to whom distribution and parallelization issues must be masked.

2.2 Polymorphic Aggregates

The SPMD model is mostly appropriate for solving problems that are data-oriented and involve large amounts of data. This model thus fits well application domains that deal with large, homogeneous data structures. Such data structures are referred to as *aggregates* in the remaining of this paper. Typical aggregates are lists, sets, trees, graphs, arrays, matrices, vectors, etc.

A computation can be efficiently parallelized only if the cost of synchronization, communications and other processing paid for managing parallelism is compensated by the performance improvement brought by the parallelization.

Most aggregates admit several alternative representation layouts and must thus be considered as *polymorphic* entities, that is, objects that assume different forms and whose form can change dynamically. Consider the example of matrix aggregates.

Although all matrices can share a common abstract specification, they do not necessarily require the same implementation layout. Obviously dense and sparse matrices deserve different internal representations. A dense matrix may be implemented quite simply as a bi-dimensional array, whereas a sparse matrix requires a smarter internal representation, based for example on lists or trees. Moreover, the choice of the most appropriate internal representation for a sparse matrix may depend on whether the sparsity of this matrix is likely to change during its lifetime. This choice may also be guided by considerations on the way the matrix is to be accessed (*e.g* regular vs irregular, non-predictable access), or by considerations on whether memory space or access time should be primarily saved.

The problem of choosing the most appropriate representation format of a matrix is even more crucial in the context of distributed computation, since matrix aggregates can be partitioned and distributed on multi-processor machines. Each distribution pattern for a matrix (distribution by rows, by columns, by blocks, etc.) can then be perceived as a particular implementation of this matrix.

When designing an application program that deals with matrices, the choice of the best representation layout for a given matrix is a crucial issue. PALADIN for example encapsulates several alternative representations for matrices (and for vectors as well, though this part of PALADIN is not discussed in this paper), and makes it possible for the application programmer to change the representation format of a matrix at any time during a computation. For example, after a few computation steps an application program may need to convert a sparse matrix into a dense one, because the sparsity of the matrix has decreased during the first part of the computation. Likewise, it may sometimes be necessary to change the distribution pattern of a distributed matrix at run-time in order to adapt its distribution to the requirements of the computation. PALADIN thus provides a facility to redistribute matrices dynamically, as well as a facility to transform dynamically the internal representation format of a matrix (see section 4).

2.3 One Abstraction, Several Implementations

To implement polymorphic aggregates —be they distributed or not— using the facilities of EPEE, we propose a method based on the dissociation of the abstract and operational specifications of an aggregate. The fundamental idea is to build a hierarchy of abstraction levels. Application programs are written in such a way that they operate on abstract data structures, whose concrete implementation is defined independently from the programs that use them.

Eiffel provides all the mechanisms we need to dissociate the abstract specification of an aggregate from the details relative to its implementation. The abstract specification can be easily encapsulated in a class whose interface determines precisely the way an application programmer will view this aggregate.

The distribution of an aggregate is usually achieved in two steps. The first step aims at providing transparency to the user. It consists in performing the actual distribution of the aggregate on the processors of a DCS, while ensuring that the resulting distributed aggregate can be handled in a SPMD program just like its local counterpart in a sequential program. The second step mostly addresses performance issues. It consists in parallelizing some of the features that operate on the distributed aggregate.

One or several distribution patterns must be chosen to spread the aggregate over a DCS. Since we opted for a data parallel approach, each processor will only own a part of the distributed aggregate. The first thing to do is thus to implement a mechanism ensuring a transparent remote access to non local data, while preserving the semantics of local accesses.

When implementing distributed aggregates with EPEE, a fundamental principle is a location rule known as the *Owner Write Rule*, which states that only the processor that owns a part of an aggregate is allowed to update this part. This mechanism is commonly referred to as the *Exec* mechanism in the community of data parallel computing. Similarly, the *Refresh* mechanism ensures that remote accesses are properly dealt with. Both mechanisms have been introduced in [4], and described formally in [3]. The EPEE toolbox provides various facilities for implementing these mechanisms, as illustrated in the following sections with the implementation of distributed matrices.

2.4 Matrices and Vectors in PALADIN

PALADIN is built around the specifications of the basic entities of linear algebra: matrices and vectors.

The abstract specifications of matrices and vectors are encapsulated in classes MATRIX and VECTOR. Both classes are generic and can thus be used to instantiate integer matrices and vectors, real matrices and vectors, complex matrices and vectors, etc.

Classes MATRIX and VECTOR are deferred classes: they provide no details about the way matrices and vectors shall be represented in memory. The specification of their internal representation is thus left to descendant classes. This does not imply that all features are kept deferred. Representation-dependent features are simply declared, whereas other features are defined —i.e., implemented— directly in MATRIX and VECTOR, as shown below.

In the following we mainly focus on the content of class MATRIX. Class VECTOR is designed in a very similar way. The class MATRIX simply enumerates the features that are needed to handle a matrix object, together with their formal properties expressed as assertions (preconditions, postconditions, invariants, etc.), as illustrated in example 2.1.

For the sake of conciseness and clarity, the class MATRIX we consider here is a simplified version of the real class implemented in PALADIN. The class notably includes some of the most classical linear algebra operations (sum, difference, multiply, transpose, etc.) as well as more complex operations (e.g., LU, LDL^T and QR factorization, triangular system solvers, etc.). It also encapsulates the definition of infix operators that make it possible to write in application programs an expression such as $R := A + B$, where A, B and R refer to matrices.

The resulting class can be thought of as a close approximation of the abstract data type of a matrix entity [1, 5]. A matrix is mainly characterized by its size, stored in attributes *nrow* and *ncolumn*. Routines can be classified in two categories, accessors and operators.

Example 2.1

```
deferred class MATRIX [T->NUMERIC]
feature -- Attributes
   nrow: INTEGER        -- Number of rows
   ncolumn: INTEGER     -- Number of columns
feature -- Accessors                                              5
   item (i, j: INTEGER): T is
          -- Return current value of item(i, j)
      require
         valid_i:  (i > 0) and (i <= nrow)
         valid_j:  (j > 0) and (j <= ncolumn)                    10
      deferred
      end -- item
   put (v: T; i, j: INTEGER) is
          -- Put value v into item(i, j)
      require                                                     15
         valid_i:  (i > 0) and (i <= nrow)
         valid_j:  (j > 0) and (j <= ncolumn)
      deferred
      ensure
         item (i, j) = v                                         20
      end -- put
   row (i: INTEGER): VECTOR [T] is do ... end
   column (j: INTEGER): VECTOR [T] is do ... end
   diagonal (k: INTEGER): VECTOR [T] is do ... end
   submatrix (i, j, k, l: INTEGER): SUB_MATRIX [T] is do ... end  25
feature -- Operators
   trace:  T is do ... end
   random (min, max: T) is do ... end
   add (B: MATRIX [T]) is do ... end
   mult (A, B: MATRIX [T]) is do ... end                         30
   LU is do ... end
   LDLt is do ... end
   Cholesky is do ... end
   -- ...
end -- class MATRIX                                              35
```

Accessors: Accessors are the features that permit to access a matrix in read or write mode. PALADIN provides routines for accessing a matrix at different levels. Basic routines *put* and *item* give access to an item of the matrix. The implementation of accessors depends on the format chosen to represent a matrix object in memory. Consequently, in class MATRIX, both accessors *put* and *item* are given a full specification (signature and preconditions and postconditions), but are left deferred.

Higher level accessors allow the user to handle a row, a column or a diagonal of the matrix as a vector entity, and a rectangular section of the matrix (function *submatrix*). Assume that A is a newly created 5 × 5 integer matrix. The following code illustrates the use of accessor *submatrix* to fill a section of A with random values (originally all items are set to zero).

$$A = \begin{pmatrix} 0\,0\,0\,0\,0 \\ 0\,0\,0\,0\,0 \\ 0\,0\,0\,0\,0 \\ 0\,0\,0\,0\,0 \\ 0\,0\,0\,0\,0 \end{pmatrix} \xrightarrow{A.\text{submatrix}(2,4,2,5).\text{random}} \begin{pmatrix} 0\,0\,0\,0\,0 \\ 0\,6\,1\,9\,6 \\ 0\,2\,7\,2\,8 \\ 0\,7\,3\,5\,1 \\ 0\,0\,0\,0\,0 \end{pmatrix}$$

An important feature about accessors is that most of the time they imply no copy of data. They simply provide a "view" of a section of a matrix. Thus modifying this view is equivalent to modifying the corresponding section. Views necessitate special implementations, which are encapsulated in classes ROW, COLUMN, DIAGONAL, SUBMATRIX, and SUBVECTOR.

The set of multilevel accessors actually provides the same abstractions as the syntactic short-cuts frequently used in books dealing with linear algebra, such as [7]. Assuming that A is a $n \times m$ matrix, the expression $A.submatrix$ (i, j, k, l) is equivalent to the notation $A(i : j, k : l)$. Likewise, $A.row(i)$ and $A.column(j)$ are equivalent to $A(i, :)$ and $A(:, j)$ respectively.

Operators: Operators of class MATRIX are high level routines used for performing computations implying a matrix as a whole and possibly other arguments (*i.e.*, other matrices or vectors). Typical operators include routines that perform scalar-matrix, vector-matrix and matrix-matrix operations. The class also contains more complicated routines for performing such computations as the Cholesky, LDL^T and LU factorizations, for solving triangular systems, etc. Since PALADIN provide accessors at different levels (item, vector, submatrix), defining new operators is not a difficult task. Any algorithm presented in a book can be readily reproduced in the library.

Although the class MATRIX encapsulates the abstract specification of a matrix object, this does not imply that all features must be kept deferred in this class. Unlike accessors *put* and *item*, operators such as *trace*, *random*, *add*, etc. are features that can generally be given an operational specification based on calls to accessors and other operators. Consequently, the implementation of an operator does not directly depend on the internal representation format of the aggregate considered, because this representation format is masked by the accessors.

The organization of class VECTOR is quite similar to that of MATRIX. In addition to the basic features (attribute *length*, accessors *put* and *item*, etc.), this class contains routines that perform scalar-vector, vector-vector (*saxpy*) and matrix-vector (*gaxpy*) operations.

3 Replicated and Distributed Matrices

3.1 Sequential Implementation of a Matrix

Once the abstract specification of an aggregate has been encapsulated in a class, it is possible to design one or several descendant classes (*i.e.*, classes that inherit from the abstract class), each descendant encapsulating an alternative implementation of the aggregate. This implementation can either consist in the description of a representation format to store the aggregate in the memory of a mono-processor machine, or it can be the description of a pattern to distribute the aggregate on a DCS.

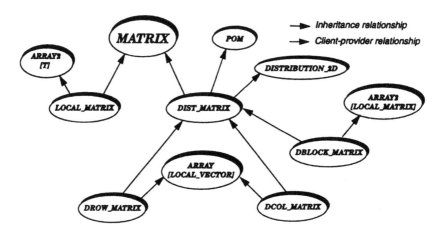

Fig. 2. Inheritance structure for matrix aggregates (partial view)

In the following, we show how the mechanism of multiple inheritance helps designing classes that encapsulate fully operational specifications of matrix objects. We first illustrate the approach by describing the design of class LOCAL_MATRIX, which encapsulates a possible implementation for local —i.e., non-distributed— matrix objects. In this class we specify that an object of type LOCAL_MATRIX must be stored in memory as a traditional bi-dimensional array.

The class LOCAL_MATRIX simply combines the abstract specification inherited from MATRIX together with the storage facilities provided by the class ARRAY2 available in most Eiffel libraries (see also figure 2). The text of LOCAL_MATRIX is readily written, thanks to the mechanism of multiple inheritance: the effort of design only comes down to combining the abstract specification of class MATRIX with the implementation facilities offered by ARRAY2, and ensuring that the names of the features inherited from both ancestor classes are matched correctly. In the example 3.1, the attributes *height* and *width* of class ARRAY2 are matched with the attributes *nrow* and *ncolumn* of class MATRIX through *renaming*.

A library designed along these lines may easily be augmented with new classes describing other kinds of entities such as sparse matrices and vectors, or symmetric, lower triangular and upper triangular matrices, etc. Adding new representation variants for matrices and vectors simply comes down to adding new classes in the library. Moreover, each new class is not built from scratch, but inherits from already existing classes. For the designer of the library, providing a new representation variant for a matrix or a vector usually consists in assembling existing classes to produce a new one. Very often this process does not imply any development of new code.

Example 3.1

```
class LOCAL_MATRIX [T->NUMERIC]
inherit
   MATRIX [T]
   ARRAY2 [T]
      rename height as nrow, width as ncolumn end          5
creation
   make
end -- class LOCAL_MATRIX
```

Unlike the abstract class MATRIX, the class LOCAL_MATRIX is a concrete (or effective) class, which means that it can be instantiated (Assuming that no operator has been left deferred in class MATRIX). It is thus possible to create objects of type LOCAL_MATRIX in an application program, and to invoke on these objects some of the accessors and operators defined in MATRIX.

3.2 Distribution of Matrices in Paladin

The PALADIN approach to the distribution of matrices is quite similar to that of High Performance Fortran (HPF) [10]. The main difference is that HPF is based on weird extensions of the FORTRAN 90 syntax (distribution, alignment and mapping directives) whereas PALADIN only uses normal constructions of the Eiffel language.

Distributed matrices are decomposed into blocks, which are then mapped over the processors of the target DCS. Managing the distribution of a matrix implies a great amount of fairly simple but repetitive calculations, such as those that aim at determining the identity of the processor that owns the item (i, j) of a given matrix, and the local address of this item on this processor. The Features for doing such calculations have been encapsulated in a class DISTRIBUTION_2D, which allows the partition and distribution of 2-D data structures. The class DISTRIBUTION_2D is actually designed by inheriting two times from a more simple class DISTRIBUTION_1D. Hence, a class devoted to the distribution of 3-D data structures could be built just as easily.

The application programmer describes a distribution pattern by specifying the size of the index domain considered, the size of the basic building blocks in this domain, and how these blocks must be mapped on a set of processors. The definition of the mapping function has intentionally been left out of class DISTRIBUTION_2D and encapsulated in a small hierarchy of classes devoted to the mapping of 2-D structures on a set of processors (see class MAPPING_2D in example 3.2).

PALADIN includes two effective classes that permit to map the blocks of a distributed matrix either row-wise or column-wise on a set of processors. In the class ROW_WISE_MAPPING, for example, the feature *map_block* is implemented as shown in example 3.3.

The keyword **expanded** in the first line of this code implies that instances of class ROW_WISE_MAPPING are value objects. Any attribute declared as being of type ROW_WISE_MAPPING can be directly handled as an object of type ROW_WISE_MAPPING.

Example 3.2

```
deferred class MAPPING_2D
feature
   map_block (bi, bj, bimax, bjmax, nproc:  INTEGER): INTEGER is
         -- Maps block(bi, bj) on a processor whose identifier
         -- must be in the range [0, nproc]                              5
      require
         bi_valid:  (bi >= 0) and (bi <= bimax)
         bj_valid:  (bj >= 0) and (bj <= bjmax)
      deferred
      ensure                                                            10
         (Result >= 0) and (Result < nproc)
      end -- map_block
end -- class MAPPING_2D
```

Example 3.3

```
expanded class ROW_WISE_MAPPING
inherit MAPPING_2D
feature
   map_block (bi, bj, bimax, bjmax, nproc: INTEGER): INTEGER is
      do                                                                5
         Result := (bi * (bjmax + 1) + bj) \\ nproc
      end -- map_block
end -- class ROW_WISE_MAPPING
```

The implementation of COLUMN_WISE_MAPPING is of course very similar to that of ROW_WISE_MAPPING. Any user could easily propose alternative mapping policies (random mapping, diagonal-wise mapping, etc.): the only thing a user must do is design a new class that inherits from MAPPING_2D and that encapsulates an original implementation of the feature *map_block*.

Figure 3 shows the creation of an instance of DISTRIBUTION_2D. The creation feature takes as parameters the size of the index domain considered, the size of the building blocks for partitioning this domain, and a reference to an object whose type conforms to —*i.e.*, is a descendant of— MAPPING_2D. The instance of DIS-TRIBUTION_2D created in figure 3 will thus permit to manage the distribution of a 10 × 10 index domain partitioned into 5 × 2 blocks mapped column-wise on a set of processors. Figure 3 also shows the resulting mapping on a parallel architecture providing 4 processors.

Each distributed matrix must be associated at creation time with an instance of DISTRIBUTION_2D, which plays the role of a distribution template for this matrix. The distribution pattern of a matrix can either be specified explicitly —in that case a new instance of DISTRIBUTION_2D is created for the matrix—, or implicitly by passing either a reference to an already existing distributed matrix or a reference to an existing distribution template as a parameter. Several distributed matrices

```
local
   my_dist: DISTRIBUTION_2D;
   my_mapping: COLUMN_WISE_MAPPING;
do
   ...
   !!my_dist.make (10, 10, 5, 2, my_mapping);
   ...
```

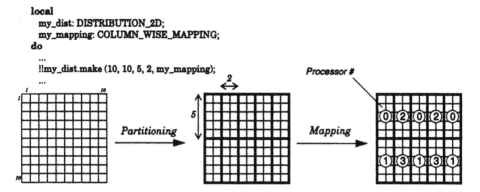

Fig. 3. Example of a distribution allowed by class DISTRIBUTION_2D

can thus share a common distribution pattern by referencing the same distribution template.

3.3 Implementation of Distributed Matrices

The accessors declared in class MATRIX must be implemented in accordance with the *Exec* and *Refresh* mechanisms introduced in section 2.3. This is achieved in a new class DIST_MATRIX that inherits from the abstract specification encapsulated in class MATRIX (see example 3.4).

Accessors such as *put* that modify the matrix are defined so as to conform to the *Owner Write Rule*: when an SPMD application program contains an expression of the form M.put(v, i, j) —with M referring to a distributed matrix— the processor that owns item (i,j) is solely capable of performing the assignment. In the implementation of the feature *put*, the assignment is thus conditioned by a locality test using the distribution template (feature *dist*) of the matrix (see the lines 20–25 of the example 3.4).

Accessors such as *item* must be defined so that remote accesses are properly dealt with: when an SPMD application program contains an expression such as v := M.item(i, j), the function *item* must return the same value on all the processors. Consequently, in the implementation of the feature *item*, the processor that owns item (i,j) broadcasts its value so that all the other processors can receive it (see the lines 16–19 of the example 3.4). The invocation M.item(i, j) thus returns the same value on all the processors implied in the computation (the communication primitives are provided by the class POM of the EPEE toolbox).

The same principle applies to row, column and submatrix accessors as well. The the distribution of data is thus dealt with, but the actual *access* to local data. This problem must be tackled in the local accessors *local_put* and *local_item*, etc. whose implementation is closely dependent on the format chosen to represent a part of the distributed matrix on each processor. Since there may be numerous ways to store a distributed matrix in memory (*e.g.*, the distributed matrix may be dense or sparse), these local accessors are left deferred in class DIST_MATRIX. They must be defined in

Example 3.4

```
indexing
    description: "Abstract matrix distributed along a template"

deferred class DIST_MATRIX [T->NUMERIC]
inherit                                                              5
    MATRIX [T]    -- Abstract specification
feature -- Creation
    make (rows, cols, bfi, bfj: INTEGER; alignment: MAPPING_2D) is
        deferred end
    make_from (new_dist: DISTRIBUTION_2D) is  deferred end           10
    make_like (other: DIST_MATRIX) is deferred end
feature -- Distribution template
    dist: DISTRIBUTION_2D
feature -- Accessors
    item (i, j: INTEGER): T is                                       15
        -- element (i,j) of the Matrix, read using the Refresh mecanism
    do
        if dist.item_is_local(i, j) then
            Result := local_item (i, j)   -- I am the owner
            POM.broadcast (Result)   -- so I send the value to others 20
        else -- I'm not the owner, I wait for the value to be sent to me
            Result := POM.receive_from (dist.owner_of_item (i, j))
        end -- if
    end -- item
    put (v: T; i, j: INTEGER) is                                     25
        -- write the element (i,j) of the Matrix, the Owner Write Rule
    do
        if dist.item_is_local(i, j) then
            local_put (v, i, j) -- Only the owner writes the data
        end -- if                                                    30
    end -- put

feature {DIST_MATRIX}   -- Communication features
    POM: POM
                                                                     35
end -- DIST_MATRIX [T]
```

classes that descend from DIST_MATRIX and that encapsulate all the details relative to the internal representation of distributed matrices.

The class DBLOCK_MATRIX presented in example 3.5 is one of the many possible descendants of DIST_MATRIX (see figure 2). It inherits from DIST_MATRIX as well as from ARRAY2[LOCAL_MATRIX], and therefore implements a dense matrix distributed by blocks as a 2-D table of local matrices. Each entry in this table references a building block of the distributed matrix, stored in memory as an instance of LOCAL_MATRIX (see figure 4). A void entry in the table means that the local processor does not own the corresponding block matrix. In DBLOCK_MATRIX, the

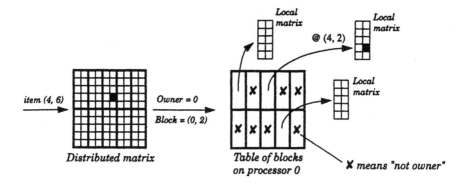

Fig. 4. Internal representation of a matrix distributed by blocks

Example 3.5

```
indexing
   description: "Matrix distributed by blocks"

class DBLOCK_MATRIX [T->NUMERIC]
inherit                                                         5
   DIST_MATRIX [T]
   ARRAY2 [LOCAL_MATRIX[T]]
      rename
         make as make_table,
         put as put_block, item as local_block               10
      end
feature  -- ...
end -- class DBLOCK_MATRIX [T->NUMERIC]
```

local accessors *local_put* and *local_item* are defined so as to take into account the indirection due to the table.

The class hierarchy that results from this approach is clearly organized as a layering of abstraction levels. At the highest level, the class MATRIX encapsulates the abstract specification of a matrix entity. The class DIST_MATRIX corresponds to an intermediate level, where the problem of the distribution of a matrix is solved, while the problem of the actual storage of the matrix in memory is deferred. At the lowest level, classes such as DBLOCK_MATRIX provide fully operational and efficient implementations for distributed matrices (up to 1.7 Gflops for a matrix multiply on a 56 nodes Paragon XP/S [8]).

Besides DBLOCK_MATRIX, the class hierarchy of PALADIN includes two classes DCOL_MATRIX and DROW_MATRIX that encapsulate alternative implementations for row-wise and column-wise distributed matrices. In these classes, distributed matrices are implemented as tables of local vectors. This kind of implementation fits well application programs that perform many vector-vector operations. Other kinds of distribution patterns or other kinds of representation formats could be proposed.

One could for example think of exotic distribution patterns based on a decomposition into heterogeneous blocks or on a random mapping policy. One could also decide to provide an implementation *ad hoc* for triangular or band distributed matrices. With the object-oriented approach, the extensibility of a class hierarchy such as that of PALADIN has virtually no limit. It is always possible to incorporate new classes seamlessly in a pre-existing class hierarchy.

4 Dealing with multiple representations

4.1 Interoperability

One of the major advantages of this class organization is that it ensures the interoperability of all matrices and vectors. A feature declared —and possibly implemented— in class MATRIX is inherited by all the descendants of this class. Hence a feature such as *cholesky*, which performs a Cholesky factorization, can operate on any matrix that satisfies the preconditions of the feature: the matrix must be square symmetric definite positive. This feature therefore operates on a local matrix as well as on a distributed one. In the library, a parallel version of the Cholesky algorithm is actually provided for distributed matrices, but this optimization remains absolutely transparent for the user who keeps using the feature the same way.

Interoperability also goes for algorithms that admit several arguments. For example class MATRIX provides an infix operator that computes the sum of two matrices A and B and returns the resulting matrix R. The user may write an expression such as $R := A + B$ while matrix R is duplicated on all processors, A is distributed by rows and B is distributed by columns. Interoperability ensures that all internal representations can be combined transparently.

4.2 Dynamic Redistribution

Complementary to the interoperability of representation variants, a conversion mechanism is available for adapting the representation of a matrix or vector to the requirements of the computation. A row-wise distributed matrix, for example, can be "transformed" dynamically into a column-wise distributed matrix, assuming that this new representation is likely to lead to better performances in some parts of an application program. The conversion mechanism therefore plays the role of a redistribution facility.

An algorithm that permits to redistribute a matrix can be obtained quite simply using the communication facilities provided by class POM and the distribution facilities provided by class DISTRIBUTION_2D. Such a redistribution facility was implemented as shown below in class DBLOCK_MATRIX.

In this code, a temporary instance of DBLOCK_MATRIX named *tmp_matrix* is created according to the desired distribution pattern. Block matrices are then transferred one after another from the current matrix to *tmp_matrix*. Once the transfer is over, the attribute *dist* of the current matrix is re-associated with the new distribution template. Its former distribution template can then be collected by the garbage collector of the runtime system, unless this template is still used by another

Example 4.1

```
redistribute (new_dist: DISTRIBUTION_2D) is
   require
      new_dist_valid: (new_dist /= Void)
      compat_dist: (dist.bfi = new_dist.bfi) and (dist.bfj = new_dist.bfj)
   local                                                                      5
      bi, bj, source, target: INTEGER
      tmp_matrix:  DBLOCK_MATRIX [T]
   do
      !!tmp_matrix.make_from (new_dist)
      from bi := 0 until bi > dist.nbimax loop                                10
         from bj := 0 until bj > dist.nbjmax loop
            source := dist.owner_of_block (bi, bj)
            target := tmp_matrix.dist.owner_of_block (bi, bj)
            if (source = POM.my_node) then
               -- Send block matrix to target                                15
               local_block (bi, bj).send (target)
            end -- if
            if (target = POM.my_node) then
               -- Receive block matrix from source
               tmp_matrix.local_block (bi, bj).recv_from (source)            20
            end -- if
            bj := bj + 1
         end -- loop
         bi := bi + 1
      end -- loop                                                            25
      dist := tmp_matrix.dist
      area := tmp_matrix.area
   end -- redistribute
```

distributed matrix. Likewise, the attribute *area*, which actually refers to the table of block matrices of the current matrix, is re-associated so as to refer to the table of *tmp_matrix*. The former block table can then be also collected by the garbage collector. When the feature *redistribute* returns, the current matrix is a matrix whose distribution to the pattern described by *new_dist* and its internal representation relies on the newly created table of block matrices.

Notice that this implementation of the feature *redistribute* can only redistribute a matrix if the source and the target distribution patterns have the same block size (see the precondition in the code of the feature *redistribute*). The code of the feature *redistribute* reproduced here is actually a simplified version of the code implemented in DBLOCK_MATRIX. The real code is more flexible (a matrix can be redistributed even if the size of blocks must change during the process), it does not rely on a temporary matrix but directly creates and handles a new table of block matrices. Moreover, the garbage collection is performed on the fly: on each processor the local blocks that are sent to another processor are collected by the garbage collector immediately after they have been sent. Data exchanges are also performed more efficiently: the sequencing constraints imposed by the *Refresh/Exec* model in the

Example 4.2

```
local
   A, B: DBLOCK_MATRIX [DOUBLE]
do
   !!A.make (100, 100, 5, 2, ROW_WISE_MAPPING)
   !!B.make (100, 100, 7, 3, COLUMN_WISE_MAPPING)          5
      ...(1)...
   B.redistribute (A.dist)
      ...(2)...
end
```

former code are relaxed so that the resulting implementation of *redistribute* allows more concurrency. The real code encapsulated in the feature *redistribute* is thus more efficient than the code reproduced above, but it is also longer and more complex. This is the reason why we preferred to reproduce a simple implementation of *redistribute* here.

Anyway, whatever the actual complexity of the algorithm encapsulated in the feature *redistribute*, it does not shows through the interface of class DBLOCK_MATRIX. From the viewpoint of the application programmer, an instance of DBLOCK_MATRIX can thus be redistributed quite simply. Consider the small SPMD application program of the example 4.2.

Imagine that in this application the requirements of the computation impose that matrices A and B be distributed differently in the first part of the concurrent execution. On the other hand, the second part of the computation requires that A and B have the same distribution. Then the redistribution facility encapsulated in class DBLOCK_MATRIX can be used to achieve the redistribution.

Other classes of PALADIN (*e.g.*, DIST_MATRIX, DCOL_MATRIX, DROW_MATRIX) also encapsulate a version of the feature *redistribute*, whose implementation fits the characteristics of their distribution pattern.

4.3 Matrix type conversion

Eiffel, like most statically typed object-oriented languages, does not allow for objects to change their internal structure at runtime: once an object has been created, its internal organization is in a way "frozen". Thus, in PALADIN, there is for example no way one can transform an object of type LOCAL_MATRIX in an object of type DBLOCK_MATRIX. However, we can go round this constraint and propose a close approximation of "polymorphic" matrices, using the only really polymorphic entities available in Eiffel: references.

Whenever we need to change the internal representation of a matrix aggregate, the conversion must be performed in three steps. At first, a new matrix aggregate must be created, whose dynamic type conforms to the desired internal representation. Next, data must be "transferred" from the original aggregate into the new one. Finally, the reference associated with the original aggregate must be re-associated with the newly created one. This conversion procedure is illustrated below.

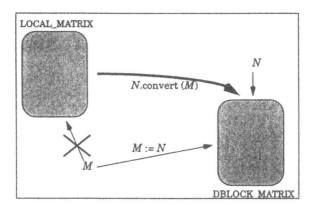

Fig. 5. Example of matrix conversion

Assume that in an application program a local matrix is created and associated with reference **M**. After some computation (part 1) it becomes necessary to transform this local matrix into a distributed one. An instance of type DBLOCK_MATRIX is created and associated with a temporary reference **N**. The information encapsulated in the original local matrix is copied in the distributed one using routine *convert*. Once the copy is complete, attribute M is re-associated with the newly created matrix thanks to a polymorphic assignment, so that the programmer can still refer to the matrix using attribute M in the remaining of the application program. The computation goes on using the distributed matrix (part 2). The conversion process is illustrated in figure 5.

Conceptually, the feature *convert* simply performs a copy from the source matrix into the target one. It simply requires that both matrices have the same size. In class MATRIX, the feature *convert* can be given a very simple implementation, based on two nested loops and calls to accessors *put* and *item*. However, this implementation, which does not depend on the internal representation formats of the source and target matrices, should only be considered as a default implementation. Better implementations of *convert* can be encapsulated in descendants of class MATRIX, using some of the optimization techniques discussed in [8].

Notice that this method to change the type of an aggregate actually requires that a new object be created. This is acceptable, since the Eiffel garbage collector ensures that the object corresponding to the "obsolete" representation of the aggregate will be collected after the conversion is over. Actually, the main problem with this conversion mechanism lies in the lack of transparency for the application programmer, who must explicitly declare a temporary reference, create a new aggregate of the desired dynamic type, invoke the feature *convert* on this object and eventually reassign the reference bound to the original object so that it now refers to the new object.

Another problem concerns *aliases*. An application program may reference the same matrix through many variables. The type conversion method presented above does not deal with this aliasing problem. A number of approaches have been proposed to solve this kind of problem. For example, we can maintain a table referencing all

Example 4.3

```
class POLY_MATRIX
feature {NONE} -- Reference to a matrix container
   container: MATRIX
feature -- Basic Accessors
   item (i, j: INTEGER): DOUBLE is do Result := container.item (i, j) end      5
   put (v: like item; i, j: INTEGER) is do container.put (v, i, j) end
   ...
feature -- Operators
   ...
end -- POLY_MATRIX                                                            10
```

the objects that may be subject to type conversions. All subsequent accesses to these objects then go through this table. Another method consist in keeping a list of client objects in each polymorphic object. Such an object can then inform its clients upon type conversion.

Because they are costly to implement, none of these approaches is fully satisfactory. A better solution would be to encapsulate the type conversions.

4.4 Towards Full Polymorphic Matrices

The only feasible solution to provide full polymorphic matrices in the context of a language such as Eiffel is to introduce a level of indirection. This boils down to introducing a distinction between the data structure containing the matrix data and the concept of a polymorphic matrix. A polymorphic matrix is just a client of the matrix class defined previously, and is thus able to dynamically change its representation.

A POLY_MATRIX has the same interface as the class MATRIX, but privately uses a MATRIX for its implementation (this is the meaning of the clause {NONE} in example 4.3). Its basic accessors *put* and *item* are defined so as to access the data stored in the container, which can be any subtype of the class MATRIX. In the same way, each operator of the class POLY_MATRIX is defined as to call the corresponding operator in the container.

A new set of routine is also available in the POLY_MATRIX class for it to be able to dynamically change its internal representation, that is to polymorph itself. For example, a POLY_MATRIX can acquire a LOCAL_MATRIX representation with the procedure *become_local* presented in example 4.4).

The performance overhead of the extra indirection is paid only once for each operation. It is thus negligible with respect to the algorithmic complexity of the operations on the large matrices considered in PALADIN.

4.5 Using Polymorphic Matrices

In PALADIN, the powerful abstraction of polymorphic matrices, together with features such as *become_xxx*, *redistribute* or *convert* are made available to the application programmer. Yet, they could also be invoked automatically within the library

Example 4.4

```
class POLY_MATRIX
   ...
feature -- Internal representation conversion
   become_local is
      local                                                          5
         new_container: like container;
      do
         -- Create a new matrix container with type as required
         !LOCAL_MATRIX!new_container.make (nrow, ncolumn);
         -- Transfer data from old matrix container to new one    10
         new_container.convert (container);
         -- Adopt new matrix container and discard old one
         container := new_container;
      end; -- become_local
   ...                                                              15
end -- class POLY_MATRIX
```

whenever an operator requires a particular distribution pattern of its operands. For example, any operator dealing with a distributed matrix could be implemented so as to systematically redistribute this matrix according to its needs prior to beginning the actual computation. If all operators in PALADIN were implemented that way, the application programmer would not have to care about distribution patterns anymore, all matrices being redistributed transparently as and when needed. Yet, redistributing a matrix —or changing its type— is a costly operation, so that this approach would probably lead to concurrent executions in which most of the activity would consist in redistributing matrices or vectors. The best approach is probably an intermediate between manual and automatic redistribution.

5   Conclusion

An OO library is built around the specifications of the basic data structures it deals with. The principle of dissociating the abstract specification of a data structure (somewhat its abstract data type) from any kind of implementation detail enables the construction of reusable and extensible libraries of parallel software components. Using this approach, we have shown in this paper that existing sequential OO languages are versatile enough to enable an efficient and easy use of DCSs. Thanks to the distributed data structures of a parallel library such as PALADIN, any programmer can write an application program that runs concurrently on a DCS. The parallelization can actually proceed in a seamless way: the programmer first designs a simple application using only local aggregates. The resulting sequential application can then be transformed into a SPMD application, just by changing the type of the aggregates implied in the computation. For large computations, we have shown that the overhead brought about by the higher level of OO languages remains negligible. Using the same framework, we are in the process of extending PALADIN to deal with sparse computations and control parallelism.

Although our approach hides a lot of the tedious parallelism management, the application programmer still remains responsible for deciding which representation format is the most appropriate for a given aggregate. Hence, when transforming a sequential program into an SPMD one, the programmer must decide which aggregate shall be distributed and how it shall be distributed. This may not always be an easy choice. Finding a "good" distribution may be quite difficult for complex application programs, especially since a distribution pattern that may seem appropriate for a given computation step of an application may not be appropriate anymore for the following computation step. Dynamically redistributing aggregates as and where needed (as is possible in PALADIN) might be a way to go round this problem. The redistribution could be controlled by the user, or even encapsulated with the methods needing special distributions to perform an operation efficiently. On this topic the OO approach has an important edge over HPF compilers that can only bind methods to objects statically, thus producing very inefficient code if the dynamic redistribution pattern is not trivial.

References

1. H. Abelson, G. Jay Sussman, and J. Sussman. - *Structure and Interpretation of Computer Programs*. - MIT Press, Mac Graw Hill Book Company, 1985.
2. P. America. - Pool-T: A parallel object-oriented programming. - In A. Yonezawa, editor, *Object-Oriented Concurrent Programming*, pages 199–220. The MIT Press, 1987.
3. F. André, J.L. Pazat, and H. Thomas. - Pandore: a system to manage data distribution. - In *ACM International Conference on Supercomputing*, June 11-15 1990.
4. D. Callahan and K. Kennedy. - Compiling programs for distributed-memory multiprocessors. - *The Journal of Supercomputing*, 2:151–169, 1988.
5. L. Cardelli and P. Wegner. - On understanding types, data abstraction, and polymorphism. - *ACM Computing Surveys*, 17(4):211–221, 1985.
6. D. Gannon, J. K. Lee, and S. Narayama. - On using object oriented parallel programming to build distributed algebraic abstractions. - In *Proc. of CONPAR92*, 1992.
7. G.H. Golub and C.F. Van Loan. - *Matrix Computations*. - The Johns Hopkins University Press, 1991.
8. F. Guidec. - *Un cadre conceptuel pour la programmation par objets des architectures parallèles distribuées : application à l'algèbre linéaire*. - Thèse de doctorat, IF-SIC / Université de Rennes 1, juin 1995.
9. F. Hamelin, J.-M. Jézéquel, and T. Priol. - A Multi-paradigm Object Oriented Parallel Environment. - In H. J. Siegel, editor, *Int. Parallel Processing Symposium IPPS'94 proceedings*, pages 182–186. IEEE Computer Society Press, April 1994.
10. HPF-Forum. - High Performance Fortran Language Specification. - Technical Report Version 1.0, Rice University, May 1993.
11. J.-M. Jézéquel. - EPEE: an Eiffel environment to program distributed memory parallel computers. - *Journal of Object Oriented Programming*, 6(2):48–54, May 1993.
12. C. Pancake and D. Bergmark. - Do parallel languages respond to the needs of scientific programmers? - *IEEE COMPUTER*, pages 13–23, December 1990.
13. Leslie G. Valiant. - A bridging model for parallel computation. - *CACM*, 33(8), Aug 1990.
14. Akinori Yonezawa, Jean-Pierre Briot, and Etsuya Shibayama. - Object-oriented concurrent programming in ABCL/1. - In *OOPSLA'86 Proceedings*, September 1986.

Programming and Debugging for Massive Parallelism: The Case for a Parallel Object-Oriented Language A-NETL

Takanobu Baba, Tsutomu Yoshinaga, and Takahiro Furuta
Department of Information Science, Utsunomiya University
E-mail: baba@infor.utsunomiya-u.ac.jp

Abstract. This paper describes the two major issues of programming and debugging with a parallel object-oriented language, A-NETL. *A-NETL programming* is supported by several language facilities, such as the static definition and dynamic creation of massively parallel objects, asynchronous message passing of past, now, and future types and their multicast versions, and declarative synchronization schemes. *A-NETL debugging* requires special support for verifying the behavior of asynchronous operations. The major feature of the A-NETL debugger is the utilization of logical time, based on the "happened before" relation among events. During a test execution, the events and their logical time are recorded as an event history. The history is edited and presented to the user to provide a global view of the execution. The history is also utilized at the replay phase to provide a virtual event-level clock to a multicomputer and to keep the happened-before relation at test execution time. This not only enables cyclic debugging but also simplifies debugging by showing originally asynchronous operations synchronously.

1 Introduction

Although massively parallel computers can provide high computational rates, their effective utilization requires tools for the programming and debugging of parallel programs [4].

Firstly, for *programming*, explicit parallel languages are indispensable in order to exploit the high-degree of parallelism in massively parallel computers. Data parallel languages of the SIMD type are a promising solution for this issue [30]. However, the synchronous nature of SIMD languages restricts the natural modeling of various parallel operations. Parallel object-oriented languages are more comprehensive than their data parallel counterparts in that they allow the user to describe both synchronous and asynchronous operations flexibly.

A parallel object-oriented language, A-NETL (A-NET Language), has been designed to allow the user to describe medium- to coarse-grained parallel operations explicitly, for use in multicomputers with thousands of nodes at the system description language level [28]. The system description language level requirement means that we provide a basic framework for the description of massive parallelism, but leave out complex operations and data structures to simplify the user-interface and language implementation. In order to compare favorably with data parallel languages, the A-NETL language should provide tools to describe data parallel operations at least at the same cost as the former. Our strategy is to permit the definition of identically structured massively parallel objects statically and dynamically, and to allow the sending of multiple messages in one statement. Further, in order to naturally model both synchronous and asynchronous behaviors of massively parallel objects, the language provides facilities for various styles of message passing as well as several synchronization schemes for autonomous control.

Secondly, for *debugging*, the asynchronous nature of parallel object-oriented programs, an important source of their efficiency and their capability for natural modeling as mentioned above, makes their debugging rather more difficult than that of SIMD data parallel programs [22]. Object-oriented programs are often not deterministic thus making cyclic debugging impossible. To solve this problem, we have designed and developed an event-based debugging system utilizing the concept of *logical time* [9, 13].

A-NETL programming and debugging facilities have been implemented on the A-NET multicomputer simulator, and integrated as the A-NETL programming environment [26]. A-NET (Actors NETwork) stands for the research project that co-designs the A-NETL language and a multicomputer architecture based on a parallel object-oriented computation model [2, 5].

The rest of this paper is organized as follows. Section 2 clarifies the design principles and basic computation model of A-NETL. Section 3 describes A-NETL using several small examples. Section 4 gives an overview of the processing systems and shows some preliminary evaluation results. Section 5 highlights the verification of A-NETL programs. Sections 6 and 7 summarize the advantages of our approach and describe future work.

2 Overview of A-NETL

2.1 Design principles

The basic objective of the A-NETL design is to provide a system description level language like C, that allows the user to describe medium- to coarse-grained, explicit parallel operations consisting of thousands to tens of thousands of objects allocated to multicomputers with thousands of nodes. The followings are the design principles used to attain this objective.

Static definition and dynamic creation of objects   It is impractical to require the user to describe thousands or tens of thousands of objects one by one. In order to allow the user to describe so many objects as easily as possible, we need an appropriate language construct. We believe that if massive parallelism is to be effectively exploited, such objects should be similarly structured. We propose to provide both static and dynamic tools for the description of these objects.

To define objects statically *indexed objects* are used. Indexed objects are similarly structured objects defined at the same cost as that for a single object. Indexed object definition is simple: the user attaches the number of required objects to an object name. Then, the compiler generates these objects automatically and directs them to be allocated to multicomputer nodes. Each indexed object may be identified by its index number, and performs message passing independently from the other indexed objects. This is a major difference with similar languages, such as Concurrent Aggregates (CA), in which messages sent to an aggregate are first received by the parallel run-time system and then directed to an arbitrary member of the collection [12].

The dynamic creation of objects is done using *class objects* where the class definitions are used as templates. Class definitions are broadcast to all multicomputer nodes before execution to save on run-time transfer overhead. Thus, the cost of creating a new object is the same for every node. Currently A-NETL does not support inheritance to simplify implementation.

Note that indexed objects do not incur run-time cost overhead and are much more efficient than class objects. Thus, the user is recommended to utilize indexed objects wherever possible. Based on our experience, most of the parallel algorithms that seemingly need class definitions may be changed to equivalent algorithms that use indexed objects. Following similar reasoning, our emphasis is placed on careful scheduling before run-time and simple control at run-time. Thus, we have developed an allocator that allocates compiler-generated objects to multicomputer nodes so that inter-object communication cost is minimized [3, 6]. The use of indexed objects, along with the allocator, should enable static creation of an efficient object configuration and should minimize the effect of run-time object creation. At run time, we let the user explicitly control the dynamic creation of objects as well as their allocation.

Various styles of message passing   The importance of message passing functions is two-fold: first, to describe a target parallel algorithm as naturally and thus as easily as possible and second, to realize efficient execution of the compiled program. The basic message passing semantics of A-NETL are similar to those in ABCL/1, i.e., they consist of past, now and future types as described later [25]. For each of these types we define a *multicast* version to allow the user to send a message to multiple receivers in one statement. *Multireceive* is defined as a counterpart of multicast message passing. Notice that we do not assume the preservation of message send order at the receiver side. In general, most parallel machines do not support this preservation law at the hardware level, as the message communication time changes depending on the number of intermediate nodes and their processing time. Some message passing libraries support this law at the cost of increased software complexity. Thus, by not assuming order preservation, we can save on software overhead in common cases. And if necessary, preservation is performed using the following synchronization schemes.

Synchronization schemes   In the early stages of A-NETL design, we did not quite recognize the necessity of the synchronization schemes. However, we encountered various synchronization problems over several years of experimental use. For example, to control the order of invocations at the receiver side, we had to use synchronous messages of the now type at the sender side. We encountered this problem, for example, in the case of one-to-one interobject communication and also in the case of two messages sent from an object to a destination object through some intermediate objects. In both cases we assumed non-preservation of send-out order. The use of synchronous message passing here not only resulted in loss of natural modeling of the target algorithm but also hurt the execution-time performance. In order to deal with these issues, several synchronization schemes were defined, and these will be described in detail in later sections.

2.2 Basic computation model

The A-NETL computation model shares basic concepts with several parallel object-oriented languages, in particular ABCL/1. Each object in A-NETL consists of its local state variables and methods. Methods are invoked via messages passed between objects. Such messages are stored in a message queue.

The execution state of an object can be any of the following: *dormant, ready, active*, or *suspended*. After receiving a message, a dormant object can be activated immediately. If a receiver object is active, i.e. executing a method, an incoming message should wait in a queue until the object state changes to suspended at which point its corresponding method begins execution. If an object issues a synchronous message and waits for a reply, its state changes to suspended. When the reply arrives, the suspended object enters the ready state and, when the processor becomes available, resumes execution.

A unique feature of A-NETL is that if some synchronization conditions are attached to a method, these conditions should be checked before method invocation. If the conditions are satisfied execution begins, else the object waits for an interval before testing for condition satisfaction again.

The execution of a method includes the following operations: usual arithmetic and sequence control operations that may change the contents of state and temporary variables inside the object; and message-send operations for past, now, future and return message types and their multicast versions. The sender of a now type message suspends execution until a reply is received. The sender of a future type message suspends execution the first time it refers to the undefined return value as described later. Notice that object creation is classified as a now type message send operation.

When method execution terminates, any synchronization conditions attached to that method should be updated to reflect the termination correctly.

3 Parallel Object-Oriented Programming in A-NETL

A-NETL has been designed based on the principles described in section 2. Major language features are summarized below.

3.1 Static definition of massively parallel objects and their structure

As described in section 2, A-NETL provides tools for defining a large number of objects both statically and dynamically, for use in describing data parallel operations. If the number of objects with similar structure is statically fixed, they can be defined as *indexed objects* simply by attaching the number of required objects to the object name.

Figure 1 shows the definition of one OR, two AND, two NOT indexed objects, and an EXOR object. The EXOR object is defined by connecting the five indexed objects. The connection is established by sending a link message to the EXOR object. In the link method of EXOR itself, a further five link messages are sent to the indexed objects to initiate connection.

```
 1:  object  OR[1]
 2:  state   Next with: nil.
 3:  methods {
 4:      link: next {
 5:          Next addLast: next.
 6:      }
 7:      2 * operate: input {
 8:          @Next operate: ((input first) || (input last)).
 9:      }
10:  }
11:
12:  object  AND[2]
13:  state   Next with: nil.
14:  methods {
15:      link: next {
16:          Next addLast: next.
17:      }
18:      2 * operate: input {
19:          @Next operate: ((input first) && (input last)).
20:      }
21:  }
22:
23:  object  NOT[2]
24:  state   Next with: nil.
25:  methods {
26:      link: next {
27:          Next addLast: next.
28:      }
29:      operate: input {
30:          @Next operate: (input not).
31:      }
32:  }
33:
34:  extern  AND[2] NOT[2] OR[1].
35:  object  EXOR
36:  methods {
37:      link: next {
38:          NOT[1] link: AND[1].
39:          AND[1] link: OR[1].
40:          NOT[2] link: AND[2].
41:          AND[2] link: OR[1].
42:          OR[1] link: next.
43:      }
44:      2 * operate: input {
45:          AND[1] operate: (input first).
46:          NOT[1] operate: (input last).
47:          AND[2] operate: (input last).
48:          NOT[2] operate: (input first).
49:      }
50:  }
```

Fig. 1. Implementation of an exclusive-OR gate — static definition using indexed objects.

Each object can refer to its own index value by using **selfIndex**. This can be utilized to link the constituent objects of an indexed object, since an object can identify its neighbors by applying simple arithmetic operations to the value of **selfIndex**. An example use is identifying neighboring objects in mesh-connected indexed objects.

3.2 Dynamic creation of massively parallel objects on nodes

If the structure of a program depends on dynamic parameters, such as data amount and run-time conditions, *class objects* can be defined as templates for use in the dynamic creation of objects on nodes. The definition of a class is similar to that of an object except that 'object **objectName**' is changed to '**class className**'. A new object is created by sending a **new** message to the class object. A node number may be attached to the message to specify the node on which the created object is to be allocated. If the number is omitted, the object is created on the same node as the sender of the **new** message to the class. The created object may be deleted by sending it a **delete** message.

Figure 2 shows an example of the dynamic creation of objects. The described project consists of **manager** and **projectLeader** objects, and a **projectMember** class. In line 8, the **manager** asks the **projectLeader** to create i **projectMember** objects. In line 26, a **new** message is sent to the **projectMember** class with node number **pos**. Thus, the number of objects to be created and the nodes on which they can be created can be specified dynamically. The sender can reference the created object using the object pointer **temp**. If the sender passes the pointer to other objects, these can use it to reference the new object as well.

3.3 Parallel asynchronous message passing

(1) *Basic message passing semantics*

There are three basic message passing semantics in A-NETL, and these are similar to those in ABCL/1. They are referred to as past, now and future type message passing semantics.

```
receiver pastMessage.
?receiver nowMessage.
result = receiver futureMessage.
```

The sender of a *past* type message continues execution. The sender of a *now* type suspends execution until a reply arrives. The sender of a *future* type continues execution until it refers again to the future variable **result** in the program code. At the point of the reference, the sender checks if a reply has been received. If not, it waits until the reply arrives else it continues execution. Unlike in ABCL/1, **result** is a variable of the sender object that stores the return value. We assume, in general, that messages will not arrive in the order they are sent. The execution sequence of methods is basically determined by message arrival order.

Messages of above three types may be found in Figs. 1 and 2. For example, the **talkToLeader** method in Fig. 2 includes all the three types. The messages in lines

```
 1:  extern  projectLeader.
 2:  object  manager
 3:  state   greeting = 'Hello from manager'.
 4:          inquiry  = 'Are you busy now?'.
 5:          replyList.
 6:  methods {
 7:      talkToLeader: i {
 8:          ? projectLeader createProjectMembers: i.
 9:          projectLeader  broadcastMessageToMembers: greeting.
10:          replyList with: nil.
11:          replyList = projectLeader  broadcastInquiryToMembers: inquiry.
12:          HOST print: ('%z',replyList).
13:      }
14:  }
15:
16:  #define MAXNODE 10
17:  extern  projectMember.
18:  object  projectLeader
19:  state   membersList.
20:  methods: {
21:      createProjectMembers: number {
22:          | temp pos |
23:          membersList with: nil.
24:          while (number > 0) {
25:              pos = number % MAXNODE.
26:              temp = projectMember(pos) new.
27:              membersList addLast: temp.
28:              number = number - 1
29:          }
30:          !
31:      }
32:      broadcastMessageToMembers: message {
33:          @membersList receive1: message.
34:      }
35:      broadcastInquiryToMembers: message {
36:          | replyList |
37:          replyList = @membersList reply: message.
38:          ! replyList.
39:      }
40:      deleteProjectMembers {
41:          @membersList delete.
42:      }
43:  }
```

Fig. 2. Project simulation — dynamic creation of objects (cont. on next page).

```
44:
45: class    projectMember
46: state    messageList with: nil.
47: methods {
48:    receive1: message  {
49:       messageList addLast: message.
50:    }
51:    reply: message  {
52:       messageList addLast: message.
53:       ! 'yes'.
54:    }
55: }
```

Fig. 2. Project simulation — dynamic creation of objects.

8 and 11 are of the now and future type, respectively. The **createProjectMembers** message in line 8 should be of the now type in order to confirm project member creation before sending messages to these objects. The messages in lines 9, 10 and 12 are of the past type.

(2) *Message multicast*

Multicast versions are defined for each of the above mentioned three types.

> **@receiver** *pastMulticastMessage.*
> **?@receiver** *nowMulticastMessage.*
> **resultList** = **@receiver** *futureMulticastMessage.*

The **receiver** represents a list of receiver objects. Once the receivers are set in the list, a multicast to them can be described in one statement. **resultList** stores the replies in their arrival order. For example, the lines 23-28 of Fig. 2 fill **membersList** with a list of the pointers to created **projectMember** objects. The past and future type multicasts to these objects are described in lines 33 and 37, respectively.

(3) *Return*

In addition to the three basic message passing semantics and their multicast versions, we also define another, the *return* type. The receiver of a now or future type message notifies the message sender of the end of method execution using this type as shown below.

> **!**
> **!** *primary.*

The statement ! simply lets the sender know of the successful termination of the method. The **!** *primary* returns the result of the evaluation of the specified primary expressions, so that it may be set to the future variable in the sender object or to a compiler-generated temporary variable for the future or now type messages, respectively.

Examples of the return type message are found in lines 38 and 53 of Fig. 2.

3.4 Declarative synchronization schemes

Sometimes we encounter situations where the simple reactive operation to a message is not sufficient. For the sake of maintaining the integrity of parallel asynchronous operations, several synchronization schemes can be defined in the control section at the head of an object or class definition. The schemes explicitly control the synchronization of multiple messages as follows.

(1) *Serialization*

In A-NETL, send order is not preserved even for object-to-object communication, as has been described in section 2, and therefore some schemes are necessary to enable the receiver object to control the order of the methods' invocations, independent of the arrival order of the messages.

The following declaration specifies the order of invocations.

```
SER { mes1 > mes2 > ...> mesN }
```

If mes$i$ > mes$j$ (i, j=1,2,..,N), then the execution of mesj can not precede that of mesi.

The serialization scheme proposed here is similar to the *sequence* scheme of the path expression proposed in [11].

(2) *Multiple receive*

This specifies multiple-message reception as the condition for method invocation. The message pattern for this scheme is defined as follows:

```
mes1 & mes2 &... & mesN    " receptions of mes1 through mesN "
N * mes                    " the N receptions of mes "
```

Multiple receive can be utilized when a method should be invoked after receiving multiple messages. Usually, this is necessary in an object that collects the results sent from multiple objects. Examples of the use of the N receptions of the same message are found in Fig. 1. In lines 7, 18, and 44, two receptions of the operate message are required to activate the corresponding gate function. Another typical example is that of a main object which waits for the results of some parallel computation by slave objects.

In the case of the reception of multiple different messages, different values may be returned to different senders as below:

```
!ans1 $mes1 & mes2.
!ans2 $mes3.
```

ans1 is returned to the senders of mes1 and mes2, and ans2 is returned to the sender of mes3.

(3) *Conditional expression*

This specifies relational expressions of two variables, both either state variables or message parameters, or one from each, as an activation condition.

```
COND { mes1(vil rel1 vir), mes2(v2l re2 v2r),
                  ... , mesN(vNl relN vNr) }
```

The method for mesi (i=1,2,..,N) can only be executed when the two variables vil and vir satisfy the relation reli.

(4) *Lock*

This locks methods to prohibit double invocation. The lock scheme is provided to enable full utilization of intra-object concurrency. It can be applied to a method containing future or now type messages so that an uncommitted value will not be observed.

```
LOCK { mes1, mes2,..., mesN }
```

In the above case, none of the methods for the message selectors mes1 through mesN will be doubly activated.

The use of the above schemes make objects autonomous, and thus allows the programmer to avoid unnecessary synchronization and to increase parallelism.

As an example of use, we define three objects named customer, bureau, and account. The customer is to deposit 50000 yen into the account, and the bureau is to withdraw 50000 yen upon notification of deposit. For simplicity, just one deposit and one withdrawal are assumed. The balance of account is initialized to 0, and it should not go lower than 0.

Figure 3 shows two possible solutions. In Fig. 3 (a), the customer deposits by a now-type message, i.e., a synchronous message. After receiving a reply to the message, the customer notifies the bureau by a past type, allowing the bureau to withdraw. In Fig. 3 (b), the customer concurrently sends the deposit message to account and the notify message to the bureau since the deposit message is of the past type. The account object will receive the deposit and withdraw messages in an arbitrary order. To maintain integrity, synchronization schemes may be used.

The use of a synchronous message in Fig. 3 (a) is sufficient for maintaining integrity in that the two messages will arrive at the account object serially. However, there is no parallelism. The use of asynchronous messages together with a synchronization scheme in Fig. 3 (b) maintains system integrity whilst at the same time facilitating parallel processing.

Figure 4 is the A-NETL program that realizes the scheme of Fig. 3 (b). The COND statement of line 17 permits the invocation of withdraw only when the balance is not smaller than the withdrawal amount (wdamount).

Note that other synchronization schemes may be used as well but with different semantics. For example, the following serialization specifies that the deposit method should be invoked before the withdraw message.

```
SER { deposit > withdraw }
```

The message pattern withdraw of the account object may be replaced with a multiple receive condition expressed as deposit & withdraw. This ensures that the withdraw method can be invoked only if the deposit method has been invoked.

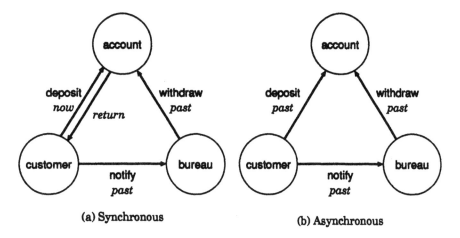

(a) Synchronous   (b) Asynchronous

Fig. 3. Bank account

From the above examples, it should be clear that the COND statement is more general than either serialization or multiple receive synchronization as it permits an arbitrary order of deposits and withdraws.

The Lock scheme may be applied in our example as LOCK {deposit, withdraw} if there is a possibility that any of the two methods deposit and withdraw might be reinvoked while current execution of the same method is suspended.

If a combination of multiple schemes are used, all the related conditions should be satisfied before a method can be invoked.

Our experimental results show that synchronization schemes allow the user to change synchronous programs to asynchronous ones with a scalable reduction of execution times [7].

4 Implementation and preliminary results

4.1 Compilation, allocation and execution

A-NETL source programs are translated by a *compiler* to A-NETL oriented, high-level machine instructions. The compiler extracts inter-object message passing information for the user. The *allocator* inputs a logical configuration of the objects and a physical network configuration of the multicomputer, and produces an allocation [3, 6].

The *linker* inputs the relocatable machine instruction code and the allocation results, and produces executable binary code to be loaded into a multicomputer or a simulator. The *simulator* performs machine instruction level simulation and produces a log for evaluation. The *evaluator* inputs the log and outputs a node-time activity graph and a user/system activity graph. The *debugger* is described in detail in the next section.

For further details of the implementation and the declaration of the logical configuration, see [8].

```
 1:  object   customer
 2:  methods {
 3:      send{
 4:          account deposit: 50000.                " past "
 5:          bureau notify.                         " past "
 6:      }
 7:  }
 8:
 9:  object   bureau
10:  methods {
11:      notify {
12:          account withdraw: 50000.               " past "
13:      }
14:  }
15:
16:  object   account
17:  control COND{ withdraw(balance >= wdamount)}   " synchronization "
18:  state   balance = 0.
19:  methods {
20:      deposit: depamount {
21:          balance = balance + depamount.
22:      }
23:      withdraw: wdamount {
24:          balance = balance - wdamount.
25:      }
26:  }
```

Fig. 4. Description of the bank account program with a synchronization scheme.

The user can use these software systems through an integrated, visual programming environment, called the A-NETL Programming Support System (APSS).

4.2 Preliminary results

An A-NETL-oriented multicomputer with 16 nodes has been developed [29]. Each node runs at about 30 MHz, and takes 35.8 μs to execute a send-past instruction. The node-to-node transfer time T_D is estimated as follows:

$$T_D = 1.9 + D + 0.066 \times n \ (\mu s)$$

D and n stand for the number of hops between the nodes and the size of a message in bytes, respectively. As the evaluator is still being built for use in total evaluation, we will only show the simulated performance evaluation for the following four sample A-NETL programs.

(1) *Gaussian Elimination* (GE): a numerical algorithm for solving an N-dimensional linear equation; one Main and N Row objects are defined

(2) *Radiosity Method* (RD): a 3-dimensional computer graphics algorithm;

one Main and N Patch objects are defined to perform repetitive computation by the Gauss-Seidel algorithm

(3) *Molecular Dynamics* (MD): modeling the behavior of molecules based on the dynamics between small particles; one Main and N Area objects are defined

(4) *N-Queens* (NQ): a search algorithm to place N Queens so that they can not take each other; one Main and N Column objects are defined

Table 1 shows the results assuming that the message transfer time is 0.25 ms on average.

Table 1. Execution time.

Problem	Execution time [ms]
GE	209.0
RD	54.7
MD	551.3
NQ	184.2

Figure 5 shows the estimated speedup ratios.

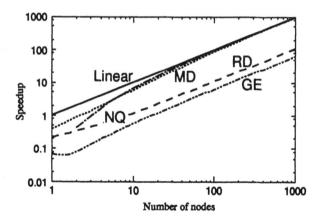

Fig. 5. Speedup ratio.

From these results, we can see that MIMD algorithms (MD and NQ), which are the major target of object-oriented computation, attain an almost ideal speedup. The speedup ratios of the SIMD algorithms (GE and RD) are not as good as those of MIMD algorithms. The reasons for this difference are that, firstly, the granularity of the MIMD programs is larger than that of SIMD programs and thus the communication overhead is smaller, and secondly, that SIMD algorithms need frequent synchronization points that are not supported by hardware. In order to improve the performance for the SIMD algorithms, we may need some hardware-supported tools, such as barrier synchronization.

5 Logical-Time Based Debugging of Asynchronous Programs

5.1 Nondeterminism and replay

The difficulty of debugging asynchronous programs must be overcome if parallel object-oriented languages are to become widely used. This difficulty stems mainly from the nondeterministic nature of such programs. The sources of nondeterminism include the asynchronous behavior of multiple nodes, asynchronous message transmissions, and the probe effect. Nondeterminism disables *cyclic debugging* [22]. In order to solve this problem, we may record all the information generated during program execution as a trace and utilize it for debugging. However, this is usually impractical due to excessive execution time overhead and the requirement of large memory space. Thus, several replay mechanisms have been proposed [21]. The major feature of our replay mechanism is that it utilizes the concept of logical time to control replay. Hereafter, we introduce our definition of event and logical time. Then, we will describe the debugging system developed based on these definitions.

5.2 Event and logical time

We classify *events* into two types: message passing and context change. The former includes message send/receive as well as object creation/delete. The latter includes the execution and termination of a method, and the suspension of execution. Notice that in a node the events between two successive message communication events are executed continuously without intervention from other nodes.

Using the so-called "happened before" relation, *logical time* is defined as follows [19].

- initialize logical time LT of all the nodes to 0;
- when an event of the context change type is executed, increment LT by one, i.e. $LT \leftarrow LT + 1$;
- when an event of the message passing type is executed, the sender attaches its logical time LT_s to the message and increments its logical time as $LT_s \leftarrow LT_s + 1$; the receiver compares its logical time LT_r with the LT_s and defines its logical time LT_r as $LT_r \leftarrow max(LT_s, LT_r) + 1$.

Figure 6 shows the application of this definition. The circles and their attached numbers indicate events and their logical times, respectively. Message passing is represented by an arrow, and the corresponding message ID is composed of the sender ID, receiver ID and the sender's logical time LT_s. Cases (a) and (b) show the effect of the difference in sending and receiving orders. Cases (c) and (d) show the different execution paths of the same program due to the nondeterminism of message arrival. In case (e), two objects O2 and O3 are allocated on the same node N2. The examples in Fig. 6 show that partial ordering is correctly represented in logical time for various cases.

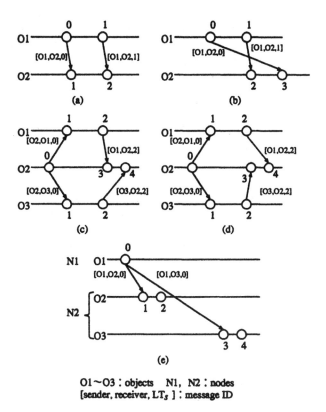

O1~O3 : objects   N1, N2 : nodes
[sender, receiver, LT$_s$] : message ID

Fig. 6. Examples of logical time determination.

5.3 Visual debugging environment

A visual debugging environment has been designed and implemented utilizing the above mentioned concept of logical time. It includes three major debugging functions: breakpoint debugging, event history diagram, and replay.

For *breakpoint* debugging, the user can set an arbitrary number of breakpoints in any of the objects at the source program level. The compiler replaces the original instruction with a system call instruction to halt. The major objective of this function is to provide the user a primitive debug function that stops the execution of the specified object without any *probe effect*. In order to enhance the applicability of the debugger to a wide range of massively parallel machines, we do not assume the existence of a common clock among multicomputer nodes. Thus, it is impossible to stop all the nodes at the same time when some object stops at a breakpoint. Instead, we provide an event history function and a replay function as high-level, inter-object debugging facilities.

Event history and *replay* debugging need a test execution for recording relevant program execution events. An event record of the context change type consists of the event type, the object ID (OID), and the logical time axis. For a message send event, the type, sender OID, send *LT*, and receiver OID are recorded. For a receive event, the type, receiver OID, receive *LT*, sender OID, and send *LT* are recorded. The receive event requires more information than the send event because of the nondeterminism of message reception.

5.4   Event history diagram

The event history diagram shows the events for each object along the logical time. Figure 7 shows the diagram for the N-queens program in A-NETL [10]. The straight and dotted horizontal lines indicate that the objects are active or idle, respectively. An arrow from an object to another one indicates message passing between them.

The user can check the outline of the program execution from the diagram. The execution starts with the user's **start** message to the HOST object on a host computer. The message is then passed to the **Main** object. The figure shows the asynchronous interactions of the 6 Column objects.

5.5   Replay

In the replay mode, the message transmission and context change events are animated according to the logical time. During replay, the event record is utilized to control the replay so that the order of execution remains the same as that of the test execution. This is realized under the control of the master debugger that keeps an event history and a logical time clock. In order to compensate for the lack of a global breakpoint, which can halt all the nodes when some node encounters a breakpoint, the replay mode allows the user to control the execution in various ways, such as *pause, step-run, stop*, and *skip*. Utilizing these execution control functions, the user can stop the whole execution at any logical time, and can observe the contents of the stopped, inter-related objects as if they were running synchronously.

Figure 8 shows the configuration of the debugging system which consists of the master debugger on the host computer and the local debuggers distributed among the multicomputer nodes. The master debugger sends message passing event IDs for a logical time to the local debuggers on multicomputer nodes and then increments the logical time of the clock. On each node, if the ID is for a send event, the local debugger executes the event immediately. If the ID is for a receive event, the local debugger searches the message buffer and executes the corresponding event. If the ID is not found in the buffer, the local debugger waits for the arrival of the specified message.

Figure 9 shows the replay window for the debugging of the N queens program. This corresponds to the vertical cut at logical time 14 on the diagram in Fig. 7.

The circles represent objects. The colors indicate the state of the objects such as message send, receive, context change, and idle.

By clicking a circle, the user can read the values of the variables in the object. If the object has sent or received a message, the contents of the message are also displayed at the same time.

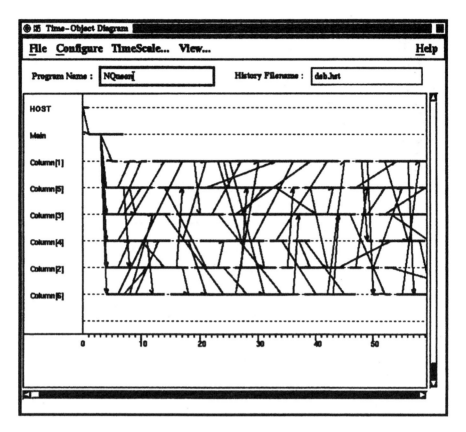

Fig. 7. Event history diagram.

5.6 Preliminary evaluation

The debugging system has been realized on the simulator of the A-NET multicomputer. The results are summarized as follows: the overhead for a breakpoint is 3.1 ms per point, the time and space overheads of event recording average 0.04 ms and 35 bytes per event, respectively. The replay takes 0.94 s to show 16 objects for one logical time.

These results prove that the system attains sufficient performance for practical use. For more detail of the replay algorithm and the preliminary test results, please see [9].

6 Related Work

The related research mentioned here emphasizes the differences from our work.

from language
processor

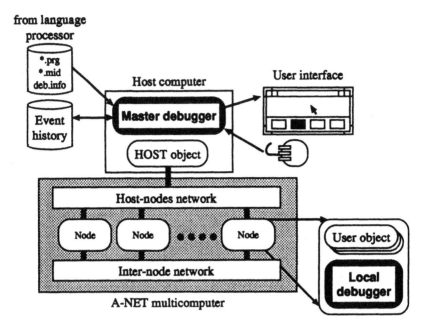

*.prg : configuration of objects and classes
*.mid : message selectors and their codes
deb.info : debug information

Fig. 8. Configuration of the debugging system.

6.1 Parallel object-oriented programming

There are many languages based on the parallel object-oriented computation model [1]. Considering the basic message passing mechanism, the future type message in ABCL/1 [25] creates an object to receive the reply. A user must explicitly test if a reply has been received or not. The future construct in Multilisp [16] forks a child task to realize this mechanism. In the case of A-NETL, no new objects or tasks are created. The availability of the future variable is automatically, and thus implicitly, checked by the tag attached to the variable. The check is supported by the underlying OS and architecture. The return type in ABCL/1 is treated as a future type message. In A-NETL, the return type simply sets a return value to the waiting variable and activates the suspended sender. Thus, it avoids the overhead incurred by method activation and termination. The utilization of intra-object concurrency in A-NETL is another major difference with ABCL/1.

For the static and dynamic creation of objects, CST [18] proposes the concept of a distributed object. However, its major purpose is to distribute the elements of a large array, and their grain size is very fine.

The Aggregate Model[12] also introduces the notion of a collection of actors, called aggregates. However, unlike our indexed objects, the aggregates are not iden-

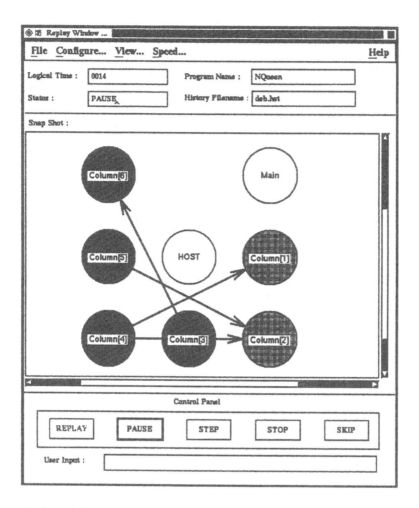

Fig. 9. Replay window.

tified from outside of the collection and a parallel run time system receives messages for the aggregate and dispatches them to the aggregate representatives.

Mentat [15] and ALBA [17] provide a similar dynamic object creation mechanism. However, details of the languages and their implementations are different.

A-NETL data is untyped. But, the recent proposals for CC++ [1] and ABCL/f [24] attract our attention as they employ data typing for efficient implementation.

6.2 Debugging parallel programs

Logical time was proposed by Lamport [19]. Our contribution is to define events for the debugging of parallel object-oriented languages. *Instant replay* proposes a replay mechanism where process-to-process communication is performed through a shared object, and the version number of data is recorded [20]. At replay, the version numbers are utilized to preserve data dependency. For a distributed memory architecture, Leu proposes a method to preserve the sequence of test execution by the control of communication primitives [21]. The major feature of our approach is the utilization of logical time. This approach can provide the user with not only the event history diagram but also virtually synchronized replay operations.

7 Conclusion

We have presented the parallel object-oriented language A-NETL mainly from its programming and debugging point of view.

We started this project in 1987, and in 1990 created an environment for description and simulation on workstations. Then, we polished up the language syntax, the execution model, the local operating system (OS), and the programming support system.

We have also co-designed a multicomputer architecture and developed the A-NET machine [5]. Currently we have a working sixteen-node prototype.

Our future goal is to encourage widespread use of the A-NETL language and the A-NET multicomputer architecture. For this purpose, the language is open to users outside of our project. Further, we have been trying to extend the A-NETL world by porting the language processor to a stock multicomputer and workstation clusters.

Acknowledgements

This research is supported in part by the Japanese Ministry of Education, Science and Culture under Grants 04555077,05219203, 07680334 and 07780225, and by the Telecommunications Advancement Foundation. The authors would like to thank other members of the A-NET project for their helpful comments.

References

1. G. Agha, P. Wegner, and A. Yonezawa, ed.: *Research Directions in Concurrent Object-Oriented Programming*, The MIT Press, Cambridge, Mass., p.532(1993).
2. T. Baba, T. Yoshinaga, T. Iijima, Y. Iwamoto, M. Hamada and M. Suzuki: A Parallel Object-Oriented Total Architecture A-NET, Proc. Supercomputing '90, pp.276-285(1990).
3. T. Baba, Y. Iwamoto and T. Yoshinaga: A Network Topology Independent Task Allocation Strategy for Parallel Computers, Proc. Supercomputing '90, pp.878-887(1990).
4. T. Baba: The Way to Massively Parallel Computers, Journal of Inf. Proc. Society of Japan, Vol.32, No.4, pp.348-364(1991).
5. T. Baba and T. Yoshinaga: Language-Architecture Integrated Approach to a Parallel Object-Oriented Total Architecture A-NET, IEICE Trans. D-I, Vol.J75-D-I, No.8, pp.563-574(1992).
6. T. Baba, A. Gunji, and Y. Iwamoto: A Network-Topology-Independent Static Task Allocation Strategy for Massively Parallel Computers, IEICE Trans. on Information and Systems, Vol.E76, No.8, pp.870-881(1993).
7. T. Baba, N. Saitoh, T. Furuta, H. Taguchi and T. Yoshinaga: A Declarative Synchronization Mechanism for Parallel Object-Oriented Computation, IEICE Trans. on Information and Systems, Vol.E78-D, No.8, pp.969-981(1995).

8. T. Baba and T. Yoshinaga: A-NETL: A Language for Massively Parallel Object-Oriented Computing, Proc. Programming Models for Massively Parallel Computers, pp.98-105 (1995).

9. T. Baba, Y.Furuya and T. Yoshinaga: Event-Based Debugging System for a Parallel Object-Oriented Language A-NETL, Trans. IEICE D-I(to be published)(1996).

10. T. Baba and T. Yoshinaga: A Parallel Object-Oriented Language A-NETL, to be included in *Massively Parallel Processing System JUMP-1*, Ohm-sha, Japan(1996).

11. R.H. Campbell and A.N. Habermann: The Specification of Process Synchronization by Path Expressions, Lecture Notes in Computer Science, Vol.16, pp.89-102(1974).

12. A.A. Chien: Supporting Modularity in Highly-Parallel Programs, in *Research Directions in Concurrent Object-Oriented Programming*, pp. 175-194(1993).

13. Y. Furuya, T. Yoshinaga and T. Baba: Program Debugging System for the Parallel Object-Oriented Language A-NETL, IPSJ SIG Notes 94-PRG-18, Vol.94, No.65, pp.129-136(1994).

14. A. Goldberg and D. Robson: *Smalltalk-80 - The Language and Its Implementation*, Addison-Wesley, p.714(1983).

15. A.S. Grimshaw: Easy-to-Use Object-Oriented Parallel Processing with Mentat, IEEE Computer, Vol.26, No.5, pp.39-51(1993).

16. R.H. Halstead: New Ideas in Parallel Lisp: Language Design, Implementation, and Programming Tools, Lecture Notes in Computer Science, Proc. U.S./Japan Workshop on Parallel Lisp, 441, pp.2-57(1989).

17. J. Hernandez, P. de Miguel, M. Barrena, J.M. Martinez, A. Polo, and M. Nieto: ALBA: A Parallel Language Based on Actors, ACM SIGPLAN Notices, Vol.28, No.4, pp.11-20(1993).

18. W. Horwat: Concurrent Smalltalk on the Message-Driven Processor, MIT MS Thesis in Elec. Eng. and Comput. Sci.(1989).

19. L. Lamport: Time, Clocks, and the Ordering of Events in a Distributed System, Comm. of the ACM, Vol.21, No.7, pp.558-565(1978).

20. T.J. LeBlanc and J.M. Mellor-Crummey: Debugging Parallel Programs with Instant Replay, IEEE Trans. on Computers, Vol.C-36, No.4, pp.471-481(1987).

21. E. Leu, A. Schiper, and A. Zramdini: Efficient Execution Replay Technique for Distributed Memory Architectures, Proc. 2nd European Distributed Memory Computing Conf., Springer-Verlag, LNCS487(1991).

22. C.E. McDowell, and D.P. Helmbold: Debugging Concurrent Programs, ACM Computing Surveys, Vol.21, No.4, pp.593-622(1989).

23. H. Taguchi, T. Yoshinaga and T. Baba: The A-NET Local OS 3rd Edition - Implementation of Message Reception Mechanism and Its Evaluation, Computer System Symposium, Inf. Proc. Soc. Japan, pp.51-58(1993).

24. K. Taura, S. Matsuoka, and A. Yonezawa: ABCL/f: A Future-Based Polymorphic Typed Concurrent Object-Oriented Language, Proc. DIMACS Workshop, American Math. Society(1995).

25. A. Yonezawa: *ABCL: An Object-Oriented Concurrent System*, The MIT Press, Cambridge, Mass.(1990).

26. T. Yoshinaga and T.Baba: A Parallel Object-Oriented Language A-NETL and Its Programming Environment, Proc. COMPSAC'91,pp.459-464(1991).

27. T. Yoshinaga and T.Baba: A Local Operating System for the A-NET Parallel Object-Oriented Computer, J. Inf. Process., Vol.14, No.4, pp.414-422(1992).

28. T. Yoshinaga and T.Baba: A Parallel Object-Oriented Language A-NETL Supporting Topological Programming, IEICE Trans. D-I, Vol.J77-D-I, No.8, pp.557-566(1994).

29. T. Yoshinaga and T.Baba: The Node Processor for a Parallel Object-Oriented Total Architecture A-NET, IEICE Trans. D-I, Vol.J79-D-I, No.2 (to appear) (1996).

30. T. Yuasa, T. Kijima and Y. Konishi: The Extended C Language NCX for Data-Parallel Programming, IEICE Trans. D-I, Vol.J78-D-I, No.2, pp.200-209(1995).

Schematic: A Concurrent Object-Oriented Extension to Scheme

Kenjiro Taura and Akinori Yonezawa

University of Tokyo

Abstract. A concurrent object-oriented extension to the programming language Scheme, called Schematic, is described. Schematic supports familiar constructs often used in typical parallel programs (future and higher-level macros such as plet and pbegin), which are actually defined atop a very small number of fundamental primitives. In this way, Schematic achieves both the convenience for typical concurrent programming and simplicity and flexibility of the language kernel. Schematic also supports concurrent objects which exhibit more natural and intuitive behavior than the "bare" (unprotected) shared memory, and permit intra-object concurrency. Schematic will be useful for intensive parallel applications on parallel machines or networks of workstations, concurrent graphical user interface programming, distributed programming over network, and even concurrent shell programming.

1 Introduction

Programmers in the world, we believe, will begin to use *concurrent* languages for various applications including demanding and intensive computation, distributed programming over networks, user interface programming and even text file processing. Although the task of concurrent programming is, in general, more difficult than sequential programming, there are many evidences and trends that support the above prospect.

- First, parallel machines will become ubiquitous. There is a strong economical demand that parallel intensive applications should run not only on dedicated parallel machines (e.g., CM5, AP1000, T3D, and Paragon), but also on networks of workstations [5, 33]. Recent research [2] has demonstrated that, with suitable communication infrastructures, intensive applications perform well on networks of workstations. Concurrent languages provide ease of programming, portability, and efficiency of applications on such computing environments.
- Second, multiple threads and synchronizing data structure (*e.g.*, concurrent objects) supported by concurrent languages allow more natural and terse description of certain types of applications. Important applications include graphical user interface (GUI) and interactive distributed computation. For example, in interactive distributed applications such as WEB browsers, the programmer in a sequential language must write a complicated scheduler loop which polls inputs both from the user and the remote server. Such

applications can be described much more concisely if the language supports multiple threads of control within a processor. In such languages, a thread can simply block when necessary data has not yet arrived. The runtime system schedules threads and guarantees that the entire application does not block as long as there is at least one runnable thread. A similar situation arises when GUI applications wish to handle multiple inputs in parallel. Since certain types of input must be synchronized with other tasks (*e.g.*, two "redraw" requests to a window must be mutually excluded), the programmer of sequential languages must suspend/restore a thread of control explicitly. This kind of mutual exclusion can be naturally expressed by multiple threads + suitable synchronizing data structures.

In summary, concurrent languages serve as a vehicle both for driving parallel machines more easily *and* expressing certain problems more naturally.

Based on the above observation, we designed and implemented a parallel extension to the programming language Scheme, named Schematic. This paper focuses on its language design. The extension is *concurrency* and *object-orientation*—the language is based on a set of flexible primitives for concurrency and a safe means for dealing with mutable data structure. We believe that the design of Schematic interests two types of concurrent language designers. First, designers who wish to extend an already popular sequential language into parallel one will be interested in how Schematic naturally *integrates* powerful concurrency primitives into existing sequential features such as function calls. Second, those who design a new parallel language, perhaps based on a concurrent calculus, will be interested in how concurrent primitives + a set of simple syntactic tricks provide a concise and familiar syntax both for sequential and parallel constructs. They are beneficial for lowering the learning barrier of the language while keeping the simplicity of the computation model and implementations of the language.

Target applications of Schematic include intensive applications (irregular symbolic or algebraic computation, in particular[1]), interactive applications (GUI in particular), and distributed programming over networks. For irregular intensive applications, Schematic supports very efficient fine-grain thread creation and communication. We have already demonstrated runtime techniques for creating and scheduling excess parallelism within a processor with very low overhead (a local thread creation + reply value communication approximately take ten RISC instructions) [30, 32]. For GUI applications, we are currently working on a GUI library where each widget is represented as a concurrent object and multiple

---

[1] We are not saying that numeric programs do not benefit from languages like Schematic. In fact, it is widely known that many numerics benefit from support of irregular data structures [8, 12, 13] and this leads to many proposals of extensions to C++ [6, 7, 11, 19]. The reason why we did not include numerics from the main target applications is just that in our initial implementation, floating point numbers have boxed (hence slow) representation for the simplicity. We are also working on a similar, but statically typed language called ABCL/f[31], which focuses on the performance of irregular numerics in fine-grain concurrent object-based languages.

events are delivered simultaneously. Since method invocations on a widget is arbitrated by the runtime system, almost no further complication is added from the programmer's point of view, while processing multiple events in parallel.

The rest of the paper is organized as follows. After giving a brief overview of Schematic in Sect. 2 and some background in Sect. 3, we introduce the basic concurrency primitives and the concurrent object-oriented extension in Sect. 4 and Sect. 5, respectively. Section 6 demonstrates some examples which highlight the main features of Schematic. Sect. 7 compares Schematic to a wide range of related languages. We finally conclude and summarize the current status of the Schematic project in Sect. 8.

2 Schematic Overview

The following is the summary of the key extensions made to Scheme:

Channels: As the fundamental primitive for synchronization, we provide first-class *channels*. A channel is a data structure on which synchronized read/write can be performed. Channels can be passed to other processes or stored in any data structure.

Future: As the fundamental construct for expressing parallelism, we introduce a variant of the *future* construct originally proposed by Halstead [14]. The value of a future expression is a channel, which we call *reply channel* of the invocation. The result of an invocation can be extracted from the reply channel of the invocation.

Explicit Reply: The reply channel of an invocation is visible from the invoked process and subject to any first-class manipulation. For example, an invocation can delegate the reply channel to another invocation, or can store the reply channel into a data structure. These features allow us to express many flexible communication/synchronization patterns in a natural way.

Concurrent Objects: Concurrent objects are supported as a safe and convenient way for sharing *mutable* data structures among concurrent processes. A concurrent object is a data structure where a method invocation can be regarded as an *instantaneous* mutation on that object. That is, the programmer is free from the complexity which comes from interleaving execution of multiple methods. An object behaves *as if* methods were serialized.

Concurrent Accesses: While achieving the instantaneous property of a method invocation, we still allow a certain amount of concurrency between multiple method invocations on a single concurrent object. In particular, we guarantee that read-only methods are never blocked by other (possibly writing) methods.

3 Background

This section briefly surveys related work which directly influenced the design of Schematic. A thorough comparison to other concurrent languages is given in Sect. 7.

3.1 Concurrent Calculi

Concurrent calculi, such as HACL [20] and π-calculus [21], have been drawing much attention and some languages have been designed based on them [23, 24]. The goal is to identify the 'core' language which expresses various computation patterns by a small number of fundamental primitives. In their simplest term, both HACL and π-calculus are based on channels communicating via processes. Channels are first-class citizens which can be passed to other processes, sent through other channels, and stored into data structures. Processes can communicate values by synchronized read/write primitives on shared channels.

Although these concurrent calculi are simple and powerful, expressing everything in the pure calculi is tedious. For example, a sequential function call would be expressed by two processes (the caller and the callee) communicating the result value via a channel. Thus, the practical concern when designing a language based on them is how to incorporate familiar constructs (*e.g.*, sequential/parallel function calls) into the language, while keeping the purity of the core.

The design of Schematic achieves both the simplicity of the core and familiar/convenient syntax for frequently used idioms such as **future** calls. A **future** call, for example, is understood as a combination of a channel creation and a process invocation. Even higher-level constructs are realized using channels and/or futures (and are defined as macros, as in Scheme).

The semantics of Schematic can be understood by encoding it into an untyped subset of HACL. Our optimizing compiler which is currently under development uses this untyped subset of HACL as the intermediate language and we are now investigating the analysis and optimization on the simple intermediate language.

3.2 Linearizable Objects

Herlihy et.al [17] defined "linearizability," which captures and formalizes an intuitively correct behavior of data structure shared by concurrent processes. An execution of a program consists of a sequence of events (history), each of which is either an invocation or a termination of a method invocation. A history is *linearizable* if events can be reordered, preserving the order of methods[2] in the original history, to a sequential history, a history in which method executions do not interleave. By definition, a method invocation in a linearizable history appears to take effect *instantaneously*. This simplifies reasoning about behavior of concurrent data structure.

Almost all concurrent object-oriented languages guarantee linearizable histories. Traditionally, many of them guarantee linearizability by, implicitly or explicitly, mutually excluding (serializing) method invocations on a single object.

As demonstrated in a separate paper by Herlihy [16], guaranteeing linearizable history, *per se,* does not require mutual exclusion. We adopt a similar implementation technique to achieve linearizability while permitting certain amount

---

[2] We say method M_1 proceeds method M_2 if the termination of M_1 proceeds the invocation of M_2.

of concurrent accesses to a single object. In Schematic, methods which do not update an object require no mutual exclusion, thus never be blocked by other methods. Methods which do update may still be blocked by other updating methods, but our scheduler never retries interrupted computation. The resulting scheduler is less permissive than Herlihy's with respect to deadlock, but will be more efficient because their implementation requires extra memory store due to the provision for possible retries.

4 Basic Parallelism and Synchronization Primitives

One of the underlying principles of the design of Schematic is the view that *a function/method invocation is, whether it is sequential or asynchronous, just a special case of a process creation.* More precisely, when we have some way for process creation and communication between processes, and we regard a Scheme lambda expression as (a template of) processes, a function call is achieved by invoking a thread which will put the result value to a communication medium. A sequential call just tries to get the result value immediately, while an asynchronous call at a later time.

In Schematic, both processes and the medium for inter-process communication, which we call *channel*, are first-class entities, just as functions are first-class in Scheme. This guarantees the flexibility of Schematic in the sense that whatever can be expressed in HACL or π-calculus has an obvious counterpart in Schematic.[3] This is true to other languages which support first-class channels and processes [24, 25]. However, Schematic better *integrates* parallel extensions with the sequential part and more concisely expresses frequent parallel programming idioms than those languages.

4.1 Channels

Channels are the fundamental entities which realize synchronization and communication between processes. Channels are *implicitly* created as the result of a process creation (see Sect. 4.3), or can be explicitly created via the following form:

(make-channel).

Let c be a channel. We can perform following operations on c:

- (touch c)—extracts a value from c. The value is supplied to the enclosing expression.

---

[3] This is not strictly true for π-calculus because writing a value to a channel in Schematic is asynchronous, while it is *synchronous* in π-calculus, in the sense that writing to a channel in a π-calculus specifies a post action which is executed *after* the reply has been completed. We presume this rarely makes difference in practice, and a synchronous call can be emulated by composing asynchronous ones, although it is tedious.

– (reply x c)—puts x in c. The enclosing expression immediately gets an unspecified value.

There may be multiple pairs of touch/reply performed on a single channel. In such cases, the extracted value is an arbitrary one which has been put until that time.

4.2 Process Templates (or Lambda)

A *process template* in Schematic is expressed by a lambda expression. As its syntax indicates, it is the analogue of a function in Scheme, but is given a name "process template" because applying values to it invokes a new concurrent process. Details about process invocations is described in Sect. 4.3 and this subsection concentrates on process templates.

The canonical form of process template has the following syntax:

(lambda (*args* ···) (:reply-to r) *exprs* ···).

In addition to the list of parameter names, (*i.e.*, (*args* ···)), a process templates takes another parameter, which we call *reply channel*. In the above, the name of a reply channel is specified as r.

For example, expression

```
(lambda (x) (:reply-to r)
  (reply (+ x 1) r))
```

represents a template of processes which reply x + 1 to the given reply channel.

A reply channel can be manipulated as first class data. In particular, a process can store it into any data structure to reply a value later. For example,

```
(lambda (x) (:reply-to r)
  (set! g r))
```

expresses a template of processes which assign the given reply channel to **g** and do not reply any value to **r** from within the processes.

This is an upper-compatible extension of Scheme in the following sense. If a lambda expression does not specify (:reply-to r) clause, it is interpreted as an abbreviation of a template of processes which reply the last evaluated value to the given reply channel. That is,

(lambda (x) *exprs*)

is an abbreviation of

(lambda (x) (:reply-to r) (reply (begin *exprs*) r)),

where r is a name which does not occur in *exprs*.

In essence, we add an extra parameter to each lambda expression, the parameter which represents the location where the result value should be stored. Explicit reply gives the programmer the ability to *decouple* the termination of a process and the delivering the result value; a process may reply a value earlier than its termination and continue some computation, reply values multiple times, or defer the reply until some synchronization/resource constraints are satisfied.

4.3 Process Invocation (or Future)

Suppose f be a process template (lambda expression). The canonical form of process creation is

```
(future (f args ···) :reply-to r).
```

This expression creates a new thread of control which executes the body of f with given arguments and the reply channel r. The entire expression returns r.

For example, when f is defined as

```
(lambda (x) (:reply-to r) (reply (+ x 1) r)),
```

code fragment

```
(let ((r (make-channel)))
  (future (f 3) :reply-to r)
  (future (f 4) :reply-to r)
  (touch r))
```

evaluates to 4 or 5, depending on which process replies the value to r first.

There are several syntactic rules which make expressions in frequent cases more concise. First, when :reply-to clause is omitted, a newly created channel is supplied. That is,

```
(future (f args···))
≡ (future (f args···) :reply-to (make-channel)).
```

Second, a function call expression found in Scheme abbreviates an expression which touches the reply channel immediately after a future call. That is,

```
(f args ···) ≡ (touch (future (f args ···))).
```

This complements the syntax rule about the abbreviation of explicit reply channel name described in the previous subsection. That is, when f is a lambda expression without explicit reply channel name, $(f\ args\ \cdots)$ can be understood just as sequential function call in Scheme.

4.4 Higher-Level Constructs

In addition to the basic primitives, we provide several useful high-level constructs. These are:

plet: a parallel version of let, which evaluates all bound values in parallel.
pcall: a parallel version of apply (evaluates all arguments in parallel)

pbegin: a parallel version of `begin`, which evaluates all subexpressions in parallel.

pmap: a parallel version of `map`, which applies a given function to all elements of the list in parallel.

pfor-each: a parallel version of `for-each`.

They are defined as simple processes and/or macros.

5 Concurrent Object-Oriented Extension

Schematic extends Scheme with concurrent objects which serve as a stylized means for safely using mutable data structure in concurrent applications. Scheme does have mutable data structures (cons cells, strings, vectors, symbols are all mutable), but they are not enough for concurrent applications; interleaving executions of multiple transactions on a single data may result in a state which were impossible in non-interleaving ones. This significantly complicates the behavior of shared data and becomes the source of irreproducible bugs.

A concurrent object in Schematic exhibits simpler and more intuitive behavior than the 'bare' shared memory. The most important property is the *instantaneousness* of a method invocation: from the programmer's point of view, a method invocation appears to mutate the state of the object at some *point* between its invocation and termination. Hence the programmer never has to reason about how potential interleaving executions of concurrent method invocations[4] may affect the result. An object behaves *as if* method invocations on the object are serialized.

This behavior, however, should not be confused with an *implementation* strategy, which really serializes all method invocations on a single object. Such implementation not only loses concurrency, but also significantly narrows the range of deadlock-free programs, enforcing unnatural description of many algorithms. The problem has been recognized for a long time and in fact many languages provide some solutions to the problem. Until recently, few of them guarantees the instantaneousness of a method invocation when the programmer specifies not to serialize certain methods [7, 9, 35]. In such languages, it was up to the programmer that guarantees the desired result on all possible interleavings.

More recent languages such as SYMPAL [3] and UFO [26, 27] propose more complete solutions. They allow concurrent accesses to a single object, while guaranteeing the instantaneousness. The basic idea is to start subsequent invocations as soon as the last update on the object is done in the current method. The remaining issue is how to detect the point where the last update is done. In UFO, updates are specified by individual assignments on instance variables and the

---

[4] Here, we say method invocations M and M' are concurrent if there are no data dependencies that guarantee they never overlap. Notice that this definition is independent of any implementation or scheduling strategy that determines if they are really scheduled in parallel.

compiler approximates the point of the last update. In SYMPAL, a special syntax called *finally* is introduced. A finally expression performs all (hence the last) updates in a method at once and continues other computation in parallel with subsequent method invocation(s). We adopted finally construct in Schematic and add a further extension to allow read-only methods to proceed without any lock.

5.1 Classes and Methods

Defining Classes. A class is defined by `define-class` and a method either by `define-method` or `define-method!`. For example,

```
(define-class point ()
  x
  y)
```

defines class called `point`, each instance of which has slots called x and y. What follows after the class name is the list of inherited classes. For example,

```
(define-class color-point (point)
  color)
```

defines `color-point` class, each instance of which now has slot `color` in addition to x and y.

A `define-class` implicitly defines a function with the class name which creates an instance of the class. For example, an instance of `point` class is created by:

```
(point 2.0 3.0).
```

Defining Methods. The following defines a method which returns the distance between the point and the origin.

```
(define-method point (distance self)
  (sqrt (+ (* x x) (* y y)))).
```

Define-method defines a process template which can read instance variables of the first parameter (`self` in this example). Invoking methods has exactly the same syntax as invoking normal process templates. For example, `distance` method can be called by:

```
    (distance p) or,
```

```
    (future (distance p)),
```

where p is an instance of `point` (or one of its subclasses).

Explicit reply channels can be used in methods as well. For example, `distance` method equivalent to the above one could be written by:

```
(define-method point (distance self)
  (:reply-to r)
  (reply (sqrt (+ (* x x) (* y y))) r)).
```

Updating States. Updating the state of an object is expressed by become construct which specifies new values for updated slots as well as the result of the entire expression. Our become is different from that of Actors [1] in that ours specifies the result value and only allows changing state variables.[5] This construct was originally proposed by Aridor [3] in the name of finally construct.

For example, the following method increments x and y by dx and dy respectively, and returns the value of (redraw! self).

```
(define-method! point (move! self dx dy)
  (become (redraw! self) :x (+ x dx) :y (+ y dy)))
```

The first argument of a become ((redraw! self) in this case) is called *result expression* of the become and specifies which value the become is evaluated to, while the rest part the updated values for instance variables.

There are two syntactic rules about the position of becomes. First, a become can only appear in the body of define-method! and cannot appear in the body of define-method. Second, inside the body of a define-method!, a become can appear only at *tail* position of the method body. A tail position of a method body is a position where a tail function call can be put. For example, we permit

```
(define-method! class (method self ...)
  (if ...
      (become ...)
      (become ...)))
```

and,

```
(define-method! class (method self ...)
  (let ((x ...))
    ...
    (become ...))),
```

because these becomes are, if replaced by a function call, tail calls. On the other hand, we reject

```
(define-method! class (method self ...)
  (+ (become ...) 10)).
```

By the second restriction, we guarantee that become is performed at most once in a method invocation. Precise definition of the syntactic restriction is not given here. It defines right places for each essential syntax and builtin Scheme macros (such as do).

5.2 Concurrency Semantics

Concurrency semantics refers to the way in which the programmer reasons about deadlock and liveness. Notice that it does not tell the programmer which pair

---

[5] Become in Actor allows us to replace the class of the object.

of methods are really scheduled in parallel. It merely tells which programs are guaranteed to run without deadlock.

In many concurrent object-oriented languages [4, 36], method invocations on a single object are serialized. In other words, the system schedules methods so that any pair of methods on a single object does not interleave. This is a very naive way to guaranteeing the instantaneousness of a method invocation and enforces unnatural coding styles just for avoiding possible deadlocks.

To illustrate the problem, consider a possible description of a relaxation step on a one dimensional mesh.

```
(define-class cell ()
   value          ; the value in the current step
   new-value      ; the value in the next step
   left           ; cell object on the left
   right)         ; cell object on the right

(define-method cell (current-value self)
   value)

(define-method! cell (relax! self)
   (let ((lv (current-value left)) (rv (current-value right)))
     (become #t :new-value (/ (- (+ lv rv) (* 2 value)) 2)))))
```

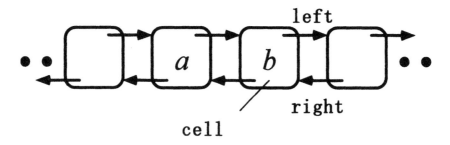

Fig. 1. Cell objects linked by `left` and `right` fields.

Many cell objects form a doubly linked list via `left` and `right`, as in Fig. 1. A relaxation step invokes `relax!` method on all the cell objects. Each `relax!` method first asks the current value of its neighbors by `current-value` method and updates itself using these values. If any pair of methods on a single object cannot overlap, invoking `relax!`s in parallel may result in deadlock. This happens when two neighboring objects start their `relax!` method almost simultaneously. Invocation of `relax!`es never terminate unless `current-values` invoked from within them terminate, but these `current-values` in this scheduling wait for the completion of `relax!`es!.

Notice that since instance variable `value` is not updated in `relax!`, there is no reason why we serialize `current-value` and `relax!` on a single object. This example suggests that we must have a finer classification of methods, which defines which types of methods can/cannot interleave with which.

The next example demonstrates another requirement for the concurrency between methods. Consider a sorted (linear) list of concurrent objects and a method which inserts a new value in the appropriate place, maintaining the list to be sorted.

```
(define-class cell ()
  value
  next)

(define-method cell (get-value self)
  value)
```

```
;;; Insert V in the appropriate place
(define-method! cell (insert! self v)
  (if (< v (get-value next))
      ;; V is smaller than VALUE of NEXT,
      ;; so we insert V between SELF and NEXT
      (become 'done :value value :next (cell v next))
      ;; otherwise recurse on the child
      (become (insert! next v))))
```

We easily see that, if we serialize methods to a *single* object, accesses to an entire list is also serialized, because `insert!` on the head object finishes only when the entire computation finishes. Since the "else" branch of the above method simply delegates the `insert!` method to `next` object, we can accept subsequent methods as soon as `(< v (get-value next))` turns out to be false. This example suggests that we must provide a way to accept subsequent methods when a method execution reaches a certain point.

Based on the above observation, Schematic refines the traditional mutual exclusion model in the following two ways.

- We classify methods into two types, *i.e.*, those defined by `define-method` (which we call **method** below) and those defined by `define-method!` (which we call **method!** below). Schematic guarantees that a **method** always progresses and can overlap with any other **methods** and **method!**s.
- For solving the second example, we breakdown execution of a **method!** into two stages, called *before-stage* and *after-stage*. After-stage evaluates the result expression of the `become` and before-stage performs all actions before the after-stage. In the **move!** method, for example,

```
(define-method! point (move! self dx dy)
  (become (redraw! self) :x (+ x dx) :y (+ y dy)))
```

the before-stage consists of evaluating (+ x dx) and (+ y dy) and updating the instance variables. After-stage invokes **redraw!** method for self. Our relaxed mutual exclusion rule is that a before-stage of an invocation cannot overlap with before-stages of other invocations, but an after-stage can overlap with other before-stages and after-stages. Hence, this example does not deadlock.

The first rule implies that, as far as deadlock is concerned, we only have to consider **method!**s. The above relaxation example never causes deadlock because it only invokes one **method!** per an object. The second rule says that a **method!** can release the mutex associated to an object earlier than its termination. The second example allows multiple **insert!**s to operate in parallel on a list because a cell object can accept subsequent methods as soon as it decides to call **next** object.

When the system results in a situation where no executing methods cannot be completed, the system simply deadlocks and never retries nor aborts unlike schedulers in many database systems.

5.3   Consistency Semantics

Concurrent objects exhibit simpler and more intuitive behavior than the regular shared memory, in that methods on concurrent objects interleave in the granularity of an entire method body, rather than individual load/store operations. This section gives the description of how to reason about possible states (*i.e.,* values of instance variables) of an object at any given time. There are two important rules.

- First, values of instance variables never change inside a body of both types of methods (*i.e.,* **define-method** and **define-method!**); their values are fixed at the beginning of the method. A mutation by a **method!** takes effect in methods *invoked after* the before-stage of the **method!**. Consider the following counter object.

```
(define-class counter ()
  value)

(define-method counter (get-value self)
  value)

(define-method! counter (add-value! self x)
  (become value :value (+ value x))).
```

Method **add-value!** increments **value** of a counter object by **x**. Referencing **value** in the result expression of the **become** still reads the *original* value of **value**. On the other hand, if we change **add-value!** method in the following way:

```
(define-method! counter (add-value! self x)
  (become (get-value self) :value (+ value x))),
```

we will obtain the value *after* value has been incremented, since get-value method is invoked after the update has been done.

- Second, become atomically updates all the instance variables, no matter how many variables are updated. Consider the following example.

```
(define-method! point (move! self dx dy)
  (become (redraw! self) :x (+ x dx) :y (+ y dy)))

(define-method point (position self)
  (list x y))

(let ((p (point 0 0)))
  (pbegin
    (move! p 1 1)
    (position p))).
```

In the last expression, we invoke position method on a point object that is moving from point $(0,0)$ to point $(1,1)$. The position method is guaranteed to return either (0 0) or (1 1). It never obtains (0 1) nor (1 0).

6 Examples

6.1 Concurrent Tree Updating

This example demonstrates how the concurrency semantics of our model, that is, classification of methods and the notion of before/after-stage, allows natural description of concurrent data structure. Consider a binary tree search algorithm where each node of the binary tree is a concurrent object. Here is the definition of each node object.

```
(define-class bintree-node ()
  ;; remember association between KEY and VALUE
  key
  value
  ;; children (#f when it does not exist)
  left
  right)
```

Each node has its key and associated value. It holds that the key of the left child is less than that of self and the key of the right child is greater than that of self. Hence binary search operation is very straightforward.

```
;;;
;;;
;;; Lookup the value associated for K.
;;;
```

```
(define-method bintree-node (lookup self k not-found)
  (cond ((= k key) value)                    ; found
        ((< k key)
         ;; look for the left subtree if K < KEY
         (if left
             (lookup left k not-found)
             not-found))
        (else
         ;; look for the right subtree if K > KEY
         (if right
             (lookup right k not-found)
             not-found)))))
```

Since this operation does not update the tree, we use **define-method**, hence multiple lookup invocations can simultaneously operate on a single tree. The following method installs a new association between key k and value **val**.

```
;;;
;;; Establish association K ↔ VAL, maintaining the
;;; following invariant:
;;;    "(KEY of LEFT) < (KEY of SELF) < (KEY of RIGHT)"
;;;
```

```
(define-method! bintree-node (insert! self k val)
  (cond ((< k key)
         (if left
             ;; if there is already left child, delegate this value
             ;; to the child, unlocking self
             (become (insert! left k val))
             ;; if there is no left child, create it
             (become #t :left (make-leaf-bintree-node k val)))
        ((= k key)
         (format #t "Warning conflicting key (~s ~s)~%" key value)
         (become #f))
        (else
         ;; the same algorithm as the first case, but for the right child
         (if right
             (become (insert! right k val))
             (become #t :right (make-leaf-bintree-node k val)))))))
```

This method first finds the appropriate place to which we insert the item and then installs a new node to that place. An interesting case happens in internal nodes; an internal node recursively calls **insert!** method for an appropriate child *after* it unlocks **self** for subsequent requests. This is expressed by

```
(become (insert! left k val))
```

at line 6 and

```
(become (insert! right k val))
```

at line 15. As has been described in Sect. 5.2, these recursive calls are in the after-stage of the method, *i.e.*, executed after `self` has been unlocked.

6.2 Synchronizing Objects

To demonstrate the expressive power of explicit reply channels, consider implementation of an object which embodies an application-specific synchronization constraint. That is, upon a method invocation, the object defers the reply of the invocation until certain synchronization constraints are satisfied *by subsequent methods*. Simply blocking computation *inside* the method does not work, because this may exclude subsequent method invocations, thus block the original computation forever!

As a simple example, consider implementing a synchronizing stack object. The synchronization constraint is that pop operation on an empty stack should block until the next push operation has been made. An instance of the following `stack` class has two instance variables `values` and `waiters`. Values is a list of pushed values and `waiters` a list of reply channels of pop requests which are not yet served. At least one of `values` or `waiters` is always empty.

```
(define-class stack ()
  values ; list of pushed values
  waiters) ; list of reply channels
```

The following `stack-pop!` method facilitates explicit reply channel feature of Schematic. The method first checks if `values` is empty. If it is, we block the caller by not replying any value to the reply channel of the invocation. In order to later unblock the caller, we insert the reply channel to `waiters` list. Otherwise we simply serve the top element of `values` by `reply` operation on the reply channel.

```
;;;
;;; Pop a value from the stack.  Block if empty, until the next STACK-PUSH!
;;;

(define-method! stack (stack-pop! self)
  (:reply-to r)   ; declare the name of the reply channel to be R
  (if (null? values)
      ;; Stack is empty.  Does not reply anything and let the caller
      ;; wait until the next value comes
      (become #t :values '() :waiters (cons r waiters))
      ;; Stack is not empty.  Simply reply the top element to R.
      (become (reply (car values) r)
      :values (cdr values) :waiters '())))
```

To make this example complete, we give the description of push operation below. The method first checks `waiters` list. If it is empty, we simply push the value to `values` for servicing later `stack-pop!`s. Otherwise it removes a channel from `waiters` and serves the value to it.

```
;;;
;;; Push VAL on the stack.
;;;

(define-method! stack (stack-push! self val)
  (if (null? waiters)
      ;; nobody is waiting, hence simply push VAL
      (become #t :values (cons val values) :waiters '())
      ;; somebody is blocking, hence resume the first guy
      (become (reply val (car waiters))
              :values '() :waiters (cdr waiters))))
```

7 Comparison to Other Languages

Schematic can be related to several groups of other concurrent languages. First, Schematic is a language whose computation model is based on a concurrent calculus which gives us the foundations of compiler optimizations. Second, Schematic supports concurrent objects which allow/guarantee more concurrency than the traditional mutual exclusion model which serialize all method invocations on a single object. Third, Schematic is an extension of a popular sequential language, which already has a philosophy to be preserved.

7.1 Languages Based on Concurrent Calculi

PICT. PICT [24] is a concurrent language based on π-calculus [21]. Its design goal is to support frequently used higher-level idioms as syntactic rules in a language directly based on π-calculus (just as Scheme is based on λ calculus and has higher-level idioms such as do loop). Although the language design is still evolving, there seems to be no constructs which directly support future or even sequential function calls. Schematic shares the same design goal and demonstrates that, by looking at function calls and lambda expressions of Scheme in a slightly different way, a language with a very small number of fundamental primitives can at the same time provide convenient constructs (such as `future` and `plet`) for typical cases.

7.2 Concurrent Extensions to Sequential Languages

Extending a sequential language to yield a concurrent dialect has many practical advantages. Among others, Multilisp and Concurrent ML are closely related to Schematic, in that Multilisp extends Scheme by future and Concurrent ML supports first class channels.

Multilisp. Multilisp [14] is the language which originally embodies the `future` construct. The central idea of `future` is that a future expression returns something which later becomes the result value. This construct or variants are later adopted not only in parallel Lisps but also in some concurrent object-oriented languages [18, 31, 34, 36].

Schematic also supports a variant of `future`. An apparent difference between the `future` in Multilisp and the one in Schematic is that in Multilisp, producer-consumer synchronization of a future invocation is implicit in value reference, whereas Schematic requires explicit `touch` operations. For example, invoking (`f` `x`) and (`g` `y` `z`) in parallel and then adds the two results is written by

```
(+ (future (f x)) (future (g y z))),
```

in Multilisp, while it is written by

```
(let ((l (future (f x))) (r (future (g y z))))
  (+ (touch l) (touch r)))
```

in Schematic.[6]

Informally, the Multilisp view of a future is that what is immediately returned by a future expression is a placeholder object, which later *becomes* the result value for itself, whereas the Schematic view is that a future expression returns a placeholder (*i.e.,* channel) *into which the result value is stored.*

There are tradeoffs between these two views. The implicit future in Multilisp, as the above example indicates, often results in a terse expression but loses some flexibility. On the other hand, by making `touch` explicit, we can distinguish a reference to a channel itself from the reference to the value which is stored in the channel by the program text. This not only guarantees fast value reference without additional compiler analysis [29], but also produces more expressive power by making channels first-class citizens. Examples have been given in Sect. 6.2.

Another difference is their treatment of shared mutable data. Multilisp provides Scheme builtin data as the basis for mutable data and some atomic memory operations such as `replace-if-eq` (analogue of *compare & swap*). No higher-level mechanisms for defining safe mutable data are provided. Schematic supports and encourages the use of concurrent objects to represent mutable data, concurrent accesses to which are arbitrated by the runtime system.

Concurrent ML. Concurrent ML (CML) [25] extends SML by first-class channels and fork (`spawn`), whereas Schematic extends Scheme by first-class channels, fork (`future`), and concurrent objects. To put concurrent objects aside, the main difference is that CML does not support any higher-level concurrent primitives (parallel calls or even `future`s).

Consider how to do two CML function calls `f` `x` and `g` `x` in parallel. Since the results must now be extracted from a channel, let us define a 'wrapper' function which takes a channel and sends the result of `f` `x` to the channel.

---

[6] As far as this particular example is concerned, `pcall` would express it more nicely.

```
fun wrapper f x c = send (f x, c)
```

What remains is to create two channels, spawn two wrappers, and wait for the result.

```
let c0 = channel ()
and c1 = channel ()
in
   (spawn (fn () => wrapper f x c0);
    spawn (fn () => wrapper g x c1);
    accept c0; accept c1)
end
```

Presumably, a fragment like this will appear very often and should be more stylized, as in Schematic. In fact, a restricted version of future can be defined in CML by

```
fun future f x =
  let c = channel ()
  in
    (spawn (fn () => send (c, f x)); c)
  end.
```

Except that it can only invoke a unary function, the above future takes any function and any argument and returns the reply channel. This is more monolithic and less flexible than futures in Schematic, in that a future now always creates a reply channel and the caller loses the chance to specify a reply channel.

Given that a function is the fundamental building block of CML programs, CML should support and encourage a convenient way for invoking functions in parallel. Schematic is designed based on this principle, while leaving chances to construct customized communication structure whenever desired.

7.3 Concurrent Object-Oriented Languages

A *concurrent object* refers to data that embodies some access arbitration mechanisms so that an execution of a method never observes inconsistent state of an object. Several object models have been proposed and they differ in the degree of concurrency on a single object. Below we compare Schematic with other languages in this respect.

Early Concurrent Object-Oriented Languages based on Actors. Some early concurrent object-oriented languages such as ABCL/1 [35, 36] and Cantor [4] achieves the instantaneousness of a method execution by mutually excluding all the method invocations on an object. This is often explained by "an autonomous object which has its own thread and message queue." Although the traditional mutual exclusion model provides the instantaneousness and a very simple model in which the programmer reasons about deadlock, it is often criticized to serialize too much. This not only loses performance gain which is otherwise possible by exploiting parallelism, but also enforces unnatural description of algorithms to solely avoid potential deadlock.

Concurrent Aggregates. Concurrent Aggregates (CA) [9, 10] supports *aggregates* in addition to regular objects. A regular object is a serializing data structure and an aggregate is internally composed of multiple objects, but externally viewed as if it were a single object. By processing multiple method invocations on an aggregate by multiple internal objects, an aggregate can serve as a non-serializing object. Maintaining the consistency among multiple internal objects, if required, is the responsibility of the programmer.

SYMPAL and UFO An object in more recent languages such as SYMPAL [3] and UFO [26, 27] allows a running method to overlap with subsequent methods, while achieving the instantaneousness of method invocations. The basic idea is to schedule subsequent methods on an object as soon as the current method finishes the last update in the method body.

Become of Schematic was originally proposed in SYMPAL as `finally` construct. A method can perform at most one `finally`, which all at once updates instance variable. The syntactic rule described in Sect. 5.1 (also described in [3]) guarantees the single update rule. Schematic extends the object model of SYMPAL by further classifying methods into two types (`define-method` and `define-method!`) and guaranteeing that `define-method` always progresses without any mutual exclusion.

UFO also enforces the single assignment rule and takes another approach for detecting the last update. A method (called procedure in UFO) updates state variables by individual assignments. The compiler statically approximates the point where the last update is done and unlocks the object at that point.

C++ Dialects. Several C++ dialects support *objectwise* concurrency control mechanisms. Here we concentrate on dialects which support this type of object model and do not discuss other types of C++ extensions such as data-parallel extensions [6].

CC++ [7] does not directly support concurrent objects, but the similar effect can be achieved by `atomic` member functions. By declaring a member function as `atomic`, the member function locks/unlocks the object at invocation/termination as in the traditional Actors. Thus the object model of CC++ has the same problems with early concurrent object-oriented languages. Non-atomic functions can run concurrently with others, but this merely leaves consistency issues for the programmer.

Objects in ICC++ [11] allows two methods M and M' to operate on a single object in parallel if there are no read/write nor write/write conflicts between them *on any instance variable of the object*. In this way, ICC++ guarantees that any method appears to take effect instantaneously, while achieving concurrent accesses to a single object. The main difference between ICC++ and the

UFO/SYMPAL/Schematic group is that the ICC++ model performs mutual exclusion on a per instance variable basis, rather than a per object basis.

The range of programs which are guaranteed to be scheduled without deadlock do not seem quite different between ICC++ and Schematic. A foreseeable problem with the ICC++ object model is that each object now potentially has to have multiple locks to serialize only conflicting methods. The worst case requires a lock per instance variable and removing redundant locks requires global information on the source code.

8 Summary and Current Status

The design of Schematic, a concurrent object-oriented extension to Scheme, has been presented. Just as most part of Scheme can be understood in terms of a very simple calculus (the λ-calculus), most part of Schematic can be understood in terms of a simple *concurrent* calculus (HACL). To make it really practical, Schematic also supports and encourages the use of familiar paradigms (*i.e.,* futures and concurrent objects) as well, achieving both the simple core of the language and the conciseness/convenience in typical programs.

A prototype on top of a sequential Scheme (Scheme->C) has been implemented and is running on AP1000 and AP1000+ massively parallel processors [15, 28]. We had developed an RNA secondary structure prediction algorithm [22],[7] which is essentially a parallel tree search with application-specific priority and a load-balancing control scheme, and Barnes-Hut Nbody algorithm. Experiments on an AP1000+ system (SuperSparc 50 Mhz × 256) indicated an usable performance, though many more improvements are necessary.

Further information is available via:

http://web.yl.is.s.u-tokyo.ac.jp/pl/schematic.html.

References

1. Gul A. Agha. *Actors: A Model of Concurrent Computation in Distributed Systems.* The MIT Press, Cambridge, Massachusetts, 1986.
2. Thomas E. Anderson, David E. Culler, David A. Patterson, and the NOW Team. A case for NOW (networks of workstations). *IEEE Micro*, 15(1):54–64, February 1995.
3. Yariv Aridor. *An Efficient Software Environment for Implicit Parallel Programming with a Multi-Paradigm Language.* PhD thesis, the Senate of Tel-Aviv University, 1995.
4. W. C. Athas and C. L. Seitz. Cantor user report version 2.0. Technical report, Computer Science Department, California Institute of Technology, 1987.
5. Nanette J. Boden, Danny Cohen, Robert E. Felderman, Alan E. Kulawik, Charles L. Seitz, Jakov N. Seizovic, and Wen-King Su. Myrinet: A gigabit-per-second local area network. *IEEE Micro*, 15(1):29–36, February 1995.

---

[7] This paper describes algorithms and results by message passing C on CM5, and we are now preparing the result in Schematic.

6. F. Bodin, P. Beckman, D. Gannon, S. Yang, S. Kesavan, A. Malony, and B. Mohr. Implementing a parallel C++ runtime system for scalable parallel systems. In *Proceedings of Supercomputing*, pages 588–597, 1993.

7. K. Mani Chandy and Carl Kesselman. CC++: A declarative concurrent object-oriented programming notation. In Gul Agha, Peter Wegner, and Akinori Yonezawa, editors, *Research Directions in Concurrent Object-Oriented Programming*, chapter 11, pages 281–313. The MIT Press, 1993.

8. Andrew Chien, M. Straka, Julian Dolby, Vijay Karamcheti, John Plevyak, and Xingbin Zhang. A case study in irregular parallel programming. In *Proceedings of the DIMACS workshop on Specification of Parallel Algorithms*, 1994.

9. Andrew A. Chien. *Concurrent Aggregates (CA)*. PhD thesis, MIT, 1991.

10. Andrew A. Chien and William J. Dally. Concurrent aggregates (CA). In *Proceedings of the Second ACM SIGPLAN Symposium on Princeples & Practice of Parallel Programming*, pages 187–196, Seattle, Washington, March 1990.

11. Andrew. A. Chien, U. S. Reddy, J. Plevyak, and J. Dolby. ICC++ – a C++ dialect for high performance parallel computing. In *Proceedings of the Second International Symposium on Object Technologies for Advanced Software (To appear)*, 1996.

12. High Performance Fortran Forum. *HPF-2 Scope of Activities and Motivating Applications*, 1994.

13. Ananth Y. Grama, Vipin Kumar, and Ahmed Sameh. Scalable parallel formulation of the Barnes-Hut method for n-body simulations. In *Proceedings of Supercomputing '94*, pages 439–448, 1994.

14. Robert H. Halstead, Jr. Multilisp: A language for concurrent symbolic computation. *ACM Transactions on Programming Languages and Systems*, 7(4):501–538, April 1985.

15. Kenichi Hayashi, Tunehisa Doi, Takeshi Horie, Yoichi Koyanagi, Osamu Shiraki, Nobutaka Imamura, Toshiyuki Shimizu, Hiroaki Ishihata, and Tatsuya Shindo. AP1000+: Architectural support of put/get interface for parallelizing compiler. In *Proceedings of Architectural Support for Programming Languages and Operating Systems*, pages 196–207, 1994.

16. Maurice P. Herlihy. A methodology for implementing highly concurrent data objects. *ACM Transactions on Programming Languages and Systems*, 15(5):745–770, 1993.

17. Maurice P. Herlihy and Jeannette M. Wing. Linearizability: A correctness condition for concurrent objects. *ACM Transactions on Programming Languages and Systems*, 12(3):463–492, 1990.

18. Waldemar Horwat, Andrew A. Chien, and William J. Dally. Experience with CST: Programming and implementation. In *Proceedings of the SIGPLAN '89 Conference on Programming Language Design and Implementation*, pages 101–109, Portland, Oregon, July 1989.

19. Yutaka Ishikawa. The MPC++ Programming Language V1.0 Specification with Commentary Document Version 0.1. Technical Report TR-94014, RWC, June 1994. http://www.rwcp.or.jp/people/mpslab/ mpc++/mpc++.html.

20. Naoki Kobayashi and Akinori Yonezawa. Higher-order concurrent linear logic programming. In *Proceedings of Workshop on Theory and Practice of Parallel Programming (TPPP)*, volume 907 of *Lecture Notes in Computer Science*, pages 137–166. Springer Verlag, 1994. http:// web.yl.is.s.u-tokyo.ac.jp/pl/hacl.html.

21. Robin Milner. The polyadic π-calculus: A tutorial. Technical Report ECS-LFCS-91-180, University of Edinburgh, 1991.

22. Akihiro Nakaya, Kenji Yamamoto, and Akinori Yonezawa. RNA secondary structure prediction using highly parallel computers. *Comput. Applic. Biosci. (CABIOS) (to appear)*, 11, 1995.

23. Benjamin C. Pierce and David N. Turner. Concurrent objects in a process calculus. In *Proceedings of Workshop on Theory and Practice of Parallel Programming (TPPP)*, volume 907 of *Lecture Notes in Computer Science*, pages 187–215. Springer Verlag, 1994.

24. Benjamin C. Pierce and David N. Turner. PICT: A programming language based on the Pi-Calculus. Technical report in preparation; available electronically, 1995.

25. John H. Reppy. CML: A higher-order concurrent language. In *Proceedings of the ACM SIGPLAN'91 Conference on Programming Language Design and Implementation*, pages 293–305, 1991.

26. John Sargeant. United functions and objects: An overview. Technical report, Department of Computer Science, University of Manchester, 1993.

27. John Sargeant. Uniting functional and object-oriented programming. In Shojiro Nishio and Akinori Yonezawa, editors, *Proceedings of First JSSST International Symposium on Object Technologies for Advanced Software*, volume 742 of *Lecture Notes in Computer Science*, pages 1–26. Springer-Verlag, 1993.

28. Toshiyuki Shimizu, Takeshi Horie, and Hiroaki Ishihata. Low-latency message communication support for the AP1000. In *The 19th Annual International Symposium on Computer Architecture*, pages 288–297, 1992.

29. Olin Shivers. Data-flow analysis and type recovery in Scheme. In Peter Lee, editor, *Topics in Advanced Language Implementation*, chapter 3, pages 47–87. The MIT Press, 1991.

30. Kenjiro Taura, Satoshi Matsuoka, and Akinori Yonezawa. An efficient implementation scheme of concurrent object-oriented languages on stock multicomputers. In *Proceedings of the ACM SIGPLAN Symposium on Principles & Practice of Parallel Programming PPOPP*, pages 218–228, 1993. http://web.yl.is.s.u-tokyo.ac.jp/pl/schematic.html.

31. Kenjiro Taura, Satoshi Matsuoka, and Akinori Yonezawa. ABCL/*f*: A future-based polymorphic typed concurrent object-oriented language – its design and implementation –. In G. Blelloch, M. Chandy, and S. Jagannathan, editors, *Proceedings of the DIMACS workshop on Specification of Parallel Algorithms*, number 18 in Dimacs Series in Discrete Mathematics and Theoretical Computer Science, pages 275–292. American Mathematical Society, 1994. http://web.yl.is.s.u-tokyo.ac.jp/pl/ schematic.html.

32. Kenjiro Taura, Satoshi Matsuoka, and Akinori Yonezawa. *StackThreads*: An abstract machine for scheduling fine-grain threads on stock CPUs. In *Proceedings of Workshop on Theory and Practice of Parallel Programming (TPPP)*, number 907 in Lecture Notes in Computer Science, pages 121–136. Springer Verlag, 1994. http://web.yl.is.s.u-tokyo.ac.jp/pl/ schematic.html.

33. Thorsten von Eicken, Anindya Basu, and Vineet Buch. Low-latency communication over ATM networks using active messages. *IEEE Micro*, 15(1):46–53, February 1995.

34. William Weihl, Eric Brewer, Adrian Colbrook, Chrysanthos Dellarocas, Wilson Hsieh, Anthony Joseph, Carl Waldspurger, and Paul Wang. PRELUDE: A system for portable parallel software. Technical Report MIT/LCS/TR-519, Laboratory for Computer Science, Massachusetts Institute of Technology, 1991.

35. Akinori Yonezawa. *ABCL: An Object-Oriented Concurrent System—Theory, Language, Programming, Implementation and Application*. The MIT Press, 1990.

36. Akinori Yonezawa, Jean-Pierre Briot, and Etsuya Shibayama. Object-oriented concurrent programming in ABCL/1. In *OOPSLA '86 Conference Proceedings*, pages 258–268, 1986.

(Thread and Object)-Oriented Distributed Programming

Jean-Marc Geib, Christophe Gransart, Chrystel Grenot, Philippe Merle

Laboratoire d'Informatique Fondamentale de Lille
Université des Sciences et Technologies de Lille
Bâtiment M3, 59655 Villeneuve d'Ascq Cedex - France
Tel: (33) 20 33 70 24 Email: {geib, gransart, grenot, merle}@lifl.fr

Abstract. (Thread and Object)-Oriented Distributed Programming is
an unifying model mixing threads and objects to design and implement
distributed and multithreaded data structures and programs. This is a
new way of imagining reusable components for distributed programming,
based on two kinds of same grained entities that are objects for data and
threads for concurrent activities.

1   Introduction

During last decade, two important evolutions have emerged in the field of distributed programming: Distributed programming with objects, and distributed programming with threads. The first one aims at preserving the well-known qualities of object orientation in the area of distributed programming. The second one aims at facilitating the programming of distributed processes which first have to respond to many asynchronous concurrent communications and events, and second have to support fine grained concurrent tasks. We submit that objects and threads are entities with the same granularity and that distributed applications designers can take advantage of mixing these two kinds of entities. Following this way, all presupposed object-oriented qualities are preserved and moreover new good properties are added to design reusable classes and complex structures for distributed programming.

In this paper we introduce the model BOX which combines an object model with a thread model. The section 2 discusses about objects and distributed programming. The section 3 presents distributed programming and threads. The model BOX is introduced in the section 4. The section 5 gives an overview of a new language (also called BOX) to support this model. We introduce Complex Active Objects which are aggregates of objects and threads, and are a foundation for reusable active components. We also describe our environment which allows the free distribution of objects and threads in a pool of processes over a network of workstations.

2   Distributed Programming and Objects

A lot of works study different environments using objects for distributed programming: Either to program the processes of a distributed application, or to define a new object-oriented model for distributed programming. Let us first introduce these two approaches:

Object-Oriented Programming of Distributed Processes

A first approach to distributed programming with objects simply promotes the use of an object-oriented language to program the different processes of a distributed application. A distributed program is then designed as a distributed set of object-oriented programs. Because a distributed application is also a set of communicating processes, this approach uses special objects which encapsulate primitives of the communicating layer. This simple view does not require any modification of object languages used for development, for example C++ or Eiffel[17], but only requests specific classes for communicating purposes.

This approach cannot be completely satisfactory because objects are here only a programming tool and not a general model for distributed programming. In that case, the qualities of object orientation are not preserved, for instance the uniformity quality: objects located in different processes cannot directly communicate using the traditional object method activation.

Distributed Object-Oriented Programming

A more ambitious approach considers a distributed program as a set of distributed objects, preserving then the uniformity quality of traditional object orientation. In this approach a specific communicating layer is needed to allow objects located in different processes to communicate in the same way as if they were located in the same process.

Moreover, besides this specific run-time, this approach has to deal with extra features: Because a distributed application always includes several execution threads, programmers have to express the cooperation of these threads in the new distributed object-oriented model. This leads to some new syntactical operations allowing the creation and the destruction of threads, and also allowing these threads to synchronize themselves. If these specific features do exist, then we really get an object-oriented model for distributed programming. These studies gave extensions of pre-existing object languages, like Concurrent C++[9], Eiffel//[5][6], or new specific distributed object-oriented languages, like Guide[16], ABCL[20], ...

3 Distributed Programming and Threads

Most current distributed applications are developed upon platforms which allow programmers to deal with several coarse grained distributed processes, such as PVM[13] or P4[4]. These processes are connected over a network and communicate by asynchronous message sending. The effective success of these platforms is essentially due to the appropriateness of the model of asynchronous communicating processes with today loosely coupled distributed architectures.

Nevertheless, many of distributed applications naturally spawn a high number of potentially elementary tasks which have to communicate and synchronize themselves. As it is not possible to spawn thousands of processes on a network of about twenty workstations, it remains a gap between a fine grained distributed design and a coarse grained distributed implementation. The solution often adopted by application developers is to set up a configuration of a few processes, each one taking charge sequentially of hundreds of elementary jobs. This approach leads to several problems: 1) If an elementary task has to wait for an event or a message, another task in the process has to be resumed, so the programmer has to program a coroutine management layer perhaps with a complex priority schema ; 2) Because asynchronous messages are transmitted between processes, there is a need for low level tasks which wait for incoming messages and dispatch them to the concerned tasks of the process. So in the case of fine grained distributed application, it is very difficult to directly program the distributed processes.

Thread-Oriented Programming of Distributed Processes

Multithreaded processes are a step towards a facilitated design of distributed processes. Threads offer pseudo parallelism inside processes. Hundreds of threads can run inside the same process. While one thread is blocked, another thread can run. So, a process is able to do computation while waiting a message, and can support many other kinds of overlapping activities. In most cases some threads interface the communication layer: Some threads wait for incoming messages from other processes and dispatch them to application threads in the process. This is a general model for fine grained distributed computing. As for objects in the previous section, this is called Thread-Oriented Programming of Distributed Processes. Programming a thread type consists in coding a function which will be concurrently spawned when such a thread is required.

Distributed Thread-Oriented Programming

Also as for objects, a more ambitious view of programming with threads is the Distributed Thread-Oriented Programming. In the previous Thread-Oriented Programming of Distributed Processes approach, threads which are located in different processes cannot directly communicate: communications are between processes, not between threads. With this new feature, a new model emerges: A distributed application is now a set of communicating threads which are distributed over a network of processes and which communicate directly by asynchronous message passing. Because the cost of a thread is low (they are also called lightweight processes), in this new model, a distributed application can be freely designed and implemented by a high number of concurrent tasks dynamically created and destroyed as threads.

Some recent works, such as PVC[8], Athapascan[19] or Chant[14] have introduced environments to support a Distributed Thread-Oriented Model. They are based on the C language and use C functions to program thread behaviors. Unfortunately they exhibit a poor integration with strong typing and loose the qualities of more structured approaches. The work introduced on BOX combines a distributed thread model with objects to obtain new qualities in data structuration and a stronger typed environment.

4 The Model BOX: Mixing Objects and Threads

In order to facilitate the design of distributed and multithreaded programs with an object approach, we propose a single and simple model, merging the main characteristics of both object design and thread design.

The object approach decomposes a program into cooperative objects. But created in the sequential programming context, the object approach does not offer any features for the decomposition of an application in concurrent activities. The thread approach decomposes a program into concurrent activities. But it looses structuration of data which, in most tools for distributed programming, is extremely poor, restricted to predefined basic data types, or using explicitly memory pointers.

These two approaches complement each other, and may exchange their respective advantages. It is the point we tackle in our model which is based on objects and threads, without real modifications of the two related models. We briefly introduce these two models, before describing BOX.

4.1 The Object Model

The usual object oriented approach, called the Object Model, introduces a few concepts and may be expressed as follows:

- *The Object Model is based on objects dynamically created from classes. An object is an instance of a class.*
- *A class describes the internal structure of its instances and the methods which can be applied onto them. A method call on an object is a procedural call executed in the encapsulated context of this object.*
- *An object can refer to some other objects. It can call methods on objects it refers to.*
- *An execution is composed of only one activity: the creation method of a root object.*

Let us take the example of a simple buffer. In the Object Model, a buffer is an object in which we can *put* or *get* some data. The buffer class describes an internal structure to store items (array, list, ...) and at least two methods to *put* and to *get* the data in a FIFO order. A buffer may be represented as in Fig.1

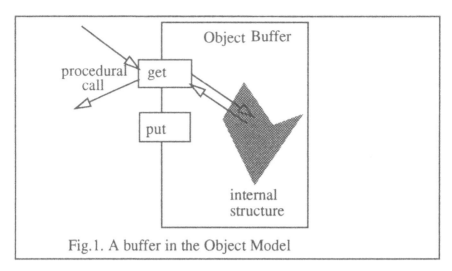

Fig.1. A buffer in the Object Model

In the sequential context, the buffer is not protected from concurrent accesses. Two concurrent activations of the *get*, for example, may corrupt the internal structure. So this buffer cannot be used immediately in a concurrent context. Several works have been done to introduce concurrent calls: 1) By introducing activation conditions on methods (for example: no active *get* to accept a new *get*) or 2) By adding a "body" to schedule incoming calls (for example: accept a *get* then a *put* and so on). We will show that our solution is slightly different because the buffer is designed as an aggregation of a traditional object and a separate thread.

4.2 The Thread Model

The Thread Model can be defined by :

- *The Thread Model is based on threads dynamically created by spawning behavioral functions.*
- *Threads are autonomous active entities.*
- *The thread behavior manages an internal structure - a private thread memory - and communications with some other threads.*
- *A thread refers to some other threads and can send asynchronous messages to them. It can also receive messages in a private mailbox and process them according to its own behavior.*
- *An execution is composed of as many execution streams as active threads.*

Let us take again the buffer example. The Thread Model leads us to design the buffer as a thread which receives messages (to *put* or to *get* data) from some other threads.

If the thread processes messages in order of arrivals, we must describe an internal structure which will store data. But this structure is redundant: 1) *put* down data are already stored in messages in the thread mailbox, 2) when a *get* out message is received, the thread has only to respond by the value of the first *put* down message of its mailbox. This requires a non FIFO management of the mailbox but it is not opposed to the model. This denotes the strongly communication-oriented aspect of the model: The buffer is only a thread which correctly manages messages it receives.

Note that asynchronous communications require an explicit management of the result recipient. In the example of the buffer, a *get* out request has to supply a name of the thread which will receive the data. The result will be sent in a return message using this name.

This buffer may be represented by Fig.2.

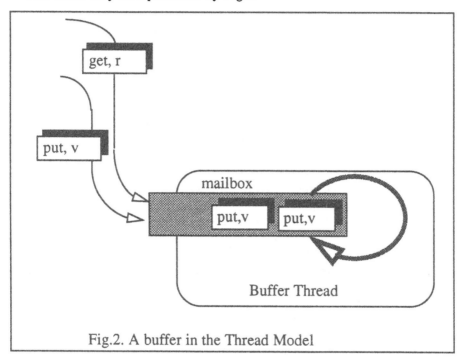

Fig.2. A buffer in the Thread Model

4.3 The Model BOX

We investigate a new model by merging the two previous ones. The result of this merge is that:

- *The Model BOX is based on objects and threads dynamically created from object classes and thread classes. An object is an instance of an object class, a thread is an instance of a thread class.*
- *A class defines the internal structure of its instances. An object class defines the methods which can be applied to its instances and a thread class defines the behaviors which can be started at creation time of its instances.*

- *An object, as a thread, refers to some other objects or threads. It can send asynchronous messages to threads it refers to, and call methods of objects it refers to.*
- *An execution is composed of as many execution streams as thread instances. Initially, there is only one implicit thread which executes the creation method of a root object.*

Thus the two previous models are preserved: if the programming is only composed of object classes we obtain a traditional object-oriented program. If the programming only includes thread classes we obtain a thread-oriented program. Then the multithreaded object-oriented programming is obtained by mixing object and thread classes.

Moreover in our environment (see section 5.5) threads and objects may be distributed in a pool of processes over a network, without any modification of the model (i.e. objects and threads may cooperate whatever their locations over the network). So we obtain a simple distributed (thread and object)-oriented model.

By merging the two models new qualities are obtained:

- Thanks to the introduction of thread classes, modularity, encapsulation, reusability and extensibility now appear in thread orientation. In the environment of the language BOX we have developed libraries of thread classes which represent all sorts of goodies in the context of distributed and multithreaded programming. Nevertheless, thread classes are slightly different from object classes: a thread class groups several behaviors together for a thread type. Each thread of a particular type runs one of these behaviors. Thread classes facilitate a modular conception of multithreaded programs.
- Because objects and threads are at the same conceptual level (neither objects nor threads are a predominant concept in BOX), we can freely mix them in aggregates. Such an aggregate contains passive entities (objects) and active entities (threads). It is a parallel data structure reusable as a whole. Different parts of an aggregate can be installed in separate processes, so it is also a distributed structure. In our opinion, it is the right way of creating reusable components for distributed programming. These aggregates are called Complex Active Objects.
- Two tools are available to express cooperation: message sending and method calls. A thread can send messages to other threads and call methods of objects. An object can call methods of other objects and send messages to threads. So the programmer can freely mix different cooperation strategies. This is of particular interest in the design of the aggregates defined above.

The introduced mixing model designs the buffer as a complex active object with two parts : an object part which offers a traditional procedural interface and a thread part (qualified as internal thread because it is hidden behind the object interface) which ensures a buffer behavior (see Fig.3).

The object is a traditional object without synchronization constraints. Its two methods translate procedural calls of clients into message based communications with the internal thread. Concurrent calls can be applied because different calling threads execute simultaneously the same code which only translates these calls into messages to the internal thread. There is no synchronization problem at this stage, the clients' synchronization being the result of the internal thread behavior. From a caller point of view, the buffer is a traditional object which can be used in a concurrent context.

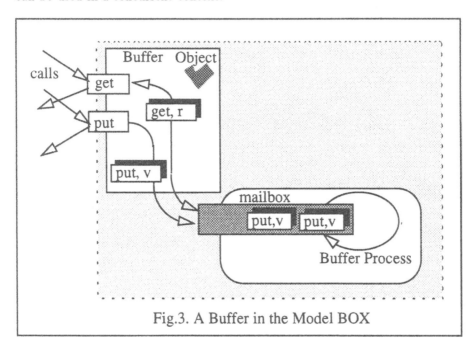

Fig.3. A Buffer in the Model BOX

5   Overview of the BOX Language

BOX is a class based language with single inheritance and genericity. It is a strongly typed language with a conformity rule based on an inheritance hierarchy.

The BOX language allows the description of objects and threads. Objects and threads are described in an uniform way by classes : each class (of objects or threads) defines typed attributes and procedures. Object classes and thread classes are at the same conceptual level: they are built by inheritance from the predefined classes OBJ and THR[1]. The class named ANY is the shared class for these two classes and also the minimal type of all BOX entities (Fig.4.)

---

[1] In a previous version of BOX, threads (THR) were called fragments (FRAG).

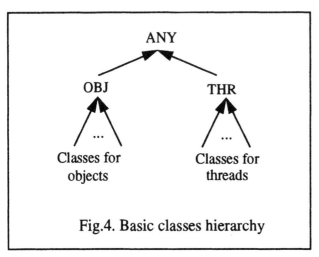

Fig.4. Basic classes hierarchy

In BOX, all items are declared preceded by their type[2] ; for examples:

- *[INT] an_integer* declares an integer attribute ,
- *[PROC] one_procedure : <args> : {<code>}* declares a procedure with its arguments and its code.
- *[C1] C2 :: <description>* declares class C2 as a sub-class of class C1 with <description> enclosing attributes and procedures introduced by the new class.

So a simple skeleton of a class is shown in Fig.5.

```
[subclass] new_class::
    -- attributs and procedures
    [INT] an_integer;
    [PROC] a_procedure :[INT] an_arg:
        { code }
    [PROC[BOOL]] boolean_function ::
        { code }
```

Fig.5. A class in BOX

5.1   BOX: an Object-Oriented Language

An object is an instance of a sub-class of OBJ ; it is a traditional object.

---

[2] Syntactically, if C is a class name, [C] denotes the type implemented by C.

The syntactic construct $e := [a\_class <-]$ creates[3] a new instance of the class, and returns a reference in e. The general form of this instruction is $[a\_class <- proc <args>]$, the procedure initializes the new object.

The dot notation is used to access to the object interface (methods and attributes). Attributes can only be read.

Fig.6. shows the skeleton of the buffer object. Note that it is a generic class (generic parameters are precised behind the name of the new class).

```
-- Object Buffer

[OBJ] BUFFER [T] ::

  [PROC] init ::
    -- Initialization
  { ...
      }

  [PROC] put : [T] elem :
    -- Put 'elem' in buffer
  {...
      }

  [PROC [T]] get ::
    -- Get an element
  {...
      }
```

Fig.6. Buffer Object Class in BOX

5.2 BOX: a Thread-Oriented Language

A thread is an instance of a sub-class of THR. Unlike objects, threads do not react to method calls, but are independent entities spawned immediately after their creation. So the procedures of a thread class are not methods but behaviors. In order to create an instance, one of these procedures must be specified. The creation request of a thread has the same appearance as the creation request of an object: $[a\_class <- proc <args>]$, this is a synchronous operation which returns a reference on the created thread executing the procedure.

---

[3] Note that [C] e; is an attribute declaration and [C<-] e; is a declaration of e followed by an instance creation of class C.

Each thread has an implicit mailbox. It receives messages in this mailbox. Asynchronous communications use specific instructions:

- Send: The <- operator.
  a_thread <- ! <value>, <value>...! sends asynchronously a message to a thread. The different values are transmitted in the message. Note that it is not a request but only values transmission. Values are basic type values or references for types described by classes.
- Receive: The -> operator.
  A thread can access to its mailbox using a receive instruction. Syntactically a thread refers to its private mailbox by the pseudo variable BOX[4]. A receive instruction message is written BOX -> ! <attribute>, <attribute>...!. A message is then extracted from the mailbox, and its content is stored in the listed attributes. Execution is waiting if there is no message in the mailbox.

The example of Fig.7. introduces these instructions: the thread class "calc" declares two threads behaviors designed first, to wait for two numbers and a thread reference, and then, return to the referenced thread the result of the addition or the multiplication of the two numbers, depending on chosen behavior at creation time.

```
[THR] calc::
   [PROC]add::
      { BOX -> ![INT]a1,[INT]a2,[THR]dest!
        dest <- !a1 + a2!
      }
   [PROC]mult::
      { BOX -> ![INT]a1,[INT]a2,[THR]dest!
        dest <- !a1 * a2!
      }
```

Fig.7. Simple Thread Class

To perform an addition, such a thread should be created by: [calc <- add] f
It will be used like: f <- ! 2, 3, BOX !
The result will be received by: BOX -> !result!
Here, BOX is the name of the client thread mailbox.

5.3 More on Receive

As in the introductory example of the buffer in the thread model, it is unsuited to force FIFO management of mailboxes. On the contrary a more complex management allows one to easily design complex behaviors. So our receive instruction

---

[4] The pseudo variable BOX is for threads the traditional SELF of the object languages.

is a little more complicated and is integrated with the strong typed feature of the language. Its partial semantic is the following:

Types of attributes which appear in a receive instruction serve as a filter to select a message in the mailbox. The selected message will be the older one for which types of inclosed values match types of attributes. If no such message exists, the instruction waits for new message arrivals.

For example if a thread executes the two following receive instructions:

```
BOX -> ! [INT] a1, [INT]a2 ! ;
BOX -> ! [THR]t !;
```

It will receive first a message enclosing two integers, then a message enclosing a thread reference, whatever the order of arrival of these two messages in the mailbox. So the mailbox is used in a non-FIFO order and is not only a communication tool but also a synchronization tool.

Another feature of the receive instruction is the possibility to add constraints over the values enclosed in messages when we want to select a particular message between several messages with the same type filter. Syntactically, a constraint is a BOX boolean expression, built with the pseudo variables ($1, $2,...) which denotes the actual values in the examined message.

For example, with the following code, a thread will only receive messages enclosing two integers; and moreover the reception order will be strictly obliged to follow the successive values of the first integer. This is a simple way to respect timestamped communications.

```
[INT] a1 := 0;
 loop
   BOX -> ! a1,[INT]a2 ! { $1 = a1+1 } ;
   ...   -- a2 in use
 end_loop
```

We can now return to the thread-oriented buffer. The code appears in Fig.8. In the procedure *behavior* of the buffer thread class, we code that the thread first selects an incoming message with a *get* request and a return reference[5], and then selects a message with a *put* request and a value. Finally, it sends the value to the referenced mailbox and then loops. The code is very simple and illustrates the power of the receive instruction.

---

[5] Note that the address is typed [BOX] which is the minimal type for threads and mailboxes.

```
-- Buffer process

[THR] BUF [T] ::

  [PROC] behavior ::
    {
    loop
      BOX -> ! [STR], [BOX] b ! { $1 = "get" } ;
      BOX -> ! [STR], [T] v ! { $1 = "put" } ;
      b <- ! v ! ;
    end_loop ;
    }
```
Fig.8. Buffer Thread Class in BOX

Shared Objects

In BOX, as in other parallel object languages, objects can be shared by threads. Because we think that synchronization is better expressed by our receive instruction, and because we do not want to deeply modify the object model, we do not provide objects with complex synchronization features. Nevertheless we must ensure that concurrent accesses to a shared object will not corrupt its internal state. In order to be able to preserve objects from this, we have only introduced a lightweight reader/writer synchronization strategy in each object. [PROC] procedures are reader declared procedures while [SPROC] procedures are writer declared procedures. In an object, writer procedures have automatically an exclusive access right to the object. This is a mechanism with a very low overhead, and in all our examples, this appears as a sufficient feature. Fig.9. shows a very simple object, protected from concurrent accesses.

```
-- Object Buffer

[OBJ]SHARED_OBJ [T] ::

  [T] value ;

  [SPROC] write: [T] new:
      -- write a new value
    { value := new
      }

  [PROC [T]] get ::
      -- read the value
    { result := value
      }
```
Fig.9. Simple Protected Shared Object

5.4 Mixing Objects and Threads

As we said previously, BOX is based on a model mixing objects and communicating processes. In BOX, object and thread attributes can refer indifferently to objects or threads. This allows the building of complex aggregates mixing active threads and passive objects; these aggregates are called **Complex Active Objects** (CAO). They allow the design of reusable distributed object-oriented software components[10][11].

```
-- Complex Object Buffer

[OBJ] BUFFER [T] ::-- Buffer Object

  [BUF [T]] bt ; -- Buffer thread

  [PROC] init ::
    -- Initialization
  {
    bt := [BUFF [T] <- behavior ];
  }

  [PROC] put : [T] item :
    -- Put 'item' in the buffer
  {
    bt <- ! "put", item! ;
  }

  [PROC [T]] get::
    -- Extract an item
  {
    [BOX <-] res ;
    bt <- ! "get", res ! ;
    res -> ! result ! ;
  }
```

Fig.10. The Buffer Object Part

We present the last version of the buffer ; this buffer is a CAO (Fig.10.) which mixes an object (instance of the object class BUFFER) and a thread (instance of the previous thread class BUF). The attribute *bt* of the BUFFER object refers to the BUF thread. Procedures of the BUFFER object use asynchronous messages to cooperate with the BUF thread. Note that the procedure *get* of the BUFFER object manages a local mailbox to wait for a result from the BUF thread. Note also that all *get* activations will use a separate local mailbox so no particular synchronization is required at the object level. On the contrary, the entire synchronization between the object and its clients is in charge of the thread which processes the request in a buffer like order.

In a more general way, we think that the Complex Active Objects idea is a good approach for the design of distributed data structures which have to encapsulate some internal concurrent activities. In most cases, such a data structure may be easily described as a set of objects and a set of threads[12]. Objects have two purposes: some objects store data, some objects implement an object-oriented interface to clients. Threads are present for several reasons: they can process in parallel concurrent requests to the data structure, maintain some properties upon the structure, manage distribution of data and serve parallel implementation of operations, ...

Let us take some examples:

- In a Complex Active Object for a binary search tree, we will find - an interface object with traditional methods, - objects which are nodes of the tree, - threads going up and down the tree to process requests, and - perhaps an internal thread which re-structures the tree as a background concurrent activity.

- A matrix is also a Complex Active Object because we can imagine that the matrix is distributed part by part on several sites - this requires a set of objects, and that a multiply operation will be supported by some threads which organize the routing of values of the second matrix towards the parts of the first one.

These examples show that distributed and parallel data structures can be more easily designed if we can freely mix objects and threads as in the model BOX.

Let us present a distributed table example to illustrate our methodology to build Complex Active Objects. The basis of such a component is a sequential table (*s_table*) with a search procedure. It is represented by a sequential object class. A distributed table is composed of several sequential tables distributed across the network. To achieve a search on this distributed table, a pool of threads is used. Each thread (*actor*) applies searches on one particular sequential table. Then, to simplify the use of this CAO, we offer to clients a procedural interface which hides the distribution and concurrent works (*d_table*).

```
[OBJ] s_table [T]:: -- sequential table class
  [ARR[T]] representation; -- array of items
  [PROC[T]] search : [ANY]criteria: -- search function
      { <sequential search algorithm> }

[THR] actor[T] :: search processes class
  [PROC] search :[s_table[T]]table:
      { loop
          BOX -> ! [ANY] criteria, [BOX] client !;
          -- wait for a request
          [T]res := table . search (criteria); -- search
           client <- ! res ! -- send the result
        end_loop
      }

[OBJ] d_table[T]:: -- distributed table class
  [ARR[s_tables[T]]] tables; -- array of sequential tables
  [ARR[actor[T]]] actors; -- array of actors

  [PROC] init :: -- components distribution
      { <component creation on different nodes
        for example for component number i
        tables [i] := [s_tables[T] <- init at node[i]] ;
        actors [i] := [actor[T] <- search ! tables[i] ! at
                                                    node[i]]
      }

  [PROC[T]] search : [ANY] criteria:
      '{ [BOX <-]b ; -- mailbox creation
         <selection of the table number i>;
         actors[i] <- ! criteria, b !;
         -- request to the actor
         b -> !result! -- waiting for the result
      }
```

Fig.11. Distributed Table in BOX

The search procedure of the distributed table can be called concurrently by several tasks. If the searches are on different sequential tables, they will be realized concurrently by the different actors prevented by messages. If searches are on the same sequential table, they will be serialized by the involved actor which processes sequentially the different messages it receives. The structure of this example is illustrated in Fig.12. It is naturally distributed on several nodes.

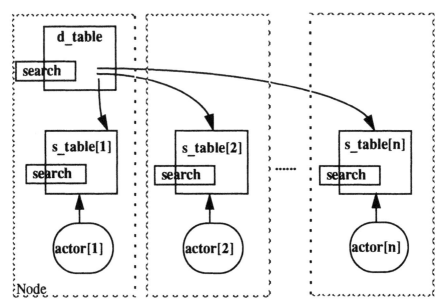

Fig.12. : Distributed Table

5.5 Distributed Environment

In the model BOX, the programmer can mix objects and threads. In our environment, objects and threads can be located as the programmer wants in a pool of processes over a network. The programmer's work takes a new dimension, that is tuning the (threads and objects) design to a particular architecture.

Let us illustrate this with our buffer.

The buffer is here an entity made of two parts, an object which presents methods to clients and a thread which implements the behavior. Installation of this entity on a distributed architecture can be done by several ways. This is illustrated in Fig.13. It shows the buffer and one of its clients. In the first case, the object is on the same site as the client, it is like a proxy[2]. The communication between the object and the thread is achieved by remote message sending, while the object and the client use local procedure calls. In the second case, the object is in the same process as the thread. The client communicates with the object by RPC (Remote Procedural Call)[3], while the object and the thread exchange local messages. The choice of one of the two solutions has to be done by taking into account global considerations (nodes load, clients location, ...). Note that as a reusable component, the buffer was designed in the language BOX, independently of these considerations. It is only in a second step (installing the application) that the BOX environment takes charge of location considerations.

100

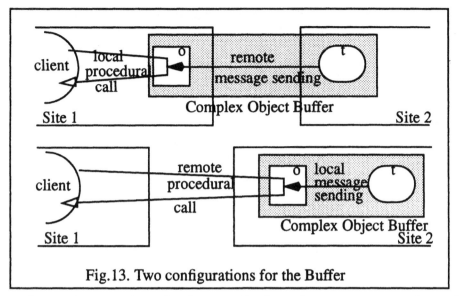

Fig.13. Two configurations for the Buffer

Our environment is made of a compiler *bc*, a cluster constructor *cluc* and a specific run-time for distributed threads (PVC[7]) based on PM2[18], a new implementation of POSIX Threads onto PVM. The run-time implements the local and remote message sending and local and remote method call mechanisms.

The compiler *bc* is able to compile a class independently of all others. It produces a C version of the class and several files, in particular a file which gives the specification of the type implemented by the class, and a file which gives the specifications of the types required by the class.

These three files compose a reusable unit for the cluster constructor. The cluster constructor takes a cluster constructor file and the units listed by the file, then checks that all types conform, and, if so, constructs the binary code files for several distributed processes.

A cluster constructor file has to detail several pieces of information:

- a list of types (i.e. a list of compiled classes) and one of them is the root class.
- a list of sites.
- a table which precises which classes have to be present on each site. If a class is present on a site, this means that instances of this class might be created on this site at execution time. At this stage, we distribute classes globally to distribute instances at execution time according to specific site features. This is a coarse tuning of distribution.

Instances of a particular class are automatically distributed[6] by the system over the different sites listed in the used cluster constructor file. But the programmer is also able to annotate the creation instructions with some location wishes. To meet this, a predefined LOCATION instance is always readable at run-time

---

[6] Some load balancing strategies have been implemented, and are under trial.

by all entities to examine the current configuration and then to take dynamic decisions over the locations. This is a fine tuning mechanism to distribute objects and threads.

Using several cluster constructor files and several annotations, the user may check several configurations for the entities of his/her distributed application, and then take the best performances. Note that cluster constructor files are also a part of the reusability concept in BOX because a cluster constructor file may be used to fix a particular good configuration for a (thread and object)-oriented data structure, and that such a cluster constructor file may be directly included in another, in an incremental design. All these features have been introduced in BOX to facilitate the design of truly reusable distributed and parallel structures.

6   Related work

Our notion of threads can be compared to the notion of actor[1]. As for actors, each of our threads has a mailbox, a procedural code and also private data. An application built using actors involves that each entity must be "an actor" but as for lots of developments, passive entities are a good complement to actors. We think that mixing active entities and passive entities is a good compromise. In the Objects+Processes model (e.g. Guide[16]) activies are not seen as objects. So a programmer designs an application using an object methodology then adds activities in the program. In the Active Objects model (e.g. Eiffel//[5][6]) programmer decomposes his/her application in terms of active entities and passive entities ; active entities are objects on which concurrent calls to methods can be executed and passive entities are traditional objects. A major problem with this approach lies in the fact that passive entities cannot be shared by several active objects (to meet this, passive entities must be redesigned in active entities). The model BOX merges these different approaches.

7   Conclusion

In distributed programming area, some works use objects, some others use threads. We submit that mixing objects and threads is an approach which preserves qualities and decreases drawbacks of the two previous approaches. We have introduced a simple model based on object and thread classes, on message sending and method call, and on Complex Active Object, i.e. aggregates of objects and threads. We have also designed a new language called BOX to support our model. This is a strongly typed class based language with all the features of modern languages. Applications produced with our language run in a distributed environment in which objects and threads may be distributed in a pool of processes over a network.

A standard library is under work. The components already developed are concurrent data structures (buffer, distributed table, linked lists and trees, ...), always with some associated configuration files for various distributed architectures.

We have also implemented an interface with Xwindow to create graphical applications, and we are investigating the model BOX for Computer Human Interfaces. We are currently working on C++ classes which implement the ideas of BOX in the C++ language.

References

1. G. Agha, C. Hewitt
   Concurrent Programming Using Actors
   Object-Oriented Concurrent Programming
   The MIT Press, 1987
2. J.K. Bennet
   The design and implementation of Distributed Smalltalk
   OOPSLA'87 Proc. of the Second ACM Conf. on Object-Oriented Programming Systems, Languages, and Applications, Orlando, Florida, October 1987, Special Issue of SIGPLAN Notices, Vol. 22, No. 12, 1987, pp. 318-330
3. A.D. Birrell, B.J. Nelson
   Implementing Remote Procedure Calls
   Xerox report CSL-83-7, October 1983
4. R.M. Butler, E. Lusk
   User's guide to the P4 parallel programming system
   TR ANL-92/17, Argonne National Laboratory, 1992
5. D. Caromel
   Concurrency : An Object-Oriented Approach
   TOOLS 2, Technology of Object-Oriented Languages and Systems, Proc., Paris, 1990
6. D. Caromel
   Concurrency And Reusability: From Sequential To Parallel
   JOOP, Journal of Object-Oriented Programming, September/October 1990, pp. 34-42
7. L. Courtrai, J.F. Roos, J.M. Geib, J.F. Mehaut
   Communicating Active Components: An environment for concurrent applications on parallel machines
   EUROMICRO'92, Paris (F), September 1992
8. L. Courtrai
   Les Composants Actifs de Communication : Outil pour la conception et l'implantation de langages parallèles à objets actifs pour machines MIMD
   PhD thesis, Université des Sciences et Technologies de Lille, Laboratoire d'Informatique Fondamentale de Lille, Octobre 1992.
9. N. H. Gehani, W. D. Roome
   Concurrent C++: Concurrent Programming with Class(es)
   Software-Pratice and Experience, Vol 18(120), 1157-1177, December 1988, pp.1157-1177
10. J.M. Geib, C. Gransart, C. Grenot
    Distributed Objects in Box
    TOOLS Europe 93 Workshop on Distributed and Concurrent Objects, Versailles, France, March 8-11, 1993
11. C. Gransart, C. Grenot, L. Courtrai
    Le projet PVC/BOX: Environnement pour la Programmation Parallèle

Journées des Jeunes Chercheurs en Systèmes Informatiques Répartis, 14-16 Avril 1993, Grenoble, France, pp 131-136

12. J.M. Geib, C. Gransart, C. Grenot
    Mixing Objects and Activities in Complex Active Objects
    ECOOP 93 Workshop on Object-Based Distributed Programming, Kaiserslautern, Germany,July 26-27 1993

13. A. Geist, J. Dongarra, R. Manchek
    PVM 3 User's Guide and Reference Manual
    Oak Ridge National Laboratory & University of Tennessee, May 1993

14. M. Haines, D. Cronk, P. Mehrotra
    On the Design of Chant : A Talking Threads Package
    Institue for Computer Applications in Science and Engineering, NASA Langley Research Center, April 1994.

15. C. A. R. Hoare.
    Communicating Sequential Processes
    Communications ACM, vol. 21, 8, pp. 666-677, August 1978

16. S. Krakowiak, M. Meysembourg, H. Nguyen Vam, M. Riveill, C. Roisin, X. Rousset de Pina
    Design and Implementation of an Object-Oriented, Strongly Typed Language for Distributed Applications.
    JOOP Journal of Object-Oriented Programming, September/October 1990

17. B. Meyer
    Object-oriented Software Construction
    Prentice-Hall, 1988

18. R. Namyst, J.F. Méhaut
    PM2 : Parallel Multithreaded Machine. A computing environment for distributed architectures
    Parco95, Gent, Belgium, September 1995.

19. J. Briat, M. Christaller, J.L. Roch
    Une maquette pour Athapascan-0
    RenPar'6, Lyon, France, juin 1994.

20. A. Yonezawa, M. Tokoro
    Object-Oriented Concurrent Programming
    The MIT Press, 1987

Distributed and Object Oriented Symbolic Programming in April

K.L.Clark[1], F.G. McCabe[2]

[1] Department of Computing
Imperial College of Science, Medicine and Technology
London
England
[2] FUJITSU Laboratories ltd.
Kawasaki
Japan

Abstract. In this paper we introduce key features of a programming language for building DAI and other types of distributed applications requiring the transmission and manipulation of complex symbolic data. Key features of the language that we will illustrate are:

1. publically named processes,
2. process identifiers as data values,
3. higher-order structure,
4. an operator precedence grammar,
5. a macro processor that works at the level of the syntax of the language.

The first two features enable one to build an environment of public servers, available to any April process simply by using its name, which can return as the response to a enquiry the identification of a non-public process. The last two allow one to tailor the syntax of the language for a particular application. We shall illustrate syntactic tailoring by showing how a simple object oriented extension of April can be implemented.

1 Overview of April

April is a process oriented symbolic language. It contains facilities for defining processes, and for allowing processes to communicate with each other in a distributed envionment in a uniform manner. It also has powerful data structuring and expression handling features as might be found in any high level symbolic programming language. April's symbolic structures are based on records, lists and sets. Overall, it is aimed at giving as convenient a vehicle as possible for symbolic programming in a distributed environment.

April has adopted and adapted features from many other languages; in particular much is owed to Parlog [1] and its object oriented extension Polka [3], PCN [6], CSP [7], Dijkstra [4], LISP [10], Prolog [2] and APL[8].

Like Java [11], April is an interpreted language which is designed to be architecture independent. However, April is more clearly oriented towards multi-agent applications and is not – in the core language – object oriented[3]

1.1 Publically named processes

All processes in April have names – called *handles* – associated with them. These names will be automatically generated by April when the process is started and can be passed around as arguments and in messages. A message is sent to a process by sending it to its handle.

In addition, a public name, a symbol such as bank0, or clark_account, can be assigned as the handle of a process when it is forked. Any April process, anywhere in the world, can communicate with this process simply by sending a message to this public name.

1.2 Communication

April incorporates a simple message passing mechanism for communicating between processes. Messages, which can be arbitrarily complex symbolic structures – including programs, can be sent between processes independently of the location of the processes involved. This is possible because the handle of a process is unique at a system wide level and the system can uniquely map each process to a single location. The message send primitive is a send to one or more process handles. The message is put into the message buffer of each identified target process, each process having *exactly one* message receive buffer.

A process uses patterns to signal the messages that it is 'willing to accept' at any given point. It can either search down the current buffer of messages, looking for one that matches a sequence of alternative patterns, or it can just test the first message against one or more alternative patterns. Since the message buffer can contain many dissimilar styles of messages, and since the message receive statement expressly filters the message buffer for interesting messages, we can easily and effectively simulate multiple input channels into the process – without needing any complex language machinery to support multiple inut channels.

A process using the buffer search pattern matching will suspend if there is no current message matching any of the alternative patterns. This is the primary process suspension mechanism of April. The process will be reactivated when a new message is put into its message buffer.

The communication primitives are based on TCP/IP, but the language interface to sending messages is somewhat higher-level than the standard socket library. This enables April to be viewed as a programming language suitable for building applications that interact across the Internet.

---

[3] It is the purpose of this paper to demonstrate how objects can be built on top of April.

1.3 Types

April is a strongly typed language. The type system in April is based on the sub-language that April uses to describe patterns. In a very real sense, there is a nearly complete equivalence between the notation for describing types and the notation for describing patterns of data. The latter are used in describing which messages to receive and the former to describe the legal values of variables in the program.

1.4 Higher-order

April is a higher order language. That means that functions are available as first class objects – they can be passed as arguments and sent in messages between processes. In addition to the classical lambda expression, April also has analogous operators for procedures – which are called mu expressions, patterns – which are called tau expressions and modules – which are called theta expressions.

1.5 Operator precedence grammar

The syntax of April is based on an *operator precedence grammar*. New operators can be declared by the programmer to provide syntactic sugar where required. This is most often used in conjunction with April's macro language features in order to enhance the underlying syntax of April.

1.6 Macro language

April's macro features make it possible to extend the syntax and functionality of April. Macros can be used to evaluate program fragments 'at compile time'; but their most important role is to implement new language features in terms of April's standard language features. Whole new language models can be built on top of April using packages of macros. This latter role is crucial to the applicability of April for building multi-agent systems, one of its intended applications [5]; and is illustrated in this paper in the context of Object Oriented programming.

Macro definitions function by matching and replacing partial fragments of April programs expressed as operator precedence grammar expressions. This is in contrast with other languages' macro-processors which function at a lower textual level. This has two main consequences – it implies that all 'replacements' for a macro must be in valid April syntax and it permits a superior form of macro patterns. In particular, it is possible to specify context sensitive macros which will only match patterns in structured contexts.

We use both user defined operator declarations and macros extensively in this paper – as the primary tehcnique for extending the syntax of April to an object oriented form.

2 Creating a publically named bank process

We shall introduce April by looking at the program for a bank process that accepts messages to create new accounts, to access an account and to close an account. The program is given below as Program 2.1.

```
acc  ::=  (handle,number);      /* declaration of type 'acc' */
bank() {
  acc[]?Accs := [];             /* declare 'Accs' as a list
                                   of acc values */
  repeat{
    (new_account,number?Deposit) -> { /* open account message */
      number?Pin := genPin();        /* generate a new pin */
      Accs := Accs<>[(fork     /* fork account process */
        mu(){account(Deposit,self(),Pin)},Pin)];
      (pin_number,Pin) >> replyto /*then return Pin as response */
    }
  | (access,number?P) -> {      /* message to access an account*/
      (handle?AcId,P) in Accs -> /* check pin number */
        (talk_to,AcId) >> replyto  /* return account process */
    | otherwise ->
        invalid_pin >> replyto /* invalid pin message*/
    }
  | (close_account,number?P) -> { /* a close account message*/
      (handle?AcId,P) in Accs -> { /* check pin number */
        sender == AcId ->  /* also test message was sent by the
                               account process for that pin */
          Accs := Accs \^ (AcId,P) /* remove details from Accs*/
      | otherwise ->
          (close_account,P) >>> AcId  /* forward to account proc*/
      }
    | otherwise ->
        invalid_pin >> replyto   /* pin was not valid */
    }
  } until quit                   /* terminate on quit message*/
}
```

Program 2.1 Bank procedure

The comments on the program should be read as initial explanation. The bank process would typically be invoked using April's *named* fork primitive:

```
bank0 public bank
```

or

bank0 public bank at M

The former forks the bank process within the current **April** invocation but it also registers the name **bank0** with the **April** name server for the local network on which that invocation is running, linking the name with the internal **April** identification of the process.

The latter forks the bank process on a named machine; actually this is forked within a special **April** execution 'shell' server called **M**. The code for the bank process and any auxiliary procedures or functions it calls, such as the code for the **account** process, will be shipped to the **M** execution server automatically. In addition, the name **bank0** will be registered with the name server for the local network of machine **M**.

The invoked bank process will initialise its local variable **Accs**, which will hold a list recording all the created accounts and their pin numbers, to the empty list. The assignment:

acc[]?Accs := [];

is a declaration as well as an initialisation. **acc[]?Accs** declares **Accs** to be a list of **acc** data items. These, via the type declaration, are pairs of handles and numbers. Handles identify processes and their associated message buffers.

The newly forked process then waits for a message to be sent to it by entering the

repeat ... until quit

loop. This is a loop of message processing that ends when the message **quit** is sent to the the **bank0** process and no other messages precede the **quit** message in its message buffer.[4]

The body of the loop comprises a three alternative *choice statement*, the alternative branches being separated by the **|** operator. The alternatives of the choice are tried sequentially. Each one is a *guarded command*, of the form:

message_pattern -> action

Such a guarded command will suspend when there are no messages in the message buffer of the process that match the pattern. So, the choice statement of the repeat loop will suspend until some message is sent to **bank0**, because each of its guarded command alternatives suspends.

A message can be sent to **bank0** by any other process AT (say), perhaps a process linked to an automatic teller machine, simply by using a message send statement of the form:

---

[4] Having a quit message summarily close down the bank process is somewhat extreme. It corresponds to having a bomb drop on the bank, all information about currently opened accounts will be lost. In the next section we will look at alternative ways of closing down processes, like this one, that maintain state information that we might want to preserve.

```
message >> handle?"bank0"
```

Here, `handle?`, tells the `April` type checker that the string `"bank0"` is actually a handle of a process registered, or preregistered, with a name server. This expression allows us to construct the name of a process from a literal string – without the actual process necessarily existing before hand. This property is important in a globally distributed application where achieving contact with a 'foreign' process must be easy to do.

A process can be preregistered which means that the name server will not respond to a query for the process until the process is started. Otherwise, the nameserver will reply to a query with **unknown** if it is asked to locate a non-existent process.

The first time process AT does such a message send, the local name server is accessed for the `April` internal identification of **bank0**. If the local name server does not record the name, other name servers, known directly or indirectly by the local name server, will be queried. If **bank0** is recorded on any such name server as a running process the message will be sent. If the name has been preregistered, but the process is not yet running, the message send is suspended until the process is started. Otherwise an error is raised. As a side effect of this name server access, the `April` identification of the **bank0** process will be returned and stored in a table of the `April` invocation in which AT is running. Subsequent message sends to **bank0**, by any other process within that `April` activation, will just access this local table.

Let us suppose that process AT executes the message send:

```
(new_account,500) >> handle?"bank0"
```

As soon as this message is put into the message buffer for **bank0** the process will be reactivated. The buffer is searched using the message pattern of the first message receive guarded command, namely

```
(new_account,number?Deposit)
```

There is a successful match, with the variable **Deposit**, which is local to the guarded command:

```
(new_account,number?Deposit)  ->  {
  number?Pin := genPin();
  Accs := Accs<>[(fork mu(){account(Deposit,self(),Pin)},Pin)];
  (pin_number,Pin) >> replyto
}
```

being bound to 500. Notice the match only succeeds if the second component of the message is a number. `April`'s message receive pattern matching does type checking. To pick up a value without type checking, we can declare a variable in the pattern to be type **any**. But this could cause a type error if the value is used in the action part of the guarded command in a context that requires a more specific type.

On successful match, the message is removed from the message buffer of bank0 and the action part of the guarded command is performed. The first statement will create a new pin number, then

```
Accs := Accs<>[(fork mu(){account(Deposit,self(),Pin)},Pin)];
```

will use April's fork function to fork a new account process. It also adds the acc type pair (...,Pin) to the Accs list.

The value returned by

```
fork mu(){account(Deposit,self(),Pin)}
```

will be the handle of the forked account process. Normally, the fork operator accepts a zero-argument procedure to execute. However, the account procedure has three arguments. By using a mu expression we can construct an anonymous procedure which will execute a single statement – a call to account;

```
account(Deposit,self(),Pin)
```

The mu expression is April's analogue of a lambda expression, the concept being equivalent except that it is a statement that is abstracted into a procedure rather than an expression being abstracted into a function.

Accs is the banks data base of accounts and associated pins. It is referred to whenever it gets a request to access an account, for withdrawal or deposit purposes, or to close an account. All such requests have to give the pin for the account. The final part of the new_account action is to send back the message (pin_number,Pin) to the reply process associated with the received message, identified by the replyto keyword. When used inside the action of a message receive guarded command: it identifies the reply process for the message that was received.[5]

For a normal message send, the reply process associated with the message is the process that sent the message. Thus the reply process associated with the (new_account,500) message sent by process AT will be AT. The sender of a message can specify another process as the reply process for the message. Thus:

```
M ‾‾ P1 >> P2
```

will make P1 the reply process for message M when it is received by P2 and *not* the process that executes the send. [6]

The expression self() passed to the forked accounts process is another April key word. It denotes the handle of the process which executes the function

---

[5] If the action part of a message receive contains another message receive guarded command: Pattern1 -> A1 and replyto is used inside A1. Then it refers to the reply process for the message that matched Pattern1.

[6] The sender of a message can always be identified by the value of sender, an April keyword similar to replyto which identifies the actual sender of a message. Testing whether sender=replyto will test if the sender has explicitly set the replyto process for the message to be a different from itself. This can be used to detect possible *passing off*. The sender associated with a message cannot be changed.

call or statement in which self() appears. In this case, self() will be the handle of the bank0 process.

AT must eventually execute a message receive guarded command of the form:

```
(pin_number,number?P) -> .....
```

in order to pick up the pin number sent back to it by bank0. If AT was linked to an automatic teller machine this would be printed out for the customer to keep. If AT is some customer assistant process, it would generally store P in some variable MyPin (say), that is global to the process, for P is only local the guarded command that receives the pin. Typically the guarded command would be:

```
(pin_number,number?P) -> MyPin := P;
```

where, MyPin, like Accs in the bank procedure, is declared at the start of the procedure for AT. After that, AT can send an

```
(access,MyPin)
```

message to bank0.

Meanwhile, bank0 has looped and is again waiting to receive a message that matches one of patterns of the three alternatives of the loop body choice statement(or quit). If, whilst it was processing the previous message, other messages have arrived, they will be waiting in its message buffer.

bank0 processes the messages in its buffer checking each in turn to see if it is a (new_account ...), or a (access,...), and so on. Any message which is not matched by one of the alternatives is kept, and skipped over, in case a later message receive statement can successfully match against the message.

Let us suppose that the bank0 process picks up the access message sent by AT. bank0 will first check that the given pin is linked to an active account. It does this with the pattern search:

```
(handle?AcId,P) in Accs
```

which succeeds if there is a pair in the list Accs which consists of a handle and P (P's contents rather than the symbol P).

This condition is the test guard of a test only (or *semantic*) guarded command:

```
(handle?AcId,P) in Accs  ->
  (talk_to,AcId) >> replyto
```

in another choice statement:

```
{ (handle?AcId,P) in Accs  ->
    (talk_to,AcId) >> replyto
| otherwise -> invalid_pin >> replyto
}
```

In general, the guard of a guarded command is of the form:

```
message_pattern :: boolean_test
```

where either the **boolean_test** or the **message_pattern** can be dropped. If a multiple choice guarded command statement has a choice which contains a pure *semantic* test, then all of the choices must also be purely tests. In the above choice statement both guards are just tests. The **otherwise** guard is a special guard that can be used as the guard of the last alternative of a choice statement. It always succeeds, so the action associated with the **otherwise** guard will be executed if no earlier guard succeeds.

If the test of the guarded command:

```
(handle?AcId,P) in Accs  ->
  (talk_to,AcId) >> replyto
```

succeeds, the handle of the process dealing with the account is returned – in the local vairable **AcId** – as a side effect of the test. This is returned in a message to the reply process associated with the received **access** message. In this way the reply process, in our scenario AT, gets access to the account process and will continue by sending messages to this process, not to **bank0**.

The last guarded command of the message processing loop of the **bank** procedure is:

```
(close_account,number?P)   -> {
  (handle?AcId,P) in Accs -> {
    sender == AcId ->
      Accs := Accs \^ (AcId,P)
  | otherwise ->
      (close_account,P) >>> AcId
  }
| otherwise ->
    invalid_pin >> replyto
}
```

The **bank** process only accepts **close_account** messages from one of its spawned **account** processes because before the account is closed all the money must be withdrawn. As with an **access** message, it checks that the given pin is for an active account. Then it also checks that the message has been sent by the process dealing with the account linked with that pin. If it is not, it forwards the message to that account process using the *forwarding* message send:

```
(close_account,P) >>> AcId
```

This is an abbreviation for:

```
(close_account,P) ~~ replyto >> AcId
```

It associates the reply process of the the `close_account` message it has just received as the reply process for this message. (Using >> would associate `bank0` as the reply process for the message sent to `AcId`.) Eventually, the `account` process will return the `close_account` message for the `bank` process to delete the account from its list of active accounts. This deletion is done by the assignment:

```
Accs := Accs \^ (AcId,P)
```

which removes all entries in `Accs` matching `(AcId,P)` (only one in this case). If the pin given in a `close_account` message is not for an active account, a suitable message is sent in reply.

3 Objects as processes

The above bank oprocedure is an example of how one models objects as processes in `April`. It is essentially the same as the way one models objects in a concurrent logic programming language ([9],[3]).

The procedure for an account process is given in Program 3.1. The main loop of this procedure is a

```
while true do {.....}
```

which only terminates on execution of the `break` primitive inside the loop body. In the account procedure, this happens when the `close_account` message is received, providing the balance is 0. Before exit from the loop, and before termination, the `close_account` message is forwarded to `Bank`, the process that spawned the account process. This alternative way of structuring the 'object' process allows for several different 'termination' messages, each of which can have a different close down action.

Notice that the procedure will only accept a `close_account` message if the balance is 0. If it is, the `close_account` message is forwarded to `Bank` for it to delete details of the account from its `Accs` data base before breaking out of the loop and terminating. It also checks for that every message, except a credit message, contains the pin for the account. If it does not, the message is simply left in the message buffer. Like the bank procedure, a more user friendly account procedure might tell the reply process of the message that it is an invalid pin. However, since accounts are assumed to be accessed from via the bank, which checks the pin, we can assume that the pin will always be valid. We check it here as extra security. However, note that our account does not object to anonymous donations!

If we recast the bank procedure in the same form as the account procedure, it would also have a

```
while true do {...}
```

loop and could be terminated on receipt of a `close_down` message which gave the handle of a bank that would take over its accounts. All that we need is to add two extra guarded commands to the main choice statement of the old bank program. We add:

```
Account(number?Balance,number?Pin,handle?Bank)
{
  while true do{
    (debit,number?amount,Pin) -> {
      Balance -:= amount;                  /* Debit the account */
      ok >> replyto}
  | (credit,number?amt) -> {
      Balance +:= amt;
      ok >> replyto                        /* Credit account */
  | (report,Pin) -> Balance >> replyto     /* Report balance */
  | (close_account,Pin) -> {
      Balance=0 -> {
        (close_account,Pin) >>> Bank;
        terminated >> replyto;
        break }
    | otherwise -> balance_not_zero >> replyto
    }
  }
}
```

Program 3.1 Procedure for the account process

```
  (close_down,handle?OtherBank) -> {
    (take_over,Accs) >> OtherBank;
    break
  }
| (take_over,acc[]?NewAccs) -> Accs <>:= NewAccs
```

3.1 Inheritance in April

There are many ways in which it is possible to model inheritance using this object-as-process model. A classical method would be to construct procedures from several class templates – this is the 'code copying' technique for modelling inheritance.

Another approach to modelling inheritance is to use different processes for each of the 'layers' in the objects definition. In order to handle inheritance in this way we need to build in to the basic loop a method which automatically 'forwards' messages that the object cannot handle to a process which models the object's super class. For example, we may have a special type of account which cannot permit the balance to go negative. This object might be represented by the code in Program 3.2.

The underlying strategy for handling objects with inheritance involves using a process for each level in the inheritance hierarchy. When an object instance is

```
NoOverdraft(number?Balance,number?Pin,handle?Bank){
  /* Create general account - super class of NoOverDraft*/
  handle?Super := fork Account(Balance,Pin,Bank);
  while true do {
    (debit,number?A,Pin) -> {
      (report,Pin) >> Super;        /*what is our balance?*/
      number?B :: sender==Super -> { /*check sender is Super*/
        B-A < 0 -> sorry >> replyto /*no overdraft allowed*/
        | otherwise -> (debit, A, Pin) >>> Super /* Super debits */
        }
    | (close_account,Pin) -> {
        handle?Reply := replyto;
        Balance=0 -> {
          (close_account,Pin) >> Super;
          { terminated :: sender==Super  -> /* terminated by Super*/
            { terminated >> Reply ; break}  /* reply and stop*/
          | any?Message :: sender==Super ->
            Message >> Reply         /* pass on other replies*/
          }
    | any?M -> M >>> Super               /* forward messages to Super*/
    }
}
```

Program 3.2 An object process with inheritance

created, its first act is to create a sub-process representing the object's super-class. It then proceeds to accept messages as normal, however all messages which cannot be handled by the object are forwarded to this super-process.

Of course, if the super class has itself inherited from another class then further super processes will be created as a result. Before the **NoOverDraft** object terminates it sends a terminate message to its super process to ensure that it terminates iirst; which may also first terminate its super processes as necessary.

Note that in the **NoOverdraft** procedure the handles of the reply process for the **debit** and **close_account** messages are remembered in a variable **Reply** using the assignment

handle?Reply := replyto

This is because in the context in which **Reply** is used, the keyword **replyto** would denote Super, not the original sender of the message to the process. Also, responses from Super are checked by:

... :: sender==Super ->

to make sure that the sender is Super and no one else.

4   An object oriented syntax layer for April

While programming **April** in this style effectively captures the essence of the run-time interpretation of object oriented programs; it is not the same as programming an object oriented language because there is no syntactic support for objects, classes and inheritance in **April**.

Our task in this section is to define a syntax which does capture the ideas of object oriented programming while preserving the flavour of programming in **April**. We also show how this syntax can be implemented straightforwardly using **April**'s parser extension and macro facilities.

4.1   micro-Object syntax

We identify two aspects of object definition – the specification of the methods of the object and the specification of the relationships between classes. Clearly, we can borrow a great deal from **April**'s existing syntax for method specification; however a more compact notation for dealing with replies to messages would be convenient.

For example, in the **NoOverDraft** class, instead of writing:

```
(report,Pin) >> Super;      /*what is our balance?*/
{ number?B :: sender==Super -> { /*check sender is Super*/
   B-A < 0 -> sorry >> Reply /*no overdraft allowed*/
 | otherwise -> (debit, A, Pin) >>> Super /*let Super do debit*/
 }
}
```

to enquire about the current balance, if would be better if we could use a more functional notation such as:

```
if super!(report,Pin)-A < 0 then  /* Would balance go negative? */
```

The expression **super!(report,Pin)** means the value returned by the **report** method from this object's super class. The identifier **super** is a new keyword giving direct access to the methods which are inherited by an object. In general, expressions such as

ObjectId!Message

would be interpreted as value obtained after sending the message **Message** to the object whose identifier is the value of the expression **ObjectId**, and waiting for the reply.

To go with the more compact notation for sending messages we also suggest a notation for replying to messages within methods. So, instead of:

```
sorry >> Reply          /*no overdraft allowed*/
```

we suggest the more compact statement:

```
!!sorry                 /*no overdraft allowed*/
```

4.2   Classes and inheritance

A complete class definition is used to identify the relationship of objects in that class to other objects; in particular any inheritance relationships must be established.

Our class notation has two parts: an infix operator – **is** – which identifies a suite of methods with a particular name – i.e., the class definition. In this notation, the complete **Account** class is written as in Program 4.1.

```
Account(number?Balance,number?Pin,handle?Bank) is {
  methods{
    (debit,number?amount,Pin) ->
      { Balance := Balance - amount;     /* Debit the account */
        !!ok
      }
  | (credit,number?amount) -> {
        Balance +:= amount; !!ok         /* Credit account */
      }
  | (report,Pin) -> !! Balance           /* Report the balance */
  | (close_account,Pin) -> {
      if Balance = 0 then {
        (close_account,Pin) >>> Bank;
        !!terminated; die
      }
      else !!balance_not_zero             /* Cant close right now */
    }
  }
}
```

Program 4.1 An object syntax account class definition

For the sake of simplicity we shall restrict our object oriented extension to single inheritance. That is, a class may inherit the methods of just one other class. Multiple inheritance is undoubtably more powerful, however the extra complications involved in implementing it would cloud the issues at this point.

Therefore, when specifing that a class is a sub-class of another, we can take a very simple approach. Here we use another infix operator – **isa** – applied to the name of the class and the super-class – to denote inheritance. This is shown in Program 4.2.

```
NoOverdraft(number?Balance,number?Pin,handle?Bank) isa
  Account(Balance,Pin,Bank) is {
  methods {
    (debit, number?A) ->
      if super!report-A < 0 then  /* Would balance go negative? */
        !!sorry                    /* no overdraft allowed */
      else
        (debit,number?A) >>> Super
  | (close_account,Pin) -> {
      any?Ans := super!(close_account,Pin);
      if Ans = terminated then {
        terminated; die
      }
      else !!Ans
    }
  }
}
```

Program 4.2 The **NoOverDraft** object definition

4.3 Macros to transform class descriptions into programs

Given our extension to the basic **April** syntax which permits us to write classes, access their methods and obtain replies in a straightforward manner, our next task is to construct a suite of macros and operator declarations which will permit use to use our notation.

April supports a mechanism for extending the valid syntax of **April** programs using an *operator precedence grammar*.[7] **April**'s grammar is actually based on an elaboration of the operator precedence grammar used for describing arithmetic expressions. In **April**'s case, the operator grammar is used to capture all of **April**'s syntax not simply arithmetic expressions. We extend the syntax of **April** by declaring new operators.

Defining new operators is not sufficient however; there must also be a means for attaching a *semantics* to a given extension. In **April** this is commonly done through the use of compile-time macro definitions. As we see below, **April**'s macro language is easily enough to cope with mapping object oriented **April** into plain 'vanilla' **April**.

The operators that we have to define for the object oriented extension are

- **is** to define a class which doesn't involve inheritance.
- **isa** to introduce a sub-class of another class.
- **methods** to introduce the methods of a class description.

---

[7] This is very similar to the technique used in Prolog for extending its syntax

- **vars** to declare the instance variables of a class.
- ! to send a message.
- !! to reply to a message.
- **super** to invoke a super communication.

We will examine each of these operators in turn, giving an example macro that will implement the feature.

Reply to a message using !! The translation of !!, in for example

!! ok

is quite straightforward. It becomes a normal **April** message send:

ok >> replyto

We can write this down quite straightforwardly, as a combination of an operator declaration and a macro, as shown in Program 4.3:

```
#op({!!},"f(*)",1100);
#macro !! ?M -> M >> replyto;
```

Program 4.3 Macro to implement !!

This declares the new syntax extension to **April** – the new operator symbol !! – which is a prefix operator of precedence 1100.[8]
   In addition, the macro definition is used to convert the newly legal statement into simpler **April** code. **April** macros use a variation of **April**'s pattern language to describe macro templates. The template:

```
#macro !! ?M -> ...
```

signifies that expressions of the form !! *anything* can be matched by this macro, and if a matching statement is found in the program, then the macro vairable **M** is bound to the right hand side of the !! operator; and the whole statement will be transformed into the message send statement:

```
M >> replyto
```

---

[8] This is the standard precedence level in **April** for encoding statement-level operators.

Send a message and wait for reply using ! This is a rather more complicated operator to implement. We are required to send a message and wait for
the response. The value of a ! expression is the reply obtained from the message.
However, we can use **April**'s **valof** construct to insert procedural statements
anywhere in expressions.

An expression of the form:

Msg ! Who

is equivalent to:

```
valof {
  Msg >> Who;
  type ? rep :: sender==Who ->
    valis rep;
}
```

Where *type* is the type of the reply and the type of the expression. Unfortunately,
it is not possible to perform type inference as part of the macro-processing of
a program. However, we can implement a facsimile of this using the macro and
operator declared in Program 4.4.

```
#op({!},"(*)f(*)",700);
#macro ?Msg ! ?Who ->
  valof {
    Msg >> Who;
    any?rep :: sender==Who ->
      valis rep;
  };
```

Program 4.4 Implementation of message send – !

Note that we declare the variable **rep** in this macro as part of the group
of statements which is waiting for the reply from the target object. It does not
matter how many times we use the '!' operator within a class as each occurrence
of the variable will be distinct – due to **April**'s scoping rules.

Implementing methods The translation of the **methods** declaration in a class
depends on whether the class is a 'base' class (i.e., one that doesn't involve
inheritance) and a sub-class of another class – which, of course, does involve
inheritance.

If we are translating the methods of a base class, then the mapping of

```
class is {
  methods {
    msg1 -> method1
    ...
  | msgk -> methodk
  }
}
```

is

```
class(){
  while true do {
    msg1 -> method1
    ...
  | msgk -> methodk
  }
}
```

with any occurence of **die** being replaced by **break**.

We can effect the toplevel part of this translation with the macro in Program 4.5.

```
#op({is},"(*)f(*)",900);
#op({methods},"f(*)",1099);
#macro class ?N is ?B./(methods ?M) ->
  (N){
    B ./ {while true do M }
  };
#macro die -> break;
```

Program 4.5 Implementation of **methods**

Using the contex search operator – ./ – allows us to search for the **method** declaration anywhere in the class. This macro will work therefore whether or not there are any instance vairables declared.

If there is inheritance involved, then the mapping is a little more complex. A typical class with inheritance, such as:

```
class isa Super is {
  methods {
    msg1 -> method1
    ...
  | msgk -> methodk
  }
}
```

is mapped into the procedure:

```
class(){
  handle?super := fork mu(){Super};
  while true do {
    msg1 -> method1
    ...
  | msgk -> methodk
  | any?M -> M >>> super
  }
}
```

We must introduce a new variable – **super** – which is given the handle of a process which represents the super-class. The super-class process is forked as part of creating the object of the sub-class. If the sub-object receives a message it cannot handle then it is forwarded to the process which is modelling the super-class.

The macro to perform this mapping – together with associated operator declaration – is given in Program 4.6. It is bigger, but not much more complicated than the one in Program 4.5.

```
#op({isa},"(*)f(*)",850);
#macro class ?N isa ?S is ?B./{ methods ?M} ->
  N{
    handle?super := fork mu(){S};
    B ./ { while true do {
            M
          | any?Other -> Other >>> super
          }
        }
  }
```

Program 4.6 Implementation of classes with inheritance

4.4 Outstanding issues

The suite of macros presented here will give a good approximation to object oriented programming – in particular concurrent object oriented programming since it is based on **April**'s process model. However, it is incomplete because an important feature of object oriented programming has not been handled, namely *self communication*.

Self communication means that the super-class part of an object can send messages to the sub-class in order to determine particular features. It is important because it allows objects to 'be aware' of the fact that they have been specialized – i.e., sub-classed. In our treatment, the super class object of an object is essentially another independent object; sending a message to an object is tantamount to sending a message to a collection of objects with the expectation that one of them 'will pick it up'. However, without self communication it is not easy for the collection to be tightly integrated.

Unfortunately, self communication involves hard technical issues which seem to imply drastic solutions. If an object sends itself a message, and waits for a reply, then deadlock is hard to avoid. Whilst it is possible to overcome this problem, it requires a radical reworking of the strategy we have outlined.

The translation into processes would require each message to 'spawn off' a special process which just deals with that message. It is beyond the scope of this case study to explore this further; except that we may note that the strategy of using macros to implement this regime would be just as effective.

What we have shown is the considerable power of April's macro language as a tool for language extension.

5 Conclusions

April is a language which is intended to build distributed symbolic applications, such as Multi-Agent systems and Distributed Artificial Intelligence applications. While it is not directly an Object-Oriented programming language, it does contain many features which are essential for Object-Oriented style programming – encapsulation of state; a uniform message passing mechanism and the ability to execute many concurrent processes simultaneously.

In addition, April has a strong strategy for extensibility – the syntax can be extended by adding new operators to the language and these operators can be given a semantics by means of a powerful macro capability.

We have seen how these features can be combined to give an Object-Oriented language 'layer' on top of April. Of course, it is a matter of some discussion whether the concept of 'process' is more basic than the concept of 'object'. What we have shown is that, in April, it is straightforward to map object oriented language features into a process language. The benefit is greater understanding of the issues in concurrent Object-Oriented programming languages and the relationship between objects and processes.

References

1. K.L. Clark and S. Gregory. Parlog:parallel programming in logic. *ACM Toplas*, 8(1):1–49, 1986.
2. W.F. Clocksin and C.S. Mellish. *Programming in Prolog*. Springer-Verlag, 1981.
3. A. Davison. Polka: a parlog object oriented language. Internal report, Dept. of Computing, Imperial College, London, 1988.

4. e.W. Dijkstra. *The discipline of programming*. Prentice-Hall International, 1977.
5. F.G.McCabe and K.L.Clark. Programming in april – an agent process interaction language. Technical report, Dept. of Computing, Imperial College, London, 1994.
6. I. Foster and S. Tuecke. Parallel programming with PCN. Internal report anl-91/32, Argonne National Laboratory, 1991.
7. C.A. Hoare. *Communicating Sequential Processes*. Prentice-Hall International, 1985.
8. K. E. Iverson. *A Programming Language*. Wiley, New York, 1962.
9. E. Shapiro and A. Takeuchi. Objected oriented programming in concurrent prolog. *New Generation Computing*, 1(1), 1983.
10. G. L. Steele and et. al. An overview of common lisp. In *ACM Symposium on Lisp and Functional Programming*, August 1982.
11. A. van Hoff. *Hooked on Java*. Addison-Wesley, 1996.

Reactive Programming in Eiffel//

Denis Caromel Yves Roudier
caromel@unice.fr *roudier@unice.fr*

SLOOP Project (http://www.inria.fr/sloop/)
I3S - CNRS - Univ. of Nice - INRIA Sophia
bât. ESSI, Rte des Colles, B.P. 145
06903 Sophia Antipolis Cedex, FRANCE

Abstract. This paper presents how asynchronous reactive programming can be achieved in the Eiffel// language. Our approach makes use of some reflection available in the language and is based on a specific communication semantics. We present some reactive abstractions that can be programmed with this mechanism and illustrate their use. The technique we developed makes it possible to transform a sequential system of objects into a reactive one. A tape-recorder example illustrates the programming technique.

1 Introduction

In an usual programming paradigm, as notably emphasized by functional languages, a program is often seen as a function of its inputs; this behavior is often referred to as *transformational*. On the other hand, some systems rather model a continuous flow of reactions to stimuli occurring throughout the program life: if the system can react immediately at the frequency imposed by external stimuli, it is said to be *reactive* to its environment (this definition was introduced in [22]). Such programs do not necessarily terminate, which can somehow change the correctness meaning.

Event-driven programming is a good example of reactivity: the arrival of an event corresponds to the triggering of a reaction. Computer Supported Cooperative Work (CSCW), or *groupware*, can fit in this category too. Real-time systems are also reactive systems, but whose reactions are associated with strict physical timing constraints. Reactive systems are also studied in Distributed Artificial Intelligence: their auto-organizing behavior seems very promising in multi-agent systems (see [9], in the robotics area).

Programming such systems with traditional tools can lead to an extreme complexity of their design, source code, and error tracing. Even object-orientation does not provide an answer on its own in this situation: in their common meaning, objects methods are transformational programs. If we want to write a reactive system in an object-oriented language, and still be able to use all the language features and reuse its libraries, we need an adequate style of programming. We would like to be able to split a reactive program into several relatively independent modules, and in this respect, features of object-oriented techniques such as encapsulation, abstraction and reuse are of great help.

In Section 2, we first give a quick overview of the Eiffel// language. Section 3 describes a first object-oriented reactive abstraction and its principle, then the techniques developed to introduce this kind of reactivity in Eiffel//. We illustrate object-oriented reactivity by the programming of a reactive tape-recorder in Section 4. More sophisticated reactive abstractions and design strategies for reactive programming are sketched in Section 5.

2   Eiffel//

The Eiffel// language [12] is a parallel extension of Eiffel. Many of the language parallel constructs extend Eiffel sequential ones and are syntactically identical. In this section, we introduce the main concepts of the language and the syntax of its parallel constructs.

2.1   Processes

One of the breakthroughs of (many) class-based object-oriented languages is the unification of module and type aspects into one construct: the class. Following this idea, Eiffel// introduces active objects, which we call processes: they unify the notions of class and task, of object and process. However, not all objects are processes: there also exist passive objects, that must be attached to a thread of control, i.e. a process, to be able to execute.

Our model makes use of inheritance for structuring object concurrency: a process is an instance of a class inheriting directly or indirectly from PROCESS.

Given a sequential class A, exporting some routines (e.g. f, g ...), we can define a parallel class (a process class) which will inherit from A and PROCESS:

```
class PARALLEL_A
  export repeat A -- same interface as A
  inherit A;
          PROCESS
feature
end; -- class PARALLEL_A
```

Creation and initialization of an object of this class are the same as for usual objects:

```
my_process:PARALLEL_A;
    ...
my_process.create;
```

After its instantiation, this process object executes its *Live* routine. This routine describes the sequence of actions that the process executes over its life. When the *Live* routine terminates, the process itself terminates. This inheritance mechanism gives the process a default behavior which is defined in the *Live* routine of the PROCESS class: requests to the process entry points are handled in a FIFO order, one at a time. Specific policies can also be programmed (see Section 2.4).

If two processes reference the same (passive) object, routine calls to this object may overlap. To address this synchronization issue, the choice has been made that each non-process object is a private object accessible by only *one* process: the process that directly or indirectly references it.

During design stage, if it appears that an object needs to be shared by several processes, the designer has to think about it and specifically program it as a process. A process and the passive objects it references form a sub-system (see Figure 1).

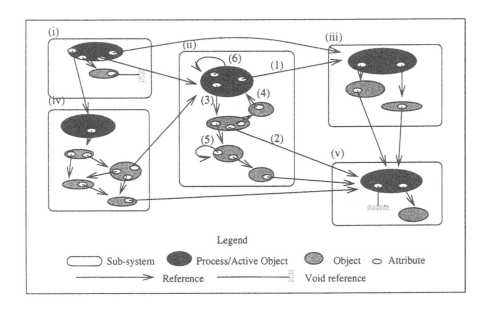

Fig. 1. Processes and objects at run-time

2.2 Communications

When an object owns a reference to a process, it is able to communicate with it: call or access one of its exported features. This basic object-oriented mechanism is used as the Inter-Process Communication (IPC) mechanism. An instruction:

```
o.f(parameters);
```

reflects either a classical feature call on the object *o*, or an IPC if *o* is a process. Moreover, the presence of polymorphism makes it possible to dynamically reference a process while *o* is statically declared as a regular object:

```
objA: A;
procA: PARALLEL_A;
  ...
objA.f;        -- routine f from A
procA.f;       -- routine f from PARALLEL_A (IPC)
objA:=procA;   -- polymorphic assignment
objA.f;        -- dynamic binding : routine f from PARALLEL_A (IPC)
```

We now define the semantics of an IPC in Eiffel// (see Figure 2).

An object *o* executing a statement *p.f (parameters)*, where p is dynamically a process, triggers the following operations:

1. Raise a specific exception, *Request*, in the context of *p*.
2. *p* is interrupted.
3. A handshake between *p* and *o* is established; an object of type REQUEST is sent from *o* to *p*.
4. *p* first releases *o* (end of rendezvous, *o* executes its next statement); then *p* enters the *receive_request* routine which handles the new request.
5. *p* resumes its previous activity when the *receive_request* routine finishes.

Later on, the process will decide to comply with the request: it will serve the request, i.e. call the routine *serve* from class REQUEST on this object. The IPC is a three-phase operation (interruption, rendezvous and asynchronous service) whose synchronous phase is small enough to globally behave asynchronously.

2.3 Synchronization

We use a specific synchronization mechanism called the **wait-by-necessity** principle: a process is synchronized, i.e. it waits, only when it attempts to use the result of a feature call that has not been returned yet. Variables that depend on an awaited result are called future variables, or futures.

This mechanism is automatic (no explicit wait on a future is necessary) and transparent (future variables do not need to be declared specifically). However, explicit waits are also possible (primitive *Wait*) as well as explicit testing of a future (*Awaited*).

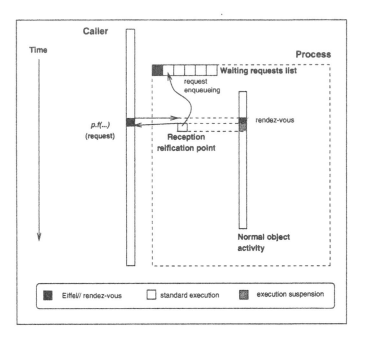

Fig. 2. Eiffel// standard communication behavior

2.4 Control

Eiffel// has a *centralized* control programming (centralized in the *Live* routine). The nature of this control can be either *explicit* or *implicit*.

Control is explicit if its definition consists of a programmed thread of control, with an explicit service of requests; otherwise it is implicit, often offering a more declarative framework. Explicit control is programmed with primitives that access the parallel structure of a process, for instance its request list. A library of specialized service routines is available to program:

- blocking services (e.g. *bl_serve_oldest*)
- non-blocking services(*serve_recent, serve_oldest_of* ...)
- timed services (*timed_serve_recent* ...)
- informations (*request_nb* ...)
- explicit wait (*wait_a_request* ...).

Implicit control is a high-level concept. Thanks to its declarative nature, it is an effective way of expressing synchronization. It usually provides the programmer with a consistent framework, where he can forget implementation details and often describe the synchronization constraints in a very synthetic and problem-adapted manner. But above all, this kind of control promotes synchronization reuse [27, 28, 17, 29, 18, 26].

In Eiffel//, implicit control is available by means of user-level defined abstractions [11, 2]. Apart from deriving his processes directly from PROCESS and programming explicitly the control, a user can derive his classes from these more general abstract frameworks. They are derived from the PROCESS class: these abstractions help programming control in a more implicit way. Libraries of such frameworks can be written (see Figure 3).

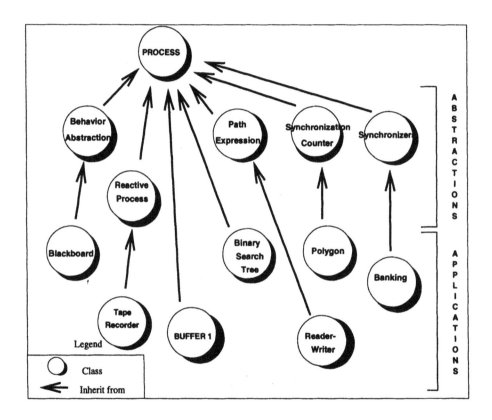

Fig. 3. An example of abstract frameworks

To conclude this presentation, let us notice that only a limited amount of reflection is available in Eiffel//:

- requests and routines are first-class objects and can be manipulated (they are reified or transformed into objects; this occurs in routines that we call reification points),
- the list of pending requests can be accessed,

– the message reception reification point (*receive_request*) can be redefined.

More details about the Eiffel// language can be found in [10, 11, 12]. The next section explains how all these mechanisms, together with the communication semantics, permit reactive programming.

3 Reactive abstractions

We first want to define a model of reactive objects: they will have to react to some stimulus or message instantaneously (in comparison with the normal duration of an activity, that is at least a method execution). We want to preserve the usual organization of a system of objects (we hope to retain as much as possible the object encapsulation), while designing a programming mode adapted to reactive applications. We will introduce a reactive behavior through several general-purpose reactive process classes that the user inherits from in order to program his reactive processes, following the same technique as the PROCESS class or the abstract frameworks.

3.1 Principle

A basic reactive process can be defined as the REACTIVE_PROCESS class; it offers fundamental reactive routines.

Reactive routines have an interruption semantics (they can be processed at any time during the execution of a process, and not only when it choses to serve them) but they also change the execution behavior of the process:

– *abort* permits aborting the current request service activity,
– *suspend* allows suspending the activity,
– *resume* resumes a suspended execution.

A reactive process is also able to answer "normal" (transformational) requests when it is not in the suspended state. During a suspended execution, normal requests are only added to the waiting list of requests, but cannot be processed, even if the process was idle before suspension.

One major enhancement of such programming is that the encapsulation of transformational methods of reactive processes is not broken by the interleaving between standard code and the scrutiny of a possible event arrival. Here, since we essentially add a special ancestor in the inheritance graph and since no code is introduced inside already written methods, reuse of existing components is allowed in general.

3.2 Example: a factory robot

Suppose that we programmed a FACTORY_ROBOT (class) with an independantly moving arm, and a soldering iron. Its work is to solder components on an empty computer motherboard. If we send it a *solder_chip* order, we want it to solder a chip with several hundred pins (a long task):

```
solder_chip is
  do
    arm.place_motherboard;
    arm.get_chip;
    arm.place_chip;
    from pin_list.go_first_pin;
    until pin_list.all_done;
      loop
        arm.get_solder;
        arm.position(pin_list.current_position);
        soldering_iron.solder(pin_list.current_position);
        pin_list.go_next_pin;
      end; -- loop
  end; -- solder_chip
```

Suppose that the price of the chip is negligible, but that we want to complete soldering on as many motherboards as possible. Unhappily, some motherboards have not been correctly produced and should be rejected. The only change we can afford is to add a testing device able to recognize these failing motherboards. However, the check takes a significant amount of time (for instance, up to half the time of the soldering process).

If the motherboard standard test has failed, a more specialized test is performed to see if the board must be rejected or if the problem is recoverable by the maintenance team; this test requires however that the robot be stopped. Its activity can be stopped with a *suspend* reactive request: if the recovery test succeeds, the soldering process will be reactivated and the board will be corrected later; the board will be rejected immediately otherwise.

A first sequential solution would be to test the motherboard and to solder the chip only if the board is valid; but because of the processing time of the test, the robot would not be working at its maximum speed. A parallel solution would be to solder the chip while testing the board (with two distinct processes) and eventually accept or reject it; still, the robot would not be working at its maximum speed.

The alternative would be to start simultaneously the testing and the soldering process and to stop the latter if the motherboard must be rejected.

Without reactivity, we can program this by interleaving each non-atomic instruction of *solder_chip* with a test to know if the robot must stop its task. This would lead to a loss of readability (the interleaving of tests) and of time (multiple testing during the soldering process until it ends or a problem happens).

We can also program this behavior by transforming the factory robot process into a reactive process class. If the first test has failed, the robot activity can be suspended while the second test is performed. If the board must be rejected, the checking process can *abort* the soldering task, otherwise, it can resume its current activity.

The resulting class layout is the following:

```
class REACTIVE_FACTORY_ROBOT
  export repeat FACTORY_ROBOT, repeat REACTIVE_PROCESS
  inherit FACTORY_ROBOT; REACTIVE_PROCESS
feature
end; -- class

class FACTORY
    ...
  board:MOTHERBOARD;
  robot:REACTIVE_FACTORY_ROBOT;
  testing_device:TESTING_DEVICE_PROCESS;
    ...
  run_assembly is
    do
      from until
        loop
          robot.get_new_board;
          robot.solder_chip;
          if not(testing_device.tested_OK) -- wait-by-necessity + test
            then robot.suspend;
                 if not(testing_device.possible_recovery)
                   then board.reject;
                        robot.reinit;
                   else robot.resume;
                        robot.chip_soldered.Wait; -- explicit wait
                        board.send_to_maintenance;
                 end; -- if
            else robot.chip_soldered.Wait; -- explicit wait
                 board.roll_out;
          end; -- if
        end; -- loop
    end; -- run_assembly
end; -- class
```

3.3 Programming technique

We introduce reactivity with messages: a message will be able to modify the normal flow of control of an object, and for instance interrupt its normal execution. In order to implement reactive classes (classes allowing reactive messages), we have to redefine the semantics of communication, and more precisely request reception.

The requests that induce an immediate reaction in the process (for instance *abort, suspend,* etc.) are not built-in: these reactive requests are normal methods of REACTIVE_PROCESS. They are handled at the reification point of message reception (*receive_request* method), so that they can be called even during the execution of a normal method. As we explained, the Eiffel// standard communication semantics, while globally asynchronous, implies an interruption of the normal execution, and a rendezvous (see Section 2.2).

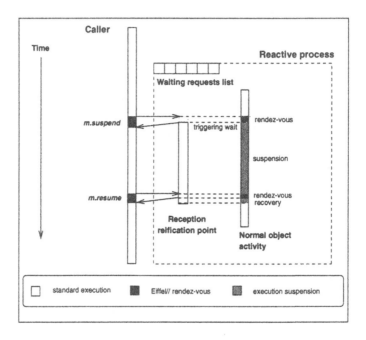

Fig. 4. The suspension mechanism at run-time

We take advantage of the interruption phase of the communication to achieve a suspension of the activity: for instance, when a *suspend* request is sent, the receiver execution is interrupted by the arrival of the request itself until a *resume* request is sent (see Figure 4).

Aborting the normal execution of a process makes use of the exception mechanism: we trigger a specific exception which is propagated along dynamic calls chain up to the higher englobing method *Live*. This method exception handler catches the exception and retries executing the Live, thus aborting the old thread of control. The object is restarted but its attributes are not reset by default to their creation values. The *abort* method leads however to the loss of the pre-post specification model: the method can no longer be considered as an atomic execution unit whose post-conditions are realized if its pre-conditions are true. For

```
   receive_request is
   do
      if new_request.feat=&resume then -- resume without suspend
         raise("reactive_failure");
(1)   elsif new_request.feat=&abort then
         new_request.serve;
         raise("start_over");
(2)   elsif new_request.feat=&suspend then  -- begin suspended mode
         from new_request.serve;
               wait_request;  -- non-active wait for an IPC
         until new_request.feat=&abort or new_request.feat=&suspend or
               new_request.feat=&resume
         loop
           if (new_request /= &abort and new_request /= &suspend and
                 new_request /= &resume) then
(3)           requests.add_request (new_request); -- old receive_request
           end; -- if
           wait_request;
         end; --loop
(4)      if new_request.feat=&resume then
            new_request.serve;
(5)      elsif new_request.feat=&abort then
            new_request.serve;
            raise("start_over");
         elsif new_request.feat=&suspend then -- suspend within suspend
            raise("reactive_failure");
         end; -- if
         -- end of suspended mode
      else
(6)      requests.add_request(new_request);  -- default behavior
      end; -- if
   end; -- receive_request
```

Fig. 5. *receive_request* in the REACTIVE_PROCESS class

the same reasons, a special processing might be necessary to maintain the class invariant of some classes; since it should be executed at each restart, this piece of code could be called from *abort*.

To illustrate these techniques, we present the programming of the REACTIVE_PROCESS class of Section 3.1. The *receive_request* message reification point is modified in the following way (see Figure 5). It normally performs the same operation as a normal process (6), i.e. it enqueues arriving requests that will be served later on by the process activity thread. If the received request is an *abort* (1), the reactive process stops its current operation and restarts its activity. On reception of a *suspend*, the reactive process switches to a suspended mode (2), where it only serves the reactive requests, and still enqueues the other requests (3); it only exits from this mode on reception of a *resume* (4) or an *abort* (5) reactive request.

4   A reactive tape-recorder

Let us take the example of a simple tape-recorder (a software tape-recorder, actually). This recorder has several buttons (*start, stop, backward, forward*) and a tape counter with a *reset* button. It can play a tape (an audio file) on the speaker.

While expressing the behavior of the system, we want to put the emphasis on the idea of event: an event (say, pressing on a button) can trigger some special processing and change of the system state. How to structure this reactive system ?

4.1   Sequential version

Our first version of the tape-recorder is *sequential*. It does not mean that one has to think of a sequentially constrained design by opposition to a parallel one, but rather that we program the application in the usual paradigm of the language, which is *imperative object-oriented*, not worrying about possible parallelism, concurrency or reactivity.

We structure this version as follows (see Figure 6): the interface relies on classes SPEAKER and TAPE_DISPLAY for the outputs, and class TAPE_COMMAND for the inputs (this class translates XWindow events into tape-recorder events).

The core of the recorder is defined in class TAPE_ENGINE; it describes and models the physical constraints, like the behavior of the *play* command.

The programming of the *play* routine is as follows: it reads and outputs the tape until it ends; we do not try to interrupt it by waiting events of a reactive nature:

```
class TAPE_ENGINE
  ...

play is
 -- normal play (until the end of the tape)
do
  from
  until end_of_tape
  loop
    one_play; -- low-level method: read a fragment of the tape
  end;
  tape_display.set_stop;
end; -- play
```

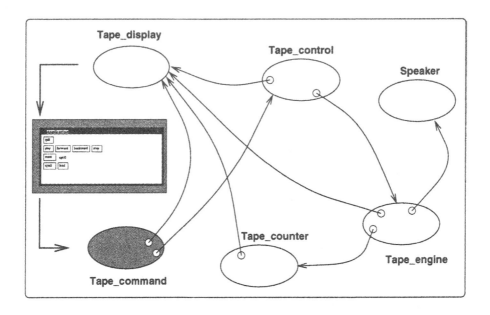

Fig. 6. Sequential tape-recorder system at run-time

Finally, the class TAPE_CONTROL represents the logical control over the recorder: it describes the available commands with their specific constraints of use, logical ordering of invocations, etc. You cannot play a tape, for instance, before there is actually one in the tape-recorder:

```
class TAPE_CONTROL
    ...

play is
  do
    if loaded then
      tape_display.set_play;
      tape_engine.play;
    else
      tape_display.message("LOAD FIRST !?");
    end;
  end; -- play
```

In this example, TAPE_CONTROL routines match the available buttons (*start*, *stop*, etc.) that can be called through the graphical interface.

This version is a complete and running system that can be tested; but since it is not reactive at all, it does not conform to the exact specifications of a tape-recorder: the operations (*play, forward, backward...*) do not take care of a possible interruption. A sequential version conforming to these specifications could possibly be obtained but at the price of a complicated thread of control (interleaving of effective actions and tests) and the loss of encapsulation.

4.2 Reactive version

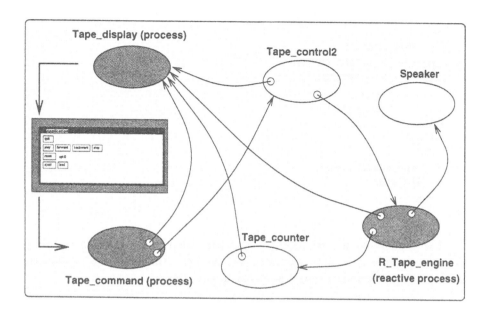

Fig. 7. Reactive tape-recorder system at run-time

The reactive version of the example (see Figure 7) is obtained by turning the sequential TAPE_ENGINE class into a reactive process. This version is working as a normal tape-recorder (the tape can be stopped any place, etc.).

The Tape_display, which now appears shared between Tape_command and R_tape_engine, has to be made an active object:

```
class P_TAPE_DISPLAY
  export
    repeat TAPE_DISPLAY
  inherit
    TAPE_DISPLAY;
    PROCESS
feature
end;
```

We then have to derive a new controller from TAPE-CONTROL (class TAPE-CONTROL2). In addition to the sequential controls previously defined and which are reused, the new controller will define the reactive behavior of the asynchronous and reactive engine. This new engine class inherits from the sequential engine (reusing the physical constraints of the recorder) and from a reactive process, which enables the interruption of methods. For example, the *stop* method of the TAPE-CONTROL class was used in the sequential version to only update the display (it could not stop the engine); it can now be redefined as follows to incorporate a reactive stop of the tape-recorder engine activity:

```
class TAPE_CONTROL2
  export repeat TAPE_CONTROL
  inherit TAPE_CONTROL
          rename stop as old_stop,
          redefine stop
feature
  stop is
  do
    tape_engine.abort;
    old_stop;
  end;
    ...
```

The application now achieves the specified behaviour of the tape-recorder.

The example can still be extended. For instance, the pause can be requested during a *play* method: a simple suspension will achieve it.

```
prior_activity: like activity;
    ...
suspend is
do
  if activity/=suspended
    then tape_engine.suspend;
         prior_activity:=activity;
         activity:=suspended;
    else tape_engine.resume;
         activity:=prior_activity;
  end; -- if
end;
```

4.3 Reuse difficulties

Coherence problems. In our example, the reactive engine methods cannot be considered atomic any more, since they have a duration and are interruptible. When needed, methods can be placed in a non-reactive critical section. For instance, if we want the information displayed on the counter to remain coherent, we need to encapsulate the engine low-level methods in such a region:

```
class TAPE_ENGINE
  ...
  one_play is
  do
    delay_requests;    -- no request acceptance: critical section
    old_one_play;
    accept_requests;   -- accepting requests again
  end;
```

The routines that need to be protected must be identified by the user when he reuses a class. If the protection granularity is smaller than the existing routine, then the method must be rewritten to include the adequate protection (factoring out this code into a separate method could be a good idea for future reuse). However, functions without side effect need no protection, and can be inherited without any adaptation.

As a more advanced mechanism, it is possible to add a declarative mechanism to reactive processes in order to express that some requests must be served in a critical section. Those requests would then temporarily turn the reactive process into a non-reactive but still asynchronous one, for instance:

```
class REACTIVE_ENGINE
  ...
  set_non_reactive(&one_play);
```

This technique promotes reuse and avoids routine redefinition.

When a programmer uses critical sections, he must be aware that the object is temporarily non-reactive: this is in accordance with the semantics of the critical section, but the granularity of protection must be well understood in order to comply with application-specific time constraints of reactivity.

Interface problems. In our example, functions like *stop* were already existing in the sequential version of the tape-recorder. This was natural, since the function corresponds in fact to an interface button.

It may happen that new request may be necessary to call reactive features when reusing an already-written sequential system, and turning it into a reactive one. This can impose to redefine the static type of some objects to be able to call their new functions. However, the problem is not specific to reactive object.

5   Perspectives

In this section, we present other reactive abstractions, extending reactive processes. We then discuss some topics related to programming design. We finally discuss related work.

5.1 Other reactive abstractions

New primitives can be introduced to program more sophisticated reactive behaviors. They are only introduced as object (not built-in) extensions: the user can define other reactive primitives he needs, and possibly provide them in libraries, following the technique we just explained.

Preemptive process. We can define a reactive process with a *preempt* reactive primitive: preemption allows the user to stop the normal flow of control of the reactive process, and to have it execute another exported method.

The caller issues a *preempt* request to the reactive process; the process execution is then suspended, and only the caller's requests and the reactive requests *resume* or *abort* are processed.

▽ example: in our previous robot example, we did not take into account the possibility that the robot might run out of solder; with a preemptive capability, we can handle this situation as follows:

```
robot.solder_chip;
  ...
-- triggered if the robot has run out of solder:
robot.preempt;
robot.arm.get_solder;
robot.reposition(last_position_soldered);
robot.resume;
```

If the methods executed during a preemption affect the object attributes used in the normal execution, the current request (or a portion of it) should be protected with a critical section. The preempt also acts as a critical section itself, because as a reactive request, it cannot be interrupted by others reactive requests.

User-defined reactive requests. The preemption mechanism, although very flexible, can become dangerous since every exported method of the reactive process can be called. We can introduce restrictions on the reactive invocations by specifying the list of reactive requests monitored in the *receive_request* routine (with a *set_preemptive* primitive).

▽ example: an event-driven system
This example shows the introduction of new reactive requests representing the sending of asynchronous events. These events trigger a routine able to process them when they arrive:

```
class EVENT_DRIVEN_SYSTEM
  export event1, event2, long_task
  inherit EVENT_REACTIVE_PROCESS
```

```
          rename Live as old_Live
  feature
     -- event-specialized routines:
   event1 is do ... end;
   event2 is do ... end;

     -- this routine is not reactive:
   long_task is do ... end;

   Live is
    do
       -- new reactive requests:
     set_preemptive(&event1);
     set_preemptive(&event2);

     old_Live; -- reactive behavior inheritance
    end;
  end -- class EVENT_DRIVEN_SYSTEM
```

A client of EVENT_DRIVEN_SYSTEM can now trigger reactively event1 and event2. As usual, the event handler duration must be appropriately defined (duration, etc.) so that the process remain reactive (to other' events, for instance).

```
  class CALLER
  feature
    sys:EVENT_DRIVEN_SYSTEM;

    method is
      do
        sys.long_task;
        sys.event1;
         -- the long_task request to sys needs not be finished
         -- to process event1
      end;
  end -- class CALLER
```

Adding such user-defined reactive requests permits a better reuse of the code of clients, because the event processing would be triggered by the event arrival itself; the new reactive requests are treated atomically and cannot be interrupted by other reactive requests. Such extension is very much suited to program event-driven applications.

5.2 Reactive systems design

What should be specifically pinpointed about the writing of a reactive system with reactive processes? In this section, we develop some ideas about the design of reactive systems.

System layout. The following points are conclusions that we drew out of experiments when programming some reactive systems:

- Sequential design derivation. It turned out that it seems better to design first a sequential version of the system and to derive it into a reactive one than to start from scratch. Although this version does not conform to the reactive specifications of the application, it permits the structuring of the application in an usual manner, possibly using sequential design methods. What is more, debugging interleaving executions is not easy in itself. This approach suppresses reactive actions interleaving at the sequential design stage: debugging at this stage eases the development process.
- Multi-level structuring. Separating different types of constraints is useful for the understanding of the system. In the tape-recorder example, the sequential tape engine *play* method is only concerned with physical limitations: it ends with the tape. In the reactive version, introducing an interruption behavior generates new constraints directed by the tape-recorder behavior, in addition to these physical constraints.
- Determination of reactive objects. Guided by the idea of interruption, the programmer should locate long tasks (regarding an application-specific time scale). In our tape-recorder example, the engine *play* method has an important duration compared to the possible arrival frequency of button-press events: the TAPE_ENGINE class that exports it is a good candidate to reactivity introduction.

Modular composition of control. It is very important for the modelling, the structuring, and above all the maintainability of a reactive system that its behavior may be broken up into modular units. Modularity of control can be achieved by separating and distributing its functionalities according to some form of control layering or delegation.

Several forms of composition can be experimented. For instance, reactive objects can be seen as interconnected blackbox-components, only communicating through events or messages. On the contrary, control can be delegated along a hierarchy, each node being responsible for its subordinates/sub-functionalities. We studied in [15, 14] the object-oriented integration of another reactive paradigm, whose control expression was based on the asynchronous reactive language Electre[16]. In that particular abstraction, the behavior of a system of reactive processes is described in a centralized fashion. We described a form of hierarchical distribution of this control, and hierarchical reactive primitives on such structure.

We are interested in further investigation about reactivity over a set of objects. This topic introduces other questions regarding relation with other mechanisms in the language. For instance, can we define frameworks for sending or dispatching reactive messages to a group of objects (which can possibly introduce deadlocks or cycles) ? How to determine the global behavior of the system?

5.3 Related work

Reactive composition and event transmission are closely linked together: a general-purpose message dispatching model could be of interest as a link between reactive objects, thus allowing different mechanisms of reaction propagation. A study[1] has been lead on the introduction of communication schemes at meta-level; it could be useful to design similar communication abstractions related to reactive programming.

Another object-oriented integration of Electre specification (see Section 5.2) has also been studied in [4, 5]. In that work, composition is achieved in a blackbox-component oriented way. The underlying communication abstraction is close to the Sophtalk [25] bus communication model. If general-purpose message dispatching components existed, they could be used to handle the interaction of reactive Electre components.

Our reactive messaging technique is somewhat similar to the express messages used in ABCL/1[33], one difference being that in our case, the interruption behavior definition takes place on the receiver side, and is always transparent to the caller; our mechanism can also globally transform a sequential class into a reactive one, which increases reuse. It might be possible to achieve a similar mechanism in a transparent manner in ABCL/R [32] which offers reflective mechanisms.

Other reactive models have been integrated with objects: for instance, [31, 6] proposes the integration of specifications based on the synchronous language Esterel inside asynchronous C++ parallel objects. [8] defines an object extension of the synchronous language Reactive C[7], which uses a notion of system-wide common instant. Each object runs the code he can execute during the current instant and waits for all other objects to do the same; when all objects have synchronized, the logical time is set to the next instant. ObjectCharts[23] and ObjCharts[19] are two extensions that provide an object-oriented integration of the synchronous StateCharts model.

Our reactive processes would also probably be an interesting base for defining other sophisticated abstractions. For instance, several mechanisms, more oriented towards real-time specification, have been described in [24] (RTC++) or [30] (DROL). We could probably program such real-time extensions around our reactive process framework through library classes (in fact, only soft real-time since we cannot react more rapidly than the runtime allows us to).

6 Conclusion

We presented in this paper a set of reactive object-oriented abstractions (reactive processes) and some techniques to program, extend and reuse them. Eiffel// allows the encapsulation of reactive behaviors inside active objects thanks to what can be called a communication *"reification point"* and the language communication semantics. This framework is built without modification of the communication syntax and without any runtime built-in extension.

Several models of reactivity have been proposed that can mainly be classified into synchronous (Esterel[3], Lustre[20], StateCharts[21]) or asynchronous approach (Electre) ; some hybrid models also exist, and rely on either approach. Our work is currently oriented towards asynchronous frameworks. However, synchronous frameworks could be implemented by using a global instant notion.

Reactivity is an unavoidable paradigm for the programming of some systems. We believe that promoting the design and implementation of a sequential system as a first-stage development can actually simplify programming and enhance structuring of reactive systems (as well as parallel systems, more generally), especially in an object-oriented environment: the programmer needs not change the usual layout of his code which limits the introduction of errors or the rewriting of existing code.

The C++// language [13] is an extension of the C++ language that we are defining on the same basis: its programming model extends and generalizes the Eiffel// one. We develop more reflective capabilities in C++//, so the techniques we presented in this paper are also valid in this language. We have defined four symmetrical communication reification points (on sending and receiving, for requests and replies) and we are currently working on addressing other issues regarding run-time meta-object protocols, composability of various parallel models, and active objects mapping policies.

References

1. M. Aksit, K. Wakita, J. Bosch, L. Bergmans, and A. Yonezawa. Abstracting Object Interactions Using Composition Filters. In O. Nierstrasz, R. Guerraoui, and M. Riveill, editors, *Proceedings of the ECOOP '93 Workshop on Object-Based Distributed Programming*, LNCS 791, pages 152–184. Springer-Verlag, 1994.
2. J.-P. Bahsoun, J.-P. Briot, D. Caromel, L. Féraud, O. Niestrasz, and P. Wegner. Panel : how could object-oriented concepts and parallelism cohabit ? In *Proceedings of the 1994 International Conference on Computer Languages*, pages 195–199, Toulouse, France, May 1994. IEEE Computer Society Press.
3. G. Berry, P. Gonthier, and G. Gonthier. Synchronous Programming of Reactive Systems: an Introduction to ESTEREL. Research report, INRIA, France, 1987.
4. F. Bertrand and M. Augeraud. Contrôle du comportement d'objets : les objets réactifs asynchrones. Rapport de Recherche No 93-3. Technical report, Laboratoire d'Informatique et d'Imagerie Industrielle, Université de la Rochelle, October 1993. In french.
5. F. Bertrand and M. Augeraud. Control of Object Behavior: Asynchronous Reactive Objects. May 1994. also available as http://www-13i.univ-lr.fr/ L3I/equipe/fbertran/ pub/dksme94.ps.gz.

6. F. Boulanger, H. Delebecque, and G. Vidal-Naquet. Intégration de modules synchrones dans un langage à objets. *In RTS'94*, 1994. In french.

7. F. Boussinot. Reactive C: An Extension of C to Program Reactive Systems. *Software - Practice And Experience*, 21(4):401–428, April 1991.

8. F. Boussinot, G. Doumenc, and J.-B. Stefani. Reactive Objects. Technical Report Technical report RR-2664, INRIA, October 1990.

9. R.A. Brooks. A Layered Intelligent Control System for a Mobile Robot. In O. Faugeras and G. Giralt, editors, *Proceedings of the Third Robotics Research Symposium*, 1986.

10. D. Caromel. Concurrency and Reusability: From Sequential to Parallel. *Journal of Object-Oriented Programming*, 3(3):34–42, September 1990.

11. D. Caromel. Programming Abstractions for Concurrent Programming. In J. Bezivin, B. Meyer, J. Potter, and M. Tokoro, editors, *Technology of Object-Oriented Languages and Systems (TOOLS Pacific'90)*, pages 245–253. TOOLS Pacific, November 1990.

12. D. Caromel. Towards a Method of Object-Oriented Programming. *CACM, 36(9)*, September 1993.

13. D. Caromel, F. Belloncle, and Y. Roudier. *The C++// System*. In *Parallel Programming Using C++*. G. Wilson and P. Lu ed., MIT Press, 1996. to appear.

14. D. Caromel and Y. Roudier. Programmation Réactive en Eiffel// (expression de synchronisations selon le modèle Electre). In *Journées du GDR Programmation - Lille*, September 1994. 10 pages. In french. http://alto.unice.fr/~roudier/RR95-10.ps.

15. D. Caromel, Y. Roudier, and O. Roux. Programmation Réactive en Eiffel// (expression de synchronisations selon le modèle Electre). Technical report, Rapport de Recherche I3S N° RR-93-70, December 1993. 100 pages. In french. http://alto.unice.fr/~roudier/RR93-70.ps.

16. F. Cassez and O. Roux. Compilation of the ELECTRE Reactive Language into Finite Transition Systems. *TCS (Theoretical Computer Science)*, 146, 1995.

17. D. Decouchant, P. Le Dot, M. Riveill, C. Roisin, and X. Rousset de Pina. A Synchronization Mechanism for an Object-Oriented Distributed System. In *IEEE Eleventh International Conference on Distributed Computing Systems*, 1991.

18. S. Frølund. Inheritance of Synchronization Constraints in Concurrent Object-Oriented Programming. In ECOOP '92 proceedings, June 1992.

19. D. Gangopadhyay and S. Mitra. ObjChart: Tangible Specification of Reactive Object Behavior. In O. Nierstrasz, editor, *Proceedings ECOOP '93*, LNCS 707, pages 432–457, Kaiserslautern, Germany, July 1993. Springer-Verlag.

20. N. Halbwachs, P. Caspi, P. Raymond, and D. Pilaud. The Synchronous Data Flow Programming Language LUSTRE. In *Proceedings of the IEEE*, pages 1305–1319, September 1991. Published as Proceedings of the IEEE, volume 79, number 9.

21. D. Harel. Statecharts: A Visual Formalism for Complex System. *Science of Computer Programming*, 8(3):231–274, 1987.

22. D. Harel and A. Pnueli. *On the Development of Reactive Systems*, volume 13, pages 477–498. In *Logic and Models of Concurrent Systems*, K.R. Apt ed., Springer-Verlag, 1985.

23. F. Hayes, D. Coleman, and S. Bear. Introducing ObjectCharts or How to Use Statecharts in Object-Oriented Design. *IEEE Transactions on Software Engineering*, 18(1):9–18, January 1992.

24. Y. Ishikawa, H. Tokuda, and C.W. Mercer. Object-Oriented Real-Time Language Design: Constructs for Timing Constraints. In *Proceedings of ECOOP/OOPSLA '90*, October 1990.

25. I. Jacobs, F. Montagnac, J. Bertot, D. Clément, and V. Prunet. The Sophtalk Reference Manual. Technical Report 150, INRIA, February 1993.

26. K.-P. Lohr. Concurrency Annotations Improve Reusability. In *TOOLS USA '92*, August 1992.

27. S. Matsuoka, K. Wakita, and A. Yonezawa. Synchronization Constraints With Inheritance: What is Not Possible – So What is ? Technical Report Technical report 10, The University of Tokyo, Department of Information Sciences, 1990.

28. C. Neusius. Synchronizing Actions. In *ECOOP '91 proceedings*, June 1991.

29. E. Shibayama. Reuse of Concurrent Object Descriptions. In A. Yonezawa and T. Ito, editors, *Concurrency: Theory, Language, and Architecture.* Springler Verlag, 1991.

30. K. Takashio and M. Tokoro. DROL: An Object-Oriented Programming Language for Distributed Real-Time Systems. In *Proceedings of OOPSLA '92*, 1992.

31. G. Vidal-Naquet and F. Boulanger. An Object Oriented Execution Model for Synchronous Modules. December 1994. Synchronous Languages Seminar, Invited Conference,Dagstuhl. Available as `ftp://supelec.fr/ pub/cs/publications/ iscore.ps`.

32. T. Watanabe and A. Yonezawa. Reflection in an Object-Oriented Concurrent Language. In *Proceedings of OOPSLA '88*, pages 306–315, September 1988.

33. A. Yonezawa, E. Shibayama, T. Takada, and Y. Honda. Modelling and Programming in an Object-Oriented Concurrent Language ABCL/1. In *Object-Oriented Concurrent Computing*. MIT Press, 1987.

Proofs, Concurrent Objects and Computations in a FILL Framework

D. Galmiche & E. Boudinet

CRIN-CNRS & INRIA Lorraine
Campus Scientifique - B.P. 239
54506 Vandœuvre-lès-Nancy Cedex
France
e-mail: galmiche{boudinet}@loria.fr

Abstract. There are several major approaches to model concurrent computations using logic. In this context, one aim can be to achieve different forms of programming as logic, object-oriented or concurrent ones in a same logical language. Linear logic seems to be well-suited to describe computations that are concurrent and based on state transitions. In this paper, we propose and analyze a framework based on Full Intuitionistic Linear Logic (FILL), logical fragment with potentialities for non-determinisms management, as foundation of concurrent object-oriented programming, following the two paradigms *proof-search as computation* and *proofs as computations*.

1 Introduction

There exists several approaches to model concurrent computations using logic or object-oriented programming. Logic programming allows to write executable specifications while object-oriented programming allows to build up complex structures and a possible challenge consists in finding an approach mixing in a same logical framework such various forms of high-level reasoning. Moreover a representation of based-on object mechanisms within a suitable logical language can provide them with a clearer semantics [7]. Trying to use, in this context, an adequate logic to represent or specify concurrency and also some interesting non-determinisms can complete the challenge. Linear logic (LL) [12] seems to be well-suited to describe concurrent or sequential computations based on state transitions [29], combining a constructive character with a finer control on resource management.

Let us recall the different ways to model concurrent computations using fragments of linear logic. A first one is based on *formulas-as-types* and *proofs-as-programs* paradigms in which propositions are interpreted as types, proofs as programs and proof normalization processes as computations. Here, main works have been devoted to term assignment for intuitionistic linear logic (ILL) [6, 23] or classical LL [1] including proposals of concurrent functional programming languages. A second way is based on the *formulas-as-states* and *proofs-as-computations* paradigms [27] where the connections with Petri nets and linear logic have been investigated. The correspondence between ILL and Petri nets [22, 27] illustrates the interest of proof search methods for proving specifications (and synthesizing programs) of distributed systems. A third complementary way is based on the *proof-search as computation* paradigm and leads to works on logic programming [3], concurrent logic programming [5, 18, 20] in fragments of LL. As in the previous approach, proof construction is essential and we need to have efficient proof search methods for the logic we consider, for example based on specific proof schemas as uniform proofs in [14, 33] or canonical proofs [8, 11]. Other proposals are based on rewriting logic as a unified model of concurrency and as a theory of concurrent objects [25].

In fact we have two main goals in this paper. The first one is to motivate the interest of the use of fragments of LL for concurrent object programming, for example with a process calculus where the basic mechanisms are at the logical level. This last point leads to the question of using logic for representing the main programming mechanisms, its interest (as a clear semantics) or difficulty (how to insert a new operator dedicated to a mechanism into the logic and the impact on proof search). The second and main one is to show that the Full Intuitionistic Linear Logic ($FILL$) [16] seems adequate as logical foundation for a framework to involve object-oriented, concurrent and logic programming (following the previously mentioned paradigms) and that to illustrate its ability to represent non-determinisms at different levels (messages, process, proof search) in the context of concurrent systems specification.

In section 2, we recall the concepts about concurrent computations in linear logic fragments, focusing on the basic ideas inside our computation model based on multiple processes. In section 3, the $FILL$ fragment is presented [16]. Unlike intuitionistic linear logic (ILL), it includes the multiplication disjunction *par*, denoted here □ and it is formalized in a sequent calculus with multiple conclusions and a familiar notation for some kind of parallel process. In section 4, we analyze the dynamics of $FILL$ through proof search and also its potentialities for non-determinisms managements and thus concurrent programming. After this analysis of the *proofs-as-computations* approach, we consider it, in section 5, in a rather different way, i.e., *proof-search as computation*. Thus we propose a new framework, based on $FILL$, that can be viewed as an extension of CPL [31] having some common features with ACL [18]. The concurrent computations are described in terms of proof construction from a process calculus, with the logical representation of concepts as communication, parallel composition. The logical system, corresponding to this calculus, can be obtained after applying our proof normalization process [11]. In section 6, we illustrate one main point, compared to other proposals, that is the introduction at the logical level of non-determinisms with the □ operator. Within this system, we are able to modelize some important concepts of concurrent object programming. The framework allows the representation of rich mechanisms for concurrent object programming that are described in a pure logical form and exhibit attractive features as a concurrent programming languages providing mechanisms for object-oriented concurrent computing (inheritance, information sharing, identifier creation). In section 7, we show that our framework allows also to model systems that can dynamically modify their state, in the perspective of *proofs-as-computations* and we also illustrate the ability to represent objects and methods in a similar way as in other frameworks [7]. To complete our work and to emphasize its interest for concurrent object programming, we consider this paradigm with extended non-deterministic Petri nets and prove that the reachability problem between two states in such a net corresponds to the provability in a fragment of $FILL$.

2   Linear logic and concurrent computations

Linear Logic (LL) is recognized as relevant for computation issues, especially concurrency and state change [2]. We briefly outline the main characteristics of LL, the formal system of which being in appendix A. From the sequent calculus point of view, LL can be seen as a substructural logic where the *contraction* and *weakening* rules are discarded in order that each assumption must be spent exactly once and thus considered as computational *resource*. With the lack of these rules we have two conjunctions $\otimes$ (*times*) and & (*with*) and two disjunctions $\wp$ (*par*) and $\oplus$ (*plus*).

2.1   Modeling concurrent computations in LL

Let us analyze the operators from the viewpoint of concurrent computation. The $\otimes$ rule means that a process connected with $\otimes$ can be decomposed into two parallel processes the environments of which are different from one another. Moreover, the & rule means that a process connected with & can be executed alternatively. LL is also characterized by a new implication $\multimap$, called *linear implication* such that $A\multimap B$ means that if we have A we can obtain B by consuming A. The modalities ! and ? allow to reintroduce the notions of weakening and contraction, but in a finer way. The cut-elimination in the *cut* rule can be seen as a communication between a process with A and a process with $A^\perp$. Thus, we can have in mind that linear logic (and its fragments) can naturally deal with properties in concurrent and distributed systems that other logical frameworks cannot represent as computational resources, communication, state transitions and concurrent execution.

There are several major approaches to model concurrent computation using fragments of linear logic. One is the approach based on *formulas-as-types* and *proofs-as-programs* paradigms in which propositions are interpreted as types, proofs as programs and proof normalization process as computation [1, 6, 23] with proposals of concurrent functional programming languages. Another approach is the one based on *formulas-as-states* and *proofs-as-computations* [22, 27] where the connections with Petri nets and Linear Logic have been investigated. It is also investigated in a rather different way in the context of logic programming [3]. Let us mention also works on linear logic programming [14], concurrent linear logic programming [18, 20] and object representation in Forum [7] that are based on *proof-search as computation* programming paradigm. Our proposal focuses an the two latter approaches for modeling concurrent computation.

2.2   Main concepts for concurrent programming

Concurrent programming languages based on asynchronous communication would become more important for massively parallel processing environments and programmers need formal frameworks for concurrent computation that can help them to transform, verify and prove concurrent programs. In such a framework, computation is described in terms of proof construction in LL, knowing that inference rules and formulas in LL are restricted so that restricted rules have a proof power equivalent to the original rules for the restricted formulas. Moreover, the mechanisms for concurrent computations are mainly described in a purely logical form.

Let us recall some simple points about linear logic and concurrent programming. More details can be obtained in [20]. We consider a computational model where multiple processes perform computation and communicate with one another via asynchronous message passing. A message disappears after having been read by a process and becomes then consumable resource. That is why it is natural to represent a message by a formula (atomic) of linear logic. Let us consider now the processes. If A is a process waiting for a message M and behaves like B after reception, A consumes M and produces B and hence A is interpreted by a linear logic implication $M \multimap B$. Then a process is represented by a formula of linear logic. Consumption of a message M by a process $M \multimap B$ is represented by the following deduction $M, M \multimap P, C \vdash P, C$ where C can be considered as other processes, messages or as an environment.

Remark. We cannot interpret it with connectives of classical logic. For example, in classical logic, we can deduce $M, M \Rightarrow B \vdash B$ but also $M, M \Rightarrow B \vdash M, M \Rightarrow B, B$ which implies that the original message M and the process $M \Rightarrow B$ may remain after the message reception. Another point here is that M is undependent of any sender and thus the communication is asynchronous. In fact, if a message has been synchronous it is consumed when it is produced.

Let us try to interpret another connectives of LL. $P \otimes Q$ means that we have both a process P and a process Q at the same time, i.e., two concurrent processes and thus $\otimes$ represents a concurrent computation. If we consider $M_1 \multimap A_1 \& M_2 \multimap A_2$, we have one of the $M_i \multimap A_i$ but not both at the same time. But even, if we have both M_1 and M_2, we can only obtain either A_1 or A_2. If we consider a predicate logic, knowing that an atomic formula $M(a)$ can be interpreted as a message carrying a value a and a predicate M as a communication channel, what does $\forall x.(M(x) \multimap A(x))$ mean ? In fact, it represents a process which receives a value of x via a message M and becomes $A(x)$. Moreover, $\exists x.A$ represents the possibility of hiding x that can be used as a private name. Moreover, there are some variants to express communication. For example, $\forall x.(M(a, x) \multimap A(x))$ receives only a message M the first argument of which matching with a and thus we can realize generative communication as in Linda.

Now, let us consider the link between proofs and process reductions. It is not always possible to interpret a provable sequent as the result of a process reduction. For example, $M_1 \multimap (M_2 \multimap P) \vdash M_2 \multimap (M_1 \multimap P)$ is provable but cannot be viewed as a reduction process. In some cases, it appears possible to characterize the sequents corresponding to a process reduction as the provable ones only with left rules (in the conjunctive case). To obtain the correspondence one can propose some choices concerning limitations of the rules application [21, 28].

3 FILL: Full Intuitionistic Linear Logic

Full Intuitionistic Linear Logic ($FILL$), unlike intuitionistic linear logic (ILL), includes the multiplication disjunction *par*. Some problems arise from the interaction between *par* and *linear implication* but a term assignment system gives an interpretation of proofs as some kind of non-deterministic function. The system does enjoy cut elimination property and is a direct result of an analysis of the categorical semantics [16].

3.1 The proof system

As soon as we try to incorporate the multiplicative disjunction *par* into the logic, we are forced to consider traditional sequents with many hypotheses and many conclusions. In *FILL par* is denoted $\Box$ because it is different of p in *LL*. It is formalized in a sequent calculus with multiple conclusions; the comma on the right-hand side of the turnstile as a vertical bar, that is a familiar notation for some kind of parallel process.

It is not easy to give a satisfactory account of the computational meaning of the proofs or term calculus for *FILL* and to give an interpretation in terms of processes. The innovation of the system is more to introduce, considering sequents with many hypotheses and many conclusions, a term assignment system and a term calculus with good properties in such circumstances [16].

The rules of the proof system are the following:

$$\frac{}{A \vdash A} \ (Id) \qquad \frac{\Gamma \vdash A \mid \Delta \quad A, \Gamma' \vdash B}{\Gamma, \Gamma' \vdash \Delta \mid B} \ (Cut)$$

$$\frac{\Gamma, A, B, \Gamma' \vdash \Delta}{\Gamma, B, A, \Gamma' \vdash \Delta} \ (Ex_L) \qquad \frac{\Gamma \vdash \Delta \mid A \mid B \mid \Delta'}{\Gamma \vdash \Delta \mid B \mid A \mid \Delta'} \ (Ex_R)$$

$$\frac{\Gamma \vdash \Delta}{\Gamma, I \vdash \Delta} \ (I_L) \qquad \frac{}{\vdash I} \ (I_R) \qquad \frac{}{\bot \vdash} \ (\bot_L) \qquad \frac{\Gamma \vdash \Delta}{\Gamma \vdash \bot \mid \Delta} \ (\bot_R)$$

$$\frac{\Gamma, A, B \vdash C}{\Gamma, A \otimes B \vdash C} \ (\otimes_L) \qquad \frac{\Gamma \vdash A \mid \Delta \quad \Gamma' \vdash B \mid \Delta'}{\Gamma, \Gamma' \vdash A \otimes B \mid \Delta \mid \Delta'} \ (\otimes_R)$$

$$\frac{\Gamma, A \vdash C \quad \Gamma', B \vdash D}{\Gamma, \Gamma', A \Box B \vdash C \mid D} \ (\Box_L) \qquad \frac{\Gamma \vdash \Delta \mid A \mid B \mid \Delta'}{\Gamma \vdash \Delta \mid A \Box B \mid \Delta'} \ (\Box_R)$$

$$\frac{\Gamma \vdash A \mid \Delta \quad \Delta', B \vdash C}{\Gamma, A \multimap B, \Delta' \vdash C \mid \Delta} \ (\multimap_L) \qquad \frac{\Gamma, A \vdash B \mid \Delta}{\Gamma \vdash A \multimap B \mid \Delta} \ (\multimap_R)$$

$$\frac{\Gamma, A \vdash \Delta \quad \Gamma, B \vdash \Delta}{\Gamma, A \oplus B \vdash \Delta} \ (\oplus_L) \qquad \frac{\Gamma \vdash A \mid \Delta}{\Gamma \vdash A \oplus B \mid \Delta} \ (\oplus_{R1}) \qquad \frac{\Gamma \vdash B \mid \Delta}{\Gamma \vdash A \oplus B \mid \Delta} \ (\oplus_{R2})$$

$$\frac{\Gamma, A \vdash \Delta}{\Gamma, A \& B \vdash \Delta} \ (\&_{L1}) \qquad \frac{\Gamma, B \vdash \Delta}{\Gamma, A \& B \vdash \Delta} \ (\&_{L2}) \qquad \frac{\Gamma \vdash A \mid \Delta \quad \Gamma \vdash B \mid \Delta'}{\Gamma \vdash A \& B \mid \Delta \mid \Delta'} \ (\&_R)$$

$$\frac{\Gamma \vdash \Delta}{\Gamma, !B \vdash \Delta} \ (!w_L) \qquad \frac{\Gamma, A \vdash \Delta}{\Gamma, !A \vdash \Delta} \ (!D_L) \qquad \frac{\Gamma, !A \vdash \Delta}{\Gamma, !A, !A \vdash \Delta} \ (!c_L) \qquad \frac{!\Gamma \vdash C \mid \Delta}{!\Gamma \vdash !C \mid \Delta} \ (!S_R)$$

3.2 Proofs and programming in FILL

Therefore, intuitively, it seems natural to investigate this logic as a model for concurrent programming based on logic. Considering the term calculus (we have not presented here) for $FILL$, it remains to give a satisfactory account of its computational meaning and also to give an interpretation in terms of processes. Our goal, in this paper, is to consider it as logical foundation for a framework to involve object-oriented, concurrent and logic programming and to illustrate its ability to represent non-determinisms at different levels (messages, process, proof search) in the context of concurrent systems specification.

From the concurrent programming point of view, we consider two complementary directions for this study based on proof search results in $FILL$, namely following the two main paradigms *proof-search as computation* and *proofs-as-computations*. In both cases, proof search management in linear logic is central as in other approaches on concurrency [18, 27] or logic (concurrent) programming [3, 13, 18]. Here, we can use a specialization of our results on proof search in fragments of LL [10, 9, 11] dedicated to $FILL$.

4 On dynamics and proof search in FILL

It is well known that Linear Logic provides us with natural encodings of based-on state transitions systems, for instance extended Petri nets [17, 27]. One main point consists in proving an equivalence between the reachability problem for such nets and the derivability problem in the corresponding LL fragment.

The classical net definition does not describe some dynamic aspects of the behavior that will be understandable through the encoding and the proof search in $FILL$ [16]. For example, we can consider that there is only one token in a net but we do not know its place, namely A or B. Thus we will introduce a "don't know" non-determinism according to the place of the token that we naturally represent in our logic. The classical token representation and behavior will be still available. To start, we illustrate the dynamics in $FILL$ through the informal definition of extended Petri nets, called $NDTN$, focusing on the proof search process.

Definition 1. In a $NDTN$ each place p_i from S will be associated with a literal p_i with the following grammar $p_i ::= a \mid p_i \otimes p_i \mid p_i \Box p_i$, a being an atomic formula. The static structure of a $NDTN$, i.e. the *transitions*, is represented by a set of proper axioms of the form $t ::= !(p{\multimap}p)$ (or $p \vdash p$ if we use the formal system with the cut rule). The tokens (*resources*) of a $NDTN$ are represented by expressions of the grammar $Tk ::= tk \mid Tk \Box Tk \mid Tk \otimes Tk$, tk being an atomic formula.

The dynamic aspects of such a net directly appears through the proof-search process into the $FILL$ system. A first example consists in considering a transition $t: !(A\Box B{\multimap}C)$, one token $A\Box B$ and to produce C. The token means that we have a token in A or a token in B but we do not know it. In fact, with the following proof of the sequent $!(A\Box B{\multimap}C), A\Box B \vdash C$,

$$\dfrac{\dfrac{\dfrac{\dfrac{\overline{A \vdash A}\ ax \quad \overline{B \vdash B}\ ax}{A\square B \vdash A|B}\ \square_L}{A\square B \vdash A\square B}\ \square_R \quad \overline{C \vdash C}\ ax}{A\square B{\multimap}C, A\square B \vdash C}\ {\multimap}_L}{!(A\square B{\multimap}C), A\square B \vdash C}\ !D_L$$

we observe that the transition t fires to produce a token at place C if and only if there exists a token at place A or a token at place B but not both at the same time. It means that only one token exists for two places A,B. The proof represents the behavior of the system including this non-determinism.

Let us consider a more specific (and significant) example to illustrate the interest of this logic to specify or modelize the behavior of concurrent systems. We study the following instance of philosophers problem in the case of *two* philosophers and *one* fork. A philosopher can eat $(Ea_i, i = 1, 2)$ only if he gets a fork to his left hand $(Hl_i, i = 1, 2)$ otherwise he gives the fork to the other philosopher in one of its hands $(Hr_i, Hl_i, i = 1, 2)$ but we cannot know the which one. When a philosopher eats, he puts the fork down to the left or right hand-side randomly.

In this problem, we have a specific non-determinism because we do not know where the fork is and how one philosopher gives the fork to the other. We can use a $NDTN$ net to represent this problem, its translation into clauses in $FILL$ and the proof search to model such situations. The set T of transitions (as proper axioms of the linear theory L_T) is composed by: $Hl_1 \vdash Ea_1, Ea_1 \vdash Hr_1\square Hl_1, Hr_1 \vdash Hl_2\square Hr_2,$ $Hl_2 \vdash Ea_2, Ea_2 \vdash Hl_2\square Hr_2, Hr_2 \vdash Hr_1\square Hl_1.$

Remark. Here, we use transitions expressed in a system including the cut rule, but the general form $P \vdash Q$ can be replaced by the expression (or clause) $!(P{\multimap}Q)$ in a system without cut rule.

In fact, the proof encodes the behavior and the evolution of this system we can consider, for example, the $Hr_1\square Hl_2$ formula as initialization, that means that the fork is in the right hand of the philosopher 1 or in the left hand of the philosopher 2. We have here a non-determinism and thus the system can change in different ways that will correspond to different proofs of the sequent $Hr_1\square Hl_2 \vdash \Sigma$ with Σ non-instanciated. They could help us to understand what could happen for this system and its behavior ? In fact we will observe that α) a philosopher can eat for ever, β) the philosophers can take and put down the fork and never eat and also γ) they can eat one after the other.

Remark. The proof is never ending. Because here we have modelize the system without constraints and this (concrete) problem is without end in reality. The proof construction is an actual representation of what happen in the system.

Let us build a proof Π of $Hr_1\square Hl_2 \vdash \Sigma$, with Σ being instanciated at each step of the proof construction process. Thus if we consider the two subproofs Π_1 and Π_2 defined by

$\Pi_1 \equiv$

$$
\cfrac{
  \cfrac{
    Hl_2 \vdash \Gamma_1
  }{}\ ax \qquad
  \cfrac{
    \cfrac{Hr_2 \vdash Hr_1 \Box Hl_1}{}\ ax \qquad
    \cfrac{
      \cfrac{Hr_1 \vdash \Delta_1}{}\ ax \qquad
      \cfrac{
        \cfrac{Hl_1 \vdash Ea_1}{}\ ax \qquad \cfrac{Ea_1 \vdash \Delta_2}{}\ ax
      }{Hl_1 \vdash \Delta_2}\ cut
    }{Hr_1 \Box Hl_1 \vdash \Gamma_2}\ \Box_L
  }{Hr_2 \vdash \Gamma_2}\ cut
}{Hl_2 \Box Hr_2 \vdash \Sigma_1}\ \Box_L
$$

and $\Pi_2 \equiv$

$$
\cfrac{
  \cfrac{Hl_2 \vdash Ea_2}{}\ ax \qquad \cfrac{Ea_2 \vdash \Sigma_2}{}\ ax
}{Hl_2 \vdash \Sigma_2}\ cut
$$

we obtain $\Pi \equiv$

$$
\cfrac{
  \cfrac{
    \cfrac{Hr_1 \vdash Hl_2 \Box Hr_2}{}\ ax \qquad \Pi_1
  }{Hr_1 \vdash \Sigma_1}\ cut \qquad \Pi_2
}{Hr_1 \Box Hl_2 \vdash \Sigma_1 | \Sigma_2}\ \Box_L
$$

Here ax corresponds to a proper axiom in the theory issued of the translation into *FILL*.

In fact, we have $\Sigma \equiv \Sigma_1 | \Sigma_2$, $\Sigma_1 \equiv \Gamma_1 | \Gamma_2$ and $\Gamma_2 \equiv \Delta_1 | \Delta_2$.

In this proof, we have made some choices. For example, we have instanciated Γ_1 with Hl_2. It is a possible choice but we could choose Ea_2 that corresponds to the fourth transition (or proper axioms). In the same way, we have fixed some choices that instantiate Δ_1 with Hr_1, Δ_2 with Ea_1 and Σ_2 with Ea_2. Therefore, from these choices, we have instanciated Σ as $\Sigma \equiv Hl_2 | Hr_1 | Ea_1 | Ea_2$.

Another proof is possible with a cut on Ea_2. In fact, we can claim that a proof encodes a process in several states (depending on the branches of the proof). Let us remark that the instantiation is a ramdom choice and thus we could go on infinitely in a branch of a proof. But with adapted instantiation we can stop the evolution of the system encoded into *FILL*. If we look on the branches of the proof, the system has terminated in one of the four following configurations: *a*) the fork is in the left hand of philosopher 2, *b*) the fork is in the right hand of philosopher 1, *c*) the philosopher 1 eats and *d*) the philosopher 2 eats. Moreover, we are able to recover the way leading to one of these states by following the adequate branch in the proof. In fact, we could build the proof of the sequent $Hr_1 \Box Hl_2 \vdash Ea_2 | \Sigma_2$ if we have in mind to force the construction of a proof branch encoding the process that leads the philosopher 2 to eat.

5 A Concurrent Logic Programming language based on FILL

We consider here the connection between Linear Logic and concurrent programming based on the *proof search as computation* paradigm. In such approach, computation is regarded as a controlled deduction in the underlying logic and several linear logic languages were proposed as refinements of logic programming [13, 14] or as new concurrent programming languages [18]. The concurrent linear logic programming we propose naturally models message-passing style asynchronous communication, with messages and processes represented in terms of linear logic formulas.

5.1 Important choices for the design

If we want to propose a concurrent logic programming language, we can use directly our results on proof search to design an interpretor of such a language as an automated theorem prover as in [4, 14, 33]. Another point consists in modelizing concurrency in a logical framework with a process calculus where formulas are considered as processes and proof search (or construction) as the process reduction [19, 28].

In fact, an important point is the choice of the *logical fragment* where we need, at the same time, efficient proof search strategies and its ability to modelize interesting systems. For example, some logical connectors cannot be used sometimes because they have no interpretation in a given process calculus. Let us recall that, for a given logical fragment of LL, we have a general method to normalize proofs [11] and to design proof search strategies [10]. For our purpose, we need to find a compromise between the modelization ability and the efficiency of the execution into the framework. The former depends on the syntax of the formulas chosen to express clauses and goals and the latter on the degree of normalization we want, knowing that we want to keep non-determinisms for execution.

Some works have proposed adequate frameworks depending on the linear logical fragments (into CLL or ILL) and on specific proof forms (uniform proofs or canonical proofs [13, 14]). One main point in our proposal consists in understanding how to interpret proof construction as a process reduction and thus to propose adequate calculi for this purpose. Such proposal is based on two complementary aspects: to propose the syntactic form (of formulas or sequents) for the interpretation of the state changes of the process, to normalize proofs in this fragment to propose a new formulation of the deductive system. In this paper, one of the goals consists in choosing $FILL$ as underlying logic to propose an approach for concurrent object programming in a logical point of view.

The interesting idea consists in considering the *formulas as processes* and the logical operations on these as algebraic operations on processes [19, 28, 35, 36]. D. Miller [28] has proposed two possibilities to compare the interpretation of linear sequents with process reduction. "P reduces to Q" can be translated as "the sequent $P \vdash Q$ is provable" (conjunctive interpretation) or as "the sequent $Q \vdash P$ is provable" (disjunctive interpretation). Thus, the representation of the operations on processes depends on the previous choice. For example, in various works, the parallel composition is represented by $\otimes$ with the first interpretation and by $\wp$ with the second one. From this choice of interpretation, it is important to focus on the representation of communication. We can decide to represent communication into or out the logic. In the latter case, we represent senders and receivers by using higher-order constants *send* or *get* that are extra-logical [28]. Moreover, in this case, the communication is asynchronous represented by a proper axiom. In our approach, as others authors, we prefer to work as much as possible in a *pure logical framework* where messages are specific formulas and linear implication ($\multimap$) represents the communication, having in mind the connections between linear logic and concurrent programming [20].

5.2 The process language

In this section, we define and analyze a new framework for concurrent computation based on linear logic, having an operational semantics described in terms of proof construction. It well captures concurrent computation based on asynchronous communication. Moreover, as other proposals like ACL or $HACL$ [20], it could provide with a new insight into other models of asynchronous concurrent computation form a logical point of view.

We define the grammar of the process and the messages (into $FILL$) of the language that is an extension of the system CPL [32] that was included in intuitionistic linear logic. Here, due to the $\Box$ connective, we are able to extend the grammar of messages and processes for representing some non-determinisms at the logical level.

The grammar to define the processes (P_r) (messages (M) and strict processes (P)) is the following

$$M ::= At|M\Box M|M \otimes M$$
$$P_r ::= M|P$$
$$P ::= I|0|M \otimes P|M\multimap P|P \otimes P|P\Box P|P\&P|\forall x P|\exists x P|!P$$

and we manipulate sequents with the form : $\Gamma \vdash P|\Sigma$ with Γ and Σ multisets of processes and P a process. Messages are considered as particular process to obtain a framework where communication is asynchronous. They are represented not only by atomic formulas as in [31] but also by formulas composed with $\Box$ and $\otimes$. The other processes, that are not messages are represented by compound formulas and the sequents are $FILL$ sequents.

5.3 Basic concepts

Let us first consider the problem of *communication*. A sender has the form $M \otimes P$, where M is the message to send and P the process activated after sending it. We will use another classical notation, from process algebras, i.e., $\underline{M}.P$. A receiver has the form $M\multimap P$ (notation: $M.P$) where M is the waited message and P the process after receipt. Furthermore, the sequent $M, M\multimap P \vdash P$ is provable in our framework and interpreted as the receipt of M by the process $M\multimap P$ that becomes P after receipt.

The operations on processes are represented by the logic connectives. $P\otimes P$ and $P\&P$ respectively represent the *parallel composition* and the *alternative choice*. Moreover, $\forall x.P$ allows the *generalization* over variables that allows communication with value passing and $\exists x.P$ allows restriction over variables, used for communication channel hiding. $!P$ represents the recursion operator which allows to manage recursive definitions of processes and the mobility in the processes structure. Finally, the constant I (unit element of $\otimes$) represents the termination process and 0 represent the abort process.

Remark. Concerning communication and operations on processes, the possible choices are similar to the ones of ACL [18] that are represented with the disjunctive form.

A main difference lies (also with Hcc [24]) on the use of the ! connector, not only for using a message several times but for expressing recursive definitions without extra logical constants.

As in other frameworks, we can represent different forms of communication. Except point-to-point communication as in the actor model, we can express the generative communication where several receivers can compete to receive a message. For instance the sequent $M, M \multimap P_1, M \multimap P_2 \vdash P_1 \otimes P_2$ is not provable because a message can only be read by one process. Broadcast communication, where a message can be read by any number of receivers, is possible as illustrated by the following provable sequent $!M, M \multimap P_1, M \multimap P_2 \vdash P_1 \otimes P_2$. Moreover, message passing and variable sharing communication can be expressed. More details about such representation can be found in [31]. Another point that arises is that it is not always possible to transfer processes in the communication. To solve it HACL [20] extends ACL in the sense that processes are parametrized by other processes but it could improve the modularity and the code reuse of concurrent programs.

5.4 The logical system

The syntax of the language being fixed, it determinates the logical fragment of FILL we have to consider. Having in mind to interpret proofs in terms of process reduction, we will apply our general method of proof normalization based on the study of permutability properties and on inference movements in a proof [11].

Starting from the permutability results for full LL we can specialized them to the rules involved in the previous sequents, i.e., $id, 0_L, I_L, \multimap_L, \otimes_L, \Box_L, \&_L, !_L, w!_L, c!_L, \forall_L, \exists_L, I_R, \multimap_R, \otimes_R, \Box_R, \&_R, !_R, \forall_R, \exists_R$ and thus to determinate the inference movements in a proof.

The inferences that can be moved up in a proof are $T_\uparrow = \{!D_L, !w_L, \multimap_L, \otimes_R, \exists_R, \Box_L\}$ and the ones that can be moved down in a proof are $T_\downarrow = \{I_L, \otimes_L, \exists_L, !c_L, \multimap_R, \&_R, \forall_R, \Box_R\}$. With these results we are able to normalize the proofs, knowing that a computation will be a bottom-up proof-search in the system.

Let us start to consider some inferences movements to define a new formal system. The $\multimap_L$ inferences (producing receivers) can be moved up to the inference introducing the active formula and thus we propose new rules obtained by merging these inferences. We can do the same with the $\otimes_R$ and then move up the weakening and contraction rules. Thus we obtain a new formal system equivalent to the original one.

1) Communication rules

$$\frac{M, P, \Gamma \vdash Q|\Sigma}{M \otimes P, \Gamma \vdash Q|\Sigma} \; S_L \qquad \frac{\Gamma \vdash Q|\Sigma}{M, \Gamma \vdash M \otimes Q|\Sigma} \; S_R$$

$$\frac{P, \Gamma \vdash Q|\Sigma}{M, M \multimap P, \Gamma \vdash Q|\Sigma} \; R_L \qquad \frac{M, \Gamma \vdash Q|\Sigma}{\Gamma \vdash M \multimap Q|\Sigma} \; R_R$$

2) Composition rules

$$\frac{P_1, P_2, \Gamma \vdash Q|\Sigma}{P_1 \otimes P_2, \Gamma \vdash Q|\Sigma} \; Par_L \qquad \frac{\Gamma_1, !\Gamma \vdash Q_1|\Sigma_1 \quad \Gamma_2, !\Gamma \vdash Q_2|\Sigma_2}{\Gamma_1, \Gamma_2, !\Gamma \vdash Q_1 \otimes Q_2|\Sigma_1|\Sigma_2} \; Par_R$$

$$\frac{\Gamma_1, !\Gamma \vdash P|\Sigma_1 \quad P, \Gamma_2, !\Gamma \vdash Q|\Sigma_2}{\Gamma_1, \Gamma_2, !\Gamma \vdash Q|\Sigma_1|\Sigma_2} \; Comp$$

$$\frac{P_1, \Gamma \vdash Q|\Sigma}{P_1 \& P_2, \Gamma \vdash Q|\Sigma} \; Alt_L \qquad \frac{P_2, \Gamma \vdash Q|\Sigma}{P_1 \& P_2, \Gamma \vdash Q|\Sigma} \; Alt_L \qquad \frac{\Gamma \vdash Q_1|\Sigma_1 \quad \Gamma, \vdash Q_2|\Sigma_2}{\Gamma \vdash Q_1 \& Q_2|\Sigma_1|\Sigma_2} \; Alt_R$$

3) Message selection rule

$$\frac{M_1, \Delta_1 \vdash \Gamma_1 \quad M_2, \Delta_2 \vdash \Gamma_2}{M_1 \square M_2, \Delta_1, \Delta_2 \vdash \Gamma_1|\Gamma_2} \; Msel$$

4) Process selection rule

$$\frac{P_1, \Delta_1 \vdash \Gamma_1 \quad P_2, \Delta_2 \vdash \Gamma_2}{P_1 \square P_2, \Delta_1, \Delta_2 \vdash \Gamma_1|\Gamma_2} \; Psel_L \qquad \frac{\Gamma \vdash Q_1|Q_2|\Sigma}{\Gamma \vdash Q_1 \square Q_2|\Sigma} \; Psel_R$$

5) Recurrence, restriction, generalization rules

$$\frac{!P, P, \Gamma \vdash Q|\Sigma}{!P, \Gamma \vdash Q|\Sigma} \; rec_L \qquad \frac{!\Gamma \vdash Q|\Sigma}{!\Gamma \vdash !Q|\Sigma} \; rec_R$$

$$\frac{P[y/x], \Gamma \vdash Q|\Sigma}{\exists P, \Gamma \vdash Q|\Sigma} \; res_L \qquad \frac{\Gamma \vdash Q[t/x]|\Sigma}{\Gamma \vdash \exists x Q|\Sigma} \; res_R$$

$$\frac{P[t/x], \Gamma \vdash Q|\Sigma}{\forall x P, \Gamma \vdash Q|\Sigma} \; gen_L \qquad \frac{\Gamma \vdash Q[y/x]|\Sigma}{\Gamma \vdash \forall x Q|\Sigma} \; gen_R$$

6) Termination rules

$$\frac{\Gamma \vdash Q|\Sigma}{I, \Gamma \vdash Q|\Sigma} \; term_L \qquad \frac{}{!\Gamma \vdash I|\Sigma} \; term_R \qquad \frac{}{0, \Gamma \vdash P|\Sigma} \; brk$$

Let us recall the notation for a receiver and a sender, that is $\underline{M}.P$ for the sender $M \otimes P$ and $M.P$ for the receiver $M \multimap P$. Let us mention the fact that this system is correct and complete w.r.t. linear logic.

Theorem 2. *A sequent $\Gamma \vdash P|\Sigma$ is provable in this new system if and only if it is provable in the FILL system.*

5.5 Non-determinisms

The $\square$ operator allows to introduce non determinisms during the specification of a process and thus to see the state of the same process in two different choices.

If we consider a sender of the form $\underline{M_1 \square M_2 \square M_3}.P$ then it corresponds to send the message M_1 or M_2 or M_3. If we consider the receiver $M_1 \square M_2.P$ then P becomes active if it receives the message M_1 or M_2. In the same way, if we consider $M_3.Q$ as receiver, Q is active if it receives the message M_3. These possibilities characterize the extension of the messages grammar compared to CPL [31, 32] where the only possibility consists in having only a *and* between messages. In fact, processes can be activated by several different messages. Moreover, the interest of $FILL$ sequents of the form $\Sigma \vdash P|\Delta$ lies in the use of non consumable messages, Then we can force some activations with a particular message and Δ is used to collect the messages that are not consumed; if we instantiate it with a given message at the beginning of the proof search then it means that we do not use effectively this message. In fact, an important point to mention is that a proof that contains n applications of the rule $\Box_L$ encodes $n + 1$ executions of process.

Remark. A possible modification of this logical framework could be to consider $\Box$ as the operator of parallel composition. In this case, due to the duality rule between $\otimes$ and $\Box$, we could propose a parallel composition rule

$$\frac{P_1, \Gamma_1 \vdash \Delta_1 \quad P_2, \Gamma_2 \vdash \Delta_2}{P_1 \Box P_2, \Gamma_1, \Gamma_2 \vdash \Delta_1 | \Delta_2} \ Par_L$$

with sequents of the form $\Sigma \vdash P_1 | P_2 | .... | P_n$, the succedent of which represents directly the parallel composition. Moreover, in this case, a rule Par_R would be not necessary.

6 On Objects and Concurrency

In this section, we illustrate the interest of this framework to modelize some important concurrent programming concepts and mainly focus on the ones involved in concurrent object-oriented style programming. In fact this framework has similar characteristics as the ACL [18] or CPL [31] languages but completed with non-determinisms management. Thus, we illustrate the interest of $FILL$ and the specific use of $\Box$ for this approach of concurrent object logic programming.

6.1 Concurrent Object-oriented style programming

We emphasize, in this part, the possibilities to represent in our logical framework objects and routines and also to modelize some features as for instance inheritance.

Objects and classes representation. Let us consider, at first, an example significant for object management [31].
An object of class *polygon* is represented by a message (atomic formula) denoted $(vertices \ : \ (id, [p_1, ..p_n]))$, the list of points p_i describing the position of polygon id. If we have other attributes, each one will be represented by an atomic formula connected by $\otimes$ to each other. The set of routines is represented by a process P_{rout} that is a parallel composition of recursive processes P_{r_i} that define the different procedures r_i. For instance, the process corresponding to the *translation* operation can be represented by the formula $P_{trans} \equiv \exists \ ad \ ! \ \forall v \ id \ (trans : (v, id)).\forall x(vertices : (id, x)).\underline{(ad \ in : (x, v))}.\forall y(ad \ out : (x, v) \ y).\underline{(vertices : (id, y))}.I \otimes P_{ad}$, with P_{ad} being a process that adds a vector v to each vertex of x.
If we want to define the class *rectangle* from the previous class then an object of this new class inherits of the attributes of *polygone* with new proper attributes as *width* and *length*. Therefore, this new object is represented by the formula $(vertices \ : \ (id, [p_1, ..p_4])) \otimes (width \ : \ (id, x)) \otimes (length \ : \ (id, y))$. It inherits from the routines and one also can add other ones to P_{rout}, using the parallel composition.

Non-determinisms. Let us precise illustrate now the interest to use $FILL$ (and in fact the $\Box$ connector) as the underlying logic to modelize some non-determinisms in concurrent systems. For that, we consider the previous example (see section 4) about the dining philosophers; it can be described by defining the behavior of each philosopher and then by connecting them, if necessary, with another process.

The process named *philo n(fork)* is represented by the formula

$P_{phi} \equiv \forall n \; f \; (fork \; in \; : (f,n)) \otimes (\; (hand \; in \; : (r,n)) \; \Box \; (hand \; in \; : (l,n))) \multimap \text{"eating"}.$

With such a process we are able to specify that a philosopher is ambidextrous and consequently that he can eat if he has a fork in the right or left hand.

As we previously mentioned, the proof construction in the $FILL$ system will represent the two possible cases into a proof.

Because of this property (to be ambidextrous), we will denote this philosopher by $P_{ambphil}$. Now, a left-handed philosopher $P_{lh-phil}$ can be considered as a particular ambidextrous philosopher that would not be able to use its right hand to eat. Then such philosopher inherits some attributes of $P_{ambphil}$ but a message of the form (r,n) on the channel $(hand \; in)$ will not activate the process named *eating*.

In this case, we have to add a new attribute, using the parallel composition $\otimes$ connective, and then we can create a new object defined by the formula $P_{lh-phil} \equiv (left\_hander : n) \otimes P_{ambphil}$ from the initial one.

Here we are in the case of a generative point-to-point communication but several processes are competing for a message.

Let us notice that we could propose an abstract syntax with guide lines of the translation in linear logic adopting a more standard and programming syntax as in [18, 20] but we prefer to emphasize the logical foundations of such languages.

6.2 Messages reception

We can provide, as in ACL, a process represented by $M_1 \otimes M_2 .... \otimes M_n \otimes P$, which waits for messages $M_1, M_2, .., M_n$ and becomes P. It can receive the messages M_i in an arbitrary order ($\otimes$ is associative and commutative). Such mechanism, with multiple messages reception, is useful for the synchronization between processes. If we come back to our example about philosophers then we can build the process $(fork \; in \; :) \otimes (hand \; in \; :) \otimes P_{ph}$ from the initial one P_{ph}.

But we can also consider partial reception of message. A receiver of a message can start some computation immediately after receiving a part of a message. Such a mechanism enables us to exploit concurrency between senders and receivers. Going back to our example, the philosopher $P_{lh-phil}$ can start to eat when he has a fork and the message $(left\_hander : n)$ can arrive after.

6.3 Dynamic restructuring of processes

Computing environments may change while programs are running. Concurrent process should dynamically adjust themselves to such changes because optimal configuration of process in a certain environment may not be optimal in another environment. The possibility to express dynamic restructuring of processes is a main motivation of proposals such as Π-calculus [30]. As in ACL or CPL, it is possible to define a process that dynamically composes or decomposes other processes to adjust their granularity. It is a main interest of this proposal with programming concepts represented at the logical level.

6.4 Synchronization and sequencing between processes

In *HACL* [20], the authors have illustrated the use of higher-order processes, in particular in a similar example about philosophers. The problem is described by defining the behavior of each philosopher and then connecting them by a process. Moreover, a specific process, named *seq*, is needed for sequencing the execution in this system.

In our example, if we consider that, when a philosopher has finished to eat, he gives the fork to the other philosopher (that is also ambidextrous) then we have to introduce sequencing in its behavior description. In our viewpoint to represent operations on processes into the underlying logic, we could consider the sequentiality through a logical connective and consequently to adapt or extend our proposal and the results we have obtained. One possible way could be to study non-commutative linear logic or linear logic extended with a sequentiality connective as in [34]. We could easily consider this connective that allows to insert sequentiality at the logical level but it would lead to other new problems about the proof search techniques to develop. Further work will consider this possible extension.

Let us assume the existence of such a sequentiality connective denoted $\triangleright$, we can define, in our example, a philosopher with the following process *philo n(fork)* that is represented by

$P_{newphil} \equiv \forall n \ f \ (fork\ in\ : (f,n)) \otimes ((hand\ in : (r,n)) \Box\ (hand\ in : (l,n))) \multimap "eating"$
$\triangleright "finish"$
$\triangleright (fork\ out\ : (f,ano(n))) \otimes (hand\ out : (r,ano(n)) \Box\ (hand\ out : (l,ano(n)))$
with $ano(n)$, represents the philosopher that is not the philosopher n.

It means that a philosopher is ambidextrous, he eats if he has a fork in the right or left hand and then, when he has finished to eat, he gives the fork to the other philosopher that is also ambidextrous.

In future work, we will consider a process calculus extending the one we present here, including sequentiality and will compare with the works on higher-order processes [20]. A main interest will be to use the representation of the process operations in a pure logical framework that is the main idea inside this approach of concurrent object logic programming.

Remark. Another point to consider in the future will be the equivalence of processes in such framework based on asynchronous message passing. We could start with a proposal based on the notion of *interface* [32] or another one based on *bisimulation* (from π-calculus) as in [15].

In this section, we have defined the representation of objects, classes and naturally concurrent objects in our framework. Now, we can come back to the *proof-as-computation* paradigm by looking if we can represent also other forms of objects and classes definitions as in [7].

7 Proofs-as-computations perspective

To complete our approach of object-concurrent programming with FILL proof, let us come back to the *proof-as-computation* paradigm. A first point consists to analyze the problem of state modification looking if we are able to consider in our system the representation of a state into a FILL sequent as in [7, 29].

7.1 More on the dynamics

One of our goal is to model, using the above language, systems that can dynamically modify their state. In some other logical models of object-oriented features [4, 26] we have methods presented by logic clauses that are used to rewrite one state into a new one. In this way, based-on Forum frameworks [29] combine both higher-order logic and linear logic and emphasize the representation of objects [7] and the proofs-as-computations perspective. It is an attempt to fit a general notion of state into a *LL* sequent.

In fact we can also represent, in our framework, the basic concepts used in these proposals. In this way we can refine the structure of the initial sequent form $\Gamma \vdash P|\Sigma$ into $!\mathcal{P}, \mathcal{S}, \mathcal{M} \vdash \mathcal{P}'|\Sigma$ where $\mathcal{S}$ can be considered as the current state of the system, $!\mathcal{P}$ is a set of definitions, $\mathcal{M}$ is the multi-set of messages (pending activities of the system), we can pick up atoms in $\mathcal{S}$ and in $\mathcal{M}$ and thus to obtain, with communication rules, a new state and a new message.

In this context, objects, methods and classes can be represented as in [7], i.e., objects are atomic formulas, classes are universally quantified formulas and auxiliary operations are expressed by atomic formulas. For instance, if objects are atoms of the form $(id\ Attrs\ (\&M_i))$ then the methods M_i are defined as $\forall x.(id\ Attrs\ Ms) \otimes (id\ Head) \multimap (id'\ Attrs'\ Ms') \otimes Msg_1 \ldots \otimes Msg_n$ where Msg_i is a message.

As example of the representation of such approach in our framework, in a proofs-as-computations perspective, we consider how to simulate the behavior of imperative paradigms as in [7].

The program executing the assignment will be expressed by the formula
$P_{ass} \equiv \forall x\ y\ v\ w\ g.(assign\ x\ y\ g) \otimes (x\ v) \otimes (y\ w) \multimap g \otimes (x\ v) \otimes (y\ w)$.

The computation to swap the values of the variables x and y is given by the following proof, knowing that $\mathcal{S}$ is initially $(x\ 1) \otimes (y\ 2) \otimes (z\ 0)$ and a program of swapping x and y is $(assign\ z\ x\ (assign\ x\ y\ (assign\ y\ z\ I)))$,

$$
\frac{
\frac{
\frac{
\frac{
\frac{!P_{ass}, I, (x\ 2), (y\ 1), (z\ 1) \vdash \Sigma}{!P_{ass}, I \otimes (x\ 2) \otimes (y\ 1) \otimes (z\ 1) \vdash \Sigma}\ R_L
}{!P_{ass}, assign(y\ z\ I) \otimes (x\ 2) \otimes (y\ 2) \otimes (z\ 1) \vdash \Sigma}\ R_L
}{!P_{ass}, (assign\ x\ y\ (assign\ y\ z\ I)) \otimes (x\ 1) \otimes (y\ 2) \otimes (z\ 1) \vdash \Sigma}\ R_L
}{!P_{ass}, (assign\ z\ x\ (assign\ x\ y\ (assign\ y\ z\ I))) \otimes (x\ 1) \otimes (y\ 2) \otimes (z\ 0) \vdash \Sigma}\ R_L
$$

The form of P_{ass} forces the computation to be deterministic because we imposed sequentiality between assignments, using continuations as the last parameter g to *assign*. Without this goal passing, we can define a non-deterministic computation (different proofs with different final states). We have forced the sequentiality in a context of the interpretation of *proofs* as *computations* where one prove that there exists a sequence of transitions from an initial to a final state ($S_i \vdash S_f$).

7.2 FILL and extended nets

We have seen in a previous section the dynamics in the proof search in $FILL$ through the definition of extended Petri net, called $NDTN$. They are extension to this fragment of the Kanovich's proposal [17]. Thus, we can consider this logical fragment as a specification logic for concurrent processes from this point of view.

In this section, we briefly consider the equivalence between the reachability problem for a $NDTN$ net and the derivability problem in the $FILL$ logical fragment.

The reachability relation between two states S_1, S_n of a $NDTN$ net P is represented by the notion of provability of the sequent $[S_1] \vdash [S_n]$ in the linear theory $L_{[P]}$, [P being the proper axioms (or clauses) that encode the transitions of P.

[.] is the function that associates to a state S_i of the net P a formula of the linear logic $[S_i]$ that encodes this state. We denote f this function $f(S_i) = [S_i]$.

Theorem 3. *Let π be a proof of the sequent $F_1 \vdash F_n$ in the linear theory L_T, there exists a $NDTN$ net P having $S_1 = f^{-1}(F_1)$ as initial state and $S_n = f^{-1}(F_n)$ as final state that is reachable from S_1 with $[P] = T$*

Proof. Let π be a proof of a sequent $F_1 \vdash F_n$ in the linear theory L_T, we proceed by structural induction considering the last inference I_l.

$\square$

Theorem 4. (Completeness) *Let P be a $NDTN$ net, S_1 its initial state and S_n a state (not necessary final) such that S_n reachable from S_1, then the sequent $[S_1] \vdash [S_n]$ is provable in the linear theory $L_{[P]}$.*

Proof. By induction on the number of transitions.

$\square$

A further work consists in analyzing deeply the relationship between this approach of proof-as-computation perspective and our based on $FILL$ framework.

8 Concluding remarks

Intuitively, it can appear natural to investigate Full Intuitionistic Linear Logic ($FILL$) as a model for concurrent logic programming, principally because it involves the representation of some non-determinisms. To validate this intuition, we have investigated the design of a logical framework for logic, concurrent object programming based on $FILL$, in order to grasp some non-deterministic cases that can occur within concurrent processes. Moreover, we have proposed a process calculus based on $FILL$ and the *proof search as computation* programming paradigm. This new framework, where computation is described in terms of proof construction, extended other proposals as ACL [18] or CPL system [31, 32]. It allows some non-determinisms in the message management and also to represent interesting mechanisms for concurrent programming that are described can be described in a pure logical form. In fact it exhibits attractive features as a concurrent programming languages providing mechanisms for object-oriented concurrent computing.

References

1. S. Abramsky. Computational interpretations of linear logic. *Theoretical Computer Science*, 111(1-2):3–58, 1993.
2. V. Alexiev. Applications of Linear Logic to Computation: An Overview. *Bulletin of the IGPL*, 2(1):77–107, 1994.
3. J.M. Andreoli and R. Pareschi. Logic programming with sequent systems: A linear logic approach. In *Int. Workshop on Extensions of Logic Programming, LNCS 475*, pages 1–30, Tübingen, Germany, December 1989.
4. J.M. Andreoli and R. Pareschi. Linear objects: logical processes with built-in inheritance. In *7th Conference on Logic Programming, MIT Press*, pages 495–510, Jerusalem, June 1990.
5. J.M. Andreoli, R. Pareschi, and M. Bourgois. Dynamic programming as multiagent programming. In *ECOOP'91 - Workshop on Object-Based Concurrent Computing, LNCS 612*, pages 163–176, Genova, July 1991. Springer-Verlag.
6. N. Benton, G. Bierman, V. de Paiva, and M. Hyland. A term calculus for intuitionistic linear logic. In *Int. Conference on Typed Lambda Calculi and Applications, LNCS 664*, pages 75–90, Utrecht, The Netherlands, March 1993.
7. G. Delzanno and M. Martelli. Objects in forum. In *International Logic Programming Symposium, ILPS'95*, Portland, Oregon, December 1995.
8. D. Galmiche. Canonical proofs for linear logic programming frameworks. In *Workshop on Proof-theoretical extensions of logic programming*, Santa Margherita Ligure, Italy, June 1994.
9. D. Galmiche and E. Boudinet. Proof search for programming in intuitionistic linear logic. In *CADE-12 Workshop on Proof search in type-theoretic languages*, Nancy, France, June 1994.
10. D. Galmiche and G. Perrier. Foundations of proof search strategies design in linear logic. In *Logic at St Petersburg '94, Symposium on Logical Foundations of Computer Science, LNCS 813*, pages 101–113, St Petersburg, Russia, July 1994.
11. D. Galmiche and G. Perrier. On proof normalization in linear logic. *Theoretical Computer Science*, 135(1):67–110, 1994.
12. J.Y. Girard. Linear logic. *Theoretical Computer Science*, 50(1):1–102, 1987.
13. J. Harland and D. Pym. On resolution in fragments of classical linear logic. In *LPAR'92, International Conference on Logic Programming and Automated Reasoning, LNAI 624*, pages 30–41, St. Petersburg, Russia, July 1992.
14. J. Hodas and D. Miller. Logic programming in a fragment of intuitionistic linear logic. *Journal of Information and Computation*, 110:327–365, 1994.
15. K. Honda and M. Tokoro. On asynchronous communication semantics. In *ECOOP'91 - Workshop on Object-Based Concurrent Computing, LNCS 612*, pages 21–51, Genova, July 1991. Springer-Verlag.
16. M. Hyland and V. de Paiva. Full intuitionistic linear logic (extended abstract). *Annals of Pure and Applied Logic*, 64:273–291, 1993.
17. M. Kanovich. Petri nets, Horn programs, Linear logic and Vector games. In *Int. Symposium on Theoretical Aspects of Computer Software, TACS'94, LNCS 789*, pages 642–666, Sendai, Japan, April 1994.
18. N. Kobayashi and A. Yonezawa. ACL - a concurrent linear logic programming paradigm. In *Int. Symposium on Logic Programming*, pages 279–294, Vancouver, October 1993.
19. N. Kobayashi and A. Yonezawa. Asynchronous communication model based on linear logic. *Formal Aspects of Computing*, 3:279–294, 1994.

20. N. Kobayashi and A. Yonezawa. Higher-order concurrent linear logic programming. In *Int. Workshop on Theory and Practice of Parallel Programming, LNCS 907*, pages 137–166, Sendai, Japan, November 1994.
21. N. Kobayashi and A. Yonezawa. Type-theoretic foundations for concurrent object-oriented programming. In *ACM SIGPLAN Conference on Object-Oriented Programming Systems, Languages and Applications, OOPSLA'94*, pages 31–45, 1994.
22. J. Lilius. High-level nets and linear logic. In *13th Int. Conference on Applications and Theory of Petri Nets, LNCS 616*, pages 310–327, Sheffield, UK, 1992.
23. P. Lincoln and J. Mitchell. Operational aspects of linear lambda calculus. In *7th IEEE Symposium on Logic in Computer Science*, pages 235–246, Santa-Cruz, California, June 1992.
24. P. Lincoln and V. Saraswat. Higher order, linear concurrent constraint programming. Manuscript, July 1992.
25. J. Meseguer. A logical theory of concurrent objects. In *OOPSLA-ECOOP '90*, pages 101–115, Ottawa, October 1990. Sigplan Notices, (25), 10.
26. J. Meseguer. Rewriting as a unified model of concurrency. In *CONCUR'90, LNCS 458*, pages 384–400, Amsterdam, August 1990.
27. J. Meseguer and N. Marti-Oliet. From Petri nets to Linear Logic. *Math. Struct. in Comp. Science*, 1:69–101, 1991.
28. D. Miller. The π-calculus as a theory of linear logic: Preliminary results. In *Workshop on Extensions of Logic Programming, LNCS 660*, pages 242–265, 1992.
29. D. Miller. A multiple-conclusion meta-logic. In *9th IEEE Symposium on Logic in Computer Science*, pages 272–281, Paris, France, July 1994.
30. R. Milner. Functions as processes. *Math. Struct. in Comp. Science*, 2(2):119–146, 1992.
31. G. Perrier. Concurrent Programming in Linear Logic. Technical Report 95-R-052, CRIN-CNRS, Nancy, March 1995.
32. G. Perrier. A model of concurrency based on linear logic. In *Conference on Computer Science Logic, CSL'95*, Paderborn, Germany, 1995.
33. D. Pym and J. Harland. A uniform proof-theoretic investigation of linear logic programming. *Journal of Logic and Computation*, 4(2):175–207, 1994.
34. C. Retoré. Pomset logic: a non-commutative extension of classical linear logic. In *Conference on Computer Science Logic, CSL'95*, Paderborn, Germany, September 1995.
35. V.A. Saraswat. Concurrent constraint programming. In *7th ACM Symposium on Principles of Programming Languages*, pages 232–245, San Francisco, California, 1990.
36. P. Volpe. Concurrent logic programming as uniform linear proofs. In *Algebraic and Logic Programming, ALP'94, LNCS 850*, pages 133–149, Madrid, Spain, 1994.

A The Linear sequent calculus

The inference system we use is the classical linear sequent calculus where, a sequent is an expression $\Gamma \vdash \Delta$ where Γ and Δ are multisets of linear formulae, i.e, formulae built on the linear primitives $0, 1, \bot, \top, ()^\bot, \otimes, \wp, \&, \oplus, \forall, \exists, ?, !$. For a complete presentation of this system we refer to [12].

1) Identity Group

$$\frac{}{\vdash A, A^\bot} \; Id \qquad \frac{\Gamma \vdash A, \Delta \quad A, \Lambda \vdash \Theta}{\Gamma, \Lambda \vdash \Delta, \Theta} \; cut$$

2) Structural Group

$$\frac{\Gamma \vdash \Delta}{!A, \Gamma \vdash \Delta} \; !w_L \qquad \frac{\Gamma \vdash \Delta}{\Gamma \vdash \Delta, ?A} \; ?w_R \qquad \frac{!A, !A, \Gamma \vdash \Delta}{!A, \Gamma \vdash \Delta} \; !c_L \qquad \frac{\Gamma \vdash \Delta, ?A, ?A}{\Gamma \vdash \Delta, ?A} \; ?c_R$$

3) Logical Group

$$\frac{A, B, \Gamma \vdash \Delta}{A \otimes B, \Gamma \vdash \Delta} \; \otimes_L \qquad \frac{\Gamma \vdash \Delta, A \quad \Lambda \vdash \Theta, B}{\Gamma, \Lambda \vdash \Delta, \Theta, A \otimes B} \; \otimes_R \qquad \frac{A, \Gamma \vdash \Delta \quad B, \Lambda \vdash \Theta}{A \wp B, \Gamma, \Lambda \vdash \Delta, \Theta} \; \wp_L \qquad \frac{\Gamma \vdash \Delta, A, B}{\Gamma \vdash \Delta, A \wp B} \; \wp_R$$

$$\frac{}{\vdash 1} \; 1_R \qquad \frac{\Gamma \vdash \Delta}{1, \Gamma \vdash \Delta} \; 1_L \qquad \frac{}{\bot \vdash} \; \bot_L \qquad \frac{\Gamma \vdash \Delta}{\Gamma \vdash \Delta, \bot} \; \bot_R$$

$$\frac{\Gamma \vdash \Delta, A \quad B, \Lambda \vdash \Theta}{A \multimap B, \Gamma, \Lambda \vdash \Delta, \Theta} \; \multimap_L \qquad \frac{A, \Gamma \vdash \Delta, B}{\Gamma \vdash \Delta, A \multimap B} \; \multimap_R \qquad \frac{\Gamma \vdash \Delta, A}{A^\bot, \Gamma \vdash \Delta} \; \bot_L \qquad \frac{A, \Gamma \vdash \Delta}{\Gamma \vdash \Delta, A^\bot} \; \bot_R$$

$$\frac{A, \Gamma \vdash \Delta}{A \& B, \Gamma \vdash \Delta} \; \&_L \qquad \frac{B, \Gamma \vdash \Delta}{A \& B, \Gamma \vdash \Delta} \; \&_L \qquad \frac{\Gamma \vdash \Delta, A \quad \Gamma \vdash \Delta B}{\Gamma \vdash \Delta, A \& B} \; \&_R \qquad \frac{A, \Gamma \vdash \Delta \quad B, \Gamma \vdash \Delta}{A \oplus B, \Gamma \vdash \Delta} \; \oplus_L$$

$$\frac{\Gamma \vdash \Delta, A}{\Gamma \vdash \Delta, A \oplus B} \; \oplus_R \qquad \frac{\Gamma \vdash \Delta, B}{\Gamma \vdash \Delta, A \oplus B} \; \oplus_R \qquad \frac{}{\Gamma \vdash \Delta, \top} \; \top_R \qquad \frac{}{0, \Gamma \vdash \Delta} \; 0_L$$

$$\frac{A, \Gamma \vdash \Delta}{!A, \Gamma \vdash \Delta} \; !_L \qquad \frac{!\Gamma \vdash A, ?\Delta}{!\Gamma \vdash !A, ?\Delta} \; !_R \qquad \frac{!\Gamma, A \vdash ?\Delta}{!\Gamma, ?A \vdash ?\Delta} \; ?_L \qquad \frac{\Gamma \vdash \Delta, A}{\Gamma \vdash \Delta, ?A} \; ?_R$$

$$\frac{A[t/x], \Gamma \vdash \Delta}{\forall x A, \Gamma \vdash \Delta} \; \forall_L \qquad \frac{\Gamma \vdash \Delta, A}{\Gamma \vdash \Delta, \forall x A} \; \forall_R \qquad \frac{A, \Gamma \vdash \Delta}{\exists x A, \Gamma \vdash \Delta} \; \exists_L \qquad \frac{\Gamma \vdash \Delta, A[t/x]}{\Gamma \vdash \Delta, \exists x A} \; \exists_R$$

Modular Description and Verification
of Concurrent Objects

Jean Paul Bahsoun[1], Stephan Merz[2], Corinne Servières[1]

[1] Institut de recherche en informatique de Toulouse, Toulouse, France
[2] Institut für Informatik, Universität München, Munich, Germany

Abstract. The design of large and complex distributed systems requires a modular approach to support reuse and verification. We propose an object-oriented programming model based on concurrently executing communicating agents (concurrent objects) and an associated proof methodology that exploits the class hierarchy to allow for modular verification.

We propose to separate protocol from functionality in class definitions, and advocate separate hierarchies of protocol classes as a way to overcome the inheritance anomaly of concurrent object-oriented programming.

We formalize an agent in Lamport's Temporal Logic of Actions. Modular verification is achieved by restricting inheritance in a way that ensures that subclasses refine superclasses. Interesting properties can thus be verified at an abstract level, ignoring unnecessary implementation detail.

1 Introduction

The object-oriented paradigm in software construction promises modular, incremental design and has therefore become very attractive to practitioners. On the other hand, its semantical foundations are still not well-understood, and few formalisms [3, 10] have been defined that allow the verification of object-oriented programs. In particular, it is notoriously hard to exploit the modular structure of object (or class) definitions in reasoning about object-oriented systems.

The lack of theoretical underpinnings is even more acute for languages that combine concurrency and object-oriented concepts, although this combination appears intuitively compelling. One of the complications that arise with concurrency is that enabling conditions have to be associated with the methods offered by an object, but that, in a parallel setting, client objects have no way of ensuring that a particular method is currently enabled. We call the collection of synchronization code that ensures that methods are executed only if they are currently enabled the *protocol* of an object. There are well-known examples where seemingly minor changes to the method suite of an object require big, non-local revisions of its protocol. This problem has been called the *inheritance anomaly* of concurrent objects in [15]; it invalidates the idea of constructing objects incrementally by localized updates to existing code.

This paper has two objectives: On the one hand, we suggest to alleviate the inheritance anomaly by distinguishing protocol code from code that provides the functionality of an object. A method can be associated with any number of protocols, which are defined in separate protocol classes, with a class hierarchy of their own. On the other hand, we propose a step towards a compositional proof system for concurrent objects, using Lamport's Temporal Logic of Actions [13] (TLA), which has proven to be an expressive and flexible formalism to specify and verify reactive systems.

We try to avoid being overly formal, but mainly proceed by a few running examples, using an illustrative syntax to present the basic ideas. Also, we do not discuss all aspects of our programming model or proof system, but concentrate on problems connected with inheritance.

Section 2 introduces our programming model, presents agents and agent classes, inheritance, and protocol classes, and shows why this separation contributes to solving the inheritance anomaly. Section 3 then shows how we formalize concurrent objects in TLA in a modular way, and how this is useful in modular reasoning about objects and object-based systems. Finally, section 4 discusses related approaches, limitations of our present model, and future work.

2   A model of concurrent objects

In this section we introduce our object-oriented programming model, where several concurrent objects (which we also call agents) may work concurrently. The agents interact with each other by message passing; we consider several modes of communication such as asynchronous and synchronous messages. We use a class-based notation, where agents are defined as instances of classes. New classes may be constructed by inheritance from previously defined classes, to allow for organization and reuse. We also argue to separate functionality and protocol of agents, and introduce separate protocol classes.

2.1   Agents, actions, and messages

The basis of the system is an agent, which acts like a sequential process and may execute concurrently with other agents. With every agent we associate:

- a unique identity,
- a private state, represented by variables (also called attributes) that are visible only to the agent itself. A variable can store data or (the identity of) another agent; this allows to model delegation and embedded objects. In particular, every agent may refer to its own identity via the predefined (constant) attribute *myself*. We distinguish between control variables and structure variables, as we explain below.
- a set of actions that constitute the agent's interface, subdivided into two disjoint subsets of *methods* and *reflexes*. Methods are executed in response to requests from other agents, while reflexes are executed spontaneously by the agent. Reflexes occur mostly at the specification level, they can be used to model actions performed by the environment or system actions triggered by events that are not visible at the current level of abstraction.

In any given state, some actions defined for the agent may be disabled. For example, a buffer can only output an object if it is not empty. We therefore associate every action with its guard, which must hold true before the action is executed. A request to execute an action that is currently disabled is delayed until the guard becomes true.

Syntactically, we express the body of an action by multiple (and possibly conditional) assignments, much as in UNITY [8], and primitives to send messages.

We insist on separating an agent's attributes into two disjoint sets of *control* and *structure* variables. The guard of a method may only contain control variables. Similarly, we subdivide the assignment section of a method into updates to the control variables and updates to the structure variables. We call *synchronization constraint* or *protocol* the guard of a method plus the assignments that update its control variables. Although this separation may appear unnecessary and complex for very small toy classes, we will see that it helps to overcome problems linked to defining classes by inheritance. Moreover, the domains of control variables are usually finite-state, which helps with the automated analysis of protocols, although we do not consider this issue in this paper.

Agents interact with each other by means of messages. We represent a message in transit by a quintuple $(s, d, m, t, \mathbf{x})$ where s is the identity of the sender, d is the identity of the destination agent, m is the mode of communication (explained below), t is the type of the message which should be the name of a method defined for the receiver, and finally, $\mathbf{x}$ is the parameter list of the message. We consider three modes of communication between agents:

- synchronous communication: after sending a message, the sender waits for a reply or acknowledgement from the receiver before carrying on with its task,
- asynchronous communication: after sending a message, the sender doesn't wait for a receiver reply or acknowledgement,
- semi-synchronous communication: after sending a message, the sender may continue with its task unless it wants to transmit another message of the same type to the same receiver, in which case it will be blocked until receipt of an acknowledgement of the first message from the receiver. Semi-synchronous message passing ensures that the order of messages of a given type between two agents is preserved and may therefore be used to establish a FIFO channel.

For the interconnection network that links the agents of a system, we assume that every message sent will eventually arrive at its destination. Because of the distributed nature of our system model, messages may get out of order, and there may be arbitrary delays. Every agent maintains a queue of unprocessed messages. Whenever a synchronous or semi-synchronous message arrives at an agent, an acknowledgement is sent back to the sender of the message.

2.2 Agent classes

We use classes as templates to describe agents. This section explains base classes that give complete descriptions of agents. Section 2.4 explains how classes may

```
class simple_buffer
  structure                 -- structure variables
    value : integer
  control                   -- control variables
    empty : boolean := true
  method put(x:integer)
    when empty              -- guard of put
    =>   empty := false     -- update of control variables
    do   value := x         -- update of structure variables
  method get(obj:agent)
    when not empty
    =>   empty := true
    do   send_asy(obj, "reply", value)
end simple_buffer.
```

Fig. 1. A class of simple buffers

inherit from existing ones.

Figure 1 contains the definition of a class of simple buffers that may store one integer value and offers two methods: *put* stores a value in the buffer if the buffer is empty, *get* sends the contents of the buffer to another object, using a message of type *reply*, and empties the buffer.

In general, the description of a class of agents consists of:

- the class name,
- possibly initialization parameters supplied at the time of agent creation (we will see examples later),
- the attributes, divided into control and structure variables, and
- the list of action definitions. As explained above, we distinguish between methods and reflexes. Agents of class simple_buf offer the methods *put* and *get*, but do not have reflexes. An action definition consists of
  - the name of the action,
  - its guard, indicated by the keyword **when**,
  - updates to the agent's control variables, preceded by =>, and
  - the proper method body which contains updates to the agent's structure variables and message transmissions. This section is indicated by the keyword **do**.

Conceptually, an agent executes an infinite loop, in which it chooses and executes some enabled action: A reflex is enabled if its guard evaluates to true. A method is enabled if its guard evaluates to true and a request to execute the method has been received from the environment. The choice between several enabled actions is arbitrary, but the implementation must be fair. Thus, we consider individual agents to behave as sequential processes, which allows us to model executions of actions as being atomic from the point of view of the environment.

```
class distributed_buffer(max: integer)
  structure
    mbuf : array [0..max − 1] of simple_buffer
    bottom : 0..(max − 1) := 0                    − − index for enq
    top : 0..(max − 1) := 0                       − − index for deq
  method enq(x:integer)
    do   send_ssy(mbuf[bottom], "put", x),
         bottom := (bottom + 1) mod max
  method deq(obj:agent)
    do   send_ssy(mbuf[top], "get", obj),
         top := (top + 1) mod max
end distributed_buffer.
```

Fig. 2. A distributed buffer

2.3 Agent systems

A software system is composed of several agents that work in parallel and communicate by means of messages. In this paper, we ignore the issue of dynamic creation of agents, but focus on static agent networks. Let us give an example of a system of agents.

We will use the class simple_buffer to define an agent which implements a distributed circular buffer that offers the methods *enq* and *deq* to enqueue and dequeue a value. This distributed buffer, whose definition appears in figure 2, embeds an array of simple_buffer agents by storing their identities in its private state. The distributed_buffer agent organizes the simple_buffer agents (which still work in parallel) in a circular fashion. The encapsulation concept allows for a hierarchy of agents, and enables to close the encapsulated agent with respect to any communication with the environment of the encapsulating agent. So our definition of the *distributed_buffer* precludes any communication between the *simple_buffer* agents and any clients of the *distributed_buffer*.

When a distributed_buffer agent receives an *enq* message (resp. a *deq* message), it sends a *put* message (resp. a *get* message) to a simple_buffer agent, using a circular policy. The distributed_buffer is an unbounded buffer because we don't have guards to accept an *enq* or a *deq* request, and the queues storing waiting requests are unbounded. But, of course, requests for *put* or *get* methods can be delayed at the level of simple_buffer agents. The circular policy is ensured thanks to:

− the use of two indexes *bottom* for *enq* and *top* for *deq*, and
− the use of semi-synchronous communication.

To illustrate some other features of our concept, figure 3 contains the definition of a very simple client-server system. An agent of class server manages the access to some resource. When executing method *Enter1*, the server sends a message *Receive1* to the client that requested the resource, informing it that the resource is free, and ready to be used.

```
class server1                          class client1(s : server1)
   control                                control
      in1: boolean := false                  owner1, waiting1 : boolean := false
   method Enter1(c : client1)             reflex Request1
      when not in1                           when (not owner1) and (not waiting1)
      => in1 := true                         => waiting1 := true
      do send_asy(c, "Receive1")             do send_asy(s, "Enter1", myself)
   method Leave1                          method Receive1
      when in1                               => (owner1, waiting1) := (true, false)
      => in1 := false                     reflex Return1
end server1.                                 when owner1
                                             => owner1 := false
                                             do send_asy(s, "Leave1")
                                          reflex Use1
                                             when owner1
                                             do  - - use resource
                                       end client1.
```

Fig. 3. Class definitions for a simple client-server system

Class client1 is parameterized by the server1 agent the client will be using. The client contains three reflexes *Request1*, *Return1*, and *Use1* to request access to the resource, relinquish the resource, or use it. In an implementation, some of these reflexes could be methods called by the client itself or some other agent.

2.4 Inheritance

We can define a class from existing ones by inheritance. The new class (called the subclass) inherits existing attributes and actions, but it may define new attributes, offer new actions, and update or redefine inherited actions.

Suppose we want to extend the behaviour of the agents of the server class: now they will have to synchronize the access to two resources that can not be used simultaneously. Figure 4 shows the server2 class, which extends the server1 class. Similarly, we define another class client2 of clients by inheritance from client1, which may use either resource controlled by the server. A server of class server2 can be used by a client of either class client1 or client2.

The class server2 inherits the control variable *in1* and the methods *Enter1* and *Leave1*. In this subclass, we add a control variable *in2* and two methods *Enter2* and *Leave2* to control access to the second resource. We also have to update the synchronization constraint of method *Enter1* to forbid the access to the first resource when the second one has been allocated. In general, we write updates to actions in the form

when *condition* => *control_upd* **do** *structure_upd*

```
class server2 inherit server1              class client2(s : server2) inherit client1
  control                                    control
    in2: boolean := false                      owner2, waiting2 : boolean := false
  method Enter2(c : client2)                 reflex Request2
    when (not in1) and (not in2)               when (not owner2) and (not waiting2)
    => in2 := true                             => waiting2 := true
    do send_asy(c, "Receive2")                 do send_asy(s, "Enter2", myself)
  method Leave2                               method Receive2
    when in2                                   => (owner2, waiting2) := (true, false)
    => in2 := false                          reflex Return2
  update method Enter1                         when owner2
    when not in2                               => owner2 := false
end server2.                                   do send_asy(s, "Leave2")
                                             reflex Use2
                                               when owner2
                                               do  -- use resource 2
                                           end client2.
```

Fig. 4. Another client-server system

much as we write action definitions. The guard of the updated method is the conjunction of the inherited guard and the condition in the update clause. The effect of the updated action is to simultaneously perform the inherited assignments and message transmissions as well as those newly defined in *control_upd* and *structure_upd*. (As before, we do not allow multiple assignments to the same variable.)

Alternatively, we may also completely redefine actions in the subclass. In this case, we give the entire definition of the action, using the keyword **redefine** instead of **update**.

On the other hand, we will see that we can obtain pleasant proof rules by using updates and redefinitions in subclasses in a restricted way. Formally, we say that a subclass *preserves encapsulation* of its superclass if the following conditions are met:

- New methods do not modify inherited attributes.
- Updates to inherited actions may only strengthen the guards.

Note that both server2 and client2 preserve encapsulation of their respective superclasses.

2.5 Protocol classes

We observe that in the two classes simple_buffer and server, the synchronization constraints of the methods have the same shape. In fact, many software systems with different functionality share the same protocol. It would therefore be useful to have a mechanism to reuse synchronization constraints in several classes. Such a mechanism, based on the syntactic separation between the definitions of

```
  protocol class mutex               class server1 constrained by mutex
     control                            method Enter1 (c : client1)
        inUse: boolean := false            use protocol acquire
     protocol acquire                      do     send_asy(c, "Receive1")
        when not inUse                  method Leave1
        =>   inUse := true                 use protocol release
     protocol release                      do - - nothing
        when inUse                      end server1.
        =>   inUse := false
  end mutex.
```

Fig. 5. Definition of server1 using a protocol class

synchronization constraints and the methods that use them, has already been suggested in [5, 4]. A class can thus be built as a composition of a class of methods that implement the functionality and a protocol class that defines the desired synchronization constraints.

A protocol class may declare control variables like an ordinary class. Instead of actions, it declares named protocols that consist of a guard and updates to the control variables declared in the protocol class. A protocol class can be inherited by an ordinary class, using the keyword **constrained by** instead of **inherits**. In this case, the control part of the protocol class is added to the control part of the new class, and any protocol defined in the protocol class can be referenced by its name in the new class. More precisely, the inherited constraints can be combined with the constraints of the new class as explained in section 2.4 above.

Let us illustrate these ideas using our examples. First, we define a protocol class called mutex, that will be reused twice to define other classes. We can build up the class server1 using the mutex protocol class as illustrated in figure 5. The server class defined in this way is identical (up to the name of the local control variable) to the server class given in figure 3.

The keyword **use protocol** can appear in the declaration of an action before its guard (if there is any), and it is followed by a list of names of inherited protocols. These protocols are combined with the constraints explicitly defined in the action declaration and those inherited from superclasses, to yield the effective synchronization constraint.

As another example, figure 6 defines the class cell: The method *put* allows to store a new value to the cell, erasing any previous value stored in the cell; the current value can be read using method *get*, even if the cell hasn't been initialized.

As shown in figure 6, class simple_buffer can be defined by inheritance from cell and mutex; this definition is again equivalent to that shown in figure 1.

```
class cell                               class simple_buffer inherit cell
   structure                                constrained by mutex
      value : integer                          update method put
   method put(x:integer)                          use protocol acquire
      do  value := x                          update method get
   method get(obj:agent)                          use protocol release
      do  send_asy(obj, "reply", value)     end simple_buffer.
end simple_buffer.
```

Fig. 6. Another definition of simple_buffer

```
class distributed_buffer2(max: integer)
inherits distributed_buffer
   method deq2(obj:agent)
      do      send_ssy(mbuf[top], "get", obj),
              send_ssy(mbuf[(top + 1) mod max], "get", obj),
              top := (top + 2) mod max
end distributed_buffer2.
```

Fig. 7. Extending class distributed buffer with method deq2

2.6 The inheritance anomaly

The term "inheritance anomaly" has been coined in [15] to designate the problem of having to update or redefine all of the inherited method definitions when introducing some new method that interferes with the inherited protocol. In this section, we will illustrate at the hand of three classical examples from [15] that the separation of functionality and protocol alleviates the problem, because we can simply refine the protocol. All of the examples are based on the distributed_buffer class defined in figure 2.

First suppose that we want to define a new method deq2 which removes the two values at the top of the buffer. Observe that the effect of this method will in general be different from a client sending two consecutive deq messages to the distributed_buffer agent because of interference from messages from other agents. However, using semi-synchronous communication between the distributed_buffer and its embedded simple_buffer agents, as shown in figure 7, achieves the desired functionality.

Second, we add a method ddeq to class distributed_buffer to obtain another subclass distributed_buffer_ddeq. Method ddeq behaves like deq, except that it must not be performed immediately after executing an enq method. Such protocol patterns occur quite frequently: some actions of a class may be sensitive to the execution of a "disabling" action. The protocol class disable of figure 8 captures this pattern of behaviour: the control variable disabled is true iff the last action performed was a "disabling" action. For our particular, example, the definition of class distributed_buffer_ddeq is defined by inheritance from class distributed_buffer and disable, giving the definition of method ddeq, and updating the synchronization constraint of the remaining actions.

```
protocol class disable              class distributed_buffer_ddeq
  control                             inherit distributed_buffer
    disabled : boolean := false       constrained by disable
  protocol sensitive                    method ddeq(obj: agent)
    when not disabled                   use protocol sensitive
  protocol insensitive                    do  send_ssy(mbuf[top], "get", obj),
    when true                                top := (top + 1) mod max
    => disabled := false              update method deq
  protocol disable :                    use protocol insensitive
    when true                         update method enq
    => disabled := true                 use protocol disable
end disable.                        end distributed_buffer_ddeq.
```

Fig. 8. Adding method *ddeq* to class distributed_buffer

```
protocol class lock                 class lockable_distributed_buffer
  control                             inherit distributed_buffer
    locked : boolean := false         constrained by lock
  protocol lockable                     method open
    when not locked                     use protocol open
  protocol close                        method close
    when not locked                     use protocol close
    => locked := true                 update method deq
  protocol open :                       use protocol lockable
    when locked                       update method enq
    => locked := false                  use protocol lockable
end disable.                        end lockable_distributed_buffer.
```

Fig. 9. Adding *open* and *close* methods to the buffer

The third example from [15] is conceptually similar: We now want to define two new methods *open* and *close*. The idea is that after executing a *close* method, all methods except *open* are disabled, and can be performed only after an explicit request to reopen the buffer. Figure 9 shows the definition of an appropriate protocol class lock as well as the definition of a class lockable_distributed_buffer based on distributed_buffer and lock. In particular, lockable_distributed_buffer preserves encapsulation of both its superclasses.

3 Formalizing agent behaviour in TLA

We will now discuss verification of agents and agent systems in a modular way. As a basis, we give an axiomatic semantics of agents using Lamport's Temporal Logic of Actions (TLA) [13]. We chose TLA because a state-based formalism seems to correspond well to the concept of state inherent in the object-oriented approach to programming. Moreover, the basic concepts of TLA have been carefully chosen such that many proof obligations can be deferred to nontemporal reasoning, enabling the use of existing theorem provers [7, 12]. Since TLA formulas, in contrast to most temporal logics, are invariant under stuttering, we get simple formal notions of refinement and parallel composition [1].

In our formalization, we propose to distinguish between two levels of reasoning about systems built from concurrently executing agents, each focusing on one particular aspect or view of agent systems.

At the *agent level*, we reason about behaviors of individual agents. We take advantage of the encapsulation of an agent's private state, which may only change by executing methods or reflexes defined for the agent. We think of an agent as an open system, and will describe aspects of communication and interaction with other agents in the form of environment assumptions. We will show that properties of superclasses can be reused in reasoning about subclasses as long as the subclass preserves encapsulation of the superclass.

The *system level* models the top-level view of the entire system by an external observer. System properties should be deduced from properties of single agents and assumptions about the communication network, in a compositional way; this form of composition is orthogonal to modular reasoning about class hierarchies.

Since TLA does not have a built-in notion of "locality" and does not enforce the proof methodology outlined above, it may in fact turn out that it is not the most suitable logic for our programming model, and we are studying more adapted logics [18]. However, the basic ideas are independent of the particular logic.

3.1 Describing a base agent

We will first explain how we model an agent of a base class in TLA. With a declaration of class A we associate a formula (we write multi-line conjunctions and disjunctions as lists bulleted by $\wedge$ or $\vee$)

$$\Phi_A(a) \triangleq \wedge \ Init_A(a) \ \wedge \ \Box[\mathcal{N}_A(a)]_{attr_A(a)}$$
$$\wedge \bigwedge_{m \in Meth_A} \Box[(\exists x : receive(a, m, x)) \ \vee \ m(a)]_{a.q_m}$$
$$\wedge \ Fairness_A(a)$$

to formalize the behaviour of an agent a of class A. We model the agent a as a record that contains one field for every attribute of class A (we let $attr_A(a)$ denote the tuple of these fields). Besides, the record contains a field q_m for every message type $m \in Meth_A$ defined in class A, representing the queue of waiting requests to execute method m. The tuple of these fields is denoted by $Msg_A(a)$.

The predicate $Init_A(a)$ defines the initial conditions for the components of record a. The initial conditions for the attributes can be directly read off the variable initializations in the declaration of class A. Additionally, we require all mail queues to be initially empty (we use ε to denote the empty sequence).

$$Init_{\text{server1}}(a) \;\overset{\Delta}{=}\; \neg a.in1 \;\wedge\; a.q_{Enter1} = \varepsilon \;\wedge\; a.q_{Leave1} = \varepsilon$$

$$Enter1(a,c) \;\overset{\Delta}{=}\; \wedge\; a.q_{Enter1} = \langle c\rangle \circ a.q'_{Enter1}$$
$$\wedge\; \neg a.in1 \;\wedge\; a.in1' \;\wedge\; send_a(\{\{\langle c, \mathsf{asy}, \text{``Receive1''}, \langle\rangle\rangle\}\})$$

$$Leave1(a) \;\overset{\Delta}{=}\; \wedge\; a.q_{Leave1} = \langle\rangle \circ a.q'_{Leave1}$$
$$\wedge\; a.in1 \;\wedge\; \neg a.in1' \;\wedge\; send_a(\emptyset)$$

$$\mathcal{N}_{\text{server1}}(a) \;\overset{\Delta}{=}\; (\exists c : Enter1(a,c)) \;\vee\; Leave1(a)$$

$$Fairness_{\text{server1}}(a) \;\overset{\Delta}{=}\; (\forall c : \mathrm{WF}_{a.in1}(Enter1(a,c))) \;\wedge\; \mathrm{WF}_{a.in1}(Leave1(a))$$

$$\Phi_{\text{server1}}(a) \;\overset{\Delta}{=}\; \wedge\; Init_{\text{server1}}(a) \;\wedge\; \Box[\mathcal{N}_{\text{server1}}(a)]_{a.in1}$$
$$\wedge\; \Box[\exists c : receive(a, Enter1, \langle c\rangle) \;\vee\; Enter1(a,c)]_{a.q_{Enter1}}$$
$$\wedge\; \Box[receive(a, Leave1, \langle\rangle) \;\vee\; Leave1(a)]_{a.q_{Leave1}}$$
$$\wedge\; Fairness_{\text{server1}}(a)$$

Fig. 10. TLA formalization of class server1

The action $\mathcal{N}_A(a)$ represents the next-state relation for the attributes of a; it is defined as a disjunction

$$\mathcal{N}_A(a) \;\overset{\Delta}{=}\; \bigvee_{\alpha \in Act_A} \alpha(a)$$

of the TLA formulas representing the actions defined for class A. These formulas are straightforward to read off the class declaration, using a predefined action $send_a(ms)$ [6] that describes the emission of a message set ms by agent a. Additionally, we add a conjunct for every method declared in class A that states that the first message waiting in the associated mail queue is consumed.

The action $receive(a, m, \mathbf{x})$ describes the receipt of a message of type m by agent a with parameter tuple $\mathbf{x}$ (of appropriate length); it is defined as

$$receive(a, m, \mathbf{x}) \;\overset{\Delta}{=}\; a.q'_m = a.q_m \circ \langle \mathbf{x}\rangle$$

Consequently, the conjunct $\Box[(\exists x : receive(a, m, x) \;\vee\; m(a)]_{a.q_m}$ states that the mail queue $a.q_m$ associated with method m for agent a only changes during the receipt of a new message of this type, or during the execution of method m by agent a.

Finally, the formula $Fairness_A(a)$ describes the fairness conditions associated with class A. These fairness conditions have been left implicit in the programming notation, but will be made explicit in the logical description. For the purposes of this paper, we simply assume weak fairness for all actions defined for an agent.

As a complete example, figure 10 contains the TLA representation of agents of class server1 defined in figure 3.

3.2 Describing an agent defined by inheritance

An agent defined by inheritance can be formalized in the same way as an agent of a base class. We will, however, here restrict ourselves to subclasses that preserve encapsulation of their superclasses, because we can formalize and reason about agents of such classes in a compositional manner.

A subclass B of class A may define additional attributes and actions as well as update existing actions by strenghtening their guards. We will in the following denote the sets of additional attributes, actions, and methods declared in B by $attr_B$, Act_B, and $Meth_B$, and the set of actions from A that are updated in B by Upd_B. The new guard associated with an updated action $\alpha \in Upd_B$ for agent b is denoted by $\mathcal{G}_{B,\alpha}(b)$.

The general form of the TLA formalization of an agent b of subclass B of class A will then be

$$
\begin{aligned}
\Phi_B(b) \triangleq{} & \Phi_A(b) \wedge Init_B(b) \wedge \Box[\mathcal{N}_B(b) \wedge attr_A(b)' = attr_A(b)]_{attr_B(b)} \\
& \wedge \bigwedge_{m \in Meth_B} \Box[(\exists x : receive(c,m,x)) \vee m(b)]_{b.q_m} \\
& \wedge \Box[attr_B(b)' = attr_B(b) \wedge \bigwedge_{\alpha \in Upd_B} \alpha(b) \Rightarrow \mathcal{G}_{B,\alpha}(b)]_{attr_A(b)} \\
& \wedge Fairness_B(b)
\end{aligned}
$$

The first conjunct states that agent b behaves at least like an agent of the superclass. This ensures that b may be used whenever an agent of class A is expected, which is essential for a robust class hierarchy. The remaining conjuncts assert the additional properties that b has to satisfy.

The initial conditions for the new attributes can be read off the definition of class B as before. Moreover, we require all mail queues corresponding to the new methods $m \in Meth_B$ to be empty.

Similarly, the action $\mathcal{N}_B(b)$, which models the new actions defined for class B, is defined as in section 3.1 above. The next-state relation for the attributes in $attr_B$ requires the inherited attributes to stay unchanged; this corresponds to our assumption that class B preserves encapsulation of class A. The next conjunct asserts that the mail queues for the additional methods from $Meth_B$ behave as expected.

The following conjunct asserts that whenever the inherited attributes of b change, the new attributes stay unchanged (because inherited actions do not modify new attributes) and that the new, stronger guard has to hold whenever an updated action is executed.

Finally, formula $Fairness_B(b)$ adds fairness conditions for the newly defined actions as in section 3.1 above.

For an agent b of class server2, which has been defined by inheritance from class server1 in figure 4, we obtain the TLA formalization shown in figure 11.

$$Init_{\text{server2}}(b) \triangleq \neg b.in2 \,\wedge\, b.q_{Enter2} = \varepsilon \,\wedge\, b.q_{Leave2} = \varepsilon$$

$$Enter2(b,c) \triangleq \wedge\, b.q_{Enter2} = \langle c \rangle \circ b.q'_{Enter2}$$
$$\wedge\, \neg b.in2 \,\wedge\, b.in2' \,\wedge\, send_b(\{\langle c, \text{asy}, \text{"Receive2"}, \langle\rangle\rangle\})$$

$$Leave2(b) \triangleq \wedge\, b.q_{Leave2} = \langle\rangle \circ b.q'_{Leave2}$$
$$\wedge\, b.in2 \,\wedge\, \neg b.in2' \,\wedge\, send_b(\emptyset)$$

$$\mathcal{N}_{\text{server2}}(b) \triangleq (\exists c : Enter2(b)) \,\vee\, Leave2(b)$$

$$Fairness_{\text{server2}}(b) \triangleq (\forall c : \text{WF}_{b.in2}(Enter2(b,c))) \,\wedge\, \text{WF}_{b.in2}(Leave2(b))$$

$$\Phi_{\text{server2}}(b) \triangleq \Phi_{\text{server1}}(b) \,\wedge\, Init_{\text{server2}}(b) \,\wedge\, \Box[\mathcal{N}_{\text{server2}}(b) \wedge b.in1' = b.in1]_{b.in2}$$
$$\wedge\, \Box[\exists c : receive(b, Enter2, \langle c\rangle) \,\vee\, Enter2(b,c)]_{b.q_{Enter2}}$$
$$\wedge\, \Box[receive(b, Leave2, \langle\rangle) \,\vee\, Leave2(b)]_{b.q_{Leave2}}$$
$$\wedge\, \Box[b.in2' = b.in2 \wedge \forall c : Enter1(b,c) \,\Rightarrow\, \neg b.in2]_{b.in1}$$
$$\wedge\, Fairness_{\text{server2}}(b)$$

Fig. 11. TLA formalization of class server2

3.3 Reasoning about an agent defined by inheritance

We will now indicate how the formal description of an agent by a TLA formula helps us to reason about local properties of the agent. More precisely, we want to obtain modular proof rules that reflect the definition of the agent by inheritance, provided the subclass preserves encapsulation of the superclass.

First, the formula that describes the superclass appears as a conjunct in the characterization of the subclass. Hence, all properties of the superclass are obviously inherited. To prove additional properties of the subclass, we will make use of the structure of its TLA description.

Suppose we want to verify that an agent of the class server2 guarantees that at no time both of the resources it manages are in use:

$$\Phi_{\text{server2}}(b) \,\Rightarrow\, \Box\neg(b.in1 \,\wedge\, b.in2)$$

The usual approach to proving invariants [13] is to prove that they are true initially, and that every action preserves the invariant. Formally, we are left with the proof obligations

$$(1)\ Init_{\text{server1}}(b) \,\wedge\, Init_{\text{server2}}(b) \,\Rightarrow\, \neg(b.in1 \,\wedge\, b.in2)$$
$$(2)\ \wedge\, [\mathcal{N}_{\text{server1}}(b)]_{b.in1}$$
$$\wedge\, [\mathcal{N}_{\text{server2}}(b) \wedge b.in1' = b.in1]_{b.in2}$$
$$\wedge\, [b.in2' = b.in2 \wedge \forall c : Enter1(b,c) \,\Rightarrow\, \neg b.in2]_{b.in1}$$
$$\Rightarrow\, (\neg(b.in1 \,\wedge\, b.in2) \,\Rightarrow\, \neg(b.in1' \,\wedge\, b.in2'))$$

Proving (1) is easy, given the definitions from figures 10 and 11. Formula (2) looks more intimidating. In fact, we would like to avoid to construct the complete next-state relation of the attributes of agent b from the definitions of $\mathcal{N}_{\text{server1}}(b)$ and $\mathcal{N}_{\text{server2}}(b)$, but rather reason separately about the next-state relations of the subcomponents. This is mostly a matter of convenience for small examples like this one, but it becomes a necessity if we want to deal with realistic examples without running into state explosion problems. Fortunately, modular reasoning is quite simple, thanks to the structure of our specifications. Formally, the following proposition allows to reason about subclasses that preserve encapsulation.

Proposition 1 *Let class* B *be a subclass of class* A *that preserves encapsulation, and let* $\Phi_B(b)$ *be the TLA formula that describes an agent of class* B *as defined in section 3.2. Let p be any action formula of TLA.*

If (i) $\mathcal{N}_B \wedge attr_A(b)' = attr_A(b) \Rightarrow p$ *and*

(ii) $\mathcal{N}_A \wedge attr_B(b)' = attr_B(b) \wedge \bigwedge_{\alpha \in Upd_B} \alpha(b) \Rightarrow \mathcal{G}_{B,\alpha}(b) \Rightarrow p$

then $\Phi_B(b) \Rightarrow \Box[p]_{\langle attr_A(b), attr_B(b) \rangle}$ *holds.*

For our example of class server2, we choose

$$p \triangleq \neg(b.in1 \wedge b.in2) \Rightarrow \neg(b.in1' \wedge b.in2')$$

which leaves us with proving

$$\mathcal{N}_{server2} \wedge b.in1' = b.in1 \Rightarrow p$$
$$\mathcal{N}_{server1} \wedge b.in2' = b.in2 \wedge (\forall c : Enter1(b,c) \Rightarrow \neg b.in2) \Rightarrow p$$

Both of these proofs are straightforward from the definitions of figures 10 and 11.

3.4 Reasoning about agent systems

We formalize an agent system as a parallel composition of its individual agents and a specification of the communication network. We have shown in sections 3.1 and 3.2 how we can formalize single agents by TLA formulas. A generic specification of a communication network for agent systems has been proposed in [6], and we will not give details in this paper.

Let us assume that we have a simple network of one agent s of class server1 and two clients $c1$ and $c2$ of class client1(s). This network is then formally described by the conjunction

$$\Phi_{server1}(s) \wedge \Phi_{client1(s)}(c1) \wedge \Phi_{client1(s)}(c2) \wedge \Phi_{Net}$$

of formulas that represent the individual agents and the network.

We deduce system properties from agent properties and properties of the network. As an example, let us prove that every request of the client $c1$ to obtain the resource from the server s will eventually be honoured:

$$Request1(c1) \rightsquigarrow \Diamond Receive1(c1) \qquad\qquad (*)$$

(The "leadsto" formula $F \rightsquigarrow G$ abbreviates $\Box(F \Rightarrow \Diamond G)$.)

We deduce this property from the following local properties of the single agents and the network:

(1) $\quad(\forall c : Enter1(c) \rightsquigarrow Leave1) \Rightarrow (receive(s, Enter1, \langle c \rangle) \rightsquigarrow Enter1(s, c))$

(2.1) $receive(c1, Receive1, \langle\rangle) \rightsquigarrow Receive1(c1)$

(2.2) $receive(c2, Receive1, \langle\rangle) \rightsquigarrow Receive1(c2)$

(3) $\quad receive(s, Leave1, \langle\rangle) \rightsquigarrow Leave1(s)$

(4.1) $Receive1(c1) \rightsquigarrow Return1(c1)$

(4.2) $Receive1(c2) \rightsquigarrow Return1(c2)$

(5) $\quad send_{c1}(\{\langle s, \mathsf{asy}, Enter1, \langle c1 \rangle \rangle\}) \rightsquigarrow receive(s, Enter1, \langle c1 \rangle)$

(6.1) $send_{c1}(\{\langle s, \mathsf{asy}, Leave1, \langle\rangle \rangle\}) \rightsquigarrow receive(s, Leave1, \langle\rangle)$

(6.2) $send_{c2}(\{\langle s, \mathsf{asy}, Leave1, \langle\rangle \rangle\}) \rightsquigarrow receive(s, Leave1, \langle\rangle)$

(7.1) $send_{s}(\{\langle c1, \mathsf{asy}, Receive1, \langle\rangle \rangle\}) \rightsquigarrow receive(c1, Receive1, \langle\rangle)$

(7.2) $send_{s}(\{\langle c2, \mathsf{asy}, Receive1, \langle\rangle \rangle\}) \rightsquigarrow receive(c2, Receive1, \langle\rangle)$

Properties (2.1), (2.2), and (3) are local liveness properties that assert that messages received by the agents will eventually be processed. These properties are verified by standard TLA reasoning about the agent specifications. Similarly, properties (4.1) and (4.2) are local liveness properties that assert that the clients will eventually release the resource after obtaining it. They follow from the fairness conditions placed on reflex $Return1$.

Properties (5), (6.1), (6.2), (7.1), and (7.2) are liveness conditions on the network that state that sent messages will eventually be delivered.

Property (1) is more interesting: it states that the server will eventually honour all requests to execute method $Enter1$, assuming that every $Enter1$ action is followed by a $Leave1$ action. Informally, this requires all agents to eventually give up their resources. Clearly, if some agent keeps the resource forever, the server could not allocate it to another agent that requests access. We will frequently make similar assumptions about the environment behaviour and use them in reasoning about an agent.

We obtain $(*)$ from (1)–(7.2) by a simple chain of reasoning: First, properties (7.1), (2.1), (4.1), (6.1), and (3), and the action definitions imply

$$Enter1(c1) \rightsquigarrow Leave1$$

and similarly for agent $c2$. Using (1), we can deduce

$$receive(s, Enter1, \langle c \rangle) \rightsquigarrow Enter1(s, c)$$

and $(*)$ follows using properties (5), (7.1), and (2.1).

Using a similar combination of local reasoning and facts about the communication network, we may conclude that the clients $c1$ and $c2$ access the resource in mutual exclusion, that is,

$$\Box \neg(c1.owner1 \wedge c2.owner1$$

4 Conclusion

The purpose of this paper has been to emphasize the importance of modularity in both program construction and verification. We have indicated a programming model based on concurrently executing sequential agents that communicate by message passing. This model appears both flexible and semantically tractable: it can readily be formalized using existing program logics such as TLA.

We advocate the separation of protocols and functionality as a way to overcome the inheritance anomaly [15] of concurrent objects. We have therefore introduced two parallel hierarchies of classes that provide functionality and protocol classes that express synchronization constraints. More generally, we may think of an object as being composed of small, relatively independent components that can be understood—and verified—separately. The inheritance anomaly has recently received a great deal of attention [11, 17, 14]. Examining the successful solutions, it appears that all rely on modular description of synchronization code. We believe that our proposal, which can be understood as pushing this idea as far as possible, is particularly simple and robust.

Compositionality is an essential prerequisite to avoid the state explosion problem in verification. It allows proof outlines to be designed such that basic verification tasks are small enough to be verified by machine and the proof structure can be checked by interactive reasoning tools.

Object-oriented concurrent systems provide two orthogonal modes of composition: First, agent systems are composed from agents that execute in parallel. This form of composition has been studied in the theory of parallel processes for many years and is rather well understood [9]. In TLA, parallel composition simply corresponds to conjunction.

Another form of composition corresponds to subclassing. It is clear that it is in general impossible to inherit properties from the parent classes, unless some discipline on modification is imposed. We have therefore suggested that subclasses preserve encapsulation of the superclasses they inherit from. We may then obtain well-structured descriptions of the subclasses, and preserve all properties derived for the parent classes. New properties can be deduced in a modular way that avoids constructing the entire next-state relation. On the other hand, the condition of preserving encapsulation is probably too restrictive for many practical applications, and it could be relaxed in a number of ways. For example, we could allow the subclass to modify inherited attributes as long as these changes can be expressed in terms of inherited actions.

Other approaches to the formal definition of concurrent objects include, most notably, the Actor model [2], the language Maude [16], as well as the POOL family of languages [3]. With the exception of relatively minor differences such as assumptions on the order of processing of incoming messages and the detailed semantics of message-passing primitives, the basic programming models of these approaches are quite similar to ours. However, few formalisms come with a logic to reason about behavioural properties of agents. For example, all reasoning in the Actor framework has to be carried out at the semantic level. The rules of rewrite logic underlying Maude, on the other hand, do not allow to prove correctness assertions, but only support properties that express the existence of a successful execution.

References

1. Martín Abadi and Leslie Lamport. The existence of refinement mappings. *Theoretical Computer Science*, 81(2):253–284, May 1991.
2. G. Agha and C. Hewitt. Concurrent programming using actors. In A. Yonezawa and M. Tokoro, editors, *Object-Oriented Concurrent Programming*. MIT Press, Cambridge, Mass., 1987. [19, pages 37–53].
3. Pierre America and F. van der Linden. A parallel object-oriented language with inheritance and subtyping. In *European Conference on Object-Oriented Programming*, Lecture Notes in Computer Science, pages 161–168, Berlin, 1990. Springer-Verlag.
4. Jean Paul Bahsoun and Louis Féraud. A model to design reusable parallel software components. In D. Etiemble and J.-C. Syre, editors, *Parallel Architectures and Languages Europe (PARLE)*, number 630 in Lecture Notes in Computer Science, pages 245–260, Berlin, 1992. Springer-Verlag.
5. Jean Paul Bahsoun, Louis Féraud, and C. Bétourné. A two degrees of freedom approach for parallel programming. In *International Conference on Computer Languages*, pages 261–270. IEEE, 1990.
6. Jean Paul Bahsoun, Stephan Merz, and Corinne Servières. A framework for programming and formalizing concurrent objects. In *SIGSOFT Conference 1993*. IEEE, December 1993.
7. Holger Busch. A practical method for reasoning about distributed systems in a theorem prover. In E. Thomas Schubert, Phillip J. Windley, and James Alves-Foss, editors, *Workshop on Higher-Order Logic Theorem Proving and Its Applications*, volume 971 of *Lecture Notes in Computer Science*, pages 106–121, Berlin, 1995. Springer-Verlag.
8. K. Mani Chandy and Jayadev Misra. *Parallel Program Design*. Addison-Wesley, Reading, Mass., 1988.
9. W. P. de Roever. The quest for compositionality – a survey of proof systems for concurrency, part 1. In E. J. Neuhold, editor, *IFIP working group on the role of abstract models in Computer Science*, pages 181–206. North-Holland, 1985.
10. José Luiz Fiadeiro and Thomas Maibaum. Verifying for reuse: foundations of object-oriented system verification. In C.Hankin, I.Makie, and R.Nagarajan, editors, *Theory and Formal Methods 1994*. World Scientific Publishing Company, 1995.
11. S. Frølund. Inheritance of synchronisation constraints in concurrent object-oriented programming languages. In O. Lehrmann Madsen, editor, *European Conference on Object-Oriented Programming*, volume 615 of *Lecture Notes in Computer Science*, pages 185–196, Berlin, 1992. Springer-Verlag.
12. Thomas Långbacka. A HOL formalisation of the Temporal Logic of Actions. In Thomas E Melham and Juanito Camilleri, editors, *Higher Order Logic Theorem Proving and Its Applications*, volume 859 of *Lecture Notes in Computer Science*, pages 332–345, Berlin, 1994. Springer-Verlag.

13. Leslie Lamport. The Temporal Logic of Actions. *ACM Transactions on Programming Languages and Systems*, 16(3):872–923, May 1994.
14. Ulrike Lechner, Christian Lengauer, Friederike Nickl, and Martin Wirsing. (OO + concurrency) & reusability—how to overcome the inheritance anomaly. Technical report, Institut für Informatik, Universität München, Munich, 1996.
15. S. Matsuoka and A. Yonezawa. Analysis of inheritance anomaly in object-oriented concurrent programming languages. In G. Agha, P. Wegner, and A. Yonezawa, editors, *Research Directions in Concurrent Object-Oriented Programming*. MIT Press, Cambridge, Mass., 1993.
16. J. Meseguer. Parallel programming in Maude. In J. B. Banatre and D. LeMetayer, editors, *Research Directions in High-Level Parallel Programming Languages*, Lecture Notes in Computer Science. Springer-Verlag, 1992.
17. José Meseguer. Solving the inheritance anomaly in concurrent object-oriented programming. In Oscar Nierstrasz, editor, *European Conference on Object-Oriented Programming*, volume 707 of *Lecture Notes in Computer Science*, pages 220–246, Berlin, 1993. Springer-Verlag.
18. Corinne Servières. *Modélisation et vérification orientées objet pour les systèmes réactifs*. PhD thesis, Institut national polytechnique de Toulouse, Toulouse, November 1995.
19. A. Yonezawa and M. Tokoro, editors. *Object-Oriented Concurrent Programming*. MIT Press, Cambridge, Mass., 1987.

CHORUS/COOL
CHORUS Object Oriented Technology[*]

Christian Jacquemot, Peter Strarup Jensen, Stephane Carrez

Chorus Systems
6 Avenue Gustave Eiffel
78182, Saint-Quentin-en-Yvelines
tel. +33 (1) 30-64-82-00
fax. +33 (1) 30-57-00-66

Abstract. CHORUS/COOL provides a unique framework for merging Object technology and CHORUS open microkernel technology.
This framework aims at providing a set of object management services ranging from simple and efficient ones for system builders, to sophisticated environments for application developers.
The design of this framework integrates the following requirements : compliance with OMG standards, performance-oriented, interoperability between applications runnning on heterogeneous systems and using different communication protocols, openess.

1 Introduction

Computing today is dominated by physically distributed systems. Networks of small machines can be found in most environments, in particular in the office and control environments. These networks offer the potential of much improved computing facilities by the use of parallel computation and more importantly, by providing an environment in which cooperative applications can support group interactions within a distributed system.

However, to date, taking real advantage of these networks has been limited by lack of the suitable infrastructure for building distributed applications. Although mechanisms have been in place for a number of years to allow machines to communicate, support that allows applications to cooperate is still lacking.

The OMG (Object Management Group) CORBA (Common Object Request Broker Architecture) is an object-oriented architecture for supporting multi-vendor applications in heterogeneous distributed environments. Support for heterogeneity was the primary motivation of the CORBA specification. CORBA provides the foundation for combining client/server and object-oriented paradigms. These two paradigms used together have proved to be an excellent approach for building robust distributed applications. Objects are encapsulated units that contain data with associated functionality. Each object exports a well defined

---

[*] This work is partially supported by the European Community under ESPRIT Project 6603 "OUVERTURE".

interface, a set of services, that are made available to other objects in the distributed system. The internals of objects are never exposed, hence they provide a unit of programming ideally suited for distribution. Interactions between objects are carried out using invocations where a request for service is dispatched to the appropriate object using the underlying infrastructure.

The concept of application has evolved to cover an ever larger class of programs. In distributed operating systems based on microkernel architectures, an operating system is a system application consisting of a set of components called system servers. On one hand different operating system personalities can cooperate on top of a given microkernel. On the other hand system servers of a same operating system can be spread out across multiple sites. The Chorus Systems' implementation of UNIX SVR4, CHORUS/MiX V.4 (Modular UNIX), is a typical example of this latter approach: several system servers (actors in CHORUS terminology) cooperate to provide the UNIX kernel personality.

Interfaces based on the client/server and object-oriented paradigms can be used in several places: between the microkernel and the operating system(s), between different operating system personalities on top of the microkernel, between system servers of a same operating system, between user applications and the underlying system(s), and inside user applications. A unique formal architecture can be used for defining the interfaces at these different levels. But it is necessary to adapt the instance of the architecture to the specific requirements of the level where it is used. For example, efficiency, scability and small memory footprint are important to implement distributed operating systems while CORBA-based user level applications are willing to trade off some efficiency and size for additional functionality such as heterogeneity.

The COOL (CHORUS Object-Oriented Layer) framework aims at providing a range of object management services ranging from simple but efficient services targeted at operating system builders to sophisticated environment for application developers. The COOL runtime support environments are based on CORBA and are implemented directly on the CHORUS microkernel or on top of an operating system personality. Different versions of the runtime exist to support different levels of functionality.

Currently three versions can be generated to match given application requirements. COOL-LD is targeted at operating system builders, COOL-ORB provides a portable ORB running on the CHORUS microkernel, on UNIX and Windows NT systems, and COOL v2 extends COOL-ORB with support for persistence and migration. Specifications are written in an IDL (Interface Definition Language) called COOL-IDL. The same object model is used for all versions of the runtime family.

The COOL framework is derived from research work performed within the European ESPRIT initiatives (COMMANDOS[2], ISA[3] and OUVERTURE) and from collaborative projects with SEPT[4].

---

[2] **COnstruction and MANagement of Distributed Open Systems**
[3] **Integrated System Architecture**
[4] **Service d'Etudes communes de la Poste et de France Telecom**

To allow system or application designers to concentrate on the application and not on management of the distribution and persistence, COOL hides these services behind the programming language (Fig. 1).

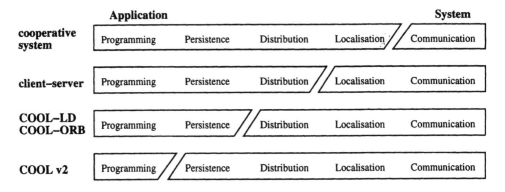

Fig. 1. Respective roles of system and application designers

2 COOL Framework

The COOL framework is composed of the following items:

- Programming Model
- Interface Definition Language (COOL-IDL)
- Runtime Family
- Services

2.1 COOL Programming Model

The COOL programming model (Fig. 2) is based on the client/server paradigm. A server consists of an arbitrary number of objects which implement arbitrary services. These objects can be invoked concurrently or sequentially by different applications. A client is an object residing in an application that performs a (remote) invocation on an object in the server.

The implementation of a server is conceptually distinct from its invocation by a client. The server encapsulates the implementation of the services it provides and exports a well-defined interface to its clients. Clients invoke the server through this interface and do not have any knowledge of the internal structure and implementation of the server.

The C++ class mechanism supports the client/server model to a certain extent. A generic interface can be implemented as an abstract base class, while derived classes, together with the late binding mechanism, provide different implementations. In this model, in order to access a server's functionality, a client needs to know only about the base class of the server.

The COOL programming model extends the C++ programming model to support distributed computation:

- the implementation of a server is separated from its invocation by a client
- the implementation inheritance tree is decoupled from the interface inheritance tree
- different policies can be implemented for the same interface by different servers
- the client interface object and the corresponding server implementation object are bound at run-time
- different interfaces can be implemented (and exported) by the same server

The COOL programming model also extends the usual message based model for distributed computation:

- a client invocation of a server is a typed procedure-oriented invocation instead of untyped message passing
- communication protocols can be optimized according to the respective locations of clients and servers

To gain access to a server, a client must first acquire an *interface object* associated with the server. An interface object is an instance of a *static* interface definition, static in the sense that the definition is fully specified at compile-time and cannot be modified dynamically at run-time.

There is a Naming Service from which one can obtain the necessary interface objects. The role of the Naming Service is to associate symbolic names to interface objects. Another way of acquiring interface objects is to have them passed as parameters of interface function invocation. Identical semantics are

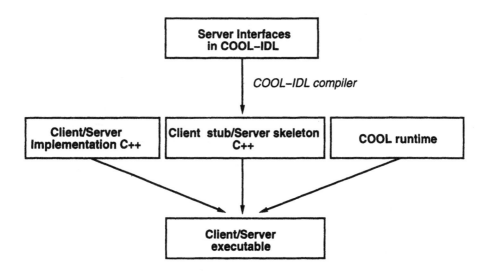

Fig. 2. COOL Programming Model

guaranteed for these objects, irrespective of whether they are obtained from the Naming Service or passed as arguments by some other server.

For each interface definition, the COOL–IDL compiler generates a C++ class with the same name. Clients operate directly on interface objects: an interface function call is a call on a function of the interface object. The interface object corresponds to the *stub* part in CORBA.

For each implementation class (distinguished from a standard C++ class by its **interface** access specifier), the COOL–IDL compiler generates a C++ skeleton class, which corresponds to the *skeleton* part of CORBA, and the conversion operator used to bind the implementation object to an interface object. The code generated for the skeleton class is statically linked with the server. The skeleton class is the server counter-part to the client stub class. It reifies the stub requests in a form that can be processed by the implementation functions.

The stub and skeleton classes are completed by a mechanism to turn message based invocations into local invocations and vice-versa. This mechanism is used to optimize communication when the server and the client are co-located in the same address space.

2.2 COOL Interface Definition Language (COOL–IDL)

The COOL–IDL specification is based on the belief that the ability to reuse existing C and C++ code will be a primary determinant in the acceptance of an interface language. The first step towards the acceptance of COOL–IDL will be through the use of interfaces encapsulating existing message based communication protocols in existing applications that are constructed using a client/server paradigm.

Most aspects of the OMG–IDL are included in COOL–IDL as pure extensions to C++ , or are adapted to fit C++ syntax and semantics. Pragmatic choices have been made about what aspects of the OMG–IDL specifications are incorporated in COOL–IDL driven mostly by experience gained from experimenting and prototyping.

Interfaces are defined using COOL–IDL. A COOL–IDL interface definition is similar to a C++ class definition in which all its members are public. A COOL–IDL interface is specified by the keyword **interface**, followed by the name of the interface and a set of definitions. The difference between an interface and a class relates to how they are implemented. Each class definition has an implementation associated with it. In the case of an interface, although the client and the server share the interface definition, the implementation of the associated implementation class is located only in the server. In the current COOL–IDL specification this sharing is static and is typically done at compile time through shared header files.

An interface object is an instance of an interface definition. A server binds an interface object to a class object implementing that interface (**binding** operation). The server may store the binding information in the Naming Service (**export** operation) or fill an interface invocation argument (**out** argument of the interface function invocation). A client that wishes to access the server initializes an interface object by invoking the Naming Service (import operation) or through an out argument of an interface invocation. The client can then use the interface object to access the server.

There is no distinction in the way C++ objects and interface objects are passed as arguments. Semantics of parameter modifiers (in, out, inout) and of return values are those specified for the proposed OMG–IDL mapping to C++ .

A server must bind an implementation to an interface before passing it to the Naming Service or to the interface function invocation. An implementation is typically a C++ program that is run in a process constituting the server. At runtime an interface object is created and bound to the implementation object in the server before the interface object is exported either to the Naming Service or to a client through an interface function out parameter. Communications between client and server are managed by the underlying object-oriented runtime system.

A COOL–IDL interface is implemented by a C++ class. The access specifier interface has been added to the C++ grammar to specify the interface(s) that are implemented by a C++ class.

When parsing an interface specification, the COOL–IDL compiler checks that all the interface functions are defined by the implementation class.

When parsing an interface access specifier, the COOL–IDL compiler generates a conversion operator for the corresponding interface. The data layout of the implementation class is not modified.

A server binds an implementation object to an interface object by assigning a class instance to an interface instance. After the binding operation is processed, the interface object can be passed by the server to the Naming Service or as argument to an interface invocation.

2.3 COOL Runtime Family

To adapt the COOL framework to specific requirements, a set of runtimes has been designed and implemented (Fig. 3). Each runtime implements an Object

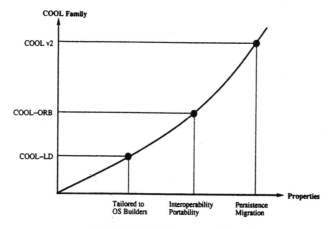

Fig. 3. COOL Runtime Family

Request Broker and is tailored to a specific use. Consequently, a runtime provides only the functions necessary for its corresponding use.

The COOL-LD runtime is ideally suited for introducing Object Oriented technology into the implementation of "component-ized" operating system kernels (e.g. CHORUS/MiX). The COOL-ORB runtime implements a complete Object Request Broker and has been designed to be portable, open and to support interoperability. The COOL v2 runtime extends COOL-ORB with support for persistence and migration. Complete interoperability is insured between COOL-ORB and COOL v2.

2.4 COOL Execution Model

In COOL, objects are passive entities. Threads of execution are independent entities which, at different points in time, can execute in different objects.

The COOL execution model is based on the **activity** abstraction.

An activity corresponds to the activation of one or more objects mapped in arbitrary address spaces. The activation of an object corresponds to the invocation of one of its methods. An activity is a logical thread of control, spanning a tree of nested and serialized object invocations. An activity is a distributed entity. When a server object is invoked on a remote site the activity **diffuses** to that site.

The COOL system is responsible for managing the resources required by the activities. When creating a new activity the system returns an interface object of the type **Activity** which allows applications to control it.

3 COOL-ORB Overview

This runtime implements a complete Object Request Broker. This runtime has been designed to be portable, open and to support interoperability.

COOL-ORB has been developed on top of the CHORUS microkernel first, and has then been ported on other Operating Systems in particular UNIX and Windows NT.

The communication component of COOL-ORB has been designed to accomodate different communication supports, in particular CHORUS IPC and TCP/IP.

3.1 Interoperability

COOL-ORB provides interoperability between clients and servers spanning networks of machines running different operating systems and using different communication protocols (Fig. 4).

Depending on the communication protocols supported by the client and by the server the invocation is done directly or through a gateway in a transparent fashion.

3.2 CGOL–ORB Architecture

The CGOL–ORB runtime is implemented as a library and a set of servers.
The main components of the library are the following:

- Core Component provides basic abstractions to manage objects and interface objects inside the library
- Execution Manager implements the execution model of CGOL based on the underlying system threads support. Depending on the underlying system, CGOL–ORB is multi-threaded or mono-threaded.
- Invocation Manager implements the invocation mechanism directly used by the stubs to mediate invocations. This mechanism can be based on different communication protocols.
- API Manager implements the Application Programming Interface of CGOL–ORB. This API is twofold, the OMG API as defined in the OMG specifications and the CGOL API.

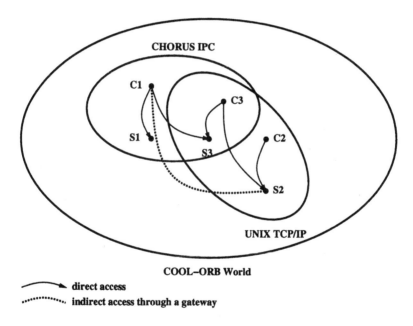

COOL–ORB World

———➤ direct access
················➤ indirect access through a gateway

Fig. 4. Interoperability

The library is completed by a set of servers. To insure interoperability, a relocation server is necessary. This server is in charge of locating objects, and defining the appropriate communication protocol to support invocation. Appropriate caching mechanisms are implemented in CGOL–ORB to minimize relocation server access time when object invocations are performed.

4   COOL v2 System Overview

This runtime extends COOL–ORB with support for persistence and migration. This extension is based on the CHORUS microkernel functions.

An object is said to be **persistent** if it outlives the application (in the sense of thread of execution) which created it. This means that a persistent object can be used by other applications after the termination of the creating application.

Persistent objects are automatically saved by the system. This might happen on application termination, or when the system or an application decides to retract the object from the address space where it is currently mapped.

The COOL v2 system integrates an efficient persistent and distributed object store providing the basic functionality needed to manage persistent distributed objects. This integration allows efficient management of persistent objects. It also provides the system and the user with alternative mechanisms to access distributed objects.

An important characteristic of the COOL v2 system is that it provides remote object invocation and object migration between address spaces in a transparent and a uniform manner (Fig. 5).

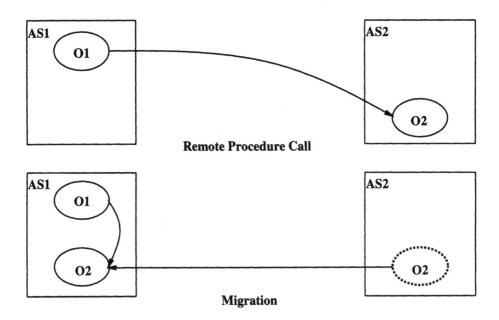

Fig. 5. Distributed object access

As an alternative to the COOL–ORB invocation mechanism, COOL v2 supports object migration. Instead of transferring the calling activity to the server it is possible to migrate the server into the client address space and perform a local invocation. Migrating an object means unmapping it from its current address space and then remapping it in the client address space, possibly at a different address.

This approach can be used to avoid unnecessary communication, by dynamically mapping objects where they are most frequently used.

The COOL v2 system allows these mechanisms to be used in uniform manner. Since the invocation semantic is not affected by the choice of the distribution mechanism, it is safe for the system to optimize invocations, based on object location.

4.1   Persistent Distributed Object Store

COOL v2 introduces an intermediate level of persistence between a complete address space and individual objects called the **cluster** (Fig. 6). From the system point of view a cluster is a unit of persistent memory, in which objects can be allocated. From a programming point of view a cluster represents objects **location**. Objects allocated in the same cluster are supposed to be strongly correlated.

Each cluster is associated with a **unit of storage** (files). **Mapping** a cluster to an address space means associating a fraction of the address space with the data contained in the cluster. When a cluster is not mapped its contents is saved in its unit of storage. An address space fragment can be associated with at most one cluster at a time.

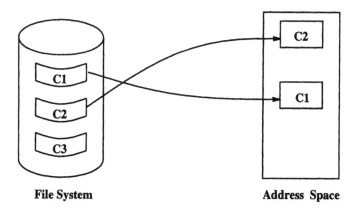

File System	Address Space

Fig. 6. Clusters

4.2   Clusters and Objects

To access objects allocated in a cluster, the cluster must be mapped into some address space. Inside a cluster, objects can be accessed using simple memory pointers (standard C++ mechanism). Since a cluster can be mapped at arbitrary addresses the pointers contained in objects allocated in a cluster must be updated each time the cluster is mapped. This is handled transparently by COOL v2. The object structural information needed to do this is provided to the runtime by the COOL–IDL compiler.

In each cluster an allocator is used to allocate memory to objects. The size of the cluster is dynamically adapted according to the size of the objects it contains.

The system does not allow pointers between objects allocated in different clusters. Instead, the notion of **interface objects** should be used to refer to objects allocated in other clusters (Fig. 7).

4.3 Clusters and Distribution

Clusters not only define the granularity level of persistence. They represent also the unit of migration.

COOL v2 does not allow migration of individual objects. When an object is migrated from one address space to another, its cluster is unmapped from the original address space and re-mapped in the new one, possibly at different addresses. COOL v2 is responsible for maintaining pointers coherence.

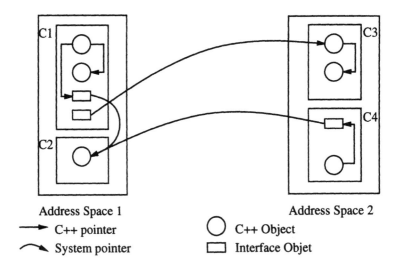

Fig. 7. Clusters and objects

4.4 Domains

Using CHORUS distributed virtual memory it is possible to map a cluster on a site independently of the site controlling its unit of storage. Uncontrolled, this could lead to an important dispersion between data and units of storage. Within a local area network such dispersion is admissible. However, for machines connected via telecommunication networks (for instance ISDN[5]) such dispersion

---

[5] Integrated Service Digital Network

could cause serious problems. The notion of **domain** has been introduced to control this dispersion.

A domain is defined as a collection of sites. Each site in a domain must have a coherent behavior. In particular, each site in a domain must simultaneously be accessible, connected and running. For instance, two sites connected via an ISDN cannot belong to the same domain. A site cannot belong to more than one domain. It is the responsibility of the network administrator to organize sites in domains.

The domain of a cluster is the domain containing the site where the cluster is stored.

Two different policies apply to cluster management:

- intra-domain cluster management, a cluster can be mapped directly in any address space on any site within its domain.
- inter-domain cluster management, the unit of storage associated to the cluster should be migrated to a site in the domain of the cluster before mapping the cluster.

4.5 Module Management

The cluster notion was introduced in order to structure object data, similarly the notion of **modules** is introduced in order to structure the code associated with objects.

The COOL v2 system allows code associated with objects to be loaded dynamically. The unit of dynamic loading is a **module**. A module is constructed by compiling and linking one or more compilation units. A module contains the code for a set of correlated classes.

The COOL v2 system supports two forms of dynamic loading: explicit loading and implicit loading. Explicit loading might be necessary before calling a constructor to create new objects. A module might also be loaded transparently by the system during object migration.

4.6 COOL v2 Architecture

The COOL v2 system is composed of two functionally separate layers:

- the COOL v2 Base layer
- the COOL v2 Runtime layer

COOL v2 Base Layer This layer is the system level layer. Its interface is a set of system calls and it encapsulates the CHORUS microkernel. It acts as a microkernel for object-oriented systems, on top of which the generic runtime layer can be built. Abstractions in this layer have a close relationship with the CHORUS microkernel and benefit from its performance.

This layer provides memory abstractions to hold objects, message passing, an execution model based on threads and a single level persistent store that abstracts over a collection of loosely coupled nodes and associated secondary storage.

This layer manages the cluster abstraction as a region of memory that contains objects. All objects referred to within a cluster are contained within this cluster.

Support for clusters is based on an external mapper and on the UNIX file system which acts as a repository for data within clusters. A mapper is a system defined entity used by the virtual memory manager to store and retrieve pages from secondary storage.

COOL v2 Runtime Layer This layer provides ORB functionality and supports object management including: creation, dynamic link/load, fully transparent invocation including location on secondary storage and mapping into context spaces.

To allow this layer to manage language level semantic information (for example C++ object layout) an upcall mechanism has been defined. These upcalls are generated by the COOL–IDL compiler and form part of the implementation skeleton that allows the runtime to manage objects. These upcalls are associated to objects on a per class basis.

The upcall information, and associated functions are used for a variety of purposes, including support for persistence, invocation and re-mapping between address spaces, any time the runtime needs access to information about objects that are only known at the language level.

5 COOL Services

5.1 Synchronization

The COOL execution model allows the same objects to be accessed concurrently by several activities. It is therefore necessary to provide some sort of concurrency control.

The COOL concurrency control is based on basic synchronization objects. This approach is a natural extension to the synchronization primitives provided by the CHORUS microkernel, and fits well with the C++ programming model. Two kinds of synchronization objects are supported.

- Local synchronization objects (standard C++).
- Distributed synchronization objects, created and managed by the system, and only accessed through interface objects.

Within each category three types of synchronization objects are defined:

- Mutex,
- Semaphore,
- Single write, multiple read lock.

5.2 Naming Service

With COOL objects are shared between applications using interface objects. The language mechanism for passing interface objects between applications is as invocation parameters. However, before an application can start invoking objects belonging to, or created by, other applications it must have at least one initialized interface object.

Interface objects can be initialized using naming service. A naming service provides a distributed name space on top of the notion of interface object. It allows saving and restoring interface objects. These information are stored and associated with information necessary for querying. Depending on the naming service queries can be based on different criteria, such as: type, symbolic name, . . .

A naming service using character strings as symbolic names is part of the COOL services. This naming service can be used in a centralized mode (a single naming server on the network) or in a distributed mode (multiple naming servers sparsely distributed around the network). In the distributed mode each instance of the naming server manages local data. The different instances cooperate to provide a single server image.

5.3 Group Service

A group represents a set of servers that implement the same interface. It allows a client to invoke an operation on one or several servers in a transparent manner: the client uses the group interface object as a target server interface object. Server interface objects are inserted or removed from the group dynamically. Insertion and removal of server interface objects is transparent as far as clients are concerned.

A group is controlled by one or several group managers. When a client invokes an operation, using a group interface object, the request is sent to one group manager. The group manager has two roles:

- It forwards the request to one or several servers according to a dispatcher policy. Basically the request is forwarded to only one or several servers. The dispatcher policy controls which server of the group will receive the request. To help the group dispatcher component decide to which server the request is to be sent, a priority is assigned to each server interface which is part of the group. This priority is an absolute value which indicates a preference when forwarding requests. Requests are sent to servers in the order of their highest priority.
- It collects one or several replies/exceptions and forwards one of them to the client. This is controlled by the collector policy.

6 Application Example: CHORUS/COOL for System Programming

6.1 CHORUS/COOL for Building Operating System Kernel

Operating systems built along the CHORUS architecture are characterised by:

- a microkernel plus independent system servers,
- system servers communicate via explicit invocation,
- system servers can be in user or system space,
- system servers can be local or remote,
- optimisations are performed when client and server are local,
- distributed algorithms enhance scaling when system servers are distributed over several nodes.

Figure 8 outlines the architecture of CHORUS/MiX, the CHORUS microkernel-based implementation of UNIX System V.4 with COOL.

The introduction of the COOL object-oriented technology for building next generation of CHORUS/MiX operating systems aims at providing an answer to the following requirements :

- smooth evolution from current CHORUS/MiX implementations, i.e., reusability of existing system server code and compatibility with the software development framework,
- improved flexibility in customizing a distributed system configuration to specific application requirements,
- improved operating system performance when interacting system objects are located on the same site, as well as when they are distributed over different nodes.

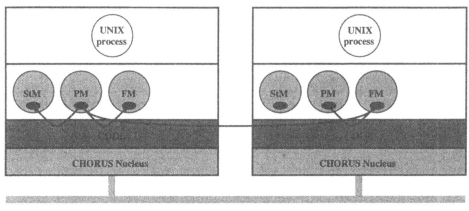

PM: Unix Process Manager   FM: File Manager   StM: Stream Manager

Fig. 8. CHORUS/MiX with COOL

The results of introducing CHORUS/COOL as the supporting object-oriented technology in the development of an operating system made out of components brings the following benefits :

- a procedure-oriented invocation mechanism instead of message passing primitives which simplifies the design and programming of interactions between system servers,
- optimizations of the invocation protocols based on server co-location, which bring 10-20% performance improvements in system calls involving single-site interactions, without impacting the performance of system call involving multiple sites,
- the ability to support new services such as transparent server migration and replication,
- the ability to implement fault tolerant system services.

6.2 CHORUS/COOL for Building Telecommunication Systems

Typical use of CHORUS microkernel technology by systems manufacturers is illustrated in the Figure 9, showing the architecture of a telecommunication equipment made of a combination of low-level real-time switching software, UNIX system servers, telecommunication specific system and application servers, off-the shelf and specific UNIX applications.

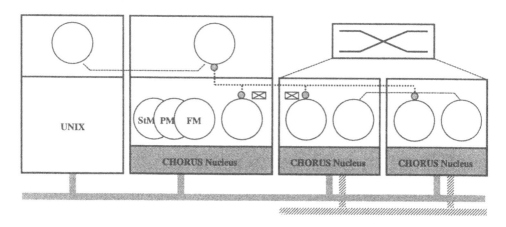

Fig. 9. Using "native" CHORUS

The introduction of the CHORUS/COOL object-oriented technology in the software architecture of such system software is illustrated on Figure 10 where interactions between specific and generic system and application servers is expressed in terms of the CHORUS/COOL invocation services instead of CHORUS/IPC and/or TCP/IP communication primitives, including for the invocation of small grain objects.

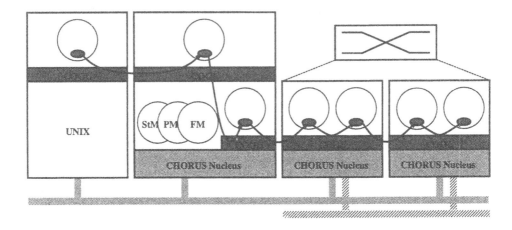

Fig. 10. Telecom system architecture using COOL on CHORUS

The introduction of the CHORUS/COOL object-oriented technology for building next generation of real-time distributed embedded systems aims at providing an answer to the following requirements:

- compliance with market standards (OMG),
- interoperability with existing systems (CHORUS based systems, UNIX, Windows NT), and communications architectures (CHORUS/IPC, TCP/IP),
- ease of customizing the configuration to support different communication means (e.g., ATM) and add new functions (e.g., Quality of Service).

CHORUS/COOL brings the following benefits to system manufacturers:

- a unified object model hiding the heterogeneity of communications architectures and protocols and systems platforms
- unified interfaces which constitute a general framework for integrating services.

7 Perspectives

On one hand, the CHORUS/COOL technology is a promising framework for building system software out of components. This framework will be extended to support efficiently the development and deployment of operating system servers (e.g. file systems, device drivers), specific value-added system servers (e.g. switching software, hard realtime application), and third party system servers and middleware (e.g. databases, graphical user interfaces).

On the other hand, CHORUS/COOL will be extended to express and operate Quality of Service functions necessary to support efficiently forthcoming intelligent network architecture and products.

8 Acknowledgements

The results reported in this paper have been produced by a team working closely together. The team members are Philippe Gautron, Jishnu Mukerji, Adam Mirowski, Pierre Lebée, Gilles Maignée, Frédéric Herrmann, Leandro Leon and the authors.

References

1. Chorus Team, "Overview of the Chorus Distributed Operating System", *USENIX Workshop on Micro-Kernels and Other Kernel Architectures*, Seattle (USA), April 1992.
2. R. Lea, C. Jacquemot, E. Pillevesse, "COOL: System Support for Distributed Programming", *Communications of the ACM*, Vol. 36, N. 9, September 1993.
3. C. Jacquemot, F. Herrmann, P. S. Jensen, P. Gautron, J. Mukerji, H.G. Baumgarten, H. Hartlage, "The CHORUS CORBA Compliant Framework", *COMPCON'94*, San Francisco, March 1994.
4. C. Jacquemot, F. Herrmann, P. S. Jensen, P. Gautron, J. Mukerji, H.G. Baumgarten, H. Hartlage, "COOL–IDL Extensions to C++ to Support Distributed Programming", *USENIX C++ Conference*, Cambridge, April 1994.
5. M.A. Goulde, "Tomorrow's Microkernel-based Unix Operating Systems", *Open Information Systems*, Vol. 8, N. 8, August 1993.
6. OMG, "The Common Object Request Broker: Architecture and Specification", *OMG Document Number 91.12.1*, 1991.
7. OMG, "IDL C++ Language Mapping Specification", *OMG Document Number 94.9.14*, 1994.
8. SunSoft, "A Spring Collection, A Collection of Papers on Spring", *SunSoft-September 1994*.
9. A. Birrel, G. Nelson, S. Owicki , E. Wobber "Network objects", *Proceedings of the Fourteenth ACM Symposium on Operating Systems Principles*, pp. 217-230, 1993.
10. C. Bryce, V. Issarny, G. Muller, I. Puaut "Towards safe and efficient customization in distributed systems", *Proceedings of the Sixth SIGOPS European Workshop: Matching Operating Systems to Applications Needs*, Scloss Dagstuhl, Germany, 1994.
11. R.H. Campbell, N. Islam, R. Johnson, P. Kougiouris, P. Madany "Choices: Framework and refinement", *Proceedings of the 1991 International Workshop on Object Orientation in Operating Systems*, pp 9-15, 1991.
12. P.Y. Chevalier, A. Freyssinet, D. Hagimont, S. Krakowiak, S. Lacoutre, J. Mossiere, X. Rousset de Pina "Persistent shared object support in the Guide system: Evaluation and related work", *Proceedings of the Ninth ACM Conference on Object-Oriented Programming Systems, Languages and Applications*, pp 129-144, 1994.
13. G. Hamilton, M. L. Powell, J.G. Mitchell "Subcontract: A flexible base for distributed programming", *Proceedings of the Fourteenth ACM Symposium on Operating Systems Principles*, pp 69-79, 1993.
14. Y. Yokote "The Apertos reflective operating system: the concept and its implementation", *Proceedings of the 1992 ACM Conference on Object-Oriented Programming Systems, Languages, and Applications*, 1992.
15. M, Nuttall "A brief survey of systems providing process or object migration facilities" *Open Systems Review*, pp 64-80, October 1994.

Adaptive Operating System Design Using Reflection

Rodger Lea, Yasuhiko Yokote and Jun-ichiro Itoh

Sony Computer Science Lab.
Takanawa Muse Bldg.
Shinagawa-ku.
Tokyo 141
Japan.

Abstract. To gain the maximum advantage of the object oriented programming paradigm, we believe it is necessary for the paradigm to be used throughout the application platform. This means that not only should applications be built using objects, but the underlying operating system should also be built using objects. Although this leads to a more modular operating system structure, perhaps more importantly it minimises the mismatch between the application programming paradigm and the underlying support infrastructure. However, ensuring that the underlying system supports individual application requirements is a difficult task. In essence it requires that the system be tailored towards application requirements. Apertos achieves this difficult task through the use of **meta-objects** and **reflection**, which allows the system to be adapted by application programmers via the reflective infrastructure. In this paper we discuss the object model that Apertos supports and how it can be tailored to support different application requirements.

1 Introduction

Any application relies on a run time support infrastructure that maps from the application programming paradigm through to the underlying operating system abstractions. It is the task of the compiler and library developer to provide a language run time environment that performs this mapping.

If the abstractions that the operating system supports are significantly different from the language, then the run-time has to bridge a larger semantic gap. Conversely, if the operating system offers abstractions close to the language then the semantic gap is small.

Various attempts have been made over the years to reduce this semantic gap, either by büilding hardware that supports a language model, e.g. the Lisp machines, by building an operating system that is close to the language semantics, e.g. Smalltalk, or even building machines and software that are suited to particular applications, such as database machines.

In most of these cases the price to pay is that the resulting system is well suited to a particular language or application but performs badly when trying to support other systems. In essence, there is a tension between the requirement for a general purpose computer platform and the desire to support well the applications that run on that platform.

With newer languages such as object oriented languages the problem has become worse. This is simply because the programming paradigm that machines and operating systems have evolved to support has been the traditional procedure oriented one.

This problem is further exacerbated by the development of distributed applications that cross process boundries. Such applications are forced to use native system functionality since the run time environment is generally restricted to a single process.

The OS research community is trying to attack this problem by developing operating systems that adapt to application requirements. Apertos[14][15] is one such approach. It uses the notion of objects as a fundamental structuring methodology within the operating system. However, it goes further by using a *meta-object* model to manage these system or **base** level objects.

The meta-object model uses a separate object to describe the interface and functionality that a base level object supports. In traditional language terms, it is a class that describes another class. By making changes to the meta-object we are able to change the way that the base level object carries out it tasks. This basic mechanism allows us to build an operating system which uses base level objects to implement basic system functionality and uses the meta-objects to describe how the operating system puts that base functionality together to provide its services. One can view the meta-objects as describing the policy, i.e. how to use the base functionality. By interacting with the meta-objects, we can change the way the operating system works and so adapt it to the requirements of any particular application. This manipulation of a run-time representation of a system via its meta-level description is known as **reflection**. The goal of this paper is to describe how Apertos supports a reflective object model to provide the basic operating system abstractions and how it can be used to reduce the semantic gap between the operating system abstractions and the applications that use those abstractions. To do this, we begin by discussing the general notion of reflection. We then show how Apertos supports reflection and outline the internal structure of Apertos. In section 5 we give some examples of the flexibility it offers, section 6 relates our work to other approaches and finally in section 7, we discuss our plans for future work.

2 Reflection

Apertos has been developed to explore the ideas of reflective computing within the framework of Operating Systems architecture. To fully understand the Apertos system, it is necessary to understand the basic ideas behind reflective systems. Thus this paper begins with a brief introduction to reflective systems.

A reflective system can be crudely described as one which can access a description of itself and change that description in such a way as to change its own behaviour. To achieve this, three steps are necessary. The first, known as *reification*, takes an abstract description of the system and makes it sufficiently concrete to allow it to be worked upon. The second step, *reflection* uses that concrete description as the subject of some manipulation. The final step, the *reflective update* modifies the reified description of the system as a result of the computational reflection and returns the modified description to the system. Thus, subsequent operation of the system will reflect the changes made to the reified description of the system.

The notion of reflection has been most commonly used in the language community, where for example, Lisp based languages such as CLOS or the Smalltalk language support the ability to carry out computation on themselves and in particular extend, at run time, the language itself. This is commonly achieved through the use of a meta-class protocol. Each object in the system has a meta-object which describes the class itself. This meta-object has an interface, the meta-class protocol, which allows programmers to access and change the behaviour of the class.

While a full discussion of the mechanisms and uses of reflection is beyond the scope of this paper, it is important to note several benefits of this model.

- The object/meta-object model means we are able to make a clean separation between the system mechanisms that support objects and the policy that dictates how those mechanisms are used.
- The model supports well a related notion of *separation of concerns*. Here the programmer concentrates on the abstractions rather than the details, thus location, virtual memory support, size, etc. of program objects are provided by the meta-space after the initial application is developed.
- The model provides a conceptually clean way of altering the behaviour of all aspects of the system. If everything in the system supports reflective computation, then all aspects of the system can be reified and manipulated.
- Lastly reflection provides a means to support a truly open and adaptable operating system. As the environment in which the operating system evolves, we are able to evolve the operating system to manipulate it.

It is this clean programming model, and in particular the ability to change system behaviour in a systematic and controlled way, that Apertos is attempting to exploit.

3   Realisation of the conceptual framework by Apertos

Apertos uses the reflective programming model described above as the fundamental structuring tool throughout the system.

Each object in the system, i.e. each piece of system functionality, has a meta-object. This meta-object describes some parts of its functionality. For example, all objects support the notion of invocation, allowing any object to be invoked by another object, irrespective of the location of the object. The actual mechanism for object invocation on any one particular object is dependent on that object's meta-object and can be different for different objects. Thus for example, one object my implement remote invocation using a RPC paradigm, while another may use an asynchronous paradigm. By manipulating the meta-object, through a reflective computation, the way that invocation is performed can be changed.

Apertos generalises the object/meta-object relationship from a one-to-one to a one-to-many. Each object is supported by a group of meta-objects whose total functionality is available to the object. A set of meta-objects is referred to in the Apertos system as a **meta-space**.

Since each meta-object in the meta-space is in fact an object, they too must have meta-objects. This leads us to define a potentially infinite stack of meta relationships known as the **meta-hierarchy**.

Apertos uses the notion of a terminal meta-space as a way of 'bottoming out' this potentially infinite recursion. Since meta-spaces provide resources and resource management for object, there are many run-time hierarchies, each supporting different sets of objects. However, one that is common to all is MetaCore. MetaCore can be considered as a terminal objects since it provides a minimal set of functionality that supports the meta-computing model. MetaCore can be likened to the micro-kernel in an operating systems such as CHORUS.

In order to manage and reason about the meta-objects that make up a meta-space, Apertos introduces the notion of a **reflector**. A reflector is a special object that sums the operations of its meta-objects and represents those meta-objects. Figure 1 depicts graphically the relationship between objects, meta-objects, meta-spaces and reflectors. The introduction of reflectors allows meta-spaces to be built into a class hierarchy. This has two benefits:

- It allows reflector programming to be put on the same footing as any other object oriented programming and thus makes it possible for system designers to re-use existing reflectors as they design and code new reflectors.
- In addition, the use of a reflector hierarchy allows us to make statements about the compatibility between reflectors. This is beneficial when we wish to migrate objects between meta-spaces. Often we will be doing so during the normal operation of a large distributed system. It is necessary to know what degree of compatibility exists between the sending and receiving meta-space to know what level of functionality the object will have when it is installed in the receiving meta-space.

In figure 1, we show the relationship between objects, meta-objects, meta-spaces and reflectors. It should be noted that the reflectors are organised into their own class hierarchy which is used for system design and compilation by system builders. This should not be confused with the meta-hierarchy, i.e. the hierarchy between the meta-spaces which is a run time notion.

4 Internal details of Apertos

In the previous sections we outlined the conceptual framework that Apertos supports, i.e. the object/meta-object model, and discussed how the Apertos system conforms to this conceptual framework. In this section we discuss in

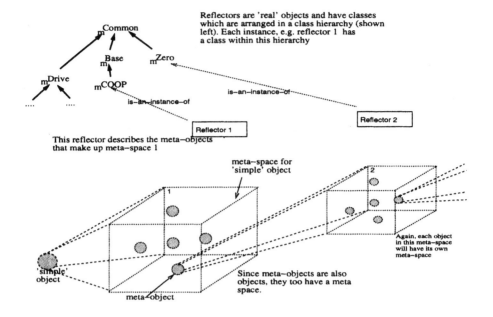

Reflectors are 'real' objects and have classes which are arranged in a class hierarchy (shown left). Each instance, e.g. reflector 1 has a class within this hierarchy

Common

Base mZero

mDrive mCOOP

is-an-instance-of

is-an-instance-of

Reflector 1

Reflector 2

This reflector describes the meta-objects that make up meta-space 1

meta-space for 'simple' object

'simple' object

meta-object

Since meta-objects are also objects, they too have a meta space.

Again, each object in this meta-space will have its own meta-space

Fig. 1. Objects and meta-spaces

more detail the actual implementation of these concepts. We begin with the key meta-spaces in the system, then describe the actual implementation of an object and finally detail how objects are created and interact using the Apertos OS facilities.

In figure 2, the abstract meta-architecture shown in figure 3 is visible as the separate meta-spaces mCOOP, $m$zero and $m$core.

4.1   MetaCore

MetaCore acts in a manner similar to that of a micro-kernel in more traditional systems. However, rather than providing a minimal set of resource abstractions, its role is restricted to supporting the object/meta-object model, the base notion of activity and interrupt dispatching. This allows a very small core object (currently around 3K) which aids both understanding and porting. MetaCore supports the following operations:

- M(meta): Make a request for meta-computing. This causes the execution of an object to be suspended and control to pass from the object to its meta-object.
- R(reflect): Resume object execution, i.e. pass control from the meta-object back to a base object.
- CBind: Specify a recipient for an interrupt.
- CUnbind: Break the association between a recipient and an interrupt.

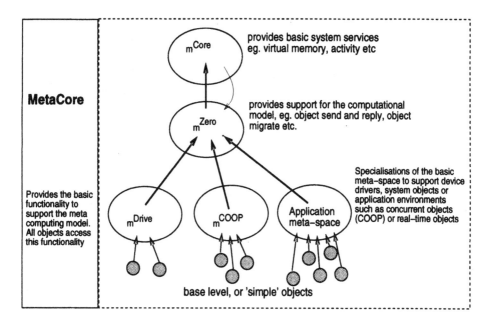

Fig. 2. Implementation hierarchy of meta-spaces

MetaCore is shown in figure 2 as the vertical box running alongside the meta hierarchy. Since MetaCore supports the basic facilities for meta-computing, i.e. the reify (Meta) and deify (Reflect) operations, it is accessible and used by all meta-spaces.

4.2 Activity in Apertos

The underlying CPU is abstracted in a structure known as a **context**. Contexts[1] are created by the meta-object *exec* which resides in mCore. Contexts are actually abstracted by a notion of **activity** which is the unit of manipulation at the meta-level (see figure 3). The context structure is seen by MetaCore as it uses this to set up the hardware to support the actual execution of an activity. The context structure contains the pointer to the meta-space for that context. This enables MetaCore to move from the currently executing context to its meta-space when the M operation is called.

m**Base** is the first level meta-space for a base level object and implements the scheduling policy.

m**Zero** is one of the terminal meta-spaces for all other meta-spaces and is thus accessed by all other meta-spaces. This allows some operations, eg. context location. to be optimised.

---

[1] Contexts in Apertos should not be confused which the general OS concept of a context as an address space. They are simply the state of the machine registers

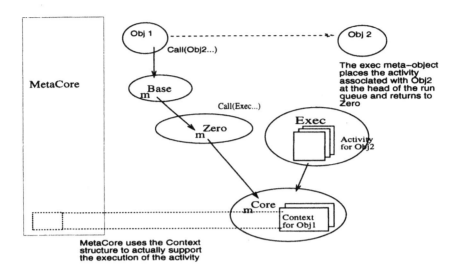

Fig. 3. Activity and the execution path

*m*Core is the reflector for *m*Zero and contains meta-objects to handle activity, physical memory and virtual memory. Although, as mentioned above, *m*Zero is the shared reflector for all others, it too needs a reflector, hence the use of *m*Core. To halt to potentially infinite hierarchy of meta-spaces we make the meta-space for *m*Core be *m*Zero. Although this introduces a circular dependency between the two it allows us to 'bottom out' when moving through the meta-hierarchy.

*m*Drive and a similar meta-space *m*System (not shown) are meta-spaces for device driver programming (see figure 2). They implement a concurrent object environment where device drivers are written in the same way as any other concurrent object application, i.e. we are able to hide the restrictions normally visible to device driver programmers. *m*Drive supports device drivers that have direct physical access to hardware and *m*system supports device drivers that have no access to hardware.

Interrupt handling requires that an interrupt is bound to a particular receiving object. The CBind operation in MetaCore does this. It sets up a dispatch entry in MetaCore which is used when the interrupt occurs. Interrupts are initially directed to MetaCore[2] which uses the dispatch table to decide on the receiving object. A standard R operation then passes control - as if it was a normal method invocation - to the context associated with the object bound to this interrupt. Thus, once an interrupt has been dispatched by MetaCore, its execution path does not differ from the normal message invocation and return path.

---

[2] In the MIPS implementation all interrupts are dispatched through a single vector.

4.3 Object creation

An object in the Apertos system consists of a set of memory segments and two meta-data structures; Activity and Descriptor. The memory segments are typed as data, code and stack.

The Descriptor is created and managed by the reflector for the object, thus the format of each descriptor is dependent on the reflector. However, certain items are common, including the memory segment information, a pointer to the context for this object, a pointer to its class and some information regarding its scheduling status.

Object creation begins by a call from an application object into its meta-space asking for the creation of an instance of a particular class of object. The first stage in creating an object is to access the class to determine the object structure. The object is then named by requesting a name from the 'namer' meta-object. Memory space is allocated by sending a request message to the VM meta-object that manages memory for this meta-space. The reflector then creates a context structure for the object so that it can be scheduled. Finally an activity is created by the meta-object *exec*.

4.4 Invocation

A particular meta-space for an object will provide the base implementation of send and reply. When an object makes a send request, control is transferred from the sending objects' context to its meta-space (m^{Base}). m^{Base} locates the receiving object's context by calling up into its meta-space (again through M) to m^{Zero}. Since m^{Zero} is shared, the location of the context, if on this machine[3], is found and the meta-space can call into the recipient object.

Referring back to figure 4, when object Obj1 attempts to call Obj2, it actually makes an M call into m^{Base}, i.e. it uses the M operation to switch to the context of m^{Base}. m^{Base} then calls into m^{Zero} as the send/receive functionality exists there. Here, the context associated with Obj2 is located. Using the *exec* meta-object, which manages the queue of activities, we place the activity associated with Obj2 at the head of the queue. m^{Zero} then exits, which is translated into an R operation, causing the scheduler to find Obj2 on the run queue and schedule it.

4.5 Meta-space migration

An important feature of Apertos is its ability to support object migration between meta-spaces. This feature allows a reflector to detach an object from its meta-space, and pass it to the reflector managing another meta-space. The protocol that does this uses information in each reflector to decide if the target reflector supports the appropriate interfaces that the object will need. If so then

---

[3] For remote objects the namer meta-object is used to locate the host for the object. The message is then sent to the m^{Zero} running on that host.

the object is passed to the target reflector which binds the new meta-space methods to the object.

Migration is a powerful technique that has two significant uses. Firstly it is used to support distributed services allowing system or application objects to be moved between hosts. Secondly it supports an extreme form of reflection by allowing an object to migrate to a meta-space that supports a completely new set of implementations for the methods that the object requires.

5 Using the mechanisms

The meta-object interface, commonly referred to as a meta-object protocol, or MOP[9], provides the means with which to change the semantics of system behaviour. As an example of this, we look at three cases of management of a simple thread abstraction.

In the first case we show the simple use of the MOP for a thread object which has an associated priority used by a priority-based scheduling algorithm. The commands to start a thread running, and to explicitly yield control are standard thread interface methods. In our system, as in any other, these would be implemented as methods of the thread class. However, the command to change the priority of a thread is one that is called not by the thread itself, but usually by the environment managing the thread. This operation is part of the thread MOP and implemented via a separate object in the meta-space for this thread. While this example is simple, it serves to illustrate the difference between base operations and meta operations. Further, it also shows the separation of concerns between the interface that the programmer must use and the interface that the environment uses. It is possible to take this basic thread object and reuse it in a different environment without any modification to the application code. All changes are made to the environment or meta-objects.

A more sophisticated use of the meta-object model is to evolve the MOP to implement extra functionality. Consider for example the case where we wish to define a new scheduler object that supports not only the priority-based scheme discussed above, but uses priority inheritance. The thread MOP is implemented through a set of meta-objects which are collectively described by a reflector object. The reflector objects are organised into a class hierarchy (see section 3). To add priority inheritance to the MOP, we derive a new reflector class object and add a method to one of the objects in the meta-space that are represented by that reflector. This method will re-order the waiting thread based on an inherited value. At run time, when the call was made to change the priority of the thread, the code executed would now take into consideration the priority of the calling object, allowing priority inheritance to take place.

Our last example illustrates the use of migration between meta-spaces. Consider the case where we wish to move our existing thread object into a scheduling regime that supports a simple quality of service (QofS) guarantee. Rather than using a pre-emptive scheme, the QofS scheduler uses fixed slots based on event arrival or pre-computation. Apertos makes this possible by allowing the thread to migrate from one meta-space to another. In the new meta-space the meta-objects that support the execution of this thread object will include a meta-object implementing this new scheduler policy. The thread would continue to use its original interface, i.e. call yield when it has finished computation, and would see no difference in its execution environment. However, the scheduler code implemented on yield is far different from the previous environment.

It is important to note that this model is consistent throughout the entire Apertos architecture and all objects have meta-objects. Thus every aspect of the system, apart from the basic operation to move from a simple object into its meta-space, is open and flexible. Not only does this approach help us solve the traditional issue of thread scheduling, but it is also used in the virtual memory system to allow us to support multiple page replacement policies, each tailored to the application they support and each dynamically changeable at run time. This method is also used in the communications system where we use these techniques to allow us to support standard send-receive, send-receive with user supplied continuations and send-receive with implicit continuations.

5.1 Performance details

In this section we give some details of the performance of an existing implementation of Apertos.

Basic system costs In table 1, we give performance figures for the basic Meta-Core operations[4]. Note that operations without trap occur when we do not cross a protection boundary. All of these calls are the basic operations that all higher level system functions must use and are therefore of great importance to the overall system performance.

Table 1. Execution cost of *MetaCore* primitives (in μsec)

primitive	on i486
M	21.1
M(w/o trap)	13.0
R	22.6
R(w/o trap)	8.8
CBind	4.1
CUnbind	3.5

Table 2 gives some brief details of execution costs for interrupt handling and use of concurrent objects in the driver meta-spaces. Details can be found in [8].

---

[4] All performance figures from a 486DX2-66MHz, 16MByte PCAT compatible.

Table 2. Costs of mDrive services, and interrupt operations (in μsec)

metaoperation	Apertos	BSD/386
Interrupt message delivery	25.0	11.5
Null interrupt handler execution	44.2	16.2
Send metacall overhead on mDrive	108.6	—
Call-Reply roundtrip on mDrive	207.8	—

Optimisations It is clear that in a pure implementation of our system, the continual rescheduling of objects as we move up and down the object hierarchy is expensive. To alleviate this cost, we implement a dynamic context hand-off mechanism [8] that allows us to reuse the calling context for the execution of the recipient. We use the reflector to hold the code that makes such a decision and which works by monitoring the use of the objects in the meta-space. When the reflector code decides that a context hand-off will not violate any system requirements, e.g. protection, then it uses the MOP to manipulate the implementation of the call-reply code such that subsequent calls use the context hand-off mechanisms. Table 3 shows the benefit of this technique within the framework of the driver meta-space.

A second technique we use is message batching which collects messages destined for the same remote object and batches them to ameliorate the message send costs. Again this technique uses the reflector object to monitor the pattern of sends from a particular object and to decide if message batching would be appropriate.

Table 3. Costs of mSystem services (in μsec)

metaoperation	Apertos
Send metacall overhead on mSystem	88.2
Call-Reply roundtrip on mSystem	772.8
Call-Reply roundtrip on mSystem(context hand-off)	7.8

In table 4, we show the macroscopic result of these performance optimisations for the implementation of an IP protocol. The protocol consists of 5 separate concurrent objects that reside within mSystem, i.e. they all have the same meta-space.

Table 4. Costs of network protocol handlers on mSystem (in μsec)

metaoperation	Apertos
ICMP echo-echoreply roundtrip	3466.0
ICMP echo-echoreply roundtrip(optimized)	362.3

6 Related work

There are many approaches to providing system flexibility; these include work that attempts to exploit modularity and work that supports run-time adaption through code modification.

Modularity is a key technique in building flexible software since it encapsulates components and makes them easier to change or evolve. Micro-kernel architectures have popularised such modularity and have demonstrated benefits in their overall flexibility[3][1]. Object oriented operating systems have extended this modularity with a finer degree of granularity and used techniques such as abstract interfaces and inheritance hierarchies to support a high degree of flexibility[10]. Systems such as Choices[6] or Isatis[2] have exploited this software engineering model to support an extremely sophisticated mix-and-match approach to the initial build phase, in some cases exploiting it to specialise systems not only for hardware but for the intended application.

Flexibility through run-time adaptation can be seen in most operating systems. For example scheduling policies are often adapted to deal with changing application loads. Recently there has been much interest in the use of more sophisticated techniques to not only choose between existing policy modules, but also to dynamically generate code that is optimised to a set of run-time constraints [13] [4].

A third type of flexibility concentrates on finding ways to allow the system interfaces to evolve over time. This type of flexibility is more difficult to achieve. Some of the work on object oriented systems has attempted to exploit type conformance [5] or similar means [7] to achieve it. Work on such languages as ABCL-R [11] also has much in common with our work, but concentrates on language level mechanisms rather than the operating system.

Although all of this work has the same goal as ours, we believe that our approach is cleaner in that we are concentrating on an overall system architecture that is designed to allow change. Our thesis is that by building this flexibility into all levels of the system we are providing a controlled mechanism that allows complete adaptability.

7 Current and future work

We are currently working on the use of Apertos in a distributed multimedia environment. In our initial setu, we have ported Apertos to a number of Sony

News 5000 workstations with MIPS R4000 processors and a video server using the R3000 processor. These machines are interconnected with a small experimental ATM network. We are experimenting with Apertos in two areas; the first uses the meta-object model to support QofS constraints and exploits our flexible architecture to adapt the resource scheduling policies to varying simulated system loads and failures. The second area of work uses Apertos in a proprietary graphics engine attached to the above network where we are experimenting with protocols for distributed shared virtual environments. In particular we are looking at the issues of distributed consistency where we are exploring the use of migration between meta-spaces to dynamically change the consistency associated with shared objects.

Efficiency is always a concern. We have chosen to explore the meta-object model to its fullest, and we have paid a price for this. We argue however, that it is necessary to get the model right first, then exploit the model to optimise. Some initial performance improvement is shown in tables 3 and 4. We are interested in exploring the use of dynamic code generation as in [13] to further improve our performance.

One of the advantages of a clean base/meta separation is that for the majority of application programmers the meta-level is hidden. However, those who wish to exploit flexibility must code at the meta-level. We have instigated some work to use compile time tools to abstract the details of the system [12], but are concerned that system users will need sophisticated tools to allow them to easily exploit the power of the meta-level model. We hope to report further as we begin to use Apertos within a number of Sony-internal development projects.

References

1. Tevanian Avadis Jr. and Richard F. Rashid. MACH: A Basis for Future UNIX Development. Technical report, Department of Computer Science, Carnegie Mellon University, June 1987.
2. M Banatra, Y Belhamissi, V Issarny, and J Routeau. Adaptive placement of method executions within a customisable distributed object based sysystem. In *Proceedings of the 15th International Conference on Distributed Computing Systems*, May 1995.
3. Nariman Batlivala, Gleeson Barry, Hamrick Jim, Lurndal Scott, Price Darren, Soddy James, and Abrossimov Vadim. Experience with SVR4 over CHORUS. In *Micro-kernel and other kernel architectures*, pp. 223–241. USENIX, April 1992.
4. Brian Bershad. SPIN - an extensible micro-kernel for application specific operating system services. In *Proceedings of the 6th ACM-SIGOPS European Workshop: Matching Operating Systems to Application Needs*, September 1994.
5. C Bryce, V Issarny, G Muller, and I Puaut. Towards safe and efficient customization in distributed systems. In *Proceedings of the 6th ACM-SIGOPS European Workshop: Matching Operating Systems to Application Needs*, September 1994.
6. Roy H. Campbell, Nayeem Islam, Ralph Johnson, Panos Kougiouris, and Peter Madany. *Choices*, Frameworks and Refinement. In *Proceedings of the 1991 International Workshop on Object Orientation in Operating Systems*, pp. 9–15. IEEE Computer Society Press, October 1991.

7. Graham Hamilton and Panos Kougiouris. The Spring nucleus: A microkernel for objects. In *USENIX 1993 Summer Technical Conference Proceedings*. USENIX Association, June 1993.

8. Jun ichiro Itoh, Yasuhiko Yokote, and Mario Tokoro. Using Metaobjects to support optimization in Apertos Operating System. Technical Report SCSL-TM-95-006, Sony Computer Science Laboratory Inc., 1995.

9. Gregor Kiczales, Jim des Rivières, and Daniel G. Bobrow. *The Art of the Metaobject Protocol*. The MIT Press, 1991.

10. Rodger Lea, Christian Jacquemot, and Eric Pillevesse. COOL: System support for distributed programming. *Communications of the ACM*, Vol. 36, No. 9,, September 1993.

11. Hidehiko Masuhara, Satoshi Matsuoka, Kenichi Asai, and Akinori Yonezawa. Compiling away the meta-level in object-oriented concurrent reflective languages using partial evaluation. In *In Proceedings of ACM SIGPLAN Conference on Object-Oriented Programming Systems, Languages, and Applications (OOPSLA '95)*, 1995.

12. Kenichi Murata, Nigel Horspool, and Yasuhiko Yokote. Design and specification of cognac. Technical Report SCSL-TM-94-006, Sony Computer Science Laboratory Inc., 1994.

13. Calton Pu and Jon Walpole. A study of dynamic optimisation techniques: Lessons and directions in kernel design. Technical Report CS/E 93-007, Oregon Graduate Institute (OGI), April 1993. Technical Report CS/E 93-007.

14. Yasuhiko Yokote. The Apertos Reflective Operating System: The Concept and Its Implementation. In *Proceedings of Object-Oriented Programming Systems, Languages and Applications in 1992*. ACM Press, October 1992. Also appeared in SCSL-TR-92-014 of Sony Computer Science Laboratory Inc.

15. Yasuhiko Yokote, Gregor Kiczales, and John Lamping. Separation of Concerns and Operating Systems for Highly Heterogeneous Distributed Computing. In *Proceedings of the 6th ACM-SIGOPS European Workshop: Matching Operating Systems to Application Needs*, September 1994.

Isatis: A Customizable Distributed Object-Based Runtime System

Michel Banâtre, Yasmina Belhamissi, Valérie Issarny, Isabelle Puaut,
Jean-Paul Routeau

IRISA, Campus de Beaulieu, 35042 Rennes Cédex, FRANCE

Abstract. This paper discusses the design and implementation of a customizable distributed object-based runtime system. Our main goal in the system's design was to provide a distributed object-based system supporting execution of various (concurrent) object-oriented languages, and that can be easily enriched with mechanisms for object management so as to fit the applications' needs. Enrichment of the runtime system with a particular mechanism is illustrated through the integration of a facility that is aimed at enhancing the applications' performance. This goal is achieved by means of a load balancing strategy that implements initial-placement of method executions and migration of data objects according to both the processors' load and the objects' features.

1 Introduction

Definition of object-oriented languages with support for distributed programming has given rise to several proposals since the last fifteen years. First proposals introduced distributed object-based programming systems [19], that is to say a concurrent object-based language together with its dedicated distributed object-based runtime system (e.g., Argus [34], Emerald [39], POOL/DOOM [2, 36]). However, this approach has not had the expected success. Although it has demonstrated that object-object oriented languages provide the adequate basis for the development of distributed applications, the efficiency of the approach has been too poor to be unanimously accepted by the distributed systems community. This inefficiency mainly came from the mismatch between the abstractions provided by operating systems and the ones offered by programming languages.

In order to increase efficiency of distributed object-based programming languages, a new approach has later been undertaken. It consists of defining generic distributed object-based runtime systems that support the execution of various programming languages. The runtime system may then be customized so as to execute efficiently applications written in a given language by implementing the best mapping between the language's abstractions and the ones of the operating system. From that perspective, micro-kernel architectures such as Amoeba [41], Chorus [40] and Mach [1] offer an adequate basis; they provide a basic set of abstractions that can be used easily for building more elaborated abstractions. Using micro-kernel architectures for building generic distributed object-based runtime systems has been undertaken by at least two projects: COOL-v2 [32] built on top of Chorus and GUIDE-v2 [18] built on top of Mach. Although the resulting systems have shown promising results from the standpoint of performance, the use of a specific underlying operating system is restrictive from the standpoint of portability. Furthermore these systems lack of flexibility in that the system's customization is addressed only at the language-level.

Due to the evolution in the fields of networking and processor technology, distributed architectures now support the execution of different kinds of applications (e.g., scientific, multimedia) having different requirements. This raises the need for application-specific operating systems (e.g., see [4]), that is to say, systems that can be customized at the application-level. The construction of application-specific operating systems brings up several issues including the ease of customization specification by the application programmers, and the provision of adequate base operating systems so as to easily support safe and efficient customization. Much work has been undertaken both in the operating system and the programming language communities in order to address these needs. This has led to complementary solutions that can be summarized as follows:

- Specialization of the system's code through partial evaluation by exploiting the applications' invariants (e.g., see [37]), which eases the process of customization specification by providing an automatic solution.
- Definition of new operating system kernels so as to support efficient and safe customization (e.g., see [13, 22]).
- System structuring in terms of high-level abstractions so as to ease the customization process both from the perspective of its specification and of its integration. Most of the existing solutions in that framework exploit the object paradigm. An example of such is the Choice operating system that is structured in terms of objects, the inheritance mechanism being used for customization [17]. Another example is the Apertos operating system that defines a reflective architecture by means of the meta-object notion [42]. This system introduces a meta-level that defines control and policy, which can be customized by modifying the meta-level components [33].

In the framework of the INRIA Solidor research group, we are investigating solutions for efficient execution of concurrent object-oriented applications through customization. Our approach follows the Choice approach. We have designed and implemented a minimal distributed object-based runtime system, called Isatis. Isatis is defined in terms of C++ objects and can be easily customized through the inheritance mechanism. We are now concentrating on the provision of solutions that allow *safe* customization of Isatis for *efficient* execution of applications that can be written in different object-based languages and that can execute on different operating systems. Our approach for safe customization relies on the exploitation of type conformance [15]. We further address enhancement of the applications' performance by designing new policies for distributed object management. This paper focuses on this last aspect by providing an introduction to the Isatis system and discussing its customization with the integration of a load balancing strategy.

This paper is structured as follows. Section 2 first introduces the Isatis architecture, discussing its object and execution models. Section 3 then illustrates the integration of an elaborated load balancing strategy within Isatis; the proposed strategy implements novel policies for transparent, initial-placement of method executions and migration according to both processors' loads and objects' features. Finally, we draw some conclusions in section 4.

2 The Isatis System

In this section, we provide an overview of the Isatis distributed object-based runtime system. We first give the background to the Isatis design. We then define the Isatis model, and introduce objects managed by the Isatis system. Finally, we examine the usage of the Isatis system from the perspective of both different object-oriented languages and different underlying operating systems.

2.1 Background

The design of the Isatis system was primarily motivated by our previous experience with the design and implementation of two distributed object-based programming systems: Gothic [6] and Arche [8]. Although this work led to promising results from the standpoint of specific object management mechanisms (e.g., fault tolerance mechanism for Gothic [7], and garbage collection for Arche [38]), the proposed distributed object-based systems were not entirely satisfactory for several reasons. Among them, let us mention the systems' poor performance and lack of portability. We thus decided to adopt a generic approach in order to solve these shortcomings but also to be able to implement more easily our research results in the field of distributed object-oriented programming, at the level of both programming languages and object management mechanisms.

Due to the wide range of research results in the field of distributed object-based systems, the approach undertaken for the design and implementation of Isatis' base features first consisted of exploiting existing proposals. The resulting process of selection led us in particular to examine work on the treatment of inter-process communications and multi-threading. From the standpoint of inter-process communication management, our goal was to support various communication methods as for instance achieved in the Network objects [14] and Concert/C [5] proposals. Due to the object-oriented framework, we based our solution on the one of Network objects that consists of defining transport objects managing connections between address spaces. Our implementation of multi-threading is based on the the Rex LWP library developed at Imperial College (London, UK) [20]. The main reason that led to this choice is that Rex LWP was the studied package embedding the least amount of hardware-dependent code.

2.2 The Isatis Model

The Isatis model is defined by its object model –i.e., the characterization of the objects it manages– and its execution model –i.e., the characterization of its execution units.

The object model. An Isatis object follows the usual definition: an object is made of a state and a set of methods that provide the only means to manipulate the object's state. Fine grain (less than a page) objects to coarse grain (segment) objects are equally supported by the system. Objects can communicate through either synchronous or asynchronous method calls. Objects are passive by default but active objects can be easily implemented by using the asynchronous method call mechanism.

Creation as well as destruction of objects is explicit by default. Although implicit destruction of objects is desirable from the perspective of reliability, its implementation requires the integration of an additional mechanism within Isatis. This obviously follows from the fact that Isatis supports programming models offering passive objects as well as models defining active objects. Garbage collection techniques being different for these two kinds of models (e.g., see [30]), their implementation depends upon the programming language to execute and hence requires system customization.

Although not addressed in the remainder of this paper, an object can be explicitly declared as being persistent, in which case its lifetime is independent of the one of its creator. Object mobility over the network is supported through a migration mechanism. However, the base Isatis system does not implement any migration policy.

The execution model. The base abstraction of the Isatis execution model is the notion of protection delegate [8]. A protection delegate is a distributed set of multi-threaded protection domains (e.g., multi-threaded processes using the Unix terminology, tasks using the Mach terminology), the number of protection domains being fixed at creation-time. A protection delegate corresponds roughly to an application and may be related to the notion of job offered in the GUIDE-v2 model [18].

Isatis objects belonging to the same application are mapped within the same protection delegate. Communication between objects belonging to the same protection delegate is achieved in two different ways depending on whether they belong to the same protection domain or not. In the former case, communication is achieved via a simple procedure call if the method call is synchronous while it leads to the creation of a thread handling the call if the method call is asynchronous. On the other hand, communication between objects belonging to distinct protection domains is carried out as for method calls involving objects belonging to different protection delegates, by means of a Remote Procedure Call (RPC).

2.3 Isatis Objects

Isatis objects are implemented in the C++ language. Customization of the objects' behavior according to the needs of either a particular application, language, or operating system then relies upon specialization of Isatis classes by system programmers by means of the C++ inheritance mechanism. We identify two kinds of Isatis objects, those implementing system-controlled functionalities and those implementing application objects. There is at most one instance of each system-controlled object per protection domain of each protection delegate. On the other hand, the number of application objects within protection delegates is application-specific.

System-controlled objects. System-controlled objects fall into three main categories that respectively correspond to the management of protection domains, multi-threading, and inter-process communication. An object managing a protection domain carries the information needed to implement system mechanisms, this includes the identification of peer protection domains and the description of the embedded application-objects.

From the standpoint of multi-threading, we have extended the Rex LWP library developed at Imperial College (London, UK) [20]. Resulting objects are those implementing threads and synchronization.

Finally, objects implementing inter-process communications follow the Network objects proposal [14] that deals with method invocations over a network. The base principle of the undertaken solution consists of implementing transport objects that generate and manage connections between protection domains (where involved domains may either belong to the same protection delegate or not). Various specializations of transport objects may coexist within the system so as to be able to deal with different communication methods. In our current prototype, we have implemented two kinds of transport objects: one that directly uses TCP and one that is implemented on top of the PVM system [24]. Connection objects are further introduced and correspond to connections that are established between domains.

Application objects. An application object translates into a set of Isatis objects: one corresponds to the object's naming, and the other to the object's representation.

Naming objects are the Isatis objects implementing references to representation objects. They are introduced in order to support mobility of actual objects. A naming object embeds the last known information about the actual object's location, that is, the identifier of the protection delegate p embedding the actual object, the identifier of the hosting protection domain d of p, and the object's address within d. A naming object further embeds a reference to either the corresponding actual object if locally present or to the local proxy otherwise. As for the location information, the reference is the last known one and hence can be erroneous in the presence of object migration. Since the base Isatis system does not implement any migration policy, information carried out by naming objects is necessarily accurate.

A given application object translates into a local and a distributed representations. The local representation corresponds to the object's actual implementation while the distributed representation enriches this base representation with distribution management. An object's local representation is implemented by means of a single Isatis object. On the other hand, the distributed representation of an application object $\mathcal{O}$ is implemented by the following Isatis objects:

- $\mathcal{O}$'s distribution manager that implements in particular policies for initial-placement of method executions and for object migration, its base behavior is described hereafter;
- $\mathcal{O}$'s proxies that manage remote references to $\mathcal{O}$, they basically implement an RPC to $\mathcal{O}$; and
- $\mathcal{O}$'s server stubs defined for both $\mathcal{O}$'s local representation and $\mathcal{O}$'s distribution manager.

Isatis objects introduced above rely on the definition of the four following C++ classes; these classes together with their descendants are called Isatis application classes in the remainder of this paper:

- t_identification that serves as a basis for implementing naming objects,
- t_generic_object that is inherited from:
  - t_remote, used for implementing remote referencing, that is to say, proxies and stubs
  - t_actual, used for implementing representation objects, that is to say, local representations and distribution managers.

The Isatis objects implementing a given application object are obtained by defining classes inheriting from t_identification, t_remote, and t_actual. Subclasses of t_identification and t_remote add method implementations for each method declared by the interface of the target application object while subclasses of t_actual provide the object's actual implementation. By default, the subclass of t_actual implementing the distribution manager of an object $\mathcal{O}$ is defined by implementing each method m of $\mathcal{O}$ according to the algorithm given hereafter.

(1)   placement: Selection of the node N for m execution
(2)   if N is remote then
(3)   migration:
(4)   Transfer of $\mathcal{O}$ within the protection domain located on N
(5)   Transfer of the call request to N
(6)   else local execution of m

Customization of Isatis from the standpoint of distribution management is in particular achieved by implementing the functions placement and migration (lines 1,3) as virtual methods. By default, the placement method selects the local node, and the migration method transfers the object's local representation for the duration of the method execution. The algorithm's structure allows a wide range of customization of object distribution management. This includes the integration of strategies for load balancing and object replication. Section 3 discusses customization of this base algorithm so as to implement a load balancing strategy according to the nodes' load and objects' features.

2.4 Using the Isatis System

We have stated that one of our main design goals for the Isatis system was to support the execution of different object-oriented languages above different base operating systems. In the following, we discuss how this goal is achieved.

Execution above different operating systems. Executing Isatis above different operating systems follows from Isatis' structure. The structure allows (system-)programmers to refine the system's classes according to the target operating system. This applies in particular to classes implementing thread management and inter-process communication. At that time, the Isatis prototype executes above nodes executing either Unix or Mach.

System classes may also be specialized so as to implement stronger semantics. For instance, the semantics of the base RPC mechanism of Isatis is the weakest one, that is, synchronous or asynchronous, maybe, single destination semantics. Depending on application requirements, more elaborated RPC semantics may have to be offered (e.g., see [26, 28]). In the framework of Isatis, integrating method calls based on RPCs with stronger semantics amounts to implement subclasses of the base RPC classes of Isatis.

Executing different object-oriented languages. Executing a given object-oriented language above Isatis requires the translation of each user-defined class in terms of the corresponding Isatis application classes. It follows that a modification of the compiler is required as in GUIDE-v2 [18]. However, given the implementation of Isatis objects described in the previous subsection, this step is quite straightforward.

At that time, our prototype supports the execution of applications written in an extended version of the C++ language as well as applications written in the Arche concurrent object-oriented language [12]. The first compiler of the Arche language generated C code to be executed on a dedicated distributed object-based runtime system [8]. Due to the features of the Isatis system, we have modified the compiler so as to generate C++ code. To give an idea of the manpower needed to execute a given language above Isatis, modification of the Arche compiler, within Isatis took us approximately 0.5 man-month.

3 Enhancing Isatis Performance through Load Balancing

Efficient execution of distributed object-based applications relies in particular on an adequate placement of objects on the system's nodes. Ideally, such a placement must be made so as to optimize the two conflicting criteria that are the number of message exchanges and the processors' loads. In general, processor allocation policies offered by existing distributed object-based systems such as Argus [34], Clouds [21], Doom [36], Emerald [39] and Guide [31], are simple. The node to be used for executing a method is selected among one of the following: object's storing node, calling node, and node explicitly mentioned by the programmer. A study has been undertaken in our group in order to integrate a transparent load balancing facility within the Arche distributed object-based system [8], dedicated to the execution of Arche applications. Results of this research are reported in [11]. Briefly stated, they consist of a migration policy that computes the objects' best storing nodes with respect to both communication costs and memory usage, and a policy, qualified as adaptive, for best initial-placements of method executions with respect to both processors' loads and objects' features. Compared to the Isatis system, the Arche system differs in several points. In particular, Arche protection domains belonging to the same protection delegate communicate through distributed shared memory, and Arche objects are (implicitly) persistent.

In the framework of the Isatis system, we have undertaken the design of a load balancing strategy based on the proposal made for the Arche system. The next subsection provides an overview of the resulting strategy. It is followed by a discussion on its integration within Isatis in subsection 3.2. Subsection 3.3 then addresses the gain due to the integration of the load balancing strategy within Isatis.

3.1 Overview of the Load Balancing Strategy

The time taken by the execution of a method invocation is given by adding the three following times:

(i) The time taken for locating the storing node of the called object,
(ii) The time taken for transferring the request to the storing node, and
(iii) The time taken for executing the method, either on the object's storing node (*local* execution) or on another node (*remote* execution).

Our goal in the design of a load balancing strategy was to provide a transparent facility that minimizes these three components, assuming a network of homogeneous workstations. This led us to define :

- An initial-placement policy for minimizing (iii), and
- A migration policy so as to co-locate communicating objects on the same node, and hence minimizing (i–ii).

In order to minimize the costs due the implementation of the load balancing strategy, the initial-placement and migration policies are coupled. However, for the sake of clarity, they are introduced separately in the following.

Adaptive initial-placement of method executions. In a message-passing framework in which objects are not replicated and communicate by synchronous method calls, the time taken by a method execution once the invocation request is received on the storing node of the called object, is given by the addition of the four following components.

1. Time required for transferring the call request to the node selected for the method's execution –it includes the time taken for moving the called object to the selected node if remote;
2. Waiting time within the chosen processor's ready queue before the method is started;
3. Method execution time, which is further split in:
    3.1. Actual execution time (cpu);
    3.2. Waiting time within the processor's ready queue, which is attributable to processor sharing;
    3.3. Waiting time resulting from interaction with other objects, that is to say, (synchronous) method calls performed by the method;
4. Time taken for returning the result to the caller.

The processor to be used for executing a method should be chosen so as to minimize the time resulting from the combination of these four components. Considering subcomponents of 3, sub-component 3.1 does not vary since a network of homogeneous workstations is considered. Hence, sub-component 3.1 is discarded. The evaluation of sub-component 3.2 depends upon the method's actual execution time (sub-component 3.1), which is not known before the method's execution. The value of 3.1 could be approximated by recording the average execution times of methods within the objects' states. However, as we have not yet foreseen if the resulting overhead would be negligible, we chose in a first approach to ignore the value of sub-component 3.2. Minimizing the value of sub-component 3.3 amounts to have communicating objects located on the same node, this is addressed through the migration policy, complementary to the initial-placement policy. Let i be any of the system's nodes on which the considered application executes, the remaining components (1,2,4) lead to the definition of two sets of decision criteria:

- T_{pro_i}, which is the decision criterion related to the nodes' loads (component 2).
- T_{trans_i} and T_{res_i}, which are the decision criteria related to the called method (components 1 and 4). T_{trans_i} is the time taken for transferring the call request on node i in a message, which is given by the input parameter size and the object's size. T_{res_i} is the time taken for transferring the result message from i to the caller's node.

At a first glance, the node i that must be chosen for executing a method is the one that minimizes the addition of T_{pro_i}, T_{trans_i}, and T_{res_i}. However, the soundness of an addition-based approach has to be demonstrated since we consider multiple, independent criteria that possibly conflict. For that purpose, we have used the multi-criteria evaluation theory (e.g., see [23]) that serves solving decision problems where multiple criteria, often conflicting, have to be taken into account. Using the multi-criteria theory, it has been shown in [11] that the decision placement for a method m of an object $\mathcal{O}$ could be taken according to the evaluation of the function $Wait$ defined as follows.

$$Wait(\mathcal{O}, \mathtt{m}, i) = T_{pro_i} + T_{trans_i} + T_{res_i}.$$

Given the function $Wait$, the algorithm computing adaptive initial-placement for the execution of a method $\mathtt{m}$ of the object $\mathcal{O}$ is straightforward; it consists of the two following steps:

- **Step 1.** Computation of the set *eligible* of eligible nodes for executing $\mathtt{m}$, that is to say, nodes $\{i_1, ..., i_n\}$ such that $\forall j \in \{i_1, ..., i_n\}$:
    - $j \in hosts(\mathcal{O})$ where $hosts(\mathcal{O})$ identifies nodes on which execute protection domains of the protection delegate embedding $\mathcal{O}$, and
    - $Wait(\mathcal{O}, \mathtt{m}, j) \leq Min(Wait(\mathcal{O}, \mathtt{m}, k), k \in hosts(\mathcal{O})) + threshold$, where *threshold* is a system-defined parameter that sets the range of selection.
- **Step 2.** Selection of the node that will execute $\mathtt{m}$ among components of *eligible*. This selection is computed randomly by default. However, it may be computed with respect to additional preference criteria specified by the programmer; for instance, this can be the preference for the node hosting the highest number of actual objects invoked by $\mathtt{m}$.

Efficient computation of the system's global load. The quality of the adaptive initial-placement algorithm depends upon the relevance of the global load information that is used. Best results are obtained when the information is close to the system's actual load and when the overhead of the algorithm handling exchange of load messages is kept as minimal as possible. The algorithm that we use is called *controlled exchange* [9] and is based on a *periodical* exchange of load information (e.g., see [10]). The periodical exchange approach is recognized as an adequate basis with respect to the global load's relevance. However, it is less satisfying from the perspective of the number of exchanged messages since it is based on message broadcasting.

Basically, the controlled exchange algorithm enhances the periodical approach as follows. Periodically, a node i sends its new local load value to a node j only if this value makes i *approximately eligible* for executing a method of an object located on j. In this definition, the eligibility notion refers to the one used by the adaptive initial-placement algorithm. Furthermore, eligibility is approximated with respect to node j, that is, if i's load is such that a local execution on j will not be preferred.

More formally, given the periodical reception of a load message from node k, node i sends a load message to node k if the following function:

$$eligible_i(k) = load_i(k) - load_i(i) + threshold > mc$$

evaluates to true, where *load* is the global load vector maintained on each node and *mc* is the cost of sending the smallest invocation message between any two pairs of nodes.

It should be noticed here that a mutual non-eligibility problem can occur if both $eligible_i(k)$ and $eligible_k(i)$ evaluate to false; load messages are no longer exchanged between i and k. In order to avoid this problem, any node i that detects the transition from $eligible_i(k)$ to $\neg eligible_i(k)$ for any node k, notifies the transition occurrence to k. Then, if i is notified the dual transition from k, one of the two nodes is selected for sending its load information on a non-controlled, periodical basis.

Object migration. In the presence of a high number of inter-object communications, a mechanism implementing an adequate placement of objects in addition to the adaptive initial-placement of method executions is required. Ideally, an object placement policy must be designed so as to reduce the applications' communication costs, which is mainly achieved by storing communicating objects on the same node. The design of such a policy has been undertaken in our group for the Arche distributed object-based system [11], and is aimed at the migration of persistent object. The proposed migration policy, that is complementary to the initial-placement policy, executes in parallel with the application. It consists of initially placing any object on the node of its creator and then migrating the object according to its interactions with other objects.

In the framework of Isatis, we have devised an alternative migration policy aimed at parallel object-based applications that is suitable for volatile objects. In order to minimize the execution overhead due to the migration policy, our solution consists of coupling the migration decision for an object together with the adaptive initial-placement decision, introduced previously. The migration of an object is examined only when one of its method is invoked. Furthermore, on the invocation of a method of an object $\mathcal{O}$ the only node considered for migration of $\mathcal{O}$ is the node selected for the method's execution. Migration of $\mathcal{O}$ then depends on its interactions with objects located on the remote node considered for migration compared to its interactions with objects located on the other nodes, including its current node. An alternative solution for selecting the node on which an object $\mathcal{O}$ is to be migrated would have been to take into account all the nodes hosting objects communicating with $\mathcal{O}$. We did not retain this solution because it increases the migration's communication cost.

The algorithm for implementing object migration is simple. Once a remote node is selected for a method execution, it is checked whether the embedding object $\mathcal{O}$ should be migrated on this node according to the number of interactions that took place between $\mathcal{O}$ and (objects on) this node compared to the interactions of $\mathcal{O}$ with the other nodes. More precisely, given the function $\mathcal{C}(N, \mathcal{O})$ that returns the number of interactions of $\mathcal{O}$ with objects located on node N, and assuming that N_i is the node selected for the method's execution by the adaptive placement policy[1], the migration algorithm is defined as follows:

· If N_i is remote and is such that $\forall N_j \in hosts(\mathcal{O})$: $\mathcal{C}(N_i, \mathcal{O}) \geq \mathcal{C}(N_j, \mathcal{O}) + threshold$,

---

[1] It can be noticed here that the information keeping count of object interactions could be taken into account in the step (2) of the algorithm implementing the adaptive placement decision so as to select for execution the node that minimizes the communication cost of the method's execution.

· then $\mathcal{O}$ is migrated on N_i

· else a copy of $\mathcal{O}$ is transferred on N_i for the duration of the method's execution.

3.2 Integrating the Load Balancing Strategy within Isatis

The integration of the load balancing strategy discussed above within Isatis leads to the following extensions:

· Introduction of system objects implementing controlled-exchange of load information,
· Refinement of the application classes so as to implement the proposed placement and migration policies.

It should be noticed here that, at that time, the proposed enhancement of Isatis has been made only for Arche applications; it follows that most of the implementation is written in the Arche language.

Implementing the controlled-exchange algorithm. The implementation of the controlled-exchange algorithm relies on two system-controlled objects defined by classes load and loadExchange.

The class load defines data-objects carrying global load information, that is, the load of processors hosting peer protection domains. In a Unix framework, which is the platform used for performance measures sketched in subsection 3.3, the local load related to a protection domain is obtained from the number of threads in the ready queue of the protection domain plus the number of processes of the processor's ready queue.

The class loadExchange defines service-objects sending their local load information to instances of load located within peer protection domains. It implements the controlled-exchange algorithm.

As for other system-controlled objects, there is a single instance of both load and loadExchange per protection domain of each protection delegate. These objects are further made known to application objects through a specialization of system-controlled objects managing protection domains (see § 2.3); each of these objects now embeds a reference to the local instance of loadExchange, and references to all the instances of load created within peer protection domains.

Implementing adaptive initial-placement and migration. The integration of the proposed initial-placement and migration policies amounts to modify the behavior of the objects' distribution manager introduced in subsection 2.3: virtual methods placement and migration are redefined so as to respectively implement the adaptive initial-placement decision, and migration policy. In particular, the migration action now consists of transferring either the object's local representation in the absence of migration but in the presence of remote execution, or both the object's local representation and distribution manager in the presence of migration. We get the following structure for the redefinitions of **placement** and **migration**:

placement:
Selection of the node N for **m** execution according to the adaptive initial-placement policy;

migration :
migrate := decision of migrating $\mathcal{O}$ on N;
if migrate
then transfer on N of
both $\mathcal{O}$'s distribution manager and $\mathcal{O}$'s local representation
else transfer on N of $\mathcal{O}$'s local representation
fi;
Transfer of the call request on $\mathcal{O}$'s local representation to N;
if not migration then gets the modified copy back of $\mathcal{O}$'s local representation fi

Let us notice here that the number of message exchanges due to a remote execution of **m** and to a migration of $\mathcal{O}$ depends on the sizes of the called object and of the input parameters.

The proposed placement and migration policies are implemented by an Arche class, called **Placement**, that can be inherited by any application class. This class redefines the virtual methods **placement** and **migration** of t_actual as sketched above. It further declares a reference to the built-in Arche class **domain** whose instance implements a system-controlled object managing the embedding protection domain (see § 2.3). Such an object allows to access system-controlled information including load information as well as the description of embedded application objects. The redefinition of **placement** subsumes computation of criteria T_{pro_i}, T_{trans_i}, and T_{res_i} so as to implement adaptive initial-placement decision. The criterion T_{pro_i} is computed by means of instances of system-controlled classes **load** and **loadExchange**. Assuming the invocation of a method **m** of $\mathcal{O}$, let us now examine the computation of method-related criteria T_{trans_i} and T_{res_i}. Criterion T_{trans_i} is evaluated from the size of $\mathcal{O}$ and **m**'s input parameters, and from the copying information for $\mathcal{O}$, which values are obtained from the local instance of **domain** that interfaces with the system. Finally, the evaluation of T_{res_i} depends upon the size of **m**'s result, which is obtained from the signature of **m**[2].

3.3 Assessment of the Load Balancing Strategy

In [9], performance measures of Isatis implementing the proposed adaptive initial-placement policy and the default migration policy have been compared with the

---

[2] Let us notice here that this applies in the case of Arche applications due to the fact that objects are passed by reference, a more complex computation would be required should objects be passed by value, due to subtyping.

ones of the base Isatis system that executes systematically a method on the storing node of its embedding object. The application considered for performance measures was a simple parallel application made of independent computations. Results show that the response times of applications using the default placement policy can be divided by up to a factor of ten when using the adaptive initial-placement policy. This figure is obtained when there is a large difference between the loads of the most and least loaded nodes. A small overhead (negligible if the method duration is important) is paid when the nodes are too lightly loaded and/or equally loaded.

So as to measure the benefits due to the migration policy, we have been running a simple parallel application made of communicating objects. As for results discussed above, the application's performance is significantly increased when the application is run on a system with unequally loaded nodes. Furthermore, the coarser grain the objects are, the higher is the gain due to our load balancing strategy.

For a complete evaluation of the load balancing strategy, we now need to run real applications. We are currently implementing well-known scientific applications in the Arche language towards this goal. However, the results we have obtained so far suggest some remarks from the standpoint of the customization process. In particular, since the load balancing strategy is mainly beneficial for coarse-grain objects, customization of application objects with the proposed load balancing strategy should be considered accordingly by the application programmers. Better performance could further be obtained by supporting dynamic customization according to the environment's features through the adaptive programming technique [25]. This would allow to execute the load balancing strategy only when the load of the system's nodes is unbalanced. However, mechanisms implementing adaptive programming technique being not mature at that time, we prefer to concentrate on static customization.

Although our first results concerning the load balancing strategy have to be complemented with performance measures of real applications, some enhancements of the load balancing strategy can already be envisioned.

As stated in subsection 3.1, the adaptive initial-placement algorithm makes the placement decision independently of the method durations (sub-component 3.1 of methods response time is discarded). This leads to underestimate the benefit of remote executions. In [9], comparison of the base adaptive initial-placement policy with a policy taking into account the methods' expected duration shows that this knowledge can further lower applications' response times if the methods' expected duration is close to their actual duration. We are currently investigating the integration of such a knowledge in the adaptive initial-placement algorithm.

Finally, it should be noticed that the proposed load balancing strategy implements initial-placement and migration among nodes hosting the application which are fixed at creation time. This strategy could be complemented by an underlying one that would allow dynamic selection of nodes hosting the application; an example of such a strategy can be found in [27].

4   Conclusion

Despite its advantages for distributed programming, the object paradigm has had a moderate success in the distributed systems community due to the poor performance exhibited by distributed object-based applications. The inefficiency of distributed object-based applications being mainly due to the mismatch between the abstractions of object-based programming languages and the ones of traditional operating systems, customizable distributed object-based runtime systems such as COOL-v2 [32] have been introduced. Such systems allow to define the best mapping between language and system abstractions, and their performance tends to make the object-based distributed programming model as good a candidate as other distributed programming models for the development of distributed applications. However, so as to make execution of applications as efficient as possible, customizable distributed object-based runtime systems must support customization at the application-level, hence allowing the development of application-specific systems (e.g., see [4]). Furthermore, mechanisms for distributed object management aimed at improving performance, like for instance load balancing, have to be devised.

Summarizing the Isatis experience. This paper has introduced the Isatis customizable distributed object-based runtime system developed at IRISA within the INRIA Solidor research group. The Isatis system is aimed at allowing the execution of distributed object-based applications written in different object-based languages, above various operating systems. It further supports customization at the application-level. The system's customizability is mainly achieved through its implementation in terms of C++ classes: Isatis customization amounts to implement subclasses of Isatis' base classes. At that time, our prototype supports the execution of applications written in either the Arche concurrent object-oriented language [12] or an extended version of C++. Furthermore, Isatis is currently implemented on top of SUN SPARC stations running SunOS, as well as on PCs running Mach.

Customization of the Isatis system has been illustrated through the integration of a load balancing strategy aimed at enhancing the applications' performance. The proposed strategy implements adaptive initial-placement of method execution and object migration. The placement policy is called adaptive as node selection for method execution is computed according to both processors' loads and objects' characteristics. The migration policy is coupled with the adaptive placement policy. On the invocation of a method of an object $\mathcal{O}$, the only node considered for migration of $\mathcal{O}$ is the node selected for the method's execution by the adaptive placement policy; migration of $\mathcal{O}$ then depends on its interactions with objects located on this node compared to its interactions with objects located on the other nodes. Integration of the load balancing strategy within Isatis is straightforward: it relies on a class implementing the placement and migration policies that can be inherited by any application class, an on the implementation of two system-level classes computing the system's global load. Performance of the Isatis system customized with the proposed load balancing strategy has been compared with the base Isatis system that does not support object migration and that implements the simple alternative initial-placement policy consisting of executing any method on the storing node of the called object. Results show that the response times of applications executing above the base Isatis system can be divided by up to a factor of ten when using the load balancing strategy.

In addition to the Isatis customization detailed in this paper, we have studied customization of the Isatis system so as to support different failure semantics for remote method calls. In particular, we have examined the implementation of the *at-most-once* failure semantics, based on the proposal of [29]. Briefly sketched, the resulting customization leads to refine transport objects so as to manage stable data structures keeping track of active remote calls, and to implement algorithms for orphan detection, orphan destruction, and detection of abnormal terminations.

Although not yet examined, another Isatis customization that could be considered is the introduction of the garbage collector dedicated to the Arche language and presented in [38]. The proposed garbage collector is comprised of a collection of local garbage collectors, loosely coupled to a global garbage collector. Each local collector identifies and reclaims the objects that can be detected to be garbage on a local basis, while it communicates with the global collector to get/provide information related to objects that possibly reference/are referenced by remote objects. The integration of such an algorithm within Isatis is close to the integration of the algorithm performing controlled exchange of load information. The local collectors together with the global collector would be implemented by means of system-controlled objects, exchanging information about object referencing.

As mentioned in the introduction, there has been much work in the field of system customization. Proposals aimed at defining new operating system kernels (e.g., see [13, 22]) should be seen as complementary to our work: Isatis could be ported above such kernels. Considering solutions oriented towards system structuring, the Isatis structuring is close to the one of the Choice operating system [17]. However, compared to this proposal, our work contributes from the standpoint of the design and integration of new policies for distributed object management.

Current and future work. In this paper, we have focused on the use of the customization approach at the application-level from the standpoint of performance enhancement. We are currently investigating complementary issues relevant to the customization process. These are mainly aimed at supporting safe system customization [15]. From the perspective of safe customization, we are examining how to enrich the type conformance relation so as to guarantee that a customized system object exhibits a behavior that is compatible with the one of the object it replaces. Briefly, our approach consists of extending the behavioral subtyping relation [3, 35] so as to integrate system-level specification within types. We are further designing new kernel mechanisms that ensure safe and efficient system customization when a type-unsafe programming language is used for implementing customized system functions [16]. Basically, the proposed mechanisms enforce isolation of the applications software components from the software components implementing the customized functions.

Acknowledgments: The authors would like to acknowledge Manuel Chevalier, Eric-Olivier Lebigot and Joel-Yann Fourré for participating to the implementation of the load balancing strategy.

References

1. M. Accetta, R. Baron, W. Bolosky, D. Golub, R. Rashid, A. Tevanian, and M. Young. Mach: A new kernel foundation for Unix development. In *Proceedings of the Usenix 1986 summer Conference*, pages 93–112, 1986.
2. P. America. Pool-T: a parallel object-oriented language. In *Object-Oriented Concurrent Programming*, pages 199–220. MIT Press, 1987.
3. P. America. A Behavioural Approach to Subtyping in Object-Oriented Programming Languages. Technical report, Philips Research Laboratory, Eindhoven, The Netherland, 1989.
4. T. E. Anderson. The Case for Application-Specific Operating Systems. Technical Report UCB/CSD 93/738, Computer Science Division, University of California Berkeley, Berkeley, California, USA, 1992.
5. J. S. Auerbach, A. S. Gopal, M. T. Kennedy, and J. R. Russel. Concert/C: Supporting distributed programming with language extensions and portable multi-protocol runtime. In *Proceedings of the Fourteenth International Conference on Distributed Computing Systems*, pages 152–159, 1994.
6. J. P. Banâtre and M. Banâtre, editors. *Les systèmes distribués : l'expérience du système Gothic*. InterEditions, 1991.
7. J.P. Banâtre, M. Banâtre, and G. Muller. Ensuring data security and integrity with a fast stable storage. In *Proceedings of the fourth International Conference on Data Engineering*, pages 285–293, 1988.
8. M. Banâtre, Y. Belhamissi, V. Issarny, I. Puaut, and J. P. Routeau. Arche: A framework for parallel object-oriented programming above a distributed architecture. In *Proceedings of the Fourteenth International Conference on Distributed Computing Systems*, pages 510–517, 1994.
9. M. Banâtre, Y. Belhamissi, V. Issarny, I. Puaut, and J. P. Routeau. Adaptive placement of method executions within a customizable distributed object-based system: Design, implementation and performance. In *Proceedings of the Fifteenth International Conference on Distributed Computing Systems*, pages 279–287, 1995.
10. A. Barak and A. Shiloh. A distributed load balancing facility for a multicomputer. *Software Practice and Experience*, 15(9):901–913, 1985.
11. Y. Belhamissi. *Placement des calculs et des données dans un système distribué à objets*. Thèse de doctorat, Université de Rennes I, Rennes, France, 1994.
12. M. Benveniste and V. Issarny. Concurrent Programming Notations in the Object-Oriented Language Arche. Research Report 1822, INRIA, Rennes, France, 1992.
13. B.N. Bershad, S. Savage, P. Pardyak, E. Gunder, M. Fiuczynski, D. Becker, S. Eggers, and C. Chambers. Extensibility, safety, and performance in the SPIN

operating system. In *Proceedings of the Fifteenth ACM Symposium on Operating Systems Principles*, pages 267–284, 1995.

14. A. Birrel, G. Nelson, S. Owicki, and E. Wobber. Network objects. In *Proceedings of the Fourteenth ACM Symposium on Operating Systems Principles*, pages 217–230, 1993.

15. C. Bryce, V. Issarny, G. Muller, and I. Puaut. Towards safe and efficient customization in distributed systems. In *Proceedings of the Sixth SIGOPS European Workshop: Matching Operating Systems to Application Needs*, Schloss Dagstuhl, Germany, 1994.

16. C. Bryce and G. Muller. Matching micro-kernels to modern applications using fine-grained memory protection. In *Proceedings of the Seventh IEEE Symposium on Parallel and Distributed Processing*, 1995.

17. R. H. Campbell, N. Islam, R. Johnson, P. Kougiouris, and P. Madany. Choices: Framework and refinement. In *Proceedings of the 1991 International Workshop on Object Orientation in Operating Systems*, pages 9–15, 1991.

18. P. Y. Chevalier, A. Freyssinet, D. Hagimont, S. Krakowiak, S. Lacourte, J. Mossière, and X. Rousset de Pina. Persistent shared object support in the Guide system: Evaluation and related work. In *Proceedings of the Ninth ACM Conference on Object-Oriented Programming Systems, Languages and Applications*, pages 129–144, 1994.

19. R. S. Chin and S. S. Chanson. Distributed object-based programming systems. *ACM Computing Surveys*, 23(1):91–124, 1991.

20. S. Crane. The Rex Lightweight Process Library. Technical report, Imperial College, London, UK, 1994.

21. P. Dasgupta, R. C. Chen, S. Menon, M. P. Pearson, R. Ananthanrayanan, R. J. LeBlanc, M. Ahamad, U. Ramachandra, W. F. Appelbe, J. M. Bernabéu-Auban, P. W. Hutto, M. Y. A. Khalidi, and C. J. Wilkenoh. The design and implementation of the Clouds distributed operating system. *Computing Systems*, 4(3):243–275, 1990.

22. D. R. Engler, M. Franz Kaashoek, and J. O'Toole. Exokernel: An operating system architecture for application-level resource management. In *Proceedings of the Fifteenth ACM Symposium on Operating Systems Principles*, pages 251–266, 1995.

23. P. C. Fishburn. A survey of multi-attributes/multi-criteria evaluation theories. In *Lecture Notes in Computer Science 155*, pages 181–224. Springer-Verlag, 1978.

24. G. A. Geist and V. S. Sunderam. Network-based concurrent computing on the PVM system. *Concurrency: Practice and Experience*, 4(4):293–311, 1992.

25. M. G. Gouda and T. Herman. Adaptive programming. *IEEE Transactions on Software Engineering*, 17(9):911–921, 1991.

26. G. Hamilton, M. L. Powell, and J. G. Mitchell. Subcontract: A flexible base for distributed programming. In *Proceedings of the Fourteenth ACM Symposium on Operating Systems Principles*, pages 69–79, 1993.

27. C. J. Hou, K. G. Shin, and T. K. Tsukada. Transparent load sharing in distributed systems: Decentralized design alternatives based on the condor package. In *Proceedings of the Thirteenth Symposium on Reliable Distributed Systems*, pages 202–211, 1994.

28. Y. M. Huang and C. V. Ravishankar. Designing an agent synthesis system for cross-RPC communication. *IEEE Transactions on Software Engineering*, 20(3):188–198, 1994.

29. V. Issarny, G. Muller, and I. Puaut. Efficient treatment of failures in RPC systems. In *Proceedings of the Thirteenth Symposium on Reliable Distributed Systems*, pages 170–180, 1994.

30. D. Kafura, M. Mukherji, and D. W. Washabaugh. Concurrent and distributed garbage collection of active objects. *IEEE Transactions on Parallel and Distributed Systems*, 1995.

31. S. Krakowiak, M. Meysembourg, H. Nguyen van, M. Riveil, and C. Roisin. Design and implementation of an object-oriented strongly typed language for distributed applications. *Journal of Object-Oriented Programming*, 3:11–22, 1990.

32. R. Lea, C. Jacquemot, and E. Pillevesse. COOL: System support for distributed object-oriented programming. *Communications of the ACM*, 36(9), 1993.

33. R. Lea, Y. Yokote, and J. Itoh. Adaptive operating system design using reflection. In *Proceedings of the French-Japanese Workshop on Object-Based Parallel and Distributed Computation*, 1995.

34. B. Liskov. Distributed programming in Argus. *Communications of the ACM*, 31(3):300–312, 1988.

35. B. Liskov and J. Wing. A new definition of the subtype relation. In *Proceedings of ECOOP'93*, pages 118–141, 1993.

36. Odjik. The DOOM system and its applications: A survey of Esprit 415 subproject A, Philips research laboratory. In *Proceedings of PARLE - Parallel Architectures and Languages Europe*, pages 461–479, 1987.

37. C. Pu, T. Autrey, A. Black, C. Consel, C. Cowan, J. Inouye, L. Kethana, J. Walpole, and K. Zhang. Optimistic incremental specialization: Streamlining a commercial operating system. In *Proceedings of the Fifteenth ACM Symposium on Operating Systems Principles*, 1995. 314-329.

38. I. Puaut. A distributed garbage collector for active objects. In *Proceedings of the Ninth ACM Conference on Object-Oriented Programming Systems, Languages and Applications*, 1994.

39. R. K. Raj, E. Tempero, H. M. Levy, A. P. Black, N. C. Hutchinson, and E. Jul. Emerald: A general purpose programming language. *Software Practice and Experience*, 21(1):91–118, 1991.

40. M. Rozier, V. Abrossimov, F. Armand, I. Boule, M. Gien, M. Guillemont, F. Herrmann, P. Léonard, S. Langlois, and W. Neuhauser. The Chorus distributed operating system. *Computing Systems*, 1(4):305–370, 1988.

41. A. S. Tanenbaum, R. Van Renesse, H. Van Staveren, G. J. Sharp, S. J. Jansen, and G. Van Rossum. Experiences with the Amoeba distributed operating system. *Communications of the ACM*, 33:46–63, 1990.

42. Y. Yokote. The Apertos reflective operating system: The concept and its implementation. In *Proceedings of the 1992 ACM Conference on Object-Oriented Programming Systems, Languages, and Applications*, 1992.

Lessons from Designing and Implementing GARF

Rachid Guerraoui   Benoît Garbinato   Karim Mazouni

Département d'Informatique
Ecole Polytechnique Fédérale de Lausanne
1015 Lausanne, Switzerland
e-mail: garf@lse.epfl.ch

Abstract. GARF is an object oriented system aimed to support the design and the programming of reliable distributed applications on top of a network of workstations. The specificity of GARF resides in its incremental programming model, and its extensible library of generic components. In this paper, we first give an overview of GARF. Then we assess its features with respect to its programming model, its abstraction library, and the implementation of its prototype. We finally present the perspectives of future design and implementation.

1   Introduction

1.1   Distribution and reliability

Programming distributed reliable applications is a hard task. The complexity of such applications is due to their *behavioral* features, i.e. concurrency expression and concurrency control, distribution and replication.

Several reliable distributed toolkits provide primitives that deal with such behavioral features. Isis [2], Psync [19], Transis [1] and Phoenix [16] are examples of such toolkits. Although powerful, these toolkits are at a too low level (Unix process level), and thus are very difficult to use for programmers without a broad experience in programming distributed and reliable applications. Systems like Arjuna [14] or Electra [15] support a higher programming level (object level) and provide adequate primitives for remote object invocation, object replication and object group invocations. Since these primitives must nevertheless be mixed with application *functional* features (i.e. sequential and centralized aspects), they hamper extensibility and modularity. For example, an application written in a centralized context cannot be directly reused for a distributed and reliable purpose. Furthermore, as stated in [20], adding new abstractions for reliable and distributed programming cannot be done in a straightforward way.

1.2   GARF Characteristics

GARF is an object-oriented system aimed to support the design and programming of reliable distributed applications, at a higher level than existing toolkits such as Isis, Psync, Transis and Phoenix. More precisely, GARF can be viewed as an intermediate between these toolkits and the application. The first prototype of GARF is actually based on Isis, and a new prototype is currently under developement on top of Phoenix. In comparison to systems like Arjuna or Electra, GARF promotes software modularity by clearly separating the behavioral features that concern concurrency, distribution and reliability, from functional ones than concern traditional sequential and centralized aspects.

GARF encourages an incremental programming methodology. First, the GARF programmer may design and implement application components in a centralized environment, focusing only on their functionalities. In further steps, without modifying the previously written code, the programmer may turn to behavioral features, by expressing and controlling concurrency, distributing the application over a network, and replicating its critical components to increase the reliability. Of course, all these steps, including the first one, may be performed concurrently, but the code written for different steps is separated.

GARF offers an extensible *behavioral* library of abstractions for various kinds of concurrency controls, remote object invocations, e.g *synchronous/asynchronous*, as well as for object group invocations, e.g *reliable/fifo/causal/atomic*. These abstractions enable to support for example both *passive* and *active* object replication [3]. GARF abstractions can be chosen according to the application semantics. An experienced programmer can implement new behavioral abstractions by combining existing abstractions, or even by using low level mechanisms provided by the *system* library of GARF. The current prototype of GARF has been implemented in Smalltalk on top of Isis. This prototype was used for the development of a reliable distributed diary manager on a network of Sun workstations [5].

1.3 Assessment and perspectives

The aim of this paper is to give a global overview of GARF, and then to present some feedbacks on its design and implementation. Among the lessons learned are:

- *Static object/behavior association is enough:* in the development of "classical closed" applications in a distributed context, there is no need for changing the behavior of objects at run-time.

- *One meta level is enough:* GARF introduce *encapsulators* and *mailers*, which can be viewed as *meta objects* [13], dedicated to describe object *communications*. The need for *meta objects* describing additionnal features such as ressource management was not identified, and the utility for *meta meta objects*, which describe the behavior of meta objects, is not obvious at all.

- *The asymmetric proxy model is too restrictive:* when considering replicated objects that can act as clients and servers in the same time, the classical proxy model (used in GARF) may lead to a proliferation of useless invocations, and even to inconsistencies in the case of updates. We discuss this issue and show how a symmetric model is more adequate in this case.

— *Behavioral classes are not independent:* the independence of the behavioral classes offered by GARF is not straightforward, and several pairs of classes are strongly coupled. This is actually not surprising as each behavioral class represents a specific abstraction for distributed programming, and these abstractions are rarely orthogonal.

— *Integrating transactions requires a flexible underlying toolkit:* the current GARF prototype is based on the Isis toolkit [2]. Although this toolkit has facilitated the implementation of GARF, the fact that it does not support transactions makes it difficult to maintain the consistency of several inter-related groups of object replicas. This situation occurs for example in the distributed diary manager application written with GARF. Porting GARF on top of Phoenix [11] will fortunately enable to circumvent this limitation.

1.4 Paper overview

We first recall the GARF programming model in Section 2. To illustrate the model, we briefly describe a reliable distributed application written in GARF: the reliable distributed diary manager. Then we give an overview of GARF architecture and implementation in Sections 3 and 4. The assessment of GARF is presented in Section 5. This assessment was done with respect to (1) the programming model, (2) the library of built-in abstractions, and (3) the current implementation. According to this assessment, we present some perspectives on GARF future development in Section 6. We finally summarize the GARF principal features and some future development.

2 GARF Programming model

In this section, we present the GARF programming model, which we illustrate through an application written in GARF: the reliable distributed diary manager.

2.1 GARF objects

GARF handles three kinds of objects: *data* objects, *behavioral* objects and *system* objects.

1. **Data objects** are passive entities that communicate in a *point-to-point, synchronous, request/reply* manner. A request is an operation invocation. It involves two objects: a *client* which invokes the operation, and a *server* on which the operation is invoked. The reply (returned to the client) represents the result computed by the server when executing the invoked operation.

2. **Behavioral objects** can be viewed as *"meta data objects"* [13], used to describe behavioral features (i.e. concurrency, distribution, and reliability) of data objects. GARF supports two kinds of behavioral objects, *encapsulators* and *mailers*.

   - **Encapsulators** are used to *wrap* data objects by controlling the way they treat incoming and outcoming requests. GARF provides a library of encapsulator classes (Section 3). For example, the class **Replica** enables to create multiple replicas of a data object, in order to increase its availability.
   - **Mailers** are used to perform (remote) communications between encapsulators. GARF provides a library of mailer classes (Section 3). For example, the mailer class **Abcast** ensures that all replicas of an encapsulator receive concurrent requests in the same order.

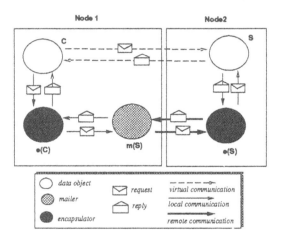

Fig. 1. data objects and behavioral objects

Figure 1 describes the runtime relation between data objects and behavioral objects. There are two data objects, C and S, two encapsulators e(C) and e(S), and a mailer m(S) that handles the communications between the encapsulators.

3. **System objects** implement the low level mechanisms on which encapsulator and mailer classes are based. For example, the system class **Group** is used by the encapsulator class **Replica**.

2.2 Programming levels

The three kinds of objects supported by GARF convey three corresponding programming levels: (1) the *data level*, (2) the *binding level* and (3) the *system level*.

1. At the **data level**, the programmer describes, in terms of data classes (classes of data objects), functional aspects of the application in a centralized environment. At this level, the programmer needs not be familiar with concurrent, distributed, or reliable programming.

2. At the **binding level**, the programmer turns to concurrency, distribution, and reliability by binding data objects to adequate behavioral objects (i.e encapsulators and mailers). At this level, the programmer has to be familiar with the meanings of concurrent, distributed, and reliable abstractions. *Behavioral* classes are chosen according to the semantics of the application (see Section 2.3).

3. At the **behavioral level**, the programmer extends the library of behavioral classes. The programmer either combines existing behavioral classes to derive new ones, or uses *system objects* [6, 7]. At this level, the programmer must be familiar with the GARF system, and even with the underlying toolkit in case he tries to define new system classes. Note that this task is only necessary if the built-in behavioral library does not contain the desired abstractions.

2.3 Example: the reliable distributed diary manager

We illustrate the GARF programming model by describing the design of a reliable distributed application implemented with GARF. We give here a brief description of the application. More details can be found in [7]. We first present an overview of the application, then we sketch the functional and binding level. There was no need for programming at the behavioral level for this application.

Overview: The aim of the application is to handle the diaries of a group of persons, by enabling the automatic planning and cancellation of meetings. A diary is associated to its owner through a diary index which manages a list of user name and diary pairs. A diary stores the list of meetings to which its owner participates. Each meeting is composed of a period and a list of participants. A diary service is a user-interface. It enables to list all diary owners, to create or delete a diary, to plan or cancel a meeting with other owners, and to list all the meetings a user is expected to attend. The required reliability feature of the application is that, as long as its machine is up, a user must always be able (1) to consult its diary, and (2) to schedule a meeting with every other user of which machine is also up[1].

Functional level: At the functional level, we designed mainly four data classes: `DiaryIndex`, `Diary`, `Meeting`, and `DiaryService`. Class `DiaryIndex` implements operations returning a diary given a user name, listing the names of all

---

[1] We do not assume link failures here.

diary owners, and adding or removing a user. This class has one instance: the **diary index**. Class **Diary** implements operations that allow to list all the meetings contained in a diary and to update the latter. This class has one instance per user. Class **Meeting** implements operations allowing to list its participants, to give the meeting period and to remove a user from the participant list. Each time a user plans a meeting, a new instance is created. Note that an instance of **Meeting** is shared by all the participants in the meeting. Finally, class **DiaryService** describes the user-interface. An instance of this class is created each time a user starts to work with the application.

Binding level: At this level, the design of the application is extended with behavioral features, using encapsulator and mailer classes.

- **Behavioral classes:** Since the application is intended to support several users at the same time, the **diary index**, **diaries** and **meetings** may be accessed concurrently.
  1. The **diary index** is a critical component. We want it to be replicated on each node where the application is running. Furthermore, the **diary index** must exist even though no user is registered.
  2. A **diary** is always present on the node of its user.
  3. The replication rate of a **meeting** depends on the number of the participants in the **meeting**. Indeed each participant has a replica of all its **meetings** on his node. This way, even though all other nodes have crashed, on can still consult its meetings through its diary.
  4. As said before, a **diary service** is the user-interface. It disappears when its user decides to stop working. Therefore it is not replicated at all and is always on the node of his user.

  The encapsulator class which provides the desired behavior for replication is the class **ActiveReplica**: it ensures that all replicas treat an invocation, and return a reply. As long as one replica is alive, a reply is returned. The mailer class **Abcast** ensures that all the replicas are invoked in the same order, and hence ensures strong consistency. Furthermore, a mailer of this class selects one reply among all (the first one to arrive), and forwards it to the encapsulator.

- **Binding behavioral objects to data objects:** Data objects of a class **D** are bound to encapsulators and mailer classes at runtime, during the execution of the specific operation **garfNew:** on **D**. This operation is inherited by every data class and invoked whenever a data object is created. By default, the **garfNew:** operation binds each data object to an encapsulator of the basic class **Encapsulator**, and to the mailer class **Mailer**. These classes only forward local communication and do not perform any particular treatment. Hence, the main programming task at the binding level consists of modifying the **garfNew:** implementation, which is done in three steps (see figure 2):

1. Creation of an encapsulator at the specified node.
2. Creation of the data object and binding the encapsulator to it [2].
3. Creating a mailer and binding the encapsulator [3] to it.

```
garfNew: aCreationMessage

(step 1)   encaps := ActiveReplica groupOn: Set new add: 'lsesun1' add: 'lsesun2'.

(step 2)   encaps buildAndBind: self sending: aCreationMessage

(step 3)   mailer:= Abcast to: encaps.

           ...
```

Fig. 2. A garfNew: operation

Figure 2 shows an example of a **garfNew:** operation, which actively replicates the **diary index** on two nodes: 'lsesun1' and 'lsesun2'. The (strong) consistency of the replicas is maintained thanks to the **Abcast** mailer class, which ensures that concurrent requests are received in the same order.

The first step consists in creating an encapsulator of the class **ActiveReplica** and replicating it on two nodes 'lsesun1' and 'lsesun2'. The second step consists in creating the data object and binding the encapsulator to it. The third step consists in binding the encapsulator to the mailer class **Abcast**. The result of the **garfNew:** operation is shown in Figure 4.

3 GARF Architecture

GARF is not intended to be used in a stand-alone fashion, but rather on top of a reliable distributed toolkit, which provides low level primitives for remote communication, group management, and reliable multicast communication. The first GARF prototype has been implemented in Smalltalk, on top of the Isis toolkit. The GARF/Isis interface is written in C (Figure 3).

The GARF system is composed of a runtime and three class libraries: the *encapsulator* library, the *mailer* library, and the *system* library:

3.1 GARF run-time

The GARF runtime manages centralized object creation and communication, as well as associations between data objects and behavioral objects, specified by programmers. GARF runtime handles these associations by intercepting data object creation and communication.

---

[2] The data object is created on the encapsulator's node.

[3] And hence the data object.

GARF System (Smalltalk)	GARF RunTime	Data classes Behavioral classes System classes	Mailer classes Encapsulator classes
			GARF Libraries
GARF / Isis (C)	GARF/RDT Interface		
(Isis)	Reliable Distributed Toolkit		
(Unix + TCP/IP)	Operating System + Network layer		

Fig. 3. GARF software layers

Each data object S is bound to an encapsulator (e(S)), and to a mailer (m1(s)) (see Figure 1). The data object and its encapsulator, i.e. S and e(S), are always located at the same node. The runtime redirects each communication to and from S through e(S). The encapsulator can thus control the behavioral features of the data object such as concurrency and replication. A clone m(S) of the mailer m1(S) is created whenever S is invoked by an object C. The mailer m(S) is located on the node of C and acts as a proxy of e(S): m(S) forwards the invocation to e(S). In Figure 4, S is bound to an encapsulator of the class **ActiveReplica** and to a mailer of the class **Abcast**. As shown in the figure, a mailer of the class **Abcast** transforms a *point-to-point* invocation into a reliable totally ordered multicast on a group of replicas. The replicas in the figures are S1 and S2, respectively attached to the encapsulators e(S)1 and e(S)2.

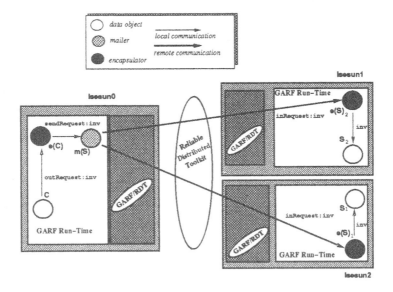

Fig. 4. GARF execution model

The GARF execution model can be described more accurately as follows:

- The GARF runtime intercepts each invocation **inv** from a data object client **C** on a data object server **S**, and *transforms* it into the invocation of the operation **outRequest:** on **e(C)**, with **inv** as an argument. The operation **outRequest:** is inherited from the basic class **Encapsulator** and redefined in the subclasses presented in Figure 5.
- **e(C)** executes operation **outRequest:** which invokes the operation **sendRequest:** on **m(S)** (with **inv** as argument). The operation **sendRequest:** is inherited from the basic class **Mailer** and can be redefined in the subclasses presented in Figure 5 (b).
- **m(S)** executes operation **sendRequest:** which forwards the invocation (possibly through a multicast as shown on Figure 4) to **e(S)** by invoking operation **inRequest:** (with **inv** as an argument) on it. Operation **inRequest:** is inherited from the basic class **Encapsulator** and refined in the subclasses presented in Figure 5 (b).
- **e(S)** executes the operation **inRequest:** and finally transmits the invocation **inv** to **S**.
- The reply follows the reverse *route*.

3.2 GARF abstractions

Encapsulator library: encapsulator classes are subclasses of the basic class **Encapsulator**, which provides two operations: **inRequest** and **outRequest**. These operations handle the way data objects receive and send requests. Defining encapsulator classes consists of programming these operations inside subclasses of **Encapsulator**. GARF provides a library of encapsulator classes (Figure 5 (a)) that handle concurrency expression (class **Active**), concurrency control (classes **Mutex** and **ReadersWriter**), and replication (classes **PassiveReplica** (passive replication), and **ActiveReplica** (active replication)). These classes are also detailed in [6] and [7].

Mailer library: mailer classes are subclasses of the basic class **Mailer** which provides the operation **sendRequest**. This operation handles the way communications are performed between encapsulators. Defining mailer classes consists of programming this operation inside subclasses of **Mailer**. GARF provides a library of mailer classes (Figure 5 (b)), which handle synchronous and asynchronous remote invocations (classes **Srpc**, and **Arpc**, as well as various models of multicasts (classes **Mcast** (reliable multicast), **Fbcast** (*fifo* reliable multicast), **Cbcast** (causal reliable multicast [2]), and **Abcast** (atomic reliable multicast [2])). These classes are also detailed in [6], [7], and [10].

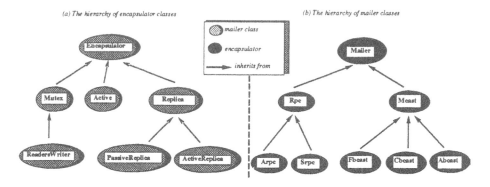

Fig. 5. GARF encapsulator and mailer classes

System library: this library contains a set of classes called *system* classes, of which instances are the *system* objects. These objects represent the main abstractions provided by the underlying toolkit. In our current prototype, the underlying toolkit is Isis, and system classes provided by GARF are for example: class **Group** for object group management, class **Future** for asynchronous invocation handling, and classes **ClassName** and **ObjectName** for invocation interception (as discussed in Section 4.1).

4 GARF Implementation

4.1 GARF runtime

The GARF runtime is in charge of centralized object management (i.e. object creation and communication), as well as associations between data objects and behavioral objects. Since the GARF runtime is an extension of the Smalltalk runtime, local object management is done by the latter.

Associations between data objects and behavioral objects are handled during data object creation and communication. The GARF runtime intercepts each invocation **new:** on a data class **D**, and transforms it into a **garfNew:** invocation on **D**. The runtime also intercepts each invocation from a data object **d**, and transforms it into an **outRequest:** invocation on **d**'s encapsulator. These interceptions are supported by two classes that we have implemented: **ClassName** and **ObjectName**.

– **ClassName:** during the initialisation phase of a GARF application, all data classes are substituted, within the Smalltalk **Dictionary**, by instances of the class **ClassName**. Hence, whenever the **new:** operation is invoked on a data class **D**, **new:** is actually invoked on the corresponding **ClassName** instance **cn(D)**. Since **cn(D)** does not provide the operation **new:**, the Smalltalk runtime raises an exception by invoking on cn(D) the operation doesNotUnderstand:, which we have implemented within the class ClassName, in such a way that it invokes the operation garfNew: on the data class D.

- ObjectName: the garfNew: operation performs the actual new:, to create a data object d, but it does not return d's reference. It rather returns an instance n(d) of the class ObjectName, which owns the reference to d. Hence, when an operation is invoked on d by a client c, it is actually invoked on n(d). Since n(d) does not provide such an operation, the Smalltalk-80 runtime raises an exception by invoking on n(d) the operation doesNotUnderstand:, which we have implemented within the class ObjectName, in such a way that it invokes the operation outRequest: on c's encapsulator.

4.2 GARF abstractions

In the following, we describe the behavioral classes presented in Figure 5, and the system classes used for their implementation.

- **Encapsulator classes:** the implementation of these classes consisted in re-defining the operations inRequest: and outRequest: inherited from the basic class Encapsulator. To implement the classes Mutex and ReadersWriter (both classes deal with concurrency control), we have redefined the operation inRequest:, so as to perform every operation of the associated data object in a *critical section* (with a well known semantic in the case of the ReadersWriter class). This implementation uses objects of the system class Semaphore provided by Smalltalk. To implement the class Active: (which offers *client asynchrony*), we redefined the operation outRequest:, in such a way that it creates a dedicated process for each invocation from the associated data object. The process is used to wait for the reply. This behavior enables the client to continue its execution after the invocation, and to obtain the reply at a later stage (using a *future* object). The implementation uses the system class Process provided by the Smalltalk environment, and the system class Future that we have implemented [6]. Neither operation inRequest: nor outRequest: are redefined in the class ActiveReplica. Indeed, an encapsulator of this class only forwards invocations and replies, to and from its associated data object: an actively replicated object acts as if it was not replicated [3]. The operation inRequest: has been redefined in the class PassReplicated, so that only one replica (the oldest created) treats an invocation, returns the reply, and then sends its state to other replicas.

- **Mailer classes:** Mailers act as proxies of encapsulators (Figure 4). In the current implementation of GARF, every encapsulator is represented by a *group* which corresponds to a set (possibly with a single element) of identical copies of an object. A group abstraction is implemented by an instance of the system class Group. To benefit from group membership monitoring and communication primitives provided by Isis, we have directly mapped

GARF encapsulator groups on Isis process groups. The GARF/Isis interface is a set of C routines called within Isis threads, for each communication between some mailer and its corresponding encapsulator (through operation sendRequest:). Every encapsulator invocation (through its group name) by a mailer is translated by the GARF/Isis interface into an Isis multicast. Object communications are coded and decoded using the BOSS (*Binary Object Streams Services* classes provided by Smalltalk.

To avoid interference between Smalltalk-80 processes and Isis threads, we implemented the GARF/Isis interface inside a dedicated Unix process.

The classes Arpc *(server asynchrony)* and Srpc *(server synchrony)* are used for non-replicated encapsulator invocation. Both classes use however the class Group, with the special case of a single element in the group. The class Arpc uses in addition the classes Process and Future (to handle asynchrony). All Mcast subclasses use class Process, and each of these classes represents a specific multicast semantics supported by Isis.

4.3   Performances

Our measurement was carried out using a Sun SPARCstation equipped with 32 Mbytes RAM and running Solaris 2.2. The measurement took place on normal workday, so the workstation had medium to high load: it was running XWindows as well as interactive applications (emacs, mosaic, etc.).

The GARF runtime introduces an overhead factor of 70 without considering distribution and reliability. Indeed, a normal (neither encapsulator nor mailer are associated to objects) Smalltalk invocation of an object has a response time of $9\mu s$. When intercepted by the GARF runtime and redirected to mailers and encapsulators, the read invocation takes $628\mu s$. The reasons for such a high factor have to do with how Smalltalk virtual machine executes and how it handles exceptions. During normal execution, the virtual machine is partially bypassed and object operations directly execute on the physical processor. When an exception is raised however, the virtual machine reinterprets the operation that caused the exception, which makes the execution much slower. This is what happens with the operation doesNotUnderstand:.

The time spent in the GARF runtime and in data objects is however small compared to $251ms$ a read invocation takes when objects are distributed and replicated. This test scenario was based on the example introduced in Figure 4, i.e. some client object interacts with a server object that is replicated twice. Using ActiveReplica encapsulators and Abcast mailers, the client invokes a read operation on the replicated server and receives an integer managed by the server as a reply.

5   Assessment

In this section, we assess the main features of GARF, considering (1) its programming model, (2) its abstraction libraries, and (3) the implementation of its prototype. The assessment is based on several developments done with GARF in extending its abstraction libraries, on the implementation of the reliable distributed diary manager, and on the performance measures. This assessment must not be viewed as a general assessment on the design and implementation of object based distributed systems.

5.1 Programming model

Incremental programming is nice: One of the fundamental characteristics of GARF is its incremental way of programming. One can focus on different aspects of an application at different stages of the development. This incremental approach was very convenient in the design and implementation of the distributed diary manager application. It was very helpful, first to test the sequential aspects, second to consider concurrency, and then to deal with distribution and reliability (i.e replication). The code written in each step has never been modified at a later step.

There are applications for which this incremental way of programming can however not be easily applied. For example, several applications are intrinsically concurrent and it is not possible to separate their sequential features from their concurrent behaviors. There are also cases where taking into account the distribution aspect, at an early stage in the object design, can lead to better performances. We believe that, in these situations, even if different aspects are treated in the same time, modularity and reusability are increased by separating the code related to each aspect.

Static association is enough: The GARF programming model is based on the associations between data objects and behavioral objects. These associations are performed at runtime (i.e dynamically), which enable for example to change the encapsulator associated to a data object. We believe however that such a feature is not necessary and these associations could be done in a static way, and once for all. Applications that would require a dynamic association scheme, are those that necessitate dynamic change of behavior. These "open" applications, such as operating systems, are actually out of the scope of GARF.

One meta level is enough: Encapsulators and mailers can actually be viewed as meta data objects since they describe how data objects behave [21]. The GARF model can thus be considered as a *pragmatic* reflexive model as it offers only *one* meta level: encapsulators and mailers do not have objects that describe their behaviors. Furthermore, encapsulators and mailers are used only for specific purpose: *communication*. We believe that such a pragmatic model is enough, and the need for a very general reflexive architecture is not obvious at all.

The asymmetric model is too restrictive: The GARF model is intrinsically asymmetric. There is a mailer which represents the server encapsulator at the client node, but there is no mailer at the server node to represent the client encapsulator. The reason of this asymmetry is that the mailer is a generalization of a proxy, and the proxy model is fundamentally asymmetric. For most of the cases we have encountered, the GARF asymmetric model suffices to describe the desired behaviors.

Nevertheless, there is a specific, yet important, case where this asymmetric model is too restrictive. This case is related to replication and the fact that objects are at the same time clients and servers. More precisely, when both a client and a server are actively replicated, there is a risk of useless invocation replication. Each replica of the client would invoke all the server replicas. If the server itself invokes another server, we will have a proliferation of useless invocations. This may even lead to inconsistencies if the invocations perform state changes. This problem is discussed in details in [17, 18], and we will sketch the way we plan to handle it in Section 6.

5.2 Behavioral abstractions

The main abstractions offered by GARF, in the form of encapsulator and mailer classes, have mainly been inspired by the underlying communication toolkit, i.e Isis. These abstractions represent various point-to-point and multicast communication primitives. We first discuss in the following the lack of orthogonality of these abstractions and its impact on programming. Second, we discuss the fact that two fundamental behaviors are difficult, if not impossible, to represent with these abstractions: persistence and transactions. Note that this is not due to the GARF model itself, but to the restricted set of abstractions offered.

Behavioral classes are not independent: Whereas the behavioral classes offered by GARF might appear at first glance independent (see Figure 5), in fact they are not. Several pairs (encapsulator class, mailer class) are actually strongly coupled and this implies that the programmer does not have a complete free choice of his combinations. This is actually not surprising as each behavioral class represents a specific abstraction for distributed programming, and these abstractions are rarely orthogonal. For example, the encapsulator class **ActiveReplica** can only be used with the mailer class **Abcast**. This is a consequence of the fact that the active replication strategy relies on a total order multicast primitive.

Persistence: In order to ensure the persistence of an object, one must store the object state on a stable storage at the end of each session, and to restore this state at the beginning of another session. This is for example necessary, in the distributed diary manager application, for the **index** which provides the correspondences between the users and their diaries. The state of the **index** must not be lost if the application stops running.

With the abstractions currently offered by GARF, no implicit support for persistence is offered. One must explicitly design and implement an encapsulator class which stores and restores, to and from stable storage, the object state.

Transactions: The abstractions offered by GARF, such as the class Abcast, are very convenient to ensure the consistency of replicated objects. A mailer of the class Abcast guarantees that invocations on a replicated object are performed on all replicas or on none of them, and concurrent invocations are performed in the same order. In the distributed diary manager application for example, this is adequate to manage the replication of the index.

A limitation of such abstractions is however that they ensure consistency when atomic activities concern a single replicated object, e.g. updating the index. There are however cases where an atomic activity concern several replicated objects. In the distributed diary application, "scheduling a meeting" is not handled correctly. Indeed, a meeting is scheduled if the date is free for all the involved users. Hence, scheduling a meeting implies an *atomic* update to several diaries. When each diary is replicated, and represented by a group, a meeting implies an atomic activity that involves several groups (i.e a transaction). Ensuring the atomicity of such activity is impossible with the GARF current abstractions. More accurately, the only way to ensure such atomicity is to create a huge super-group which contains all replica groups. This limitation is due to the Isis underlying reliable distributed toolkit (and group-oriented systems in general), where the notions of groups and consistency are strongly coupled. We will discuss in Section 6.2, how porting GARF on the Phoenix [11, 12] platform, will enable to provide such abstractions.

5.3 Implementation

Interpreter vs compiler: In GARF, redirection of invocations is a central issue, since the clear separation of functional and behavioral aspects relies on this mechanism. The GARF runtime performs these redirections while objects execute. The GARF runtime can thus be seen as an interpreter in charge or redirecting parts of the invocations. A compiler approach, based on a preprocessor, would perform redirections at compile time. The choice of an interpreter approach was motivated by our will to build a first prototype as quickly as possible. Smalltalk was a good choice for this purpose. Its reflective facilities, e.g the doesNotUnderstand: mechanism, and the flexibility in debugging, confirm the commonly agreed assertion that Smalltalk is very well suited for prototyping. Of course, basing GARF on the Smalltalk virtual machine has a negative impact on performance. However, we were quite surprised to see that although not optimized at all, GARF gives acceptable response times, as far as user driven applications (e.g diary manager) are concerned.

The underlying toolkit: Basing GARF on an existing reliable distributed toolkit, i.e Isis, presents several advantages. Reliable multicast primitives are easily implemented (at the object level) since they were all provided by Isis (at the Unix process level). The current version of Isis can be considered as a very stable technology, and our prototype has benefited from this stability, respecting the rule: "never use a prototype to implement a prototype".

However, as we have mentioned in the previous section, group-oriented systems like Isis make it difficult to ensure the consistency of activities involving several replicated objects (i.e transactions in the diary manager). Furthermore, the use of an underlying toolkit that manages groups at the Unix process level, poses the object groups/process groups mapping problem which, due to the difference in granularities, hamper performance. As we will discuss in Section 6, the porting of GARF on Phoenix will enable to handle transactions, and also to avoid the object/process mapping, since Phoenix offers groups at an object level.

Finally, as both Isis and Smalltalk have their own package of threads, we have decided to run both systems inside two different Unix processes (in order to avoid inter-schedulers interferences). This avoids rewriting the Isis scheduler, but the additional communication between the two processes was a performance penalty.

6 Perspectives

In this section, we discuss some perspectives on further design and implementation of GARF.

6.1 Towards a symmetric model

We intend to extend the GARF model, in order to deal with situations such as replication of clients and servers. The basic idea is to come up with a symmetric model where there is a mailer that represents the server at the client node, and a mailer that represents the client at the server node. This model will be used to express the pre-filtering behavior [17, 18]. The pre-filtering consists in avoiding a useless replication of invocations when a client and its server are both replicated. The client mailers will actually be used to filter the invocations, in such a way that only one invocation is forwarded to the server's encapsulator.

6.2 Porting GARF on Phoenix

Extending the basic abstractions: The major characteristic of the Phoenix platform [11, 12] is that it decouples the notion of group from the consistency issues. Phoenix provides the notion of groups to represent replicated data for example, but groups are only viewed as an addressing capability. Reliable communications with consistency guarantees are designed in an orthogonal way to the notion of group. One can thus perform an atomic multicast on a set of group, without creating a super-group for this purpose. This enables to support transactions accessing several replicated objects, such as scheduling a meeting in the distributed diary application.

Direct mapping of object groups: Phoenix is an object-oriented system in two senses [4]. First, it is itself implemented in an object-oriented language and it has a modular and extensible structure. Second, it is aimed to support an object-oriented environment. More precisely, Phoenix offers communication and structuring mechanisms at an object level (rather than at a Unix process level as in Isis). Hence, objects groups in GARF will be directly mapped on Phoenix groups which will avoid the current performance penalty due to the object groups/process groups mapping.

6.3 A pre-compiler approach

As we have mentioned, the interpretor approach has permitted us to implement in a relatively short time a first prototype of GARF. This approach leads however to some performance limitations. For example, the 70 factor overhead is due to the dynamic redirection of invocations. Since a dynamic association scheme between data objects and behavioral objects is not actually necessary, we will experiment a pre-compiler approach. The basic idea is to use a pre-compiler in order to perform the association between data objects and behavioral objects at compile time, Hence no redirection will be necessary during the execution.

Among other optimizations, we will also integrate the Smalltalk system and the Phoenix system within the same Unix process. This will avoid extra communications between Unix processes.

7 Concluding remarks

The main motivation in constructing GARF was to simplify the design and implementation of reliable distributed applications. We wanted to enable such design and implementation at a higher level than existing reliable distributed toolkits such as Isis [2]. We believe that this goal is reached. The distributed diary application was initially written in our Lab, directly in Isis (before GARF was designed and implemented), and we could appreciate the difference in writting the application with GARF.

GARF enforces an incremental programming methodology, where a reliable distributed application can be designed and implemented in several steps and by different programmers. The GARF architecture enhances software modularity, since different aspects of an application are implemented within independent classes: data classes implement functional features, encapsulator and mailer classes implement behavioral features, and system classes implement low level distribution and reliability mechanisms. This enables a programmer to modify the implementation of a behavioral class, e.g. a multicast class, without affecting the rest of the application. GARF also provides flexibility since new behavioral abstractions can be defined and added to the library. For example, by combining the mailer classes *Arpc* (asynchronous rpc) and *Mcast* (multicast), we can define a new mailer class that performs asynchronous multicasts. One of the main lesson learned from using GARF is that a pragmatic reflexive model is enough for a wide area of applications. In GARF, reflection is applied only to inter-object communication, and there is no recursivity in the model, i.e no meta meta object.

The main limitation of GARF is its abstraction library which we believe is too restrictive. As we have said in the paper, this library do not support, for example, a transaction accessing replicated objects. The porting of GARF on the Phoenix [11, 12] platform, which provides a broad range of communication primitives, will enable us to extend the GARF library and support various transaction models. Another limitation is the asymmetry of the programming model. We will extend this model towards a symmetric scheme, and experiment the new model for replication situations. Finally, the current prototype suffer from several drawbacks that hamper performance. We have sketched some possibilities to eliminate these drawbacks.

We are currently designing a new application with GARF: *a virtual private network*. This application is intended to allow the building of a logical private network by using the physical public network infrastructure instead of dedicated network resources (i.e leased lines).

Acknowledgements

A. Schiper, F. Pacull, B. Muganga and R. Mattman have all contributed in the GARF project. The GARF system is currently used in practical teaching of distributed computing (Msc projects) and we have greatly benefited from the feedbacks of the students.

References

1. Y. Amir, D. Dolev, S. Kramer, and D. Malki. *Transis: A Communication Sub-System for High Availability.* In Proceedings of International Symposium on Fault-Tolerant Computing. July 1992.
2. K. Birman and R. van Renesse. *Reliable Distributed Computing with the Isis Toolkit.* IEEE Computer Society Press. 1993.
3. F. Cristian. *Understanding Fault-Tolerant Distributed Systems.* In Communications of the ACM. February 1991.
4. P. Felber and R. Guerraoui. *Group Programming: an Object-Oriented approach.* In Proceedings of International Conference on Technologies of Object Oriented Languages and Systems. Prentice Hall. March 1995.
5. B. Garbinato, R. Guerraoui, and K. Mazouni. *Programming Fault-Tolerant Applications Using Two Orthogonal Object Levels.* In Proceedings of International Symposium on Computer and Information Science. November 1993.
6. B. Garbinato, X. Défago, R. Guerraoui, and K. Mazouni. *Abstractions pour la programmation concurrente dans GARF.* In "Calculateurs Parallèles" Journal, Hermes publisher. June 1994.

7. B. Garbinato, R. Guerraoui, and K. Mazouni. *Distributed Programming In GARF.* In Object-Based Distributed Programming. Springer Verlag, LNCS 791. June 1994.

8. B. Garbinato, R. Guerraoui, and K. Mazouni. *Implementation of the GARF replicated objects plateform.* In Distributed Systems Engineeting Journal, (2). 1995.

9. A.J Goldberg and A.D Robson. *SMALLTALK-80: The Language and its Implementation.* Addison Wesley publisher. 1983.

10. R. Guerraoui, B. Garbinato, and K. Mazouni. *The GARF Library of DSM Consistency Models.* Proceedings of ACM SIGOPS European Workshop on Operating Systems. September 1994.

11. R. Guerraoui and A. Schiper. *Transactional model vs Virtual Synchrony model: bridging the gap.* In Theory and Practice in Distributed Systems. Springer Verlag, LNCS 938. 1995.

12. R. Guerraoui and A. Schiper. *A Generic Primitive to Support Transactions on Replicated Objects in Distributed Systems.* In Proceedings of IEEE Future Trends on Distributed Computing Systems. Korea, 1995.

13. G. Kiczales, J. des Rivières, and D. Bobrow. *The Art of the Metaobject protocol.* The Mit Press, 1991.

14. M. Little, D.L. McCue, and S.K. Shrivastava. *Maintaining Information about Persistent Replicated Objects in a Distributed System.* In Proceedings of IEEE International Conference on Distributed Computing Systems. May 1993.

15. S. Maffeis. *Making Distributed Programs Object-Oriented.* In Proceedings of Usenix Symposium on Experiences with Distributed and Multiprocessor Systems. September 1993.

16. C. Malloth and A. Schiper. *View Synchronous Communications on Internet.* In Proceedings of 2nd Open Workshop of the Esprit Project BROADCAST (6360), 1995.

17. K. Mazouni, B. Garbinato, and R. Guerraoui. *Building Reliable Client-Server Software Using Actively Replicated Objects.* In Proceedings of International Conference on Technologies of Object Oriented Languages and Systems. Prentice Hall. March 1995.

18. K. Mazouni, B. Garbinato, and R. Guerraoui. *Filtering Duplicated Invocations Using Symmetric Proxies.* In Proceedings of IEEE International Workshop on Object Orientation in Operating Systems. Lund, Sweden, August 1995.

19. S. Mishra, L. Peterson, and R. Schlichting. *Implementing Fault-Tolerant Replicated Objects Using Psync.* In Proceedings of IEEE Symposium on Reliable Distributed Systems. October 1989.

20. S. Shrivastava. *Lessons Learned from Building and Using the Arjuna Distributed Programming System.* In Theory and Practice in Distributed Systems. Springer Verlag, LNCS 938. 1995.

21. Y. Yokote. *The Apertos reflective Operating System: The Concept and its Implementation.* Proceedings of ACM International Conference on Object-Oriented Programming, Systems, Languages and Applications. 1992.

22. M. Wood. *Replicated RPC Using Amoeba Closed Group Communication.* Proceedings of IEEE International Conference on Distributed Computing Systems. May 1993.

Design and Implementation of DROL Runtime Environment on Real-Time Mach Kernel

Kazunori Takashio *

Department of Computer Science,
The University of Electro-Communications
1-5-1, Chofugaoka, Chofu-shi, Tokyo, 182, Japan

Hidehisa Shitomi ** and Mario Tokoro ***

Department of Computer Science, Keio University
3-14-1, Hiyoshi, Kohoku-ku, Yokohama, 223, Japan

Abstract. This paper describes our design and implementation of a real-time object invocation model supported by the distributed real-time programming language DROL. The main characteristic of this model is the notion of least suffering. Least suffering assures users to be notified network and computer faults within a required timing constraint and supports rapid recovery from them. Consequently, this notion allows users to construct real-time applications on widely distributed environments. Through the design and implementation of a DROL runtime environment on the Real-Time Mach kernel, we examine costs of least suffering in a network-wide object invocation. We also show what functions are needed to real-time kernels to implement a distributed real-time programming environment.

1 Introduction

Now, the utility of distributed systems is widely recognized. And also, real-time computing in the distributed environment will play an important role for various applications. They include distributed multimedia systems, large scale air traffic control systems and satellite monitoring systems. These systems consist of multiple computer modules connected by high-speed networks. Thus, to construct such systems, we have to discuss how we modularize real-time software and what kinds of inter-module real-time communication protocol are required.

The main characteristic of "distributed" real-time computing is that there are network-wide interactions among real-time program modules. If we can use perfect networks and computers, it is easy to provide predictability of such a distributed real-time system. Perfect networks and computers mean that they

---

* Email: *takashio@cs.uec.ac.jp*
** Email: *shitomi@mt.cs.keio.ac.jp*
*** Email: *mario@mt.cs.keio.ac.jp*, Also with Sony Computer Science Laboratory Inc.
3-14-13 Higashi-Gotanda, Shinagawa-ku, Tokyo, 141, Japan.

never stop working, and therefore timing behavior is statically predictable. Unfortunately, networks and computers are not always reliable. Furthermore, it is not easy for an application to know when and where a certain network is disconnected or a certain computer is down. The lack of reliability and the lack of unique global view bring unexpected delays to message transmissions, or causes messages to be lost. Consequently, this makes it difficult to analyze the behavior of a distributed real-time system from a static and global viewpoint. In other words, it is hard to construct such a distributed real-time system when depending on the predictability of programs. Therefore, we need other methodologies or frameworks adaptable for widely distributed environments besides the notion of predictability.

One of the new frameworks is the notion of *least suffering* that we proposed in [10] [11] [12]. In these papers, we have pointed out that in the domain of distributed real-time computing, more autonomous real-time software modules are needed. They ought to behave as "self-defensive" activities. The notion of "least suffering" provides survivability for real-time modules[1]. That is, it notifies users of network and computer faults within the required timing constraint. Such faults include physical network faults, the overloading of router nodes and the down of computer nodes. It therefore guarantees rapid system recovery in the event of a fault. These benefits enable us to write highly modularized real-time programs and adopt these to widely distributed environments.

In [12], we introduced the notion of least suffering into the real-time communication mechanism of the *Distributed Real-time Object (DRO)* model. Moreover, to demonstrate the correctness of our programming model and to show that we can actually realize the model on real-time kernels, we designed and implemented a real-time programming language *DROL*, which is an extension of C++ based on the DRO model.

However, the previous version of DROL runtime environment implemented on the ARTS kernel [13] had several problems described below:

- Alternatives of computer architecture are limited. The ARTS kernel is running only on MC-680X0 architectures, such as Sun-3 and Sony-NEWS.

- Communication primitives supported by the ARTS kernel are based on the request/reply scheme. Thus, it provides less flexibility to construct object level communication protocols.

- The ARTS kernel does not support the trend of network media and network protocols.

To solve these problems, we have to switch the platform from the ARTS kernel to other real-time kernels.

---

[1] We also described that the modules should provide a dynamic and flexible QOS control mechanism such as imprecise computing [9] [8] [7]. We call this property *best service*. A module provides multi-modal services each of which requires different amount of computer resources. Then, a module selects an appropriate execution-mode at runtime dynamically, which is executable within a timing constraint.

In this paper, we adopted Real-Time Mach (RT-Mach) [14] as a new implementation platform, and built a DROL runtime environment *DROL/RtM* on it. Then, through the design and implementation of the runtime environment and the verification of its performance, we show the following two items:

- Costs of least suffering are lower than that of our scheme which we adopted in the ARTS kernel version, and

- What functions of real-time kernel are needed to implement a distributed real-time programming environment.

This implementation also makes a contribution to providing a distributed programming environment on RT-Mach, since it does not support any real-time language.

2 Brief Summary of DROL

An objective of our research project is to provide the framework for network-wide real-time application programming. As we discussed in [12], the main aspect of distributed real-time systems is that *applications must be guaranteed delivery of acknowledgments and notifications of network and computer failures within bounded times, so that they have time make their own decisions.* In the design phase of DROL, we have discussed the following three issues carefully:

- Fault detection, that is, how a client or a server finds the presence of network or computer fault and aborts current invocation;

- Notification of abortion, that is, whether it is necessary for the client to notify the server of the abortion; and

- Cooperative recovery, that is, how the client is guaranteed notification of a server's recovery from the failure.

We have also considered how to reflect such diversified application-level requirements in the communication model of our programming language.

In the following subsections, we will show brief summary of strategies adopted in the programming language DROL. Please, see [10] [11] [12] for details of language specifications such as object definition and creation, thread definition and creation, remote object invocation, and so forth.

2.1 Least Suffering Strategy

We can find object-oriented real-time programming models in the domain of real-time kernel [2] [6] [13] and that of real-time programming language [3] [4] [5]. Most of these models are based on the active object model and aim at modularizing real-time software. They encapsulate not only logical information but also timing information[2]. The models are sufficient for modularizing real-time software, but unfortunately are insufficient for realizing self-defensive computational

---

[2] We call this strategy *timing encapsulation*.

activities. Because they did not assume existence of unreliable communication channels.

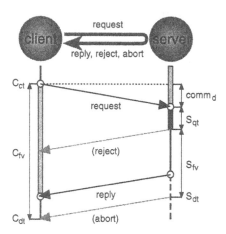

Fig. 1. Time Fence Protocol

Here, we point out a typical problem by citing an example of existing DRTS implementation, the Time Fence Protocol (TFP) [13]. TFP is a real-time remote object invocation protocol based on request/reply semantics. In TFP, the verification of an invocation timing constraint depends on a remote server object (Figure 1). In this scheme, method execution time allowed for a server, S_{fv}, is calculated using the following expression.

$$S_{fv} = C_{fv} - 2comm_d - S_{qt} \tag{1}$$

Where, C_{fv} corresponds to a timing constraint that the client object should satisfy. Notations $comm_d$ and S_{qt} show the estimated worst case delay time and the time elapsed in a server's message queue respectively. Let M_{wcet} be worst case execution time of a requested method. The timing correctness of the server object is verified by the next expression.

$$S_{fv} \geq M_{wcet} \tag{2}$$

If this condition does not hold, the server can reject the request for execution. Moreover, a server that has missed its deadline during method execution triggers a timeout and notifies the client. The client can then cause a timeout. However, if there is an unexpected delay in the message transmission, verification of the timing constraint based on expressions (1) and (2) may break down. In such situations, even if the client receives a reply message, it may be difficult to meet the client's deadline.

The semantics of the object invocation protocols proposed in DROL are based on the notion of *least suffering*. The least suffering strategy enables us to construct self-defensive software modules to guard against network and computer failures. In other words:

> *The system supports real-time object invocation for objects when it is physically possible, but if it is not, because of some network or computer fault, the system will notify the objects in bounded time, so that they will not have to wait for an indefinite amount of time.*

This provides the object with the opportunity to recover in its own way within a certain time frame, and keeps the decline of real-time facilities to a minimum.

DROL assumes the following types of faults:

- Physical network or computer troubles that cause messages to be lost; and
- Overloading of certain network segments or router nodes causing significant delay in message transmission.

Both failures result from the dynamic nature of distributed environments. In DROL, an object detects the presence of these faults by the timeout of a certain message reception. Here, we assume there is a pair of objects: one is a client object and the other is a server object. The client object invokes the server object by sending a request message. Upon receipt, the server object performs the requested service and returns a reply message. There is a strict timing constraint between the transmission of the request message and the reception of the reply message. The client informs the server of its timing constraint. Thus, the server does its best to meet the deadline. Unfortunately, if the reply message is not received by the client object by its invocation deadline, the system judges that some network or computer fault has occurred and notifies the client. Then, the client resumes its work and starts an exception.

In this way, to realize least suffering in an object invocation, DROL provide the framework for declaring a strict timing constraint as well as exception codes upon invocation [12].

2.2 Timed Object Invocation Protocols

We call invocation semantics that has a strict timing constraint and supports exceptions to realize least suffering *timed object invocation*.

DROL provides the following three synchronous invocation models as defaults[3]. Particularly, Timed Invocation (TI), Timed Invocation with Notification (TIwN) are real-time object invocation protocols based on the least suffering strategy. Each model is designed based on different application-level requirements, fault detection, notification of abortion and cooperative recovery, which are all discussed in the previous subsection. Details of protocol semantics are described in [12].

---

[3] In addition, DROL supports asynchronous remote object invocation: Asynchronous Timed Invocation with Notification (ATIwN).

Non-Timed Invocation

The semantics of *Non-Timed Invocation* (NTI) is equal to that of the Time Fence Protocol (TFP) [13] (see Figure 1). Using this semantics, a server can verify the timing correctness of a network-wide task execution. Thus, it does not support any mechanism for least suffering. Four messages are exchanged during one object invocation: *request, reply, reject notification,* and *abort notification.*

As mentioned in previous subsection, this communication semantics has some problems when used in widely distributed environments. Therefore, this is effective only in communications that do not require the least suffering strategy.

Timed Invocation

Timed Invocation (TI) is the simplest object invocation protocol supporting the least suffering strategy. Each client can trigger the timeout of an invocation if it is judged that it cannot meet its deadline. The behavior of a server object is equal to that of the TFP. That is, the object verifies whether it can complete a requested method within a client's time limit.

TI has no way to notify the server of client's timeout. Thus, this protocol is applicable only to the domain of problems where the recovery of the server object from the exception is unnecessary or is allowed to be discarded. The abortion of an invocation due to a client's timeout is caused by the serious delay or loss of a request message; a message from the server (reply, reject notification or abort notification); or overload of the server object. In this protocol, the reply message arriving after the timeout is discarded.

Timed Invocation with Notification

Timed Invocation with Notification (TIwN) is an object invocation protocol also supporting least suffering of client object. One difference between TIwN semantics and TI semantics described above is that TIwN provides a way to inform the server of client's abortion. For this purpose, the fifth and the sixth message types, *timeout notification* and *reply acknowledgment,* are introduced. Figure 2 represents an overview of the TIwN protocol.

Let's assume that a client object invokes a certain server object. The server object commits the invocation by the reception of a reply acknowledgment (reply_ack) from the client. The scenario by the client aborts the invocation goes as follows:

1. An unexpected delay occurs in the transmission of a request message or a reply message, or some trouble takes place on the server object.
2. The client that could not get the reply message before the invocation deadline causes a timeout.
3. It starts an exception immediately.
4. After that, if it receives the delayed reply message, it sends a timeout notification back to the server.

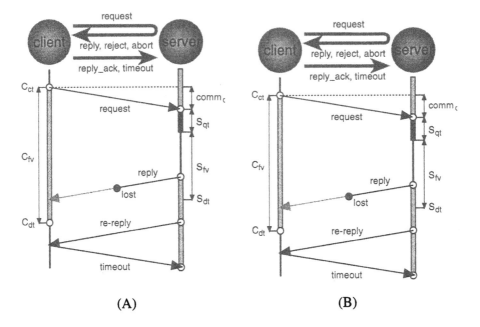

Fig. 2. Overview of TIwN Protocol

There are two scenarios for the server object that has already sent the reply message to recover its internal state. One is the case that the client has already caused a timeout.

1. The server receives a timeout notification from the client.
2. It aborts the invocation, and starts an exception immediately.

Another is the case that a reply message to the client or an acknowledgment or timeout notification from the client was lost.

1. The server causes a reception timeout.
2. It aborts the invocation, and starts an exception immediately.

The semantics of the TIwN protocol needs more message exchanges than that of the TI protocol to preserve the consistency between a client and a server. This means that chances of a message getting lost may increase. In this situation, the server cannot know which message was lost. When a reply acknowledgment is lost, though the client finished the invocation correctly, the server may abort it. This problem can be solved by introducing re-transmission and confirmation functions into the protocol[4]. However, to keep server blocking time to a minimum, the current implementation of the TIwN protocol does not support message re-transmission.

---

[4] DROL provides language constructs, called the DROL Meta Object Protocol (DROL-MOP), which make extension of invocation protocol easy.

2.3 Protocol Class and Timed Invocation Operator

The *Protocol Class Library – PCL* is a C++ class library to provide the various communication protocols introduced by the DRO model. A C++ class is defined for each protocol. A C++ object that is an instance of a protocol class, called *protocol object*, provides the semantics for inter-real-time object communication.

The root of the PCL class hierarchy is the abstract class `Protocol`, where methods[5] necessary for interfacing with the DROL runtime environment are defined. Each communication protocol is implemented as a subclass[6] of this class. Subclasses redefine these interface methods, and realize various communication protocols. The subclass `ProtoNTI` implements the semantics of the NTI protocol which only supports a timing constraint verification mechanism on the server-side. Subclass `ProtoTI` and `ProtoTIwN` implement the semantics of the timed invocation (TI) and that of the timed invocation with notification (TIwN) respectively.

A protocol object is a kind of meta-level object that provides semantics for communication between objects. The protocol class `Protocol`, the root of the class hierarchy, provides methods to define new meta objects; that is the *DROL Meta Object Protocol – DROL MOP[7]*, which is protected in the hierarchy. Programmers can design and implement original real-time invocation semantics easily by defining a new class that inherits existing classes.

DROL provides a language construct, *timed invocation operator*, to declare strict timing constraints upon each invocation. A remote object invocation takes the following form:

```
1 p_obj = new <Protocol Class>;
2 r_obj
3    -> (p_obj , <TF Val>) method();
```

In the first argument, we specify the protocol object. `<Protocol Class>` means a protocol class provided by the library PCL. An instance `p_obj` is a protocol object that realizes the communication semantics defined in the protocol class. The second argument, `<TF Val>`, denotes a timeout value to be used for the least suffering strategy. The use of the timed invocation operator allows us to support various invocation protocols in a unified language primitive. Please see [12] for details of DROL language specifications and its programming examples.

3 Runtime Environment DROL/RtM

In this section, we first summarize characteristics of Real-Time Mach [14]. Then, we describe our design and implementation of DROL/RtM.

---

[5] Member functions in C++ terminology

[6] Derived class in C++ terminology.

[7] In the previous version of DROL [10], DROL MOPs were provided as language specifications. Now, they are included in the PCL framework. How to use DROL MOP is discussed in other papers.

3.1 Overview of Real-Time Mach

Mach Operating System [1] is a micro-kernel-based operating system being developed at Carnegie Mellon University. Real-Time Mach is an real-time extension of the Mach kernel. One of its goals is to extend the system functions for real-time applications without changing the original interface. For reflecting resource requirements of applications, we can specify attributes for objects provided by the kernel such as threads, processor sets, mutex variables, and IPC ports. Especially, the *thread attributes* allow us to specify timing attributes, and the *processor set attributes* are used to change processor scheduling policies.

Real-Time Mach has several advantages to build a DROL runtime environment, which can make up for the problems of the ARTS kernel.

- **Variety of target architecture** · · · While the ARTS kernel is implemented on limited CISC architectures such as Sun3 and Sony CISC-NEWS, Real-Time Mach is implemented on i386/486 architecture, and is being ported on new architectures such as the PowerPC architecture and the SPARC architecture.

- **High adaptability to many communication models** · · · Real-Time Mach provides many useful programming environments, such as Real-Time Server (RTS) and Network Protocol Server (NPS). NPS supports UDP-like one way message passing. We can construct various communication models more flexibly by using NPS.

- **Support of high-speed communication media** · · · Real-Time Mach supports high-speed communication media and real-time network protocols such as FDDI. The use of them enables us to realize high-speed and real-time inter-object communications.

In consideration of these advantages, we build DROL runtime environment on the Real-Time Mach kernel.

3.2 Design Policies

At the design stage of DROL/RtM, we considered the following four items:

- To keep portability of real-time programs written in DROL, we have to avoid introducing Real-Time Mach specific language constructs. Thus, we do not change basic construction of distributed real-time objects and DROL language specifications.

- In Real-Time Mach, network communication primitives are provided by the Network Protocol Server (NPS). Therefore, we have to separate remote communication model and mechanisms from those of local IPC.

- While an ARTS object can create and use only one communication port, in Real-Time Mach, a programmer can assign multiple ports to one task. By creating a port for each thread, we can reduce cost of message dispatching and improve total communication cost.

- While the ARTS kernel supports interruptive timer primitives, Real-Time Mach does not supply such timer primitives. Thus, we have to implement a new timeout mechanism for least suffering.

In the following subsections, details of the communication model are described.

3.3 Communication Mechanisms in DROL/RtM

Here, we discuss a communication mechanism in DROL/RtM, and make its differences from that of the ARTS kernel version [12] clear. One of the biggest modifications in DROL/RtM is that it uses NPS primitives for network-wide communication while it uses Mach IPC primitives for local communication. NPS is a network protocol server that provides various network services. However, these differences can be absorbed in Protocol Class Library (PCL). Therefore, we need not change the language specifications of DROL.

Direct Reception of Reply Messages

Since the ARTS kernel can create only one communication port per one object, a special thread has to deal with all message reception, which is called "message dispatcher." Reception of a reply message causes a context switch from a slave thread to the dispatcher thread. Then, the context transfers from the dispatcher thread to the slave thread again. In contrast, Real-Time Mach supports multiple port creation. As shown in Figure 3, by creating a port for each slave or master thread, each thread can receive reply messages directly. Thus, we can reduce cost of message dispatching (context switches) and improve total communication cost.

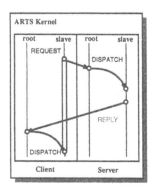 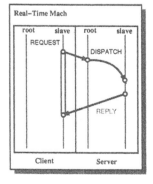

Fig. 3. Reception of Reply Messages

Local Object Invocation

To realize the notion of least suffering, a timeout mechanism on client side is needed. However, Real-Time Mach does not support any interruptive timer primitives, such as WithinPrimitive() of the ARTS kernel. We adopted a Mach IPC primitive mach_msg() as a base of the implementation model for least suffering, to which we could declare a timeout value as an argument.

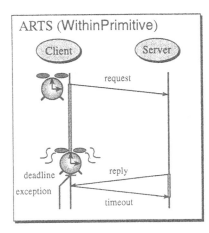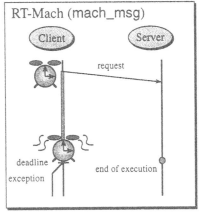

Fig. 4. Timeout Detection in Local Invocation

Figure 4 depicts a model of local communication with the TIwN protocol [12]. In this case, the runtime environment DROL/RtM uses a Mach IPC primitive mach_msg(). Here, an argument for timeout value of mach_msg() is used to realize least suffering. To detect timeout of a client object, the runtime system works as follows:

1. It sets a timeout value declared in program codes to an argument of the mach_msg() primitive.
2. It calls the primitive to receive a reply message.
3. If it cannot obtain the reply message within the timing constraint, the mach_msg() finishes abnormally and notifies a timeout to an application.
4. It starts an exception program, immediately.

In this way, least suffering in the client object is achieved.

At the end of method execution, a server object can verifies whether it could finish a requested service before its deadline or not. At this time, it can also recognize a condition of the client whether it has time-outed or not. This is because they can use the same local clock in a local object invocation. Consequently, the server do not need a timeout notification or a reply acknowledgment from the client, which are indispensable in the runtime environment on the ARTS kernel[8].

---

[8] In the previous implementation of DROL runtime environment on the ARTS kernel, we had to use same network primitives for both cases: local invocations and remote invocations.

Remote Object Invocation

In case of remote communication, we can use a net_receive() primitive provided by NPS. However unlike the mach_msg() primitive, it does not support any timeout scheme. Thus, we designed and implemented a new version of this primitive, called net_receive_to(), which needs argument to set a timeout value.

Application program first calls this primitive. Then, an application-side stub routine is called. The stub routine calls a NPS-side stub routine with mach_msg(). We took notice of this mach_msg() primitive. We implement the net_receive_-to() adding one new argument. This argument means timeout value to be used in the mach_msg(). The new primitive has the following specification:

```
1 kern_return_t net_receive_to(
2         mach_port_t     receive_port,
3         char            *msg,
4         int             size,
5         int             timeout,
6         boolean_t       type )
```

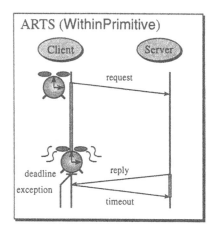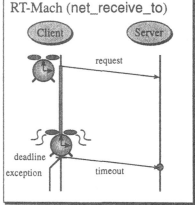

Fig. 5. Timeout Detection in Remote Invocation

Figure 5 shows a scenario of remote object invocation with the TIwN protocol. A big difference between the implementation on the ARTS kernel and that on the RT-Mack kernel is behavior of the client which missed its deadline. While in the former scheme, a client has to wait a delayed reply message before it sends a notification message, in latter scheme, a client can send a timeout notification to a server immediately. This is because, on RT-Mach, we can use one-way message passing primitives of NPS. On the contrary, in the previous implementation, all invocation protocols were constructed by using two-way communication primitives provided by the ARTS kernel.

In contrast to the local model, the server object cannot recognize whether sending a reply message commits in success or not from a return value of net_receive_to(). Thus, the server has to wait for the reply acknowledgment.

4 Performance and Discussions

In this section, we evaluate cost of communication between two distributed real-time objects using DROL/RtM in real-time. Then, we compare the result with the previous version of runtime environment implemented on the ARTS kernel.

All measurements were made in the following environment: two PC/AT compatible machines (CPU Intel Pentium, Clock 90 MHz) connected by Ethernet. We set it up so two objects were located on different hosts and communicated with each other through the network. Two real-time servers, RTS (Real-Time Server) and NPS (Network Protocol Server), were also running on each host.

A client object sends a message whose message size is 1,024 bytes as a request with 100 milliseconds' deadline. Here, it uses the NTI protocol or the TIwN protocol. A server provides one method that has null method body. We measured average communication times by repeating the invocations 100 times. All programs were written in DROL. The programs were transferred to C++ code by the DROL compiler. Translated C++ source code was compiled into executable code by the GNU C++ compiler (gcc).

By comparing the performance result of TIwN with that of NTI, we examine the cost of carrying out least suffering. The performance of remote object invocations, of message size 1,024 bytes, is 22.5 milliseconds in the TIwN protocols and 18.2 milliseconds in the NTI semantics. The difference between these invocation times, that is 4.3 milliseconds, corresponds to the cost of the least suffering strategy in DROL/RtM.

Table 1. Cost for Least Suffering in TIwN (RT-Mach)

Factors	Cost (μsec)	
Context Switch (2 times)	—	
Msg. Allocation and Deallocation	218	(5.1%)
Msg. Operation	111	(2.6%)
Timer Start-up and Verification	937	(21.8%)
Ack. or Timeout Msg. Transmission	3,034	(70.6%)
Total	4,300	

Details of the cost are represented in Table 1. In this table, we also depicted percentages of main factors of this overhead. Table 2 indicates those of the ARTS

Table 2. Cost for Least Suffering in TIwN (ARTS)

Factors	Cost (μsec)	
Context Switch (2 times)	510	(13.3%)
Msg. Allocation and Deallocation	90	(2.3%)
Msg. Operation	120	(3.1%)
Timer Start-up and Verification	190	(4.9%)
Ack. or Timeout Msg. Transmission	2,929	(76.1%)
Total	3,839	

version. However, we cannot compare two strategies by using real-time data directly. Because all measurements of the ARTS version were made in different environment: two SONY NEWS workstations (NWS-1450: CPU MC68030, Clock 25MHz) connected by Ethernet. Therefore, we use the percentages of factors for comparison.

There is one factor of which we took notice. It is the overhead of context switches. The rate of context switches is reduced in DROL/RtM obviously. This is because a server object can send a reply message to the specific thread of a client directly, which sent a request message. In the implementation model on the ARTS kernel, an object using the TIwN protocol had to receive a reply as a message delivered no to a specific thread but to the object. In contrast, the NTI protocol was implemented by using a request/reply communication primitive provided by the ARTS kernel. Thus, the thread that sent a request message can receive a reply directly [12]. The object needs two more context switches to dispatch the received reply message to an appropriate thread than the case of NTI. Consequently, the existence of context switches was a primary factor of the overhead of least suffering in the ARTS model. A context switch takes much time as compared with other factors. Therefore, this reduction of context switches contributes to decreasing total cost of object invocation.

Finally, we summarize what functions are needed to real-time kernels to implement a distributed real-time programming environment, which we recognized through above measurement and discussions.

- To assign multiple ports to one object is effective to reduce overhead of context switches.

- Support of one-way communication primitive allows users to design various communication protocols easily in user level.

- Provision of communication primitives that support interruptive timer functions makes it easy to realize the notion of least suffering.

5 Conclusions and Remarks

This paper pointed out that it is hard to construct a distributed real-time system depending only on the traditional predictability of programs. Thus, we needed other methodologies or frameworks adaptable to widely distributed environments other than the notion of predictability.

We first summarized the notion of *least suffering* which is proposed in [12] as the new framework. This notion improved the survivability of real-time objects. It assures that the system notifies the objects of the presence of fault within bounded time, so that they do not have to wait for an indefinite amount of time. This provides the object with the opportunity to recover in its own way within a certain time frame, and keeps the decline of real-time facilities to a minimum.

We discussed how the notion of least suffering was achieved in the programming language DROL. Then, with a runtime environment implemented on the Real-Time Mach kernel, the overhead of the least suffering strategy was evaluated. Finally, we depicted what are essential functions of real-time kernels to implement a distributed real-time programming environment.

Our research also contributed to constructing a distributed real-time programming environment on Real-Time Mach that did not support any real-time specific programming language.

Acknowledgment

We would like to thank Yutaka Ishikawa for his valuable comments. We also thank Hideyuki Tokuda for their comments on improving the manuscripts. Finally, we wish to express gratitude to participants of the workshop for their helpful comments on an earlier draft of this paper.

References

1. M. Accetta, R. Baron, W. Bolosky, D. Golub, R. Rashid, A. Tevanian, and M. Young. Mach: A New Kernel Foundation for UNIX Development. In *USENIX 1986 Summer Conference Proceedings*, June 1986. USENIX Association.

2. P. Gopinath. CHAOS: Why One Cannot Have Only An Operating System for Real-Time Applications. *Operating System Review*, 23(3), July 1989.

3. A. S. Grimshaw, A. Silberman, and J. W. S. Liu. *Real-Time Mentat, A Data-Driven, Object-Oriented System*. 1989.

4. Y. Ishikawa, H. Tokuda, and C. W Mercer. Object-Oriented Real-Time Language Design: Constructs for Timing Constraints. In *Proceedings of ECOOP/OOPSLA '90*, October 1990.

5. K. B. Kenny and K.-J. Lin. Building Flexible Real-Time Systems Using the Flex Language. *IEEE COMPUTER*, 24(5), May 1991.

6. S. T. Levi, S. K. Tripathi, S. D. Carson, and A. K. Agrawala. The MARUTI Hard Real-Time Operating System. *Operating System Review*, 23(3), July 1989.

7. J. W. S Liu, K.-J. Lin, C. L. Liu, W. K. Shih, and J. Y. Chung. Imprecise Computations: A Means to Provide Scheduling Flexibility and Enhance Dependability. In Y. H. Lee and C. M. Krishna, editors, *Readings in Real-Time Systems*. IEEE Computer Society Press, 1993.

8. W.-K. Shih and J. W. S. Liu. On-line Scheduling of Imprecise Computations to Minimize Error. In *Proceedings of 13th IEEE Real-Time Systems Symposium*, 1992.

9. W.-K. Shih, J. W. S. Liu, and J.-Y. Chung. Fast Algorithms for Scheduling Imprecise Computations. In *Proceedings of 10th IEEE Real-Time Systems Symposium*, 1989.

10. K. Takashio and M. Tokoro. DROL: An Object-Oriented Programming Language for Distributed Real-time Systems. In *Proceedings of ACM OOPSLA '92*, October 1992.

11. K. Takashio and M. Tokoro. Time Polymorphic Invocation: A Real-Time Communication Model for Distributed Systems. In *Proceedings of IEEE 1st Workshop on Parallel and Distributed Real-Time Systems (WPDRTS'93)*, April 1993.

12. K. Takashio and M. Tokoro. Least Suffering Strategy in Distributed Real-Time Programming Language DROL. *Real-Time Systems*, 9, 1996. To be appeared.

13. H. Tokuda and C. W. Mercer. ARTS: A Distributed Real-Time Kernel. *Operating System Review*, 23(3), 1989.

14. H. Tokuda, T. Nakajima, and P. Rao. Real-Time Mach: Towards a Predictable Real-Time System. In *Proceedings of USENIX Mach Workshop*, October 1990.

ActNet: The Actor Model Applied to Mobile Robotic Environments

Philippe Darche *, Pierre-Guillaume Raverdy, Eric Commelin
Laboratoire MASI, Institut Blaise Pascal, Université Pierre et Marie Curie
4 Place Jussieu, 75252 Paris Cedex 05, FRANCE
Tel: +33.1.44.27.34.23 Fax: +33.1.44.27.62.86
E-Mail: {darche,raverdy,commelin}@masi.ibp.fr

Abstract. Mobile computers using wireless communication bring new challenges for resources access and cooperative work. Such devices, especially for robots control, may be dynamically specialized by adding cards thus changing computer functionalities. Systems should also manage resource mobility (due to localization change) and resource unavailability (due to failures or disconnections). Actor model is well suited for such environment where location and functionality changes need to be managed transparently from the user applications.

This paper describes ActNet, an actor based system designed for a robotic environment and its dynamic resource management. The ActPL programming language model associated to this system is also presented.

Keywords: Mobile robotic, Wireless networks, Actors, Resource management.

Introduction

This paper gives an overview of the ActNet project that aims to provide a robotic platform for the design and test of cooperative applications. ActNet is composed of a set of mobile robots using wireless communication among themselves, but also to access resources on a wired local area network. Field of application is primarily education [10]. Other domains are distributed artificial intelligence [18] as well as decentralized artificial intelligence [11].

Mobile robotic environments exhibit numerous needs, often conflicting. To allow quick response time in a robotic environment, software architecture should be reactive. On the other hand, highly complex tasks should be performed such as image processing and planning. Also, failure of any component, software or hardware, should be handled by the system and be harmless for the tasks performed. Moreover, the constant emerging of new technologies leads to highly heterogeneous systems (e.g., processors, devices). Applications may even access unknown resources (not available at design time).

---

* Affiliation: UFR Informatique, Université Paris V

Introducing wireless communications brings new challenges for resource and cooperative application management [4]. Due to mobility, the location of hosts, applications, and resources can change. A mobile host needs to continue its work while disconnected and to connect transparently to the network from various locations. The obligation to deal with unreliability and limited bandwidth of wireless communications are also important for the design of distributed algorithms.

Because actual embedded systems become closer to distributed systems [24], a centralized architecture for the control system [22] is no more applicable. Other approaches, behavioral [7] or connectionist [26] are also not practical due to communication bottleneck.

In ActNet, the actor model is used to control hardware and software resources and build user applications. Actor concept [16] allows to deal with this heterogeneity in a transparent manner. Actors are autonomous entities that use message passing for communication. Key principles of actors are modularity and re-usability. Each node of the network is a hardware actor that carries out software actors (applications).

A set of system actors manages users applications and provide an efficient access to the resources distributed in the system (load balancing) and help for disconnect work and reconnection (fault tolerance).

To build application actors, the programmer needs a programming model that allows to deal with concurrency in a way that is compatible with modularity. ActPL (ActNet Programming Language) uses active objects to embed actors because their concurrency management is compatible with modularity.

The first section presents the mobile computing model with wireless communications, resources mobility, and robotic constraints. Section 2 describes our hardware actor model and justifies the use of actors for mobile robots. Section 3 depicts our actor network for mobile robots and it resource management. The programming language used in ActNet is then described in section 4 and we conclude in section 5.

1 Mobile Computing Model

In this section, we present our mobile robotic environment where wireless communications and hardware constraints have a great influence on system design.

1.1 Wireless Communication

Communication characteristics are, (1) the medium, (2) the network topology and protocol, and (3) the communication link specificities.

The atmosphere used in wireless communication is often subject to various interferences (e.g., scrambling) and consequently is an extremely noisy channel. Information is carried out by a wave characterized by its frequency : coherent laser transmission, infrared or radio frequency. Due to their easyness of use, only the two last domains are used in mobile systems. Laser is mostly used for static point-to-point communication.

Topology of wireless networks is mainly of three types: bus, star, and ring. Wireless Local Area Networks (WLAN) [23] generally use the bus topology and the access type is usually Pure-Aloha type or Slotted-Aloha type [1].

In order to preserve energy and allow more users, transmission power is generally low. As a consequence, wireless communication is more sensitive to electrical or physical interferences and its quality is more subject to change than wired network [23]. Even without any channel attenuation, communication throughput is very low compared with wired links. Communication area is divided into cells. In each cell, a data concentrator allocates one or several frequencies to one mobile.

This allocation does not change during the communication if the mobile stays in the same cell. Cells are linked to the wired network via wireless gateways or radio-frequency relay (see Figure 1). To allow a mobile computer to continue its communication while changing of cell, specific protocols have to be implemented [5, 8].

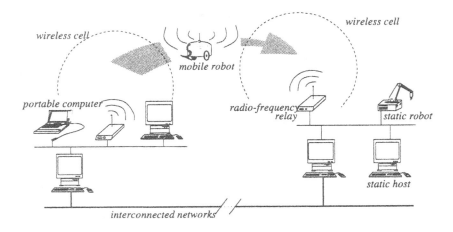

Fig. 1. Mobile Robotic Network

1.2 Mobile and Robotic Constraints

Compared with traditional distributed systems, mobile computers and robots present more pronounced features. Mobile computing is characterized by a highly dynamic environment and emphasize energetic concern. Robotic systems are composed of highly heterogeneous devices and are more subject to mechanical, electronical and software errors.

Because energy is limited (battery), embedded devices must be equipped with electronic modules with minimum current consumption. System design must also take this limitation into consideration. Specific algorithm should be implemented to make less use of components with high energetic needs [3]. This is fundamental because it has a direct effect on system lifetime and on transmission power, and as a result on the maximal distance of communication.

Because mobile robots are moving around the wired network, resources location on these entities are changing. Also, from the point of view of the applications executing on the robots, the environment is completely changed after a location change.

Due to mechanical, electronical or software faults, applications in mobile robotic environment are more subject to faults. These faults need to be managed as transparently as possible for the running applications.

As a conclusion, this section that briefly introduced our environment constraints shows the needs for our system to be highly modular in order to handle external, as well as internal changes.

2 Actors for Mobile Robots

The basic entity of ActNet, the actor, is used to manage software and hardware resources and their mobility. Actors also carry out activities of user applications.

2.1 The actor model

The actor concept is prompted by the social organization model of communicating experts and has been defined in [16]. Actors are autonomous cooperating entities which communicate through messages. Several implementations of the actor model exist like PLASMA [16], ABCL/1 [28] et Actalk [6].

Actors abide by the encapsulation principle of usual objects, but have the additional possibility of internal activity independently of any external communications. An actor has a limited and local knowledge of its environment: a list of other actors (acquaintances) with whom it can exchange messages. The actor is accessed from the external world by the address of its mailbox; mailboxes are linked to waiting lists where received messages are stored until their evaluation. When an actor receives messages, it has to follow a specific behavior described with a script.

When a message is evaluated, the actor may undertake one or more of the following actions:

- sending messages to some of its acquaintances or to itself (self-addressing),

- creating new actors,

- evaluating expressions of the invoked message pattern (i.e., execution of threads in its work space).

Asynchronous communication via message passing is the sole possible interaction between actors. Actor model ensure that any message will arrive to its destination but there is no obligation for the receiver to handle it.

The actors family is subdivided into two sets : serial actors and parallel actors. A serial actor computes only one message at once and explicitly specifies its new state in order to compute the following message. A parallel actor can evaluate several messages at the same time. Actor model allows to express "naturally" concurrent activities. If a calculation has to be executed in a sequential way, the sequentiality will be expressed by actors themselves,

Actor in accordance with Agha [2] can be considered as not serial, because its behaviors are computed at the same time. In ABCL/1 model [28], actor is serial.

2.2 Actor adequacy for mobile robots

The actor model is well suited for robotic systems because they exhibit a high degree of concurrency. Robotic programs need to (1) wait for external and/or handle interrupts, (2) deal with concurrent activities, (3) synchronize actions with external events, and (4) communicate with other robots and processes.

The actor model simplifies the design of the robot system by allowing the direct expression of concurrent activities. It also simplifies the coordination and cooperation of robot activities as well as providing high-level communication facilities between multiple robots and other devices.

Actors allow the programmer to dynamically customize the system depending on robot configuration and environment (e.g. sensor failure).

Actors offer a uniform communication scheme among all the entities of our mobile system, hardware or software, static or mobile. Message passing allows to deal transparently with mobility and disconnection. Messages can be buffered in a representative of the disconnected actor. At reconnection time, after localization step, the pending messages will be forwarded to the new location of the actor. This mechanism respect the communication scheme (obligation of receiving, but no obligation of evaluation).

2.3 The hardware actor

The actor model has been extended to deal with the fine management of hardware, introducing the hardware actor (H-Actor) [9]. A H-Actor is composed of a generic command card, a network interface and possibly specific interfaces. Opposed to H-Actor, we call as software actors (S-Actors), those that do not manage any hardware. With this decomposition, everything in the system is an actor. Some peripherals have to be managed in critical section. The serial actor model evaluates messages in a sequential way and is, therefore, well adapted to the atomic management constraint of tasks.

In order to be coherent with the actor model, the H-Actor should keep message as communication model. Thus, hardware interrupts are encapsulated in messages that are assigned different priorities in order to ensure real-time constraints.

The hardware actor (H-Actor) model extends the software one to hardware level, so that, from the outside, a hardware actor behaves just like a software actor, but has exclusive management of the inputs/outputs (I/O).

The H-actor has four states:

- Dead : the actor is not powered.

- Passively waiting : waiting queues are empty and the actor is sleeping.

- Active : the actor evaluate a message.

- Actively waiting : the actor is in an explicit waiting of a message.

At power-up, the actor initializes its central processing unit and its peripherals. Unlike software actors, hardware ones are not permanent. When a H-actor is not powered, it is considered as dead.

3 The ActNet System

3.1 ActNet: a Robotic Network

ActNet is a robotic platform that allows to design and test actors based applications [10]. From a hardware point of view, ActNet is a heterogeneous actors network, which can be split between hardware actors and software actor on top of hardware actors

We have characterized two types of hardware actors :

- Static Robotic Actor (SRA),

- Mobile Robotic Actor (MRA).

Executive subnetworks of moving actors (M.A.S.N.) and sedentary actors (S.A.S.N.) are associated with each kind of hardware actor. Gateway Actors manage communications between sub-networks. Moreover, a user sub-network (U.S.N.) is dedicated to the development and control of user applications (see Figure 2 and 3).

Thus, the network is heterogeneous because of its topology (M.A.S.N, ring or bus), and also because of its kind of processors on each node. The U.S.N. is a local commercial network with a variable topology defined by computers supporting the developments of the users (in our implementation, it is composed of a PC base equipped with an interface board for S.A.S.N.). To increase reliability and insure a high and warranted speed for the flow of data, the S.A.S.N. is a double ring, with opposite directions,

A wired communication link with mobile robots is only considered in the following cases:

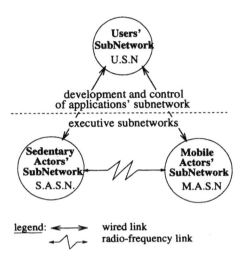

Fig. 2. ActNet Topology

- when a failure occurs in the embedded energy supplying system; an external energy supply is then necessary for the electronic devices and for reloading the batteries; the power line of the network should fulfills this part,

- in the implementation phase for fast downloading of a software prototype or for debugging applications,

- when failure of the radio frequency system occurs.

Since the set of hardware actors is similar to a distributed system, some interesting properties may be observed:

- Heterogeneity: Because of message passing communication, that are independent of hardware architecture, a hardware actor may be assigned to any kind of processor board and each network node may be assigned a different processor.

- Generality: We proposed a generic control board[10] of robots, which saves designer concern with interface problems, or at least reduces the degree of such concern. All actors may be equipped with this same I/O control board. Using such a normalized I/O interface, the ActNet architecture is generic enough and may support complex robot control schemes.

- Modularity: We adopted a modular design of hardware actors in order to ease evolution of robot control systems. H-Actor or S-Actor may be easily removed or added; such modifications do not affect the whole architecture. Thus, fault tolerance mechanisms may be implemented via redundancy.

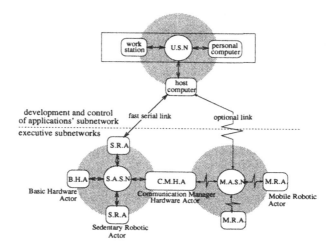

Fig. 3. ActNet Topology: Details

- Flexibility: The system may be tested in simulation or in real world solely with S-Actors; H-Actors may be next used in real world to achieve better performance.

- Distributiveness: S-Actors may be moved from one H-Actor to another one, for instance in order to achieve load balancing. By taking the distribution of processor units into account, a designer may make the system fault-tolerant: when a H-Actor fails, S-Actors migrate on other H-Actor.

3.2 Cooperative Applications in Mobile Systems

Cooperative applications management in a local network of static hosts already poses many problems like remote access, resources or actors migration, fault tolerance, and load sharing. This management is even more complex in the case of mobile computers due to:

- frequent disconnection of mobile computers,

- resources replication to allow disconnected work,

- reconnection after a location change,

As a consequence, the system must be highly dynamic. It must support mechanisms to allow disconnection, to ensure information consistency during disconnection and to allow cooperating actors to resume their communications after host reconnection.

After a reconnection, actors located on a mobile host need to locate the remote resources they were accessing and resources managed by the mobile host should also be made visible to the other ones. Change of location also influences the global system performances by introducing load imbalance due to communication delay. It may be efficient for actors to migrate in order to reduce communication and response time.

Here, we outlines the dynamic management of ActNet that allows an efficient use of the resources distributed over the network and improves cooperative work between static and mobile units.

Application Model

Concerning the applications, each robot is a communicating entity. Hence, application objectives can be considered as collaboration between hardware and software actors.

We consider independent applications composed of communicating actors. These actors use resources (hardware of software actors) distributed over the whole network. Resources may be software or hardware and can be located on static or mobile hosts. Message exchange occurs mostly between actors of the same application or between an actor and a resource. So, we can neglect communications between actors of different applications in regard of load balancing decisions.

An application can be described by a dynamic execution graph that represents resource utilization and communication between actors. In this graph, there are two kinds of nodes, one represents the different resources and the other one the application activities. The nodes are connected by valued links representing the use of resources or the communication between processes (see figure 4).

Migration orders are decided according to execution graph by using attraction/repulsion mechanisms like in CFM [25], EOS [15] or Bellorophon [12]. Concurrent access to resource (e.g., processor) defines repulsion forces between actors whereas communication defines attraction forces.

Application Management in Mobile Systems

We introduce the **Execution Territory** (ET) to allow an efficient control of cooperative applications. An ET, associated with an application, is composed of the set of nodes on which application and resources actors are located. Each application has a central manager or **Territory Manager** (TM) that keeps track of message activity between application and resources actors. These statistics allow the TM to maintain an execution graph of the application and to detect any load imbalance due to inefficient communication link or resource contention. The TM is also in charge of preserving application state consistency during disconnection.

Resource managers (RM), dispatched over the network, help TM to find the most suitable resource when a load imbalance due to resource access is detected.

RM are part of a connected graph mapping the global network topology. They keep track of the different resources (and their actual use) in the nodes under their authority. RM can manage a LAN or interconnected LANs but can also be associated with mobile robots.

When a mobile host moves, it can create a load imbalance due to actors or system resources on the mobile host. For instance, an actor on the mobile host was formerly using a nearby resource located on a static host. After location change and due to network latency, requests to this resource may be overwhelming. Load imbalance can also be the result of application evolution (e.g., start of new actors).

If the load imbalance is due to application actors, the execution manager can initiate actor migration. In the case of inefficient resource access, and depending of the resource, the territory evolves differently.

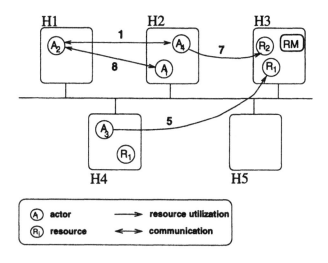

Fig. 4. Execution graph

Figure 4 presents an execution territory composed of five hosts, H1, H2 H3, H4 and H5. After statistics retrieval, the TM will detect that host H2 is overloaded and that execution of actor A4 (resp. A3) is slowed by access to resource R2 (resp. R1). Because actors A2 and A1 have a high communication level, the TM decides to transfer actor A1 onto host H1. And send request to the RM of R2 (resp. R1) with hints about resource accesses. With these hints, and according to other accesses on these resources, the RM decides that resource R2 should be moved on H2 and that A3 should access another instance of R1 (see Figure 5).

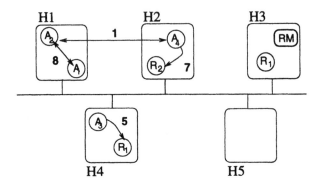

Fig. 5. Execution graph (2)

Resources in Mobile Systems

To define the localization method of resources after a reconnection, we classified resources in three types:

- **Static resources** that have a specified location on the network. An actor using these resources still uses the same ones after it migrates or its host moves (e.g., printer device).

- **Replicated resources** that have fixed locations but are replicated on the network. After the actor migration, the actor will use the closest version of the resource to improve performances.

- **Mobile resources** that can migrate with an actor to better answer to the application need and to improve their performances.

Actor migration for load balancing, can introduce inefficient access to resources. Reconnection of a mobile computer from another location can also introduce such effect. These cases are managed cooperatively by TM and RM. The TM detects such problems from the execution graph and send information to the RM. According to the kind of resource used by reconnected or migrated actors, (1) the same instance is used, (2) the RM tries to find a copy, or (3) the RM asks the resource migration.

Mobile host reconnection implies :

- update location information of the actors and resources located on the mobile host,

- forwarding of pending messages,

- computation of the new execution graph and possibly deciding actor migration or resource hunting.

4 The ActPL Programming Model

ActPL stands for ActNet programming language. It implements ActNet's actors (S-Actors, H-Actors) through active objects.

This section describes the specification and functionalities of this language. Its implementation is under way.

4.1 Actors through Active Objets: Actor-Objects

ActPL is designed to fulfill the needs of S-Actors and H-Actors. In ActPL, actors are implemented through active objects, so they are called actor-objects, or AO, for short.

Unlike some others actor-based languages (such as ABCL [28] or BOX [14]), PRAL-RT [13] and Charm++ [21] use an existing object language: C++. They extend C++ with new keywords and use a modified compiler.

ActPL also uses C++, because this commonly used object-oriented language provides all needed functionalities to support AO. However, in ActPL, C++ is used **as is**, and without any modification of the compiler. An actor-object is a classical C++ object which class inherit of a provided class.

The object model is used for its modularity and code reuse facilities through inheritance, but we also allow the programmer to use every facility of an object language, such as operator overloading and dynamic binding. The actor model is used because concurrent programming with actors can be compatible with the modularity of the object model.

An AO is made of three entities bound together:

1. an **object**, which methods define the behavior of the AO,

2. a **mailbox**, which contains the messages to be processed by the AO,

3. an **activity**, which executes the object's methods corresponding to the messages extracted from the mailbox.

Messages sent to an AO are enqueued in its mailbox to be extracted and computed by its bound activity. According to the destination AO, a message in the mailbox is a **task**[2] to perform. Like Charm++ [21], we associate one message type to each *public* method of the AO.

An AO has only one activity at construction time, but the programmer is free to create new activities. It is then the programmer responsibility to maintain the consistency of AO's data thanks to synchronization primitives.

The mailbox is not a FIFO queue: each message has an associated priority and/or deadline that will define its insertion position inside the destination mailbox. Moreover an AO can register (and unregister) any of its public methods as an *interrupt-method* according to its internal state. Thanks to this functionality, the current task performed by the AO can be interrupted by the arrival of a

---

[2] set of sequential operations

message that corresponds to a interrupt-registered method in the mailbox. The AO's current task may only be interrupted by such message arrival.

Orient 84/K [20] also associates message types to methods and provides priorized execution of methods within an object. The execution of a low priority method is suspended by the arrival of a higher priority message. After executing the high priority method, the suspended method is resumed. In R^2 [17](a real-time extension of ABCL), a computation can also be suspended, but only to receive notification of deadline miss from the Alarm-Clock object. The computation is then aborted.

With ActPL, the programmer can specify inside an interrupt-method how the interrupted task should behave when resuming. Two choices occur:

1. let it be resumed as if nothing happened, when the message computed by the interrupt-method does not influence the current task,

2. raise an exception in the task, if the event notified by the interrupt-method must influence the current task.

In the last case, the exception can be handled afterwards in the interrupted method, when the interrupt-method ends. The use of an exception mechanism allows the interrupted method to deal with consistency problems that can be handle efficiently only in the context of the interrupted task. The raise of an exception can be used, for example, to receive a deadline miss notification from an alarm-clock AO, as in [17], or to handle a hardware interrupt.

4.2 A Replacement Behavior Mechanism in ActPL

Reflexivity is the ability for an object to access its own representation and to control its own execution semantic. Reflexivity is used to build 'intelligent' programs which are able to reason and act upon themselves [19]. A reflexive language has data which abstracts its computation process. The computation process is modified indirectly when this *meta-level* representation is modified. In mobile robotic applications programming, reflexivity is useful to program hardware actors that change their behavior to fit their environment. It can also be useful to enable debased mode execution according to the state of the internal components.

ActPL is not a full reflexive language. Nevertheless, it proposes a reflexive mechanism that allows the programmer to specify a new behavior for any AO. That means changing the task to be performed when a specific message is received. One can notice the similarity of this behavior change and the dynamic link of object-oriented languages.

ActPL allows AOs to change their behavior by exchanging the object bound to the message box with one of another class. The only restriction is that the new object's class must implement at least the same messages. In fact, a mailbox is associated with a class C, and can be bound to objects of any public derived classes from C. The rule is the same as the one used with object pointers assignment in C++.

This replacement mechanism is the *become* of the actor model. In Agha's model, an actor can create a new actor to compute the next message of the message box. The new actor can start its execution before the old one ended. In ActPL, the same activity executes the new object's methods, so there is no parallel computing between the new and the old behaviors.

This access to the object used by the thread of the AO is the only meta-level feature of ActPL at this time.

4.3 Actor-Objects for Mobile Computing Environment

The environment of a mobile computer changes frequently, due to the mobility of the device or to the unreliability of its transient and possibly wireless link with the network. Applications in the mobile computing environment need to act accordingly in response to these changes in order to provide the user with the best quality of service for the current environment. A mobile robotic application has the same requirements, but it also must adapt in case of mechanical failures. To reach these aims, the actors of the applications need to adapt their behavior dynamically so that they match the environment:

- a hardware component replaces a software computation, to improve the system performance, or because the mobile system can access a new resource the S-Actor is replaced by a H-Actor,

- a H-Actor or a S-Actor becomes unreachable, due to communication or hardware failure, a new local actor can simulate the missing one to offer a debased mode behavior.

H-Actors and S-Actors must be exchangeable. ActPL allows the programmer to built H-Actors and S-Actors in an uniform way and uses inheritance to build a set of compatible actors that implement different behaviors. The replacement mechanism is used to swap dynamically the behaviors.
H-Actors can handle interrupt message and decide when an interrupt must suspend or destroy its current computation. It is also a way to adapt to the environment.

TM and RM actors handle *static resources, replicated resources* and *mobile resources.* ActPl provides an object oriented interface for the territory management: a class library offers the basic code for resources as in Mobject [27], but in ActPL events are send to actor via messages, in the same way that messages from actors. The programmer can register dynamically messages as event with the *interrupt-method* mechanism. This way the set of events supported is highly flexible.
The replacement mechanism of ActPL allows to deal with communication failure and dynamic quality of service: when a distant service becomes unreachable the local proxy can change to become a buffer. On the other hand, A local server can become a simple proxy to forward its requests to another server on a faster

computer when it becomes reachable.

Let us also take a robotic example: when one of the robot's leg has a failure, the H-Actor that manages it can become a S-Actor that sends requests to the others legs' actors to make them make up for the broken one.

4.4 Communication Semantics in ActPL

While keeping simplicity in mind, we want our model to provide a wide range of message passing semantics, like PRAL-RT [13] (a parallel extension of C++) which offers four different semantics:

1. When using **synchronous** message passing, the caller is blocked until the receiver has computed the reply. The receiver also cannot continue its computation after the sending of the reply. This is the same semantic that the present mode of ABCL,

2. **Asynchronous** message passing allows the caller to send a imperative message that do not require reply,

3. With **delayed synchronous** message passing the caller is allowed to get a reply to its request and will be blocked only when the reply becomes necessary for its current computation (it also could be called a 'lazy wait'),

4. **Loose synchronous** message passing allows the receiver to continue the computation initialized by the arrival of the message after having sent its reply.

ActPL offers a single but flexible message passing way that achieves all the functionalities shown in PRAL-RT: (1) synchronization between caller and receiver, (2) asynchronous message sending, (3) wait for a reply when needed (lazy wait), (4) response without ending the current task.

In ActPL, a task can only send asynchronous messages. To receive answers, it uses references to shared objects. Such object is only **available for one AO at a time**. This way, the caller can give the shared object access to the receiver at construction time. The sender can then try to access the answer object, and be suspended if it is not ready. The receiver AO must release the answer object when it is assigned with the answer, releasing the eventually waiting caller. The receiver can continue its task (as with the loose synchronous message passing mode) or stop there (like with the delayed synchronous and synchronous message passing modes).

5 Conclusion

The use of mobile computers and embedded systems implies more secure and flexible operating systems because both applications and resources are mobile.

One major advantage of actor model is its scalability and suitability for mobile systems. The H/S-Actor paradigm is an interesting way because there is no separation between hardware and software modules during analysis and implementation phases. The designer uses only components.

To control the application needs and then decide which actor to migrate or which resource to use, we introduced the execution territory. This allows to dynamically benefit from all available resources according to application needs.

We are currently implementing our system for the robotic actors network **ActNet** [10]. This network is representative because it includes mobile entities (mobile robotic actors) and static ones (static robotic actors, workstations).

ActPL, the programming model associated to ActNet, provides active objects to handle the inherent concurrency of embedded applications. It also allows the programmer to use all the functionalities of the object model (like inheritance and dynamic binding) both with active and passive objects.

References

1. N. Abramson. Development of the ALOHANET. *IEEE Transactions on Information Theory*, 2(32):119–123, March 1985.
2. G. Agha. *Actors: a Model of Concurrent Computation in Distributed Systems*. The MIT Press ISBN 0-262-24026-2, Cambridge, Massachusetts, 1986.
3. R. Alonso and S. Ganguly. Energy efficient query optimization. Technical Report MITL–TR–33–92, Matsushita Information Technology Laboratory, Princeton, NJ 08542-7072, December 1992.
4. B. R. Badrinath, Arup Acharya, and Tomasz Imielinski. Impact of mobility on distributed computations. *ACM Operating Systems Review*, 27(2):15–20, April 1993.
5. Ajay Bakre and B. R. Badrinath. Handoff and systems support for indirect TCP/IP. In *2nd USENIX Mobile and Location-Independent Computing Symposium*, pages 11–24, Rutgers University, April 1995. USENIX.
6. Jean-Pierre Briot. Actalk: a testbed for classifying and designing actor langugaes in the smalltalk-80 environnement. In S. Cook, editor, *British Computer Society Workshop Series*, pages 109–129. European Conference on Object-Oriented Programming, Cambridge University Press, July 1989.
7. Rodney A. Brooks. A layered intelligent control system for a mobile robot. *IEEE Journal of Robotics and Automation, RA-2*, pages 14–23, April 1986.
8. G. D. Culp. Cellular intersystem handoff: Creating transparent boundaries. In *36th Vehicular Technology Conference*, pages 304–310, Texas, USA, May 1986.
9. Philippe Darche. *Le Paradigme Acteur Appliqué aux Systèmes Embarqués Communiquants : ActNet, un Réseau d'Acteurs Robotiques*. PhD thesis, Université Paris 6, 4 place Jussieu, 75252 PARIS cedex 05, France, March 1994.
10. Philippe Darche and Gérard Novak. Actnet: A heterogenous network of actors for learning of parallelism, communication and synchronication. *Control Technology in Elementary Education, NATO ASI Series F*, 116:pages 289–307, 1993.
11. Yves Demazeau and Jean-Pierre Muller. Decentralized artificial intelligence. In *Proceedings of the first European Workshop on Modelling Autonomous Agents in a Multi-Agent World*, pages 5–13, Cambridge, UK, August 1989. Elsevier Science Publisher.

12. Peter William Dickman. *Distributed Object Management in a Non-Small Graph of Autonomous Networks with Few Failures*. PhD thesis, University of Cambridge, september 1991.
13. G. Fouquier and F. Terrier. Introducing priorities into C++ based actor language for multithread machines. *Pacific TOOLS 94*, 1994.
14. J.-M. Geib, C. Gransart, and C. Grenot. Mixing objects and activities in complex active objects. July 26-27 1993.
15. Olivier Gruber and Laurent Amsaleg. Object grouping in EOS. In *Proceedings of the International Workshop on Distibuted Object Management*, pages 184–201, Edmonton, Canada, August 1992.
16. Carl Hewitt. Viewing control structures as patterns of passing messages. *Artificial Intelligence*, 8(3):323–364, June 1977.
17. Yasuaki Honda and Mario Tokoro. Soft real-time programming through reflection. Technical Report SCSL-TR-92-016, Sony Computer Science Laboratory Inc., November 1992.
18. Michael N. Huhns. *Distributed Artificial Intelligence*. London, UK, 1987.
19. Jun ichiro Itoh, Rodger Lea, and Yasuhiko Yokote. Using meta-objects to support optimisation in the apertos operating system. Technical Report SCSL-TM-95-006, Sony CSL, 1995.
20. Yutaka Ishikawa and Mario Tokoro. A concurrent object-oriented knowledge representation language: Orient84/k: Its features and implementation. *OOPSLA*, pages 232–241, 1986.
21. Laxmikant V. Kale and Sanjeev Krishnam. Charm++: A portable concurrent object oriented system based on C++. *OOPSLA*, pages 91–108, 1993.
22. Sundar Narasimhan, David M. Siegel, and John M. Hollerbach. A standard architecture for controlling robots. *AI Memo, M.I.T*, (977), July 1989.
23. K. Pahlavan. Wireless intraoffice networks. *ACM Transactions on Office Information Systems, Practice and Experience*, 6(3):277–302, 1988.
24. Lynne E. Parker. *Heterogeneous Multi-Robot Cooperation*. PhD thesis, Massachusetts Institute of Technology (USA), February 1994.
25. Mario Tokoro. Computational Field Model: Toward a New Computing Model/Technology for Open Distributed Environment. In *2nd Workshop on Future Trends in Distributed Computing Systems*, Cairo, September 1990.
26. Elpida S. Tzafestas. A cellular control architecture for autonomous robots. In *Proceedings of International Workshop on Intelligent Robotics Systems*, Grenoble, France, July 1994.
27. Girish Welling and B. R. Badrinath. Mobject: Programming support for environment directed application policies in mobile computing. *ECOOP'95 Workshop on Mobility and Replication*, August 1995.
28. Akinori Yonezawa. *ABCL: An Object-Oriented Concurrent System*. ISBN 0-262-24029-7. The MIT Press, Cambridge Massachussetts, 1990.

Component-based Programming and Application Management with Olan

Luc Bellissard*, Slim Ben Atallah**, Alain Kerbrat *** and Michel Riveill**

IMAG-LSR [†] - Projet SIRAC [‡]
BP 53, 38041 Grenoble Cedex 9

Abstract. Efficient system mechanisms for distributed object management are becoming increasingly available. Application developers need appropriate tools to fully exploit the power of these facilities. A distributed application is conveniently viewed as a set of components, some of which are developed specifically, while others are legacy applications, encapsulated within components. While engineering issues for the development of individual components are reasonably understood, many research issues are open in the management of software configurations made up of a number of distributed components. In this paper, we introduce a component-based programming model supported by a module interconnection language for large scale distributed application development and administration. The contribution of the Olan model is to separate the interconnection requirements of the application from the implementation and from the constraints of the underlying architecture. The flexibility of this model is well suited to large scale application requirements in terms of components distribution and dynamic evolution. As a first experiment, we have developed a teleconferencing application, whose description highlights the advantages of our approach.

1 Introduction

This paper presents a programming model based on the concept of *component*, a basic unit for construction and management of large and complex distributed applications. Such applications typically involve several possibly distant users working on a set of workstations, sharing information and interacting to complete a common task. Examples of such applications are teleconferencing, cooperative edition, software development environments or workflow applications. These applications may be considered as a set of interacting software entities, basically including existing pieces of software which have to be integrated within

---

* Institut National Polytechnique, Grenoble
** Université de Savoie, Chambéry
*** INRIA-Rhône-Alpes
[†] IMAG-LSR is a joint laboratory of Centre National de la Recherche Scientifique (CNRS), Institut National Polytechnique de Grenoble, and Université Joseph Fourier, Grenoble
[‡] SIRAC is a joint project of IMAG and INRIA

the global application. These entities, as they may be reused from other software, must be integrated as they were initially defined.

The *construction* of applications refers to the description of the software entities involved, the definition of interactions between them and a framework for the evolution of both sets throughout the lifetime of the application. *Management* deals with the accurate use of system resources according to application requirements, such as placement of components on a distributed system, observation of executions, access control to components, etc. Both actions are commonly referred to as *configuration*, the former from a software engineering point of view, and the latter from an administration point of view.

The *software configuration* of a distributed application is the description of the software entities involved, that can be either already existing or specially developed for the application. Granularity may vary from a single object to a set of libraries. The configuration also describes interactions between the entities, not only from a functional dependency point of view, like in current programming languages with include and export directives, but also from a communication point of view. Current languages are not adapted to the description of communications between entities. Interactions such as a method call to an object are currently buried in the implementation code, which makes modification uneasy to achieve.

More complex interactions, such as event broadcasting are even more complicated to express with existing tools. Moreover, current tools do not allow easily to identify components by their properties rather than by their name.

Finally, the structure of the entities as well as the interactions between them are also prone to evolve during execution. For instance, an entity will accept to serve a given request at a given time and will refuse the following requests when it becomes busy. No support is really provided to express this evolution in a more general way than writing specific code and maintaining adequate structures.

This paper presents a programming model which addresses the following issues:

- encapsulation of existing or hand-made software entities whose granularity may vary,
- expression of interactions between software entities, in terms of functional dependencies and communication types,
- decoupling interactions from the implementation,
- construction of complex interactions,
- language and runtime support for the dynamic evolution of the structure and the interactions along multiple executions of an application, and
- management of distributed applications.

We submit that these actions should be based on a single unifying model that brings together features not always available in current programming models.

2 Related Work

The OMG [10] framework may be considered as an attempt to ease construction of distributed applications. CORBA is the first layer of the framework. It enables to define objects with a clear interface, described in a specific language, the IDL. Inter-object communication is carried out by the ORB (Object Request Broker) with an RPC-like mechanism. It provides a pure client-server model of interactions.

Nevertheless, there is no way, neither at the IDL level nor at the ORB level, to specify relations between objects. Interfaces stand alone at the broker level, so the deployment of an application with all required interfaces is still a painful task. Moreover, CORBA offers no way to describe dynamicity inside an application, like creating or destroying a previously called object, or even to create a set of identical interfaces on different nodes of the system. CORBA has been enriched with Object Services that enable specification of relations and dependencies between interfaces. However, no overall vision of the application is available; Object Services are helpful for a bottom-up approach to construction.

Message Bus [9, 12] are another approach to constructing distributed applications. Objects or modules involved in the application are able to publish on the bus what services they can offer. Then, whenever a service is needed, the message bus transmits the requests that will be completed if an object has published a service. It is an extremely dynamic approach because providers can publish as many services as needed and clients can request services without having to name the provider. The bus is in charge of the association between the requester and the provider of the service.

However, Message Bus are the sole providers of communication protocols between entities or objects. Adaptation of communication protocols to specific requirements is impossible unless the bus offers those features. Moreover, the vision of the overall configuration, in terms of component organization and interactions, is not highlighted at all.

Module Interconnection Languages are means for isolating program structures from the execution context. The developer is able to concentrate on functional requirements of the modules and then, using a higher level language, he can describe the interactions between modules. POLYLITH [11] is an example of such an approach. It offers modules and a module interconnection mechanism independently from the deployment platform. The runtime support of POLYLITH encapsulates the communications between modules as well as data transformation, so that the treatment of interfacing requirements is decoupled from that of functional requirements. Programmers are not to pay constant attention to constraints imposed by the underlying architecture, the language processors or the communication media. Furthermore, when an application has been configured for one execution environment, its execution within another environment is treated separately, automatically and independently from the implementations of modules. The problem with POLYLITH is that the application is seen as a flat collection of modules that are tightly coupled but no means are available for the composition of modules.

Conic [6] and more recently Darwin [8] offer a more flexible approach than POLYLITH. The structure of an application is made of components, a very similar notion to modules, except that a component is an instance of a class and may be composed of several already defined instances of components. The application is seen as a hierarchy of interacting components defined by the application designer using the Darwin configuration language. The management process of a distributed application, for instance execution monitoring, becomes easier because the manager and the designer of the application have the same view of the application. They can now focus on communication between components, placement on nodes of the distributed system, without having to modify the code of basic components.

Our approach extends that proposed by Darwin by elaborating the notions of interaction through connectors [1]. In Darwin, connectors are simple bindings between a source and a set of well-defined destinations. No naming facilities compared to those of message bus are provided and communications are assimilated to method call - within a same node - or RPC between nodes. We want to express more information in connectors. Referring to [15] and [1] shows that this approach is a realistic one.

Section 3 introduces the Olan component-based programming model and the derived language. Components refine and extend the notions of modules and objects by emphasising the properties of inter-module communications.

Section 4 illustrates the use of the Olan programming model to build collaborative teleconferencing applications. Finally, Section 5 addresses the deployment and the administration of distributed applications.

3 Component-based Programming Model

The Olan model allows an application to be expressed as a hierarchy of interacting components. As in object-oriented models, components are instances of classes from which they are instantiated. We thus distinguish:

- The *component class:* it consists of three parts:
    • an interface that provides informations for a correct use of the component,
    • an implementation which is a description of how the functions of the interface are realised,
    • an administration part that describes the behaviour of the components regarding the use of available system resources in the runtime environment.
- The *component instance* or *component*: it is the execution unit derived from the class.

All examples presented in this section are issued from the description of a platform for teleconferencing applications named CoopScan [3], initially prototyped on a distributed Unix platform and redesigned with Olan. This application is presented in section 4.

3.1 The Interface

The interface of a component class is composed of information that allows the component to be used without knowledge of its implementation. We have extended the usual concept of an interface, as described for example in the CORBA IDL, to include the description of all the properties required from a component to work properly. The interface defines *services* and *notifications* [4] either required or provided by the implementation. The interface therefore contains both input and output "plugs" to the component, described as follows:

- *Services* are functions or procedures that can be executed or requested by a component. They may be compared to extern or import directives in programming languages like Ada. *Provided services* are those offered by the implementation of a component while *required services* are those expected to be called by the component.
- *Notifications* are events whose broadcasting may trigger the execution of *reactions* by other components. Notifications have a name and can carry parameters. Every component which receives the notification signal can choose either to react by executing an internal handler, or to ignore it. At the interface level, this is represented by *Reactions*.

Services and notifications differ from each other by an intrinsic property: a service in an interface must always be supplied. A notification may or not be treated by the components included in the application. A runtime property also makes both notions different: a call to a service is always synchronous, while a notification is asynchronous.

An interface includes public *attributes*: attributes, either user-defined or predefined are typed variables whose value is set at instantiation and may change during execution. The value of a given attribute can be: a) imported from the implementation, or b) set from outside of the component. Finally, predefined attributes directly control system mechanisms for administration purposes (Section 5).

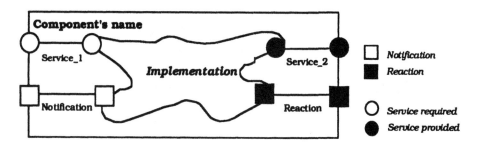

Fig. 1. A component class interface

In figure 1, we present a graphical representation of a component interface, with some bindings with the component's implementation. The graphical syntax is an extension of the one used in the configuration language Darwin.

3.2 Connectors

Connectors are the units that mediate interactions between components. They establish the rules that drive component interactions and specify the required protocol at the runtime level. Rules at the connector level specify:

- the interface conformity such as type conformity and interconnection homogeneity (e.g. "connecting *required* services to *provided* ones"),
- protocols used for the communication (e.g. asynchronous event broadcasting, remote procedure call, etc.),
- specification of an expected behaviour and a set of QoS requirements (e.g. for supporting multimedia communication).

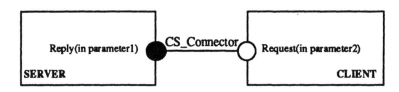

Fig. 2. The client-server communication

In figure ??, the CS_Connector implements a method call between two components. It can be described as follows:

```
connector CS_Connector {
    input requirement (IN parameter2);
    output provision (IN parameter1);
    implementation methodcall;
}
```

Input and **output** are intended to check the conformity of services that can be interconnected (signatures compatibility). The **implementation** stands for the communication protocol involved.

The concept of a connector has already been introduced in the literature. In [1], connectors are defined using a subset of the CSP process algebra. This, combined with the inclusion of some CSP specifications in the interface of components, allows compatibility checking between components and connectors to be performed.

For now, the Olan platform supports several kinds of connectors that are part of a connector library available to the application designer. Among them, there is one connector for synchronous method call facility (with no concern about remote or local call, because this task is handled at deployment time, c.f. section 5), another one for asynchronous event broadcasting, etc.

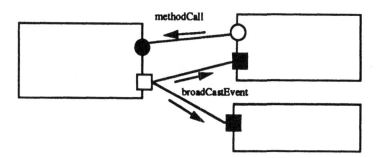

Fig. 3. Connectors

The **methodCall** connector selects one destination among a set of possible ones. The **broadCastMethodCall** connector reaches every possible destination. The **broadCastEvent** uses an asynchronous event service to broadcast an information to a set of destinations.

The definition of more complicated connectors is not yet supplied at the OCL level (Olan Configurartion Language). The application designer shall use one of the connector included in the library package. We are in the process of defining either an implementation pattern for user-defined connectors and an OCL description of connector behavior. However, those features will not be available to the average application designer, as they are considered as advanced utilities.

3.3 The Implementation

The implementation of a component class defines how the services and notifications described in the interface are realised. Implementation is defined by a set of software units or other components and by the interconnections between them. As in Darwin, we distinguish two kinds of implementations that leads to two kinds of component classes, the *primitive* component and the *composite* component.

Primitive Components The *primitive component* is the basic unit of code reuse. The implementation of a primitive component is made of pieces of software that the programmer supplies. For instance, an implementation can be composed of a set of C++ classes, a set of modules or libraries or any combination of the above. Services provided at the interface level must be implemented in the component. Attributes may also be public variables of the implementation.

The concept of a primitive component suits well the approach we adopt for building teleconferencing applications using the Olan model. In fact, our goal is to integrate already existing single-user applications in a co-operative environment without modifying their code. However, a primitive component may also encapsulate one single object (e.g. a single instance of a C++ class).

An example of primitive component is the component **SharedApplication**, which encapsulates the binary code of an existing application.

- The *Init* provided service is called for application initialisation.
- The *SendOperation* required service enables locally executed actions to be communicated to other components.
- The *ReceiveOperation* provided service enables another component to perform an action on the application. It is linked to the API of the encapsulated application.

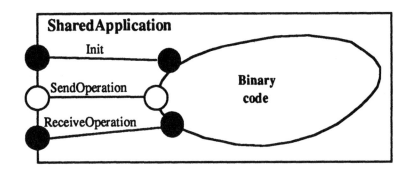

Fig. 4. The SharedApplication primitive component

We give the textual description of the component in OCL (Olan Configuration Language):

```
interface SharedApplicationItf {
  provide Init (in long launchMode);
  provide ReceiveOperation (in string encodedAction);
  require SendOperation (in string encodedAction,
            out long result);
}
primitive implementation SharedApplicationImp :
          SharedApplicationItf {
  // reference to binary code
}
component class SharedApplication {
  interface SharedApplicationItf;
  implementation SharedApplicationImp;
}
```

Composite Components The *composite component* class is the structuring unit. Its implementation is made of sub-components and interconnections between them. Sub-components are instances of component classes described elsewhere. Compared to usual programming languages, it does not describe how functions are supplied, but what are the components needed to achieve the interface definition, and how these components communicate with each other. Figure 5 gives an example of a composite component.

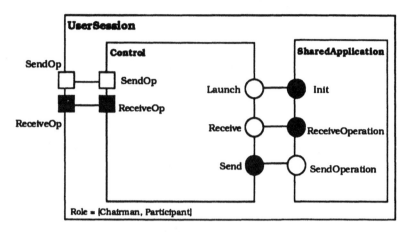

Fig. 5. Composite component class

inst defines the declaration of a "sub-component". The keyword **=>** defines an interconnection which uses a connector specified in the **using** statement.

```
interface UserSessionItf {
  notify SendOp (IN string encodedOperation);
  react ReceiveOp (IN string encodedOperation);
  attribute Role in [Chairman, Participant];
}
implementation UserSessionImp : UserSessionItf {
  // sub-components declaration
  theController = inst Control;
  theApplication = inst SharedApplication;
  // connections between enclosing component interface
  // and sub-components interfaces
  theController.ReceiveOp => ReceiveOp ;
  SendOp => theController.SendOp;
  // sub-component inter-connections
  theController.Launch => theApplication.Init
      using methodCall;
  theController.Receive
      => theApplication.ReceiveOperation
      using methodCall;
  theApplication.SendOperation
      => theController.Send
      using methodCall;
```

```
};
component UserSession {
  interface UserSessionItf;
  implementation UserSessionImp;
}
```

Collections In order to facilitate the design of co-operative applications, we introduce the concept of a *collection*. A collection is a set of instances of a same component class. The number of possible instances at execution time is specified with a minimum and maximum cardinality. Collections allow an easy manipulation of a set of entities which can evolve dynamically. Instances contained in the same collection are commonly manipulated through an unified interface. The interest of the collection appears if we try to build a new composite component consisting of several interconnected instances of the component **UserSession**. Defining all the possible bindings between all the instances would be tedious, especially if we consider a variable number of instances.

In figure 6, we present the **DistributedApplication** component, which is based on a collection of components **UserSession**. The collection is specified by the component class name and the cardinality. Internal links are interactions between the different component contained in the collection.

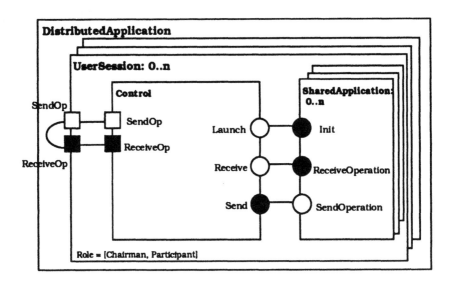

Fig. 6. Composite component with a collection

```
implementation DistributedApplicationImp :
            DistributedAplicationItf {
  everyUser = collection [0..n] of UserSession;
  everyUser.SendOp => everyUser.ReceiveOp
      using broadcastEvent;
}
```

Collections are the keystone of dynamic instantiation of components. In order to realise creation and destruction of components, each collection provides **create** and **delete** services.

Introducing collections raises a new issue concerning the naming requirements of components. In a distributed system, objects are generally named by their object identifier (Oid). This naming scheme seems somehow restrictive and incompatible with collections, where the destination of a communication is a priori not known. Therefore, we introduce associative naming facilities based on the run-time value of components attributes. Among these attributes, one can find for example, an instance's identifier, so a direct naming is still possible. Figure 7 presents an example of such associative naming.

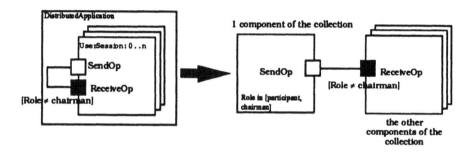

Fig. 7. Associative naming with connectors and collections

The *SendOp/ReceiveOp* interaction of the previous example becomes:
```
everyUser.SendOp => everyUser.ReceiveOp
where everyUser.Role ≠ chairman
using broadcastEvent
```
In this example, the communication is achieved with a broadcast event mechanism according to an associative designation (the **where** condition) to identify component destinations.

4 CSCW Application Construction

4.1 CoopScan: functional description

CoopScan is a generic framework for developing teleconferencing applications [3]. Conferencing refers to the use of an application (or a set of applications) by multiple users simultaneously to achieve a multiparty communication. In CoopScan, conferencing is implemented by:

- distributing the visual interface of an application to remote workstations thereby allowing remote users to see the actions of one another, and

– providing input paths from each participant back to the application so that any participant in the conference may interact with the application.

The design of our architecture has been driven by a general principle: to support synchronous co-operation over networked computer systems using already existing applications (e.g. editors, drawing programs, text processing utilities). This has led us to provide a set of control protocols, used for all conferencing services, and which allow concurrent access to shared data, and transparent dynamic participation to the conference.

Therefore, generic control modules can be used for various shared applications. For instance, CoopScan can be used as a support for a teleconferencing session in which geographically distributed users cooperate simultaneously through a shared synchronous editor (Grif [12]) and a shared white board panel (xfig). In this scenario, two shared applications are integrated using the same control mechanisms.

4.2   The CoopScan Architecture

The CoopScan architecture is defined as a hierarchical set of interconnected modules possibly located on several sites. This architecture has been designed according to a fully replicated scheme where each node contains an instance of the shared applications, called a *UserSession*. Basically, a *UserSession* is made of a conferencing controller and of a set of shared applications. The conferencing controller provides services to enable shared application access and dynamic user participations. The shared applications allow specific access to the shared co-operation space (e.g. a set of common documents).

The collaboration task is achieved as follows:

– any action performed on a shared application is forwarded to the conferencing controller. If the user is allowed to do an action, the action is effectively performed and the controller broadcasts it to the other controllers,
– actions received from controllers of other sessions, i.e. from another user, are replayed on the local instance of the shared application.

From a functional point of view, the Controller is made of a *LocalAgent* module and a set of *DistantAgents* each one being located on a remote conferencing node. The role of the *LocalAgent* is to grab actions from local applications, validate these actions and broadcast them to the remote sites while *DistantAgent* receive actions from their corresponding *LocalAgent* and ask local applications for a replay.

4.3   Component Based Description

The key direction of using a component based model for designing CoopScan is to provide a direct implementation out of an architectural scheme described in OCL.

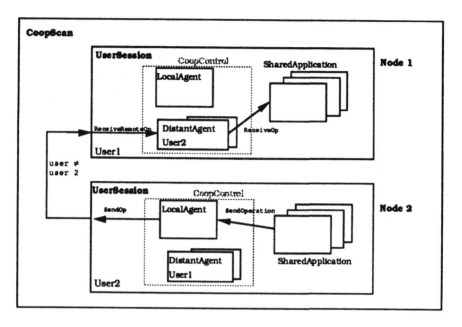

Fig. 8. CoopScan Execution Scheme

CoopScan primitive components Each CoopScan participant has access to the following primitive components :

- the *LocalAgent*: it essentially controls user connections, shared application access, and user interactions,
- the *DistantAgent*: each *LocalAgent* is associated to a set of *DistantAgents* located on every remote node involved in the co-operation task. The *LocalAgent* broadcasts local user actions to all its *DistantAgents*, which allow them to be remotely executed,
- a set of shared application components which carried out actual collaboration tasks. User actions on shared applications are transmitted to the *LocalAgent* before being executed. According to the user role, the action is either validated, locally performed and broadcast to all remote *DistantAgents* (the current user is the floor holder), or ignored (the current user does not hold the floor).

Some primitive components were specifically built for CoopScan (local and distant agents) while other components encapsulate the code of the existing applications.

Using Olan composite components to describe the CoopScan architecture In the Olan model, the CoopScan application is defined as a collection of *UserSession* components. Each CoopScan user is represented by one of the *UserSession* component of the collection. At the lowest description level, a

UserSession is made of a control component *CoopControl* connected to a collection of [0..n] *Shared application* components.

CoopControl is a composite component composed of a *LocalAgent* component and a collection of *DistantAgents* components. Each *DistantAgent* component is associated to a fixed remote user.

Using Olan connectors to describe CoopScan communications The first implementation of CoopScan on top of a Unix platform using sockets as a means to implement interagent communication, has proved carry a high development cost with lots of reimplementation when changing the communication protocol from TCP to UDP. At the opposite, the configuration with Olan makes the implementation of communications independent from that of the primitive components. Thus, the developer uses appropriate Olan connectors to implement communications provided the interfaces of its components are correct.

In the current prototype of CoopScan, communications are implemented using three kinds of connectors: a broadcast method call, a simple method call wich are based on a RPC service provided by the run-time support, and a broadcast event.

- The *broadcastMethodCall* connector is used to implement communications between one source and a set of potential destinations using a synchronous method call service combined with an associative designation service. For example, encoded messages containing a user action on a shared application (delivered from the *LocalAgent* component) are broadcast from a *UserSession* component to all remote *UserSession* components.
- The *methodCall* connector is used to implement communication from one source to a well known destination. The protocol and the mechanism used by the runtime support to do the communication may be of different kind. If the components are on the same node, it may be a classic method or procedure call. If the components are on different nodes, it may be an RPC or simply a message sending through sockets. We actually rely on the resources of the underlying platform.
- The *broadcastEvent* connector implements an event based communication allowing asynchronous event communication between one source and n potential destinations.

5 Application Management with Olan

The overall purpose of distributed application management is to adapt the application behaviour to the resources actually provided by the underlying host environment. This is especially difficult because the same application may run on a wide variety of distributed architectures, ranging from a single machine to tens or hundreds. Referring to [7], we decompose distributed application management into four issues:

- *configuration* of applicative components according to available resources and application requirements,
- *deployment* and *initialisation* of the application in an orderly way,
- *monitoring* of application behaviour and performance measurement,
- *tuning* the application behaviour according to monitored information.

The goal of the Olan framework is to help and ease the configuration process of a distributed application by providing the same programming model for software configuration (process dedicated to the application designer) and for management configuration (dedicated to the application administrator) which includes the first two points previously stated as well as monitoring. We claim that using the same approach and model for both activities will help us take into account application requirements to enhance usage of available system resources.

Usually, adapting an application to specific environment needs such as varying workloads on nodes, environment changes or failures, requires re-programming and re-deploying part of the application. We would like to make the programming and management processes as independent as possible.

Research activity has already focused on that area. Meta [7] provides a collection of tools that perform monitoring and control of the behaviour of an application. The Meta system presents a control program, in charge of managing the application, clearly separated from the functional aspects of the application. Defining this controller with Meta requires three steps:

- instrumenting the application with *sensors*, that gather and monitor the desired information, and *actuators* that modify the behaviour of application components;
- describing the application structure and the environment in which it runs with object-oriented data modelling facilities;
- expressing the *policy rules* which describe the intended behaviour of the system and can make direct calls to sensors and actuators.

With Olan, management facilities rely on the application description previously introduced. This description is the basis for configuration, deployment and installation of the application as well as the setting up of instrumentation for monitoring and tuning purpose. The following section describes how the instrumentation of an application is achieved, and how it is used to define management policies that drive the application behaviour.

5.1 Management Description

In order to isolate management information from the rest of the definition of the component's class, we introduce a specific interface dedicated to management issues and a policy section that describes:

- the instrumentation used to achieve management activities, and
- the way attributes are to be modified at run-time.

Isolating management issues provides protection by preventing unallowed users to perform management actions. This approach tends to be a common issue in the management of complex object-based systems [16].

Management interface The management interface contains a special kind of attribute called *management attributes* which may be readable or writable; their related values are collected from either system calls or from private variables within the implementation of primitive components. These attributes are declared in the interface; the policies will create the relations between attributes and the instrumentation provided in the Olan runtime environment.

Management attributes are defined as:

management attribute [readonly] <type_name> <attribute_name>

The readonly attribute indicates if the attribute only forwards a sensor value or if an actuator is associated to it.

As an example, let us add to the ConfTool primitive component a management attribute in charge of setting the "display" name where the teleconferencing user interface should appear:

```
interface SharedApplicationItf {
  provide Init (in long launchMode);
  provide ReceiveUIOperation (in string encodedAction);
  require SendUIOperation (in string encodedAction,
out long result);
}
implementation SharedApplicationImp : SharedApplicationItf {
    // cf. previous section
}
management interface SharedApplicationMgmt {
  management attribute string display;
}
component SharedApplication {
  interface SharedApplicationItf;
  implementation SharedApplicationImp;
  management SharedApplicationMgmt;
}
```

The management interface is only in charge of defining the values or parameters which may be monitored and tuned before, during or in between executions.

Management policies The management policies are in charge of the definition of:

- the *relationship* between management attributes and instrumentation,
- the *relevant "events"* supposed to change an attribute value,
- the *reactions* associated to a change of an attribute value.

Policies are declared for each attribute. They are composed of a condition and a reaction triggered when the condition is fulfilled. Conditions may either be predefined events, like reading an attribute (e.g. attribute `display` {on read do <something>}) , changes of an attribute value, or more generally request for a requirement defined in the component's interface (e.g. on `sendUIOperation do`), request for a provided service of the component (e.g. on `receiveUIOperation do`), boolean condition based on attribute values (e.g. on `display = ''unix:0'' do`). A condition may also be logical combination of events (e.g. on `(display = ''unix:0'') and (sendUIOperation)`).

We have not supplied an exhaustive definition of relevant events, neither have we a definite syntax for expressing the policies. The reader should refer to [17] for ideas about how to define such policies. A set of default policies will be provided depending on values of predefined attributes.

5.2 Configuring an Application

Configuration for management purpose consists in setting particular attributes before and during execution. The management policies associated with these attributes will then act on the instrumentation with obtain the desired behavior. For example, changing the host where the component resides will enact the migration of the component to another node: the policy associated to changes of the host name attribute invokes the actuator in charge of migrating components.

So far, the human configurator has a limited number of management attributes available. The instrumentation associated as well as the policy are still built-in features within the Olan runtime support. Customization of the management behavior is part of the work in progress. Available attributes and their related policy are listed in figure 9.

6 Conclusion

We claim that *constructing* and *managing* distributed applications require the use of a common model. Such a model should enforce a clear separation between software entities and the interactions between these entities. It should facilitate the integration of existing code, but also the description of the evolution of the structure and interactions along the execution of the application. And finally, the model should provide management facilities that ease the utilisation of available system resources.

The Olan model presented in this paper fulfils these requirements. Software entities are encapsulated into *primitive components*. Interactions are described by *connectors*, which define what kind of components may be interconnected and what communication protocols they use. This model offers a hierarchical structuring of the application, as *composite* components can be built from primitive components and connectors. Dynamic aspects such as creation and deletion of components during an execution are handled with collections. Other dynamic

Attribute name	Sensor	Actuator
nodeName : string *toua.imag.fr*	getHostName	loadOnHost migrateToHost
On instantiation or loading, map the component on host nodeName On changes of nodeName, migrate component to new host nodeName		
nodeType : string *AIX4.1*	getMachineType	loadToMachine migrateToMachine
On instantiation or loading, map component on a host of type nodeType On changes of nodeType, migrate component to a host of type nodeType		
persistent : boolean persistentName : string	isPersistent *none*	registerComponent lookupComponent
If persistent, on instantiation, register the component in name server If persistent, on loading, lookup the component from name server		
owner : name *bellissa@imag.fr*	getOwnerName	belongToOwner migrateToOwner
On loading or instantiation, set ownership to ownerName On changes of ownerName, set ownership to new ownerName and migrate component into a correct context		
...	...	...
Other predefined management attributes are provided They will not be detailed here but they deal with storage location, protection parameters, etc.		

Fig. 9. Available attributes

aspects such as the candidates at a given time to be receivers of a communication are chosen depending on evolving properties with the *associative naming* scheme.

The *management* requirements are expressed directly at the component's level. A component includes management *attributes* and management *policies* which are used to configure the application with respect to its requirements and the system resources.

We have demonstrated the benefits of the Olan model by the description of an existing framework for the development of cooperative applications. This framework, CoopScan, requires the encapsulation of existing code, and the description of generic interactions, independently of the location and implementation of existing software entities. Using the Olan model for CoopScan has allowed a straightforward description of a fairly complex application.

Current status The basic design of the Olan model has been completed, as well as the definition of the runtime environment. The runtime layer has been developed on a network of AIX workstations running OODE [5], a distributed CORBA compliant object-oriented environment, that supports object sharing, distribution and persistence.

We have recently completed the construction of the first version of the teleconferencing CSCW application presented in the paper.

Future work Our current work concerns: tools for visual programming and monitoring based on previous work described in [18]; and the construction of the Olan compiler that will generate the skeleton of the application for our runtime.

Conceptual efforts are made to define more precisely: the connectors and their formal specification, the management policies as well as the instrumentation formalism, and the runtime support for dynamic reconfiguration.

Acknowledgement This work is currently part of the SIRAC project. It has been partially supported by the European ESPRIT project Broadcast and CNET (France Télécom Research Center). We would like to thank the SIRAC team and especially Roland Balter, Fabienne Boyer, Sacha Krakowiak, Emmanuel Lenormand, Vladimir Marangozov, and Jean-Yves Vion-Dury, as well as André Freyssinet and Serge Lacourte from Bull Research Center / Open Software Systems.

References

[1]   Allen R., Garlan D., *Formal Connectors*, (CMU-CS-94-115), School of Computer Science Carnegie Mellon University, Pittsburgh, PA 15213, March 1994.

[2]   Balter R., Bernadat J., Decouchant D., Duda A., Freyssinet A., Krakowiak S., Meysembourg M., Le Dot P., Nguyen Van H., Paire E., Riveill M., Roisin C., Rousset de Pina X., Scioville R., Vandôme G., "Architecture and Implementation of Guide, an Object-Oriented Distributed System", *Computing Systems*, Vol.4 (No.1), pp. 31-67, 91.

[3]   Balter R., Ben Atallah S., Kanawati R., "System Architecture for Synchronous Groupware Development", *Proceedings of the Sixth International Conference on Human-Computer Interaction, (HCI International '95)*, Vol.1, pp371-379, ed. Elsevier, Tokyo, Japan , 9-14 July 1995

[4]   Boyer F., "Coordinating Software Development Tools with Indra", *7th Conference on Software Engineering Environments (SEE'95)*, pp. 1-13, IEEE Computer Society Press, Noordwijkerhout (Netherlands), 5-7 April 1995.

[5]   Bull Open Software Systems, "OODE: Une plate-forme Objet pour les Applications Coopératives", Congrès AFCET, Paris - France, Novembre 1994.

[6]   Kramer J., Magee J., Sloman M., "Constructing Distributed Systems in Conic", *IEEE Transactions on Software Engineering*, Vol.15 (No.6), pp. 663-675, 1989.

[7]   Marzullo K., Cooper R., Wood M. D., Birman K. P., "Tools for Distributed Application Management", *IEEE Computer*, Vol.24 (No.8), pp. 42-51, August 1991.

[8]   Magee J., Dulay N., Kramer J., "A Constructive Development Environment for Parallel and Distributed Programs", *Proceedings of the International Workshop on Configurable Distributed Systems*, Pittsburgh, March 1994.

[9]   Oki B., Pfluegl M., Siegel A., Skeen D., "The Information Bus - An Architecture for Extensible Distributed Systems", *ACM Proc. 14th Symposium on Operating Systems Principles (SOSP'93)*, pp. 58-67, Dec. 1993.

[10]   Object Management Group, "The Common Object Request Broker: Architecture and Specification", (91.12.1), December 1991.

[11]   Purtilo J.M., "The POLYLITH Software Bus", *ACM TOPLAS*, Vol.16 (No.1), pp. 151-174, Jan. 1994.

[12]   Quint V., Vatton I., "Active Document as a Paradigm for Human-Computer Interaction", *Workshop on Research Issues in the Intersection of Software Engeneering and HCI*, Sorrento, Italy, May 1994.

[13]   Reiss S., "Connecting Tools Using Message Passing in the FIELD Environment", *IEEE Software*, pp. 57-66, July 1990.

[14]   Shaw M., "Procedure Calls Are the Assembly Language of Software Interconnection: Connectors Deserve First-Class Status", *in Proceedings of Workshop on Studies of Software Design*, LNCS Springer-Verlag, 1994.

[15]   Shaw M., DeLine R., Klein D. K., Ross T. L., Young D. M., Zelesnik G., "Abstractions for Software Architecture and Tools to Support Them", *IEEE Transactions on Software Engineering*, Vol.21(No.4), pp. 314-334, April 1995.

[16]   Sloman M., *Chapter 12 of Network and Distributed Management*, ed. by M. Sloman, Addison-Wesley, pp 303-347, 1994.

[17]   Sloman M., *Policy Driven Management for Distributed System*, (DoC 93/48), Imperial College Department of Computing, 180 Queen's Gate, London SW7 2BZ UK, June 1994.

[18]   Vion-Dury J.-Y., Santana M., "Virtual Images: Interactive Visualisation of Distributed Object-Oriented Systems", *Proc. of the Ninth Annual Conference on Object-Oriented Programming Systems, Languages and Applications (OOPSLA)*, Portland, Oregon, October 1994.

The Version Management Architecture of an Object-Oriented Distributed Systems Environment: OZ++

Michiharu Tsukamoto[1], Yoichi Hamazaki[1],
Toshihiro Nishioka[*2], and Hideyuki Otokawa[*3]

[1] Electrotechnical Laboratory, 1-1-4 Umezono, Tsukuba, Ibaraki 305, Japan
[2] Mitsubishi Research Institute, Inc., 2-3-6 Otemachi, Chiyoda-ku, Tokyo 100, Japan
[3] Sharp Corporation, 2613-1 Ichinomoto, Tenri, Nara 632, Japan

Abstract. Internet based information retrieval software attracts attention because of potentially great impact on our society brought about by its usefulness in information dispatch, sharing, and distribution. However, it is difficult to share, distribute, and reuse of software on wide-area network environment. OZ++ system is a software system to conquer this problem. Based on the concept of object-orientation, the system provides automatic distribution and upgrading function of software over networks. Using the system, software can be brought together from all over the network; furthermore, it has become possible to run such software immediately. This paper introduces the version management mechanism of the most attractive feature of OZ++. Its version management is based on the interface of classes.

1 Introduction

Internet based information retrieval software attracts attention because of Internets potentially great impact on our society brought about by its usefulness in information dispatch, sharing, and distribution. However, many software developers remake and reintroduce similar softwares the world over, and this makes difficult to improve productivity and software reliability. It is considered that mutual sharing and reuse of software through Internet will improve the quality of shared and reused software, and enable us to concentrate our efforts on the new software development. That is, we expect not only data sharing, distributing and reusing on Internet, but also development of the software system, which will enable program sharing, distribution and reuse.

1.1 Object-Oriented Approach to the problems

The object-oriented approach is considered to be the most suitable approach for realizing a software system that enables sharing, distribution and reuse of programs because of its ability to devise parts and reutilize software resources. The development and execution methods based on this approach are as follows:

---

* Researcher, Tsukuba Laboratory, Open Fundamental Software Technology Project

- **Development phase**
  On the network environment, programming with a class sharing function, inter-utilizing and/or customizing the opened class library if necessary, will be enabled.
- **Execution Phase**
  When receiving a class object made like this, whenever the need arises, the customized class is obtained and executed by a function of class distribution.

For smooth implementation of this kind of development and execution, however, requires as follows:

- If various customizations exist, it does not matter if a class uses an old version.
- On customizing the class, only necessary parts are recompiled.
- When a program is executed, various coexisting class versions can be executed at the same time.

1.2 Contents of this Paper

OZ++ is a software system that meets these requirements. It operates in a distributed object-oriented environment that takes into consideration the wide-area network environment consisting of the OZ++ language system, an executing system, a management system and the development environment[1],[2],[3]. The characteristic functions are class sharing, class distribution, class version management and class certification function in the network environment. The prelemenary evaluation of OZ++ will be published in [4].

This paper discusses the concepts of class, version management systems and version propagating systems on the OZ++ system. Section 2 presents a discussion of related work in distributed systems, Section 3 discusses class sharing and upgrading, Section 4 introduces class to OZ++, Section 5 explains interface and version, Section 6 mentions the information managed by the object management system, Section 7 describes the basic version management system and Section 8 deals with the version distribution method.

2 Related Works

Some former studies of programming to utilize object-oriented languages include Eden[5], Argus[6], Emerald[7], Distributed Smalltalk[8] and OZ+[9]. They are however, basic studies because they applied object-based language on small-scale networks such as LAN, or aimed at design and execution systems for object-oriented languages.

OZ++ language is multiple-inheritance object-oriented languages which has week type system. OZ++ doesn't use uniform objects model as in Emerald and Smalltalk but network-wide global objects and local objects model as in Argus and Eden. Because many of objects has locally of access and the performance of access to global objects and local objects differs greatly in large-scale network environment. In OZ++ language, global or local is not a property of class but that of variable bound to object. This gives freedom of choice to programmer who uses classes available on networks in his/her programs.

Studies have recently started on C+@[10] and JAVA[11] which are intended for the large-scale Internet environment. OZ++ comes into this category. Both OZ++ and Java have mechanisms to gather executable codes over networks on demand. Java is designed to be used to extend functions of world wide web's browser, and its applications are rather small. In the other hand, OZ++ is designed to be used for large scale applications which are distributed widely over internet.

The large-scale Internet environment requires classes, naming of objects, co-existence of various versions and security countermeasures which do not exist in the small-scale LAN environment. Naming has been studied as an important system of distributed operating systems. When it is subjected to programming, it is necessary to add peculiar contrivances to the programming language. However, there have been insufficient studies in this field. For version management, there are schema-evolution [12], [13], which are designated to template changes in the field of the object-oriented database, and a study on the object management system focused on interrelationships between objects [14]. Version management of OZ++ has the point aimed at interface of classes.

3   Common Use and Upgrading of Software on Distributed System

For efficient programming on a distribution system, it is first necessary to verify whether or not there is an object that provides a required service (function). If there is, you will have to search for an interface to utilize it. It can be listed for this purpose that traders of CORBA/OMG[15] which enables you to discover the location of the object from contents of a service. If you can not find it with this way, you will have to program it.

On programming, the nearest class that can realize the purpose is verified, and started to customize, the nearest function when it is verified. When it shortens the function or does not exist, the search will be started to find useful parts. If this job can be repeated easily, it is easy to make an objective program instead of building a new program. No attention need be paid to others when you make your own program. Your purpose will be achieved on the Internet environment on which only you exist or a plural number of people coexist, however, you very frequently want to run two programs at the same time, in both of which you have already utilized parts of others programs and your this-time-remodeling-program. In this case, th e existing program can not be rewritten, and it is necessary to make your remodeling program run simultaneously. Then, if the program is very sophisticated, has been, frequently improved, it is necessary to enable the latest program to be used by referring to the originals instead of using copied programs. OZ++ aims at this kind of programming environment. What, generally speaking, are necessary to develop the potentials of these programming environments?

3.1 Modularity

In a wide-area network environment, there are few relations between software sources supplier and users, and it is difficult to assume that they have common purposes. To have software sources in common in this occasion requires the following mechanism:

- A clear expression of the interdependency between supplier and user
- Ability to utilize software sources without detailed knowledge about the environment of the supplier

That is, software resources must have clear interfaces and high modularity. Fortunately, the object-oriented paradigm is consistent with this purpose.

3.2 Distribution-Transparency

The most important point is whether or not both the supplier and the user of software resources have a common environment or not when they are assumed to have common software resources. However, this can not generally be assumed on a wide-area network. It is assumed that minimum environment preparations are made for a software in advance instead of the user preparing for it each time it is provided. That is, each environment is assumed to be ready beforehand. Thus, it is necessary to provide:

- A mechanism that can take advantages of software sources with distribution-transparency independently of its location

3.3 Variation of Software

Software is always being upgraded. Softwares used on network environments are no exceptions to this tendency. Now, even if a software is upgraded, it can not waste data generated by the old version. Nevertheless, you want to use the new one, so it is necessary to allow plural version software to exist and run, or to translate data from old software to a new one with the assistance of schema-evolution. When there is a drastic upgrading of software, the schema-evolution can not handle it. Moreover, the user is sometimes requested to use same version or a different version at the same time when he is provided a software by a third party. Thus, it is necessary to introduce:

- A mechanism that can manage both new and old software versions without conflict

3.4 Software Upgrading

In a wide-area network environment, various kinds of software are requested for various needs. Changing needs prompt the software to change and expand, and to be newly featured. The following mechanisms are required to respond to these changes:

- One that can expand and add functions to existing software
- One that can customize a realization of a function to suite a users own purposes as using existing software
- One that can utilize the functions when a software is upgraded by expanding functions and/or fixing bugs

4 Designing the OZ++

As described in the previous section, to satisfy the demands for distribution-transparent software resources, modularity, and software upgrading and versions, the OZ++ employs the following methods:

- It considers the class to be the unit of software resource. It also considers it to have high modularity and supports multiple inheritance.
- It introduces the class management system, and provides information concerning classes throughout the network.
- It manages the versions using the class management system.

These methods were employed because:

- In the framework of object-orientation, it is both natural and comprehensive to consider class as the unit of software resources.
- The concept of OZ++ that the object, being the unit of service in the network, enables the introduction of a class management system which implements the distribution-transparent class.
- Software resources can be effectively utilized out by version management.

4.1 Class as Unit of Software Resources

In OZ++, the class is introduced as the module of software development, and it can be shared as a unit of software resources. For this reason, in OZ++, the class is given an identifier (ID) which is unique worldwide. Both the language processing system (compilers) and program execution system (executors) can refer to classes through this ID.

To generate unique IDs for classes distributed worldwide, centralized approach is not realistic, so hierarchical approach is used in OZ++. In OZ++, objects are held and their methods are executed by executors. Several executors may work on a computer. A group of computers which can communicate each other using both unicast and broadcast makes a site, and all executors on those computes belong to the site.

Unique IDs for classes are 64 bits numbers which consist of three parts, site ID, executor number, and item number which are 16 bits, 24 bits and 24bits respectively. Site-IDs are assigned uniquely by an organization as like as IP-addresses of internet. Executor numbers are generated in sequence in each site and they are not reused to make them unique in the site. Item numbers are generated in sequence in each executor and not reused to make them unique in the executor. We assumed that thirty thousand sites are enough for experimental use of OZ++ system worldwide. Millions of executors in a site and millions of items for a executor are enough in the lifetime of OZ++ system. The combination of Site ID and executor number is used for executor's ID, and the combination of executor's ID and item number is used for ID of classes. These IDs are unique in the world, and no communication between sites is necessary to generate them.

This class ID is affixed to objects, and objects belonging to the same class share this ID.

Classes in OZ++ support multiple inheritance, enabling the existent classes to be utilized either as extensions of present classes or as parts for other softwares. This in turn clarifies the parts of mutual existence between the clients and servers of classes. In this way, the OZ++ measures the effective utilization of software resources as a library. Furthermore, the interface is clearly described, and the safe utilization of classes is guaranteed to some extent through static checks of types. This leads to the re-utilization of software resources.

4.2 Distribution-Transparent Classes and the Class Management System

An ID unique to each class is given to every class in the world, enabling unique reference to them. For this reason, the management system is introduced, and information concerning the classes is provided as a service in the network. This unique ID must be shown to access information about classes, and a request for the particular information must be made. The class management system is realized by a group of OZ++ objects of same kind, the classes, so it can be extended, and customized.

4.3 Class Management System, Language Processor and Executor

The OZ++ has three subsystems as shown in Fig.1: the class management system, the language processors and the executors. The OZ++ user develops or utilizes classes using these subsystems.

The registration of classes by the language processor to the class management system and the acquisition of class information by the executor from this class management system are performed as follows:

– The language processor compiles the source codes and registers the resulting memory configuration and executable codes in a class which is a part of the class management system.

When compiled results are registered in a class, unique IDs are generated by the executor on which the class exists and those IDs are assigned for each classes.

- The class, based on the interface, manages this information as a version. Each versions has unique ID.
- Using the unique class ID placed in the object, the executor obtains information whenever necessary from the class management system.

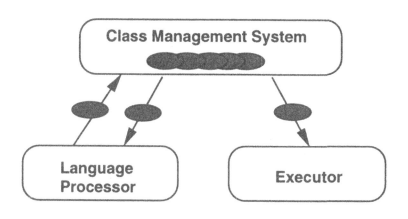

 : **Executable Code, Interface, etc.**

Fig. 1. The Class Management System, the Compiler, and the Executor

4.4 Obtaining Information from the Class Management System over Networks

Classes are identified by their unique IDs and executors can obtain information from the class management system when necessary. Classes are created by many programmers at any location over networks day and night. It is not appropriate to manage those classes in centralized fashion, so they are managed objects 'the classes' distributed over networks.

Broadcast is used to search the location of information in a site, because broadcast is most suitable way to find information in unknown location within small area like OZ++'s site. In the case of inter-site service, the class management system in a site is responsible to provide information about classes generated in the site. Originated site of the information can be decided form its ID, and inter-site communication mechanisms for searching information is provided in OZ++.

The procedure to obtain information from the class management system is as follows:

1. The executor raise a request of obtaining information with its ID to the class which exists on it when necessary.
2. If the class has that information, it gives the information to the executor. Otherwise, the class begins to find the information over networks.
3. At first, the class broadcasts the request to all classes in its own site. If some of classes have that information, they respond to the requesting class, and the class can get the information from one of responding classes. Thereafter the class manages the information gotten from other class.
4. If there is no response after several retrial, the class send the request to the class service object of the site where the information is generated initially. The site can be determined from the class ID, because it contains site ID. When the class service object receives request, it searches the information in the site and respond it if found.

4.5 Delayed Acquisition of Class Information

The following can be said about the acquisition of access and information by the executor from the class management system:

- The acquisition of information concerning the memory configuration of objects can be delayed until objects are instantiated.
- The acquisition of executable codes can be delayed until methods are invoked.

In the OZ++, these delays are used effectively, whenever necessary, to obtain and access service from the class management system. Thus, when executing methods or instantiating objects, there is no need to prepare in advance executable codes and information concerning memory configurations of objects.

As a result, there is no need for unnecessary copies or transfers. Thus, a very effective sharing of distribution-transparent software resources can be realized.

This also means that implementation particulars can be delayed until objects are instantiated. From this, the user can change the particulars of implementations according to the situation. Flexible operations can be performed with this function.

4.6 Guarantee of Safe Sharing

From the realization of the distribution-transparent class management system, a framework for using the class is provided. Moreover, to advance sharing effectively, there is a need for a safe mechanism for sharing classes. Class management which does not cause contradiction in operations is necessary.

In the OZ++, this problem is solved by performing static checks on the inheritance relationship of classes at the time of compilation, on the signature of methods, and on types of variables. Also an approach is taken to manage each version of classes based on the interface.

The interface is clearly defined. Thus, if class management performance is based on an interface, the class of a different interface can never be used mistakenly. This makes it possible to realize a mixture of objects using both old and new classes.

5 Interfaces and Versions of Classes

In OZ++, interfaces of classes are described clearly and the types are checked at the time of compilation. This section explains the interfaces and versions of classes in OZ++.

5.1 Uses of Classes

There are two ways to use classes: within the inheritance tree, and from outside the tree. The former uses the class as a superclass. This is called use for inheritance. The latter uses the class for instance variables and automatic variables. This is called the use for external reference.

5.2 Access Control in OZ++ Language

Specifying whether or not any of the class elements (class members) hidden from or exposed to the exterior of the class is called access control. In OZ++, the access control of the class members is performed in the following ways:

- **public**
  Among class members, this can be used to specify only methods. Class members specified as public, can not only be used for inheritance, i.e. using the class within the inheritance tree, but also for external reference, i.e. using the class from outside the inheritance tree.
- **protected**
  This can be used to specify all class members. Class members specified as protected, can only be used for inheritance, i.e. using the class within the inheritance tree. Thus, the use of the class for external references, i.e. from outside the inheritance tree, is forbidden.
- **private**
  This can be used to specify all the class members. Class members specified as private can be used for neither inheritance nor external references.

5.3 Interface of Classes and Their Versions

In OZ++ language, parts of classes specified as public and protected in the above access controls are interfaces, and parts specified as private are not interfaces but are details of implementations. In OZ++, a version is given to each part, public, protected or private, and employs system performing management. That is, the class version is expressed in terms of these three combinations of numbers expressing the public interface, the protected interface, and the implementation. The corresponding parts expressing the versions are the parts of public, protected, and implementation.

By handling the version in three parts corresponding to the mechanism of information hiding of the class, the need to re-compile programs using the class can be restricted.

The version structure of classes is shown in Fig.2. A unique ID is given to all versions in the world. The OZ++ system provides a mechanism for providing information concerning the version shown by this ID.

Along the interface, the class development is performed according to the following three steps:

1. The version of public interface of a class is developed.
2. After specifying the version of the public interface, its protected interface is developed.
3. After specifying the version of the protected interface, its implementation interface is developed.

If a class uses another class, depending in the method of use, the version of the class which uses the other class is specified.

- **If used for external reference**
  The public interface version of the class, using the other class, is specified.
- **If used for inheritance**
  The protected interface version of the class using the other class is specified.

Precautions must be taken if the first development step stated above is taken, where it is necessary to specify the version of the protected super classes.

5.4 OZ++ Compiler

When writing programs in OZ++ language, the class name is a meaningful character string only to programmers. The programmer specifies the following to the compiler:

- The class development step
- The source program
- The corresponding table between class name and the version IDs of classes specifying the interface

The compiler, by using the correspondence table, replaces the class name appearing in the source program into the version ID of the class capable of checking interface adaptability.

According to the steps described above and by using the specified versions, the OZ++ compiler checks the adaptability of method calls and reference by variable names.

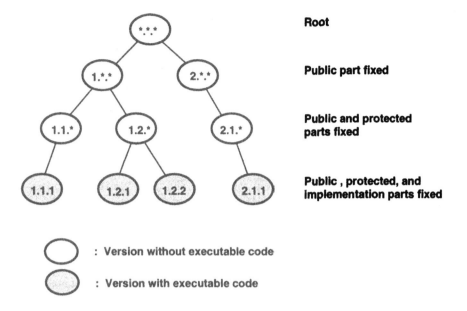

Fig. 2. The Version Structure of Classes

6   The Information Managed by the Class Management System

The class management system which manages the classes as versions based on the interface handles the following information:

- The Inheritance Tree:
  The language processor generates and registers this tree. It is used when the language processor compiles the source codes, and when the executor generates the configuration and dispatch table.
- The Public Method Signature:
  The language processor generates and registers this signature and uses it at the time of compilation.
- Protected Method Signature:
  The language processor generates and registers this signature and uses it at the time of compilation.
- Memory Allocation Information:
  This is used when the executor either generates or encodes/decodes objects.
- Executable Codes:
  These are generated and registered by the language processor and are used when methods are executed.
- Class Information at Runtime:
  This is the information required when the executor runs the method of an object.

7 The Configuration Management

The OZ++ executor loads on-demand the executable codes generated by the language compiler. This section explains the mechanism of deciding and managing the versions of the implementation parts of classes at the time of instantiation.

7.1 The Configuration

As described in the previous section, the class, described in OZ++ language is used for inheritance, and must be specified up to the version of the protected part. If the class is used for external references, the public part is specified. In either case, the version of the implementation part is not specified at the time of compilation, but at the time of instantiation.

Let us consider class hierarchy as shown in Fig.7.1. When using this class D, specification of the implementation version must be done not only for D, but also for A, B, and C. After specifying the A, B, C and D versions, it is necessary to deal with the generated objects as a combined version (i.e. combination of versions).

In this way, if the combined version of the implementation parts of a class and all its super classes is specified up to the implementation part, it is called a configuration. An ID is also given to the configuration. This ID is called configured class ID (configuration is the combination of the class version ID and this configured class ID).

Since the configuration is only a part of the information concerning the class version, it is generated and managed by the class objects. The configuration is generated in the following cases:

- Before generating instances, if the user specifies which instance to use as the implementation part.
- If configurations are necessary, however, the user generates instances without generating configurations.

In this way, deciding only the interface part of the classes at the time of compilation enables the dynamic specification of the implementation part by configurations at the time of instantiation.

Using the mechanism of this dynamic specification, the user, by specifying configurations, can to some extent select the behavior of generating instances.

7.2 Generation of Instances

When generating instances of a class, information concerning the expression of instance structure and the execution of methods is needed for the executor to fix the data space and to execute the constructor. However, this information belongs to the part which is determined by the version of the implementation part of the classes. Therefore, at the time of compilation, the implementation part generates a configuration to the given version ID of an unknown version. Later,

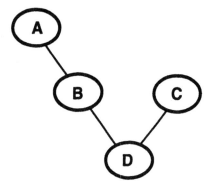

Fig. 3. An Example of Class Hierarchy

the implementation part must specify its version (This version ID is referred to as compilation version ID from below).

For this reason, the process related to the configuration between the executor and the management system takes place in the following manner (Fig.4):

- The executor queries the class management system about configured class ID corresponding to compilation version ID.
- The class management system returns configured class ID if the configuration exists for the received compilation version ID.
- If a configuration does not exist for the compilation version ID, the class management system generates a new configuration, returns its configured class ID.

Next, the executor allocate data space and executes the constructors in the following manner:

- Obtains the execution-class-information from the class management system, using configured class ID.
- Inserts configured class ID into the object management information inside the data space. Even if this object is copied into other executors, the execution-class-information is obtained by the proper execution of methods.
- After the data space allocation is terminated, the constructor is executed and the instance generation is completed.

7.3 Execution of Methods

On the basis of the execution class information, the executor prepares the class management information as shown in Fig.5. The class management information contains the version ID of the version fixed by the implementation part of each constituting class. (This version ID is referred to as the execution version ID.)

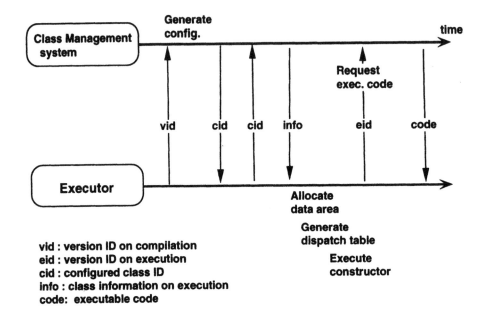

Fig. 4. Generation of Instances

The execution version ID is used when the executable codes are loaded dynamically.

The executor runs the method as follows:

- If the dispatch table of the method does not exist in the executor, the execution class information is obtained from the class management system on the basis of the configured class ID. Thus, the dispatch table is created, and the executable codes to be loaded are fixed.
- If the executable codes do not exist in the executor, the execution version ID is passed to the class management system, and the dynamic load of the executor is activated.
- After loading the executable codes, the function to be executed is selected by using the selector allocated to the method during compilation. Thus, the function is executed.

7.4 Specifications of Configuration

When classes like class D shown in Fig.6-(a) are used for external references, their public parts are fixed during compilation. When class D is compiled, the versions of protected parts in the super classes A, B and C are also fixed.

Specifying of class D configuration means fixing the versions specific to the implementation parts of A, B, C and D.'

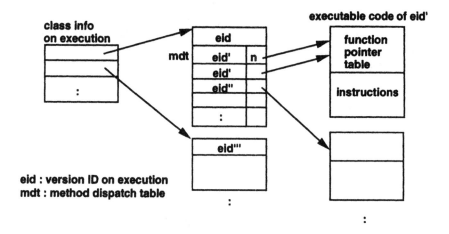

Fig. 5. Class Management Information

For each class shown in Fig.6-(b), there are many versions which are specific up to the implementation part. By selecting any of these versions, a combination of versions can be fixed as shown in Fig.6-(c).

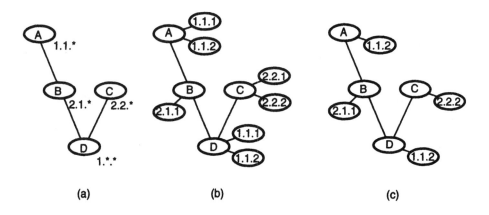

Version number = public-part . protected-part . implementation-part

Fig. 6. Fixation of Configurations

8 Propagation of Configurations

A big advantage is that the latest version can be always used. However, there are many particular versions of softwares whose functions are definitely guaranteed.

Thus, we introduced the mechanism of propagating the configuration sets in OZ++. The configuration set is the set which regulates the configuration of each class constituting the software. Moreover, this set is used at the time of instantiation of classes.

8.1 The Application Range of Configuration Sets

The application range of a particular configuration set is the execution range of the software. However, where different users have the same softwares and where one user has different softwares, in general, different configuration sets are produced. Furthermore, the execution range of the software (i.e. the application range of a particular operation set) is not determined clearly, since an object is passed as a parameter of a method invocation or as a return value of the method in the OZ++ network.

The configuration is used only during the generation of instances. It is enough to know which software the instantiation belongs to. The following two methods can be considered:

- **Method of Focusing on the Process**
  An instantiation performed by a first process or a second process forked by the first process is considered to belong to the software of the first process.
- **Method of Focusing on the Object**
  An instantiation performed by the method of an object is considered to belong to the object of the software.

A method that focusing on the process is not proper, because the chain of method invocation is emphasized, and use configurations beyond what a software developer or a software user can think of. Thus, a method that focusing on the object where configurations familiar to the software user or developers are used, is employed. That is, the configuration sets are put into the object.

8.2 Method of Propagating Configuration Sets

The following methods are employed to set up the software configuration and to give a configuration set to each object:

- The launcher which activates the software contains an initial configuration set corresponding to it.
- The object contains the configuration sets when its instantiation starts.
- Instantiation inside the objects uses its own configuration set.

By these methods, the configuration is kept by each object, and the initial configuration set is propagated one object to the other serially. Moreover, when a method of another object is invoked, its configuration set is used.

8.3 Efficient Propagation

The problem is how efficiently the configuration set is propagated. To resolve this problem, we first propose to divide the large-scale software into several modules. This will set the configuration in each module. However, there will still be cases when the configuration set needs 1.6 KB for a medium scale module of 100 configurations. In this case, copying this configuration set frequently is not a good idea.

In the computation model of the objects in OZ++, there are independent memory spaces in the form of units called cells [3]. Objects inside the cells are accessed by pointers. Objects outside the cell are accessed by object ID. However, in latter cases, the memory itself can not be accessed directly. Therefore, the configuration set, when it generates instances from inside the cell, simply copies the pointers. Thus, there are no overhead collisions. In reality, copying becomes necessary in the following cases:

- creating another new cell,
- transmitting the object as a parameter for method invocation of another cell,
- returning objects as return values for method invocation to another cell.

Since it is very rare to create a new cell, we do not consider this case. There are problems in exchanging objects frequently among cells. However, objects are transferred to carry the data and the algorithms. It is thought that in objects which are transferred to another cell, generation of instances does not take place so frequently. Therefore, to improve performance, a cautious programmer will empty the configuration set before transmitting unnecessary objects.

By considering what is being realized by the configuration set, the performance drop can be maintained at to an acceptable level, if the drop is limited to the case of generating instances in another cell.

Since the compiler outputs the codes when using the configuration set described here, and when copying passed by the network in generating instances, an ordinary programmer does not need to know much about the propagation mechanism of configuration sets.

9 Conclusion

This paper proposed a method of enabling the class as distribution-transparent and as a unit of common software resources, and a method of version management giving heed to class interfaces. It also described the class management method and distribution method of configuration to materialize it. Problems waiting solutions after this are as follows:

- To incorporate some beneficial fruits of schema-evolution into OZ++, and to improve the treatment of expansion and improvement unrelated to interface, even of super class.

- To enable the parts specified as private which are not interfaces to select the same implementations by interfaced private, and to give OZ++ flexibility for debugging.

The information, software and documents of OZ++ system are available via the following Internet addresses.

`http://www.etl.go.jp:8080/etl/bunsan/OZ/OZ.html`

Acknowledgments

This research is conducted under the Open Fundamental Software Technology Project of Information-Technology Promotion Agency, Japan (IPA). Design and implementation of OZ++ derive from the great contribution of researchers in the OZ++ Project, Mr.Yu Nakagawa (Fuji Xerox Information Systems, Co., Ltd.), Mr. Masao Onishi (Toyo Information Systems, Inc.), Mr. Yasumitsu Yoshida (Nihon Unisys, Ltd.), Mr. Hiroaki Kago (Mitsubishi Research Institute, Inc., currently Waseda University), Mr. Masaki Ishikawa (Mitsubishi Research Institute, Inc.), Mr. Yutaka Niibe (Mitsubishi Research Institute, Inc.), Mr.Takayuki Suzuki (Sharp Business Computer Software, Co., Ltd.), Mr. Eiji Yoshiya (Fuji Xerox Information Systems, Co., Ltd.), and Dr. Akihito Nakamura (Electrotechnical Laboratory). We wish to thank these colleagues.

References

1. Tsukamoto, M., Hamazaki, Y. et al.: Distributed Programming with Sharing and Transfer of Classes, Proc. of 13th IPA Conference (Oct. 1994) 197-215 (in Japanese)
2. gNiibe, Y., Otokawa, H., Nishioka, T., Ishikawa, M., Nakagawa, Y., Hamazaki, Y., and Tsukamoto, M.: The Version Management Mechanism of OZ++ Compiler, Proc. of SWoPP '94 (July 1994) (in Japanese)
3. Hamazaki, Y., Tsukamoto, M., Onishi, M., and gNiibe, Y.: The Object Communication Mechanisms of OZ++: An Object-Oriented Distributed Systems Environment, Proc. of 9th ICOIN (Dec. 1994) 425-430
4. Tsukmaoto, M., Hamazaki, Y. et al.: The Design and Implementation of an Object-Oriented Distributed System Based on Sharing and Transfer of Classes, Trans. on IPSJ (Spring 1996) (in Japanese)
5. Almes, G.T., Black, A.P., Lazowska, E.D. and Noe, J.D.: The Eden system: A Technical Review, IEEE Trans. Softw. Eng. SE-11, 1 (Jan. 1985) 43-58
6. Liskov, B.: Distributed Programming in Argus, CACM 31, 3 (Mar. 1988) 300-312
7. Jul, E., Levy, H., Hutchinson, N., and Black, A.: Fine-grained Mobility in the Emerald System, ACM Trans. Comput. Syst. 6, 1 (Feb. 1988) 109-133
8. Benett, J.K.: The Design and Implementation of Distributed Smalltalk, Proc. of OOPSLA '87 (Oct. 1987)
9. Tsukamoto, M., Hamazaki, Y., Mizutani, I., Shinohara, H., Kaziura, H. et al.: Development of Object-Oriented Open Distributed System OZ+, Bull. of ETL 56, 9 (Sep. 1992) 1049-1071
10. Internet news group "comp.object" (only discussions)
11. Goshing, J. and McGilton, H.: The Java Language Environment - A White Paper, Sun Microsystems Computer Co. (May 1995)

12. Peney, D.J. and Stein, J.: Class Modification in the GemStone Object-Oriented DBMS, Proc. of OOPSLA '87 (1987) 111-117
13. Banerjee, J., Chou, H-T, Garza, J., Kim, W., Woelk, D. and Ballou, N.: Data Model Issues for Object-Oriented Application, ACM Trans. on Office Info. Syst. 5, 1 (Jan. 1987) 3-26
14. Lippe, E. and Florijn, G.: Implementation Techniques for Integral Version Management, Proc. of ECOOP '91 (July 1991) 342-359
15. The Common Object Request Broker: Architecture and Specification, OMG TC Doc. (Dec. 1991)

Formal Semantics of Agent Evolution in Language Flage

Yasuyuki Tahara[1*] , Fumihiro Kumeno[1**] , Akihiko Ohsuga[1***] ,
and Shinichi Honiden[1*]

Information-Technology Promotion Agency, Japan (IPA)
Shuwa-Shibakoen 3-Chome Bldg., 3-1-38 Shibakoen, Minato-Ku, Tokyo 105, Japan
ytahara,kumeno,ohsuga,honiden@caa.ipa.go.jp

Abstract. In this paper, we propose new concepts, *Evolutional Agents* and *Field Oriented Programming*. The main purpose of the work is to provide a framework for building software which adapts to changes of requirements autonomously.

Such adaptability is essential in open networks. Meanwhile in networks, many free applications exist and have a great potential for software reuse. We focus on the point and incorporated concurrent object oriented model with meta-architecture and a concept called *field*. In our model, evolutional agents are autonomous objects with meta-architecture which adapts to changes by acquiring components scattered over networks as their own functions. Fields are receptacles of software components in networks. Agents evolve into adaptive ones by moving among fields and acquiring components from the fields.

Flage language is a framework for describing such a software architecture. Moreover, formal semantics of agent evolution in Flage is proposed because it is necessary to rigorous verification of specifications and programs in software development in practical situations of industrial fields. The semantics of Flage is based on an algebraic framework to enable automatic verification procedures.

1 Introduction

With the advance of downsizing and computer networks such as Internet in recent years, distributed systems have come to the main stream of information systems. Meanwhile in software development, the efforts to increase the productivity by software reuse are being made and the reuse of free software has become popular. However, there are the following problems with reusing free applications available from networks as software components.

- In a network, a wide-area network especially, a large number of free applications are being scattered over several sites, many of them having similar

---

* Also in Toshiba Corp.
** Also in Mitsubishi Research Institute.
*** Currently in Toshiba Corp.

functionality. If one wants to use an application for some purpose, one needs a means to retrieve the most suitable one.

- In general, many free applications have only a few functions or are made for general purpose use. So even if one has found a suitable application, one must often add some functions to it, or customize it.
- A modified program is often released as a modified version if it can be in general use. A user of the original version can choose the most suitable one among such variants if his requirements change and the original does not satisfy them. But the suitable one does not necessarily satisfy all of the requirements.

To provide a solution to these problems, we propose a new concept in software architecture, *evolutional agents*.

- We define active objects, *agents*, that serve users' requirements.
- We also define *fields*, receptacles of software components which compose an application at a node which represents a computer or a transparent subnetwork in networks. An agent works as an application that serves the user's requirements by entering the field and acquiring the components in it.
- An agent can move among fields. It searches a field that has a component implementing the desired function by referencing addresses of other fields which represent applications related to the present field.
- An agent evolves into one with several application functions by going around to several fields and acquiring components in them.
- An agent resolves inconsistency among application functions and merge them with itself by utilizing the correct usage of the components given in the fields.

We also propose a framework for building such an architecture, *Field Oriented Programming Language, Flage.* An outline is as follows.

- Agents are active objects with attributes and methods. Each agent has its own processing power and the contents of its attributes can be accessed only by itself. For a user's requirement expressed by a *message*, an agent responds by executing the method which matches it.
- Fields are inactive objects which have methods and constraints on using the methods imposed on agents.
- When an agent is in a field, it has the methods of the field as its own definition, as well as the imposed constraints. An agent can move among fields and nodes as occasion demands. A field can have constraints imposed on agents when they enter or exit it.
- An agent can change values of its attributes and its own definition(attributes, methods) dynamically, to satisfy the constraints to enter or exit a field and to adapt changes of user's requirements.
- An agent can have methods of a field after exiting it.

If we develop software by evolutional agents in a practical field, it is important to verify that the software satisfies the users' requirements. Although various verification techniques have been proposed, there are some problems in verification of agent evolution. Therefore, we propose formal semantics of Flage to solve these problems.

In the section 2, we propose a language for specification and programming of agent evolution, *Flage*, and sketch the evolution mechanism in Flage. In the section 3, formal semantics of agent evolution in Flage is proposed. The semantics is the basis of formal verification procedures. In the section 4, related works are summarized, separated into reuse technology and semantic issues. Finally in the section 5, there are some concluding remarks.

2 Flage – Field Oriented Language for Evolutional Agents

2.1 Agents

Agents have a description of their attributes and methods. They behave concurrently, communicating messages with each other asynchronously. However, the internal actions of each agent are sequential. They can communicate by one-to-one messages and broadcasting. Moreover, they can handle their own definitions as data and can modify them dynamically in order to adapt to changes of fields and requirements.

Meta-architecture realizes this function. Agents have hierarchical structures which consist of $meta_0$, $meta_1$, ... levels. We call $meta_{i+1}$ level *meta* from the viewpoint of the $meta_i$ level, and conversely call the latter *base*. In the meta, we define a computation model of the base and a mechanism which handles definitions in the base.

Definitions of agents are represented by terms separately in each metalevel as follows:

$$\{ \quad aid \quad | \quad \langle\textbf{attribute}\rangle \; attr, \ldots, attr; \, ;$$
$$\langle\textbf{method}\rangle \quad mtd, \ldots, mtd; \, ;$$
$$\langle\textbf{spec}\rangle \qquad spec, \ldots, spec; \, ;$$

where *aid* is the identifier of the agent, *attr*'s are pairs of the names and the values of its attributes, *mtd*'s are pairs of the message patterns and the internal procedures, and *spec*'s are the algebraic definitions of the functions. The syntax rules of this term are shown in figure 1.

2.2 Fields

Compared with agents which are active objects behaving according to their own definitions, fields are inactive ones representing actions and constraints of agents under an environment. Since these definitions are common to agents in the environment, that is, in the field, it is natural to describe them separately from each agent definition.

Considering the dynamic entrance and exit of agents into and out of fields, items of definitions described in fields are listed as follows.

```
agent-exp ::=  "{" aid "|"
   [ "⟨attribute⟩" attr "," ... "," attr ";;" ]
   [ "⟨method⟩" mtd "," ... "," mtd ";;" ]
   [ "⟨spec⟩" spec "," ... "," spec ";;" ]   "}"
aid ::= symbol | "m(" aid ")"
attr ::= atid ":" val
atid ::= symbol
val ::= term
mtd ::= msg-pttn ":" proc
msg-pttn ::=  "(" mid [ term...term ] ")"
mid ::= symbol
proc ::= dest "<=" msg
   |  "!(" dest "<=" msg ")"
   | atid "=" "(" dest "<=" msg ")"
   | atid "=" term-with-atid
   |  "!" term-with-atid
   | proc ";" proc
   | "if" term-with-atid "=" term-with-atid
     "then" "(" proc ")" [ "else" "(" proc ")" ]
dest ::= aid | fid
fid ::= symbol
msg ::=  "(" mid [ term-with-atid...term-with-atid ] ")"
spec ::= sort-decl | op-decl | var-decl | eqn-decl
sort-decl ::= "sort" sid...sid
op-decl ::= "op" opid...opid ":" sid...sid "->" sid
var-decl ::= "var" variable...variable ":" sid
eqn-decl ::= "eq" term "=" term
```

Fig. 1. Syntax of Flage

Field Constraints *Field Constraints* are constraints on attributes of agents in each field. They are formulae of conditions for attributes, that is, composition of terms for boolean values using logical connectives, for example, $A = B$ and $A \leq B$, where A, B are formulae of functions including attributes as arguments. There are three kinds of constraints on attributes: 1) those for entering fields, 2) those for exiting fields, and 3) those always which must always be satisfied in fields.

Field Methods *Field Methods* define methods proper to each field. Agents set these methods as their own definition in each field.

For example, even if an agent has a method named methodA as its own definition, when it enters a field in which methodA is defined, the agent acquires the definition of methodA from the field, and it refers this definition rather than the original one. If the agent has no definition of methodA, it can obtain the method immediately after it enters the field.

Field methods consist of definitions of methods added to agents in the fields, functions called by them, and attributes accessed by them.

Each method proper to a field can be specified whether agents preserve its definition or not after going out.

Field Attributes *Field Attributes* define attributes proper to each field for preserving common knowledge. Read/Write procedures for attributes can be designated. There are built-in attributes for preserving information about agents entering and exiting fields and for preserving the definitions of the fields themselves.

These items are defined for each designated kind of agents (classified by the designation of names of attributes and methods of agents) in one metalevel.

A field can be created and modified dynamically by specific agents.

2.3 Evolutional Agents in Flage

We describe a problem domain as follows to explain our concept, *Evolutional Agents*. We assume that an application program has been developed, which manipulates data in a file at a node, and several variants of it have also been developed in other nodes. They are upward compatible, that is, inherit the original functions, and can read files saved by the original application. We also assume that the author knows their names and on which nodes they exist.

In this situation, we would like to construct flexible software. This means that even if its requirements are changed, it adapts the changed ones autonomously by retrieving additional and expanded functions of variants and reusing them.

As a specific example, we define a database for data whose keys are integers. In this database, data are represented by a list whose elements are pairs of integers as keys and contents of the data. The database provides the commands: **open**, **search**, **add**, **delete**, **import**, **save**, **save new**, and **new**. We call this database a list DB.

At two other nodes, separate extensions of this database are carried out. At one node, a database whose data structure is modified into binary search trees (called btree DB in the following explanation) is built, and at another, modified into ordered lists (called ordList DB). Each database has its own additional commands; for example, btree DB has functions to calculate min/max, and ordList DB has a function "showlist" to sort the data according to their keys in increasing order and display them.

The problem is to enable the original list DB to handle the data of the two other databases and also to use the commands proper to them.

2.4 Modeling The Example

File Agents and Data Manipulate Agents List DB is modeled by file agents and data manipulating agents (called DM agents afterwards) as follows(figure 2).

1. When a DM agent receives an **open** or **save** message, it reads and writes data of the file agent by message passing. Data is preserved in an attribute (called *data*).

2. When it receives a **search,add,delete**, or **import** message, a DM agent manipulates *data*.

3. When a DM agent receives a **save new** message, it creates a new file agent with *data*.

4. When a DM agent receives a **new** message, it create a new file agent with the data designated by the message.

The structure of data that file agents and DM agents preserve is defined by a field since it is a common constraint on the attribute *data*(figure 2).

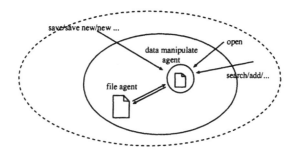

Fig. 2. File Agent, Data Manipulate Agent and ListDB model in Flage

The methods for *data* of DM agents are also defined as field methods of the same field, because the definitions of methods to manipulate *data* depend on the structure of *data* . For example, in list DB field, the data structure of *data* must be lists whose elements are pairs of integers and data, and the methods of DM agents must be defined so that they can handle such *data*.

Field Constraints

$$always \rightarrow (data\ is\ sort\ intDatalist)$$
$$sort\ intDatalist,\ intDatapair$$
$$op\,[\,]\ :\ intDatalist$$
$$op\,[\_|\_]\ :\ intDatapair\ intDatalist\ \rightarrow$$
$$intDatalist$$
$$op\,(\_,\_)\ :\ Int\ Term\ \rightarrow\ intDatapair$$

Field Methods

$$search(sender, x, data) \; :$$
$$if \, data = [(x, Data)|_\lrcorner]$$
$$then \, sender \Leftarrow search Reply(Data)$$
$$else$$
$$if \, data = [_\lrcorner|tdata] \, then$$
$$search(sender, x, tdata)$$
$$else \, sender \Leftarrow search Reply(\bot).$$
$$add((x, Data)) \; : \; data := [(x, Data)|data]$$
$$delete(x, data) \; : \; ...$$
$$import(DataSet) \; : \; ...$$

The field methods above are defined as being left in DM agents after they exit the field.

In the field, there are several file agents and DM agents, and many-to-many message communication is executed among file agents and DM agents. We also define exclusion control of data writing to file agents in the field. By defining control mechanisms as field methods, the mechanisms are added to the file agents without fully describing them in the file agents.

The database can be extended by modification of the definition of the field. As for the btree DB, the field constraints and methods are defined as follows:

Field Constraints

$$always \rightarrow (data \, is \, sort \, btree)$$
$$sort \, btree, \, int Datalist, \, int Datapair$$
$$op \, [] \; : \; btree$$
$$op \, [_\lrcorner, _\lrcorner, _\lrcorner] \; : \; int Datapair \; btree \; btree \; \rightarrow \; btree$$
$$var \, X \; : \; btree, A, B \; : \; Int$$
$$eq \; (X = [(A, _\lrcorner), [(B, _\lrcorner)|_\lrcorner], _\lrcorner]) \; \rightarrow \; B < A$$
$$var \, X \; : \; btree, A, B \; : \; Int$$
$$eq \; (X = [(A, _\lrcorner), _\lrcorner, [(B, _\lrcorner)|_\lrcorner]]) \; \rightarrow \; A < B$$

Field Methods

$$min(sender, data) \; :$$
$$if \, data = [(x, Data), [], []]$$
$$then \, sender \Leftarrow min Reply(Data)$$
$$else$$
$$if \, data = [[(y, Data_y), BTL_y, BTR_y], _\lrcorner, _\lrcorner] \, then$$
$$min(sender, [(y, Data_y), BTL_y, BTR_y])$$
$$else \, sender \Leftarrow min Reply(\bot).$$
$$max(sender, data) \; : \; ...$$
$$search(sender, x, data) \; : \; ...$$
$$...$$

In order to keep upward compatibility, btree DB field and ordList DB field have methods whose function are the same as those of list DB field methods, we keep the methods to move from list DB field to each field in the built-in attribute of each field. Then, each function which transforms the data structure (*list → Btree* and *list → OrdList*) is held in the attribute of each field by the same name, *trans_field(frm, to, data)*.

The names of btree DB field and ordList DB field are held in the built-in attribute of list DB field.

Evolutional Agents in The Model The desired agent which provides a solution to the example is the DM agent which can manipulate data from file agents in each field of list DB, ordList DB, and btree DB and also can apply all field methods to the data.

In order to construct such a DM agent, we define a metalevel method of a DM agent(called agentA temporarily) in the list DB field; by executing the method with fields designated, agentA goes around to the fields and returns to list DB field at last.

If this method is called with ordList DB and btree DB, the agent executes the following action(figure 3):

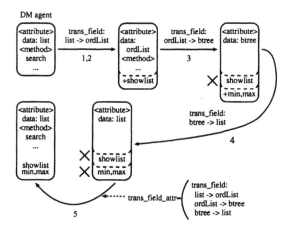

Fig. 3. Method acquirement mechanism

1. agentA moves from list DB field to ordList DB field. In this movement, agentA must transform the data structure of *data* attribute from list to ordered list. agentA searches the transformation function in the definition of itself (the function definition in the metalevel attribute *trans_field_attr* described later) and in built-in attributes of ordList DB field successively. If not found, agentA reports this information to the agent which had activated this metalevel method (DB user) and requests the transformation function.

In this case, moving from list DB field to ordList DB field, the function is already provided in the built-in attribute of ordList DB.

2. By the transformation function obtained in this way, agentA transforms the data in *data* and enters ordList DB field.

   By this procedure the ordList DB field method(*showlist*) is added to agentA. The transformation function is preserved in the metalevel attribute (called *trans_field_attr* temporarily) of agentA. This attribute is for preserving ways to enter a field. If the transformation function is newly composed, it is preserved in the built-in attribute of the field.

3. Next, agentA moves to btree DB field. In this movement, agentA behaves in the same way as the movement from list DB field to ordList DB field. By the movement, however, the method *showlist* becomes unavailable to *data* although it is one of the methods of the agent, because it has to have ordered list data as its argument.

4. agentA moves from btree DB field to list DB field in the same way. In this situation, any of *showlist*, *min*, and *max* obtained in the other fields become unavailable to *data*.

5. At this moment, however, agentA has each transformation function of lists → ordered lists → binary search trees preserved in *trans_field_attr*. So agentA transforms all of the methods so that they are available if they have arguments of whichever types of data. In this way, if *data* has whichever data structure of lists, ordered lists, and binary search trees, all of the methods become available to the data.

By the above actions, we can obtain the desired DM agent.

In this example, the agent adapts to changed requirements by visiting to all of the fields because the number of the fields is small.

Searching fields which have required methods is based on pointers to other fields preserved in an attribute of each field, but if a number of fields exists, a blind search is inefficient. A search strategy to the problem is discussed later.

3 Formal Semantics of Agent Evolution in Flage

In this section, formal semantics of agent evolution in Flage is proposed. If we develop software by evolutional agents in a practical field, it is important to verify that the software satisfies the users' requirements. Although various verification techniques have been proposed, there are some problems in verification of agent evolution. Therefore, we propose formal semantics of Flage to solve these problems.

Formal semantics of Flage is given by the following process (see figure 4).

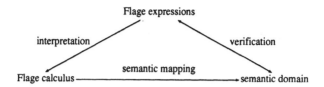

Fig. 4. Formal semantics of Flage

1. Since the most essential characteristics of Flage to realize agent evolution is the metalevel architecture, we present a formal system to give semantics of metalevel architecture, called *Flage calculus.*
2. Formal semantics of Flage calculus is given based on an algebraic framework, especially, a category-theoretic framework.
3. Finally, rules to interpret Flage expressions to notions of Flage calculus are given. In this way, algebraic semantics of Flage is established.

3.1 Overview of Flage Calculus – a Formal System for Metalevel Architecture

Flage calculus is a formal system which models metalevel architecture of Flage language and is a basis to give formal semantics of agent evolution in Flage. Characteristics of Flage calculus is shown as follows.

– In Flage calculus, behaviors of systems are described based on state transition model similar to that of rewriting logic. Although states of systems are denoted by equivalence classes of terms by equality relations and transitions by rewriting of terms, in Flage calculus behaviors of systems are denoted by transitions between pairs of equivalence classes of terms and rewrite theories which represent specifications. In this way, dynamic modifications of specifications are expressed.

Rewriting logic is an algebraic formal system which is based on multi-sorted (or order-sorted) conditional equational logic and also treats (one-directional) rewrite rules as axioms. By rewriting logic, we can formulate the Flage agent model as follows.

  • States of each metalevel are represented by multisets of terms which stand for agents, messages left unattended and fields. Hence concurrent behaviors of agents are modeled.
  • Constraints of fields are represented by conditions in conditional rewrite rules. Therefore, we adopt conditional rewriting logic.

For example,

  • The term stands for an agent **dm** in the meta-0 level which has an attribute **data** is:
    `{ dm | data: ... field: [...] fldToEnter: [...] }`

where attributes `field` and `fldToEnter` represent the fields to which `dm` now belongs and those which `dm` declares to enter respectively.
- Terms for messages left unattended are as follows:
  (`msg open(FileAg) from ... to dm`)
- Terms for fields are as follows:
  `<< ordListDB >>`
- Flage calculus has characteristics to model metalevel architecture.
  - It uses systems of symbols which are distinguished into those of baselevel and those of metalevels and a mapping between them is given.
  - It has primitives to handle baselevel expressions.
  - It has inference rules which reflect transitions in metalevels to those in baselevel among general rules which derive transition relations.
- Also in the same way as rewriting logic, algebraic semantics is given based on category theory. Therefore rigorous and automatic verification is possible.

3.2 Components of Flage Calculus

Components of expressions of Flage calculus is shown as follows.

- Enumerablly infinite set S of baselevel symbols. S needs to include all of the primitives to handle baselevel expressions mentioned later. For each baselevel symbol π, the metaexpression of it is denoted by π' which is a constant symbol of sort `Sym` also mentioned later. In the rest of this paper, the set of all metaexpressions of baselevel symbols is denoted by S_+ and the union set with that of all baselevel symbols by $S_* = S_+ \cup S$.
- A specification is a rewrite theory $\mathcal{R} = (S, \Sigma, V, E, L, R)$, where
  - S is a set of sorts $\subseteq S$,
  - $\Sigma = \{\Sigma_{\bar{s}s} | \bar{s} \in S^{*2}, s \in S\}$ is a family of sets of constant symbols and function symbols distinguished by the sorts of their arguments and values which satisfies
    * $\bigcup_{\bar{s} \in S^*, s \in \Sigma} \Sigma_{\bar{s}s} \subseteq S_*$
    * $S_+ \subseteq \Sigma_{\varepsilon \mathbf{Sym}}$ where `Sym` is the sort of baselevel symbols mentioned later,
  - $V = \{(v_i, s_i) | v_i \in S, s_i \in S\}_{i=1,\ldots,n}$ is a finite set of pairs of variables and their sorts where $S \cap \{v_i\}_{i=1,\ldots,n} = \phi$,
  - $E \subseteq \mathrm{Term}^2_{S,\Sigma,V} \times (\mathrm{Term}^2_{S,\Sigma,V})^*$ is a set of conditional equations, where if $((t_1, t_2), ((t_3, t_4), \ldots, (t_{n-1}, t_n))) \in E$, we denote

  $$t_1 = t_2 \text{ if } t_3 = t_4, \ldots, t_{n-1} = t_n,$$

  - $L \subseteq S$ is a set of labels of rewrite rules and
  - $R \subseteq L \times \mathrm{Term}^2_{S,\Sigma,V} \times (\mathrm{Term}^2_{S,\Sigma,V})^*$ is a set of conditional rewrite rules, where if $(l, (t_1, t_2), ((t_3, t_4), \ldots, (t_{n-1}, t_n))) \in R$, we denote

  $$t_1 \to t_2 \text{ if } t_3 \to t_4, \ldots, t_{n-1} \to t_n,$$

---

[2] This is different from S_* and denotes the set of all finite sequences (including the empty sequence) of elements of S.

- The specification of the primitives to handle baselevel expressions is as follows. The rewrite theory of this specification is denoted by $\mathcal{R}_0$.

```
sort Sym Term Arr Obj Op Var Eq Rl Spec .
sort SymList ...
        % Sorts of lists of each sorts above.
op termCon : Sym -> Term .
op id : Obj -> Term .
        % Components of categories.
        % The others are _~_, p1, p2, pair, unit, (), objCon, _x_,
        % dom, cod, _o_, arrPair.
op spec : SymList OpList VarList EqList
        RlList -> Spec .
op opCon : Sym SymList Sym -> Op .
        % Components of specifications.
        % The others are varCon, eqCon, rlCon.
op reifySym : Sym -> Term .
op reify : Term -> Term .
ops reifySpec : Spec -> Term .
        % The reifier.
vars T T1 T2 : Term .
        % Declarations of variables.

eq arrCon(T1 ~ T2, Sp) = arrCon(T1, Sp) o arrCon(T2, Sp) .
eq arrCon(pair(T1, T2), Sp)
    = arrPair(arrCon(T1, Sp), arrCon(T2, Sp)) .
eq cod(arrCon((), Sp)) = 'unit .
eq reifyObj(objCon(S)) = reifySym(S) .
eq reifyObj(O1 x O2)
    = '_x_ ~ pair(reifyObj(O1), reifyObj(O2)) .
eq reify(termCon(S)) = reifySym(S) .
eq reify(p1(O1, O2))
    = 'p1 ~ pair(reifyObj(O1), reifyObj(O2)) .
        % Specifications of the reifier.

rl mp : arrCon(T1, spec(Sl, Ol, Vl, El, Rl))
        => arrCon(T2, spec(Sl, Ol, Vl, El, Rl))
    if (member(rlCon(R, [T1, T2 | RRest]), Rl)
        and rewAll(RRest, spec(Sl, Ol, Vl, El, Rl))) = true .
```

- For a term t and a rewrite theory $\mathcal{R} = (S, \Sigma, V, E, L, R)$, *reification* terms which are metaexpressions of the term and theory are defined as follows.
   - If $s \in \Sigma \cap S$, $\uparrow(s, \mathcal{R}) = \texttt{termCon}('s)$.
   - If $s \in \Sigma \cap S_+$, $\uparrow(s, \mathcal{R}) = \texttt{reifySym}(s)$.
   - If $(v_i, s_i) \in V$, $\uparrow(v_i, \mathcal{R})$
     $= \texttt{p1}(s_i \texttt{ x } (s_{i+1} \texttt{ x } \ldots \texttt{ x } s_n))$
     $\tilde{} \; \texttt{p2}(s_{i-1} \texttt{ x } (s_i \texttt{ x } \ldots \texttt{ x } s_n))$
     $\tilde{} \; \ldots \tilde{} \; \texttt{p2}(s_1 \texttt{ x } (s_2 \texttt{ x } \ldots \texttt{ x } s_n))$
   - $\uparrow(f(t), \mathcal{R}) = (\uparrow(f, \mathcal{R})) \circ \uparrow(t, \mathcal{R})$

- $\uparrow(f(t_1,\ldots,t_n),\mathcal{R}) = (\uparrow(f,\mathcal{R})) \circ \mathtt{pair}\,(\uparrow(t_1,\mathcal{R}),\mathtt{pair}(\ldots,\mathtt{pair}(\uparrow(t_{n-1},\mathcal{R}),\uparrow(t_n,\mathcal{R}))\ldots)$
- $\uparrow(S,\Sigma,V,E,L,R) = \mathtt{spec}(\uparrow S,\ldots,\uparrow R)$ where $\uparrow S$ and others are lists of metaexpressions of elements of each of the sets. For example, if
  $t_1 = t_2$ if $t_3 = t_4,\ldots,t_{n_1-1} = t_{n_1}$;
  $\ldots;t_{n_2} = t_{n_2+1}$ if $t_{n_2+2} = t_{n_2+3},\ldots,$
  $t_{n_3-1} = t_{n_3}$ in E,
  $\uparrow E = [\mathtt{eqCon}([\;\uparrow(t_1,\mathcal{R}),\ldots,\uparrow(t_{n_1},\mathcal{R})]),\ldots,\mathtt{eqCon}([\;\uparrow(t_{n_2},\mathcal{R}),\ldots,\uparrow(t_{n_3},\mathcal{R})])]$

3.3 Inference Rules of Flage Calculus

In Flage calculus, behaviors of systems are denoted by transition relations between pairs of equivalence classes of terms by equality relations representing states of the systems and rewrite theories representing specifications. Such equality and transition relations are given by the following inference rules.

- A State of systems is denoted by a pair of an equivalence class of a term and rewrite theory $([t]_{\mathcal{R}}{}^3,\mathcal{R})$.
- The inference rules for equality relations are given as follows.
  - If $t = t'$ is derived in $\mathcal{R}$ by the usual inference rules of equational logic, we can deduce $t = t'$ in $\mathcal{R}$.
  - (Reflection of Equation)
    $t = t'$ in $\mathcal{R} \Leftrightarrow \mathtt{arrCon}(\uparrow(t,\mathcal{R}),\uparrow\mathcal{R}) = \mathtt{arrCon}(\uparrow(t',\mathcal{R}),\uparrow\mathcal{R})$ in $\mathcal{R}$
- $([t]_{\mathcal{R}},\mathcal{R}) \to ([t']_{\mathcal{R}},\mathcal{R})$ where the transition induces no modifications of the rewrite theory is also denoted by $[t]_{\mathcal{R}} \to [t']_{\mathcal{R}}$ in $\mathcal{R}$.
- The inference rules for transition relations are as follows.
  - If $[t]_{\mathcal{R}} \to [t']_{\mathcal{R}}$ is derived in $\mathcal{R}$ by the usual inference rules of equational logic, we can deduce $[t]_{\mathcal{R}} \to [t']_{\mathcal{R}}$ in $\mathcal{R}$.
  - (Reflection of Rewriting)
    $([t]_{\mathcal{R}},\mathcal{R}) \to ([t']_{\mathcal{R}},\mathcal{R}') \Leftrightarrow [\mathtt{arrCon}(\uparrow(t,\mathcal{R}),\uparrow\mathcal{R})]_{\mathcal{R}} \to [\mathtt{arrCon}(\uparrow(t',\mathcal{R}'),\uparrow\mathcal{R}')]_{\mathcal{R}}$ in $\mathcal{R}$

3.4 Algebraic Semantics of Flage Calculus

Since Flage calculus is based on rewriting logic as explained so far, we can examine algebraic semantics based on category theory in the same way as rewriting logic. Moreover, Flage calculus has characteristics for modeling metalevel architecture which are reflected in the semantics.

Semantic domains are given as (2-)categories similarly as rewriting logic. However, they reflect the characteristics of metalevel architecture of Flage calculus in the following way (see figure 5).

---

[3] Since equality relations depend on rewrite theories, there is a subscription.

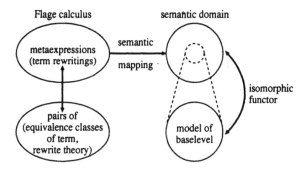

Fig. 5. Algebraic semantics of flage calculus

- The domains have elements corresponding to the primitives to handle baselevel expressions mentioned earlier.
- There are isomorphic functors between domains for baselevel and metalevels corresponding to the reflection rules.

Definition 1 *A semantic domain C is an $\mathcal{R}_0$-system[4] with isomorphic functors $\sigma_C : C \to C^r, \delta_C : C^r \to C$ where $C^r = (C_0^r, C_1^r, C_2^r, \mathrm{dom}^r, \mathrm{cod}^r, 2\mathrm{dom}^r, 2\mathrm{cod}^r$ is a cartesian 2-category and σ_C satisfies the following conditions.*

- $C_0^r = [\![\mathtt{Obj}]\!]_{C_0}$[5]
- $C_1^r = \{f \in [\![\mathtt{Arr}]\!]_{C_0} | [\![\mathtt{arr?}]\!]_C(f) = [\![\mathtt{true}]\!]_C\}$
- *The components as a cartesian category is given by the corresponding ones of $\mathcal{R}_0$ in such a way as $\mathrm{dom}(f) = [\![\mathtt{dom}]\!]_C(f), g \circ f = [\![\_\circ\_]\!]_C(g, f)$.*
- $C_2^r = \{\tau \in [\![\mathtt{Arr}]\!]_{C_1} | \mathrm{dom}_{[\![\mathtt{Arr}]\!]_C}(\tau),$
  $\mathrm{cod}_{[\![\mathtt{Arr}]\!]_C}(\tau) \in C_1^r\}$
- $2\mathrm{dom}(\tau) = \mathrm{dom}_{[\![\mathtt{Arr}]\!]_C}(\tau), \ 2\mathrm{cod}(\tau) = \mathrm{cod}_{[\![\mathtt{Arr}]\!]_C}(\tau)$
- *For each sort s of $\mathcal{R}_0$, $\sigma_C([\![s]\!]_C) = [\![\mathtt{objCon}('s)]\!]_C$.*
- *For each $f : [\![\mathtt{unit}]\!]_C \to [\![\mathtt{Arr}]\!]_C, r : [\![\mathtt{unit}]\!]_C \to [\![\mathtt{Spec}]\!]_C$,*
  $\sigma_C([\![\mathtt{arrCon}]\!]_C \circ \langle f, r \rangle)$
  $= [\![\mathtt{arrCon}]\!]_C([\![\texttt{'\_~\_}]\!]_C([\![{}'\mathtt{arrCon}]\!]_C,$
  $[\![\mathtt{pair}]\!]_C([\![\mathtt{reify}]\!]_C(f([\![{}'()]\!]_C)),$
  $[\![\mathtt{reifySpec}]\!]_C(r([\![{}'()]\!]_C)))), r([\![{}'()]\!]_C))$

By defining semantic domains as categories in this way, metalevel operations (that is, partial handling of terms and dynamic modifications of rewrite theories) are formulated algebraically. Moreover, reflection of metalevel operations to baselevel behaviors is also managed algebraically by the notion of functors.

---

[4] A category which is a semantic domain of $\mathcal{R}_0$ in semantics of rewriting logic. cf. [9]

[5] $[\![]\!]_C$ denotes the semantic function to C as an $\mathcal{R}_0$-system. Moreover, $[\![s]\!]_C$ where s is a sort is a category with terms of the sort s as objects and rewritings between terms as morphisms.

Soundness of this semantics is shown by the following facts.

Lemma 2 $t = t'$ *in* $\mathcal{R} \Rightarrow [\![\mathrm{arrCon}(\uparrow(t,\mathcal{R}),\uparrow\mathcal{R})]\!]_{\mathcal{C}} = [\![\mathrm{arrCon}(\uparrow(t',\mathcal{R}),\uparrow\mathcal{R})]\!]_{\mathcal{C}}$ *in* $\mathcal{C}$

Theorem 3 $[t]_{\mathcal{R}} \rightarrow [t']_{\mathcal{R}}$ *in* $\mathcal{R} \Rightarrow \exists r : [\![\mathrm{arrCon}(\uparrow(t,\mathcal{R}),\uparrow\mathcal{R})]\!]_{\mathcal{C}} \rightarrow [\![\mathrm{arrCon}(\uparrow(t',\mathcal{R}),\uparrow\mathcal{R})]\!]_{\mathcal{C}}$ *in* $\mathcal{C}$

Corollary 4 $(t,\mathcal{R}) \rightarrow (t',\mathcal{R}') \Rightarrow \exists r : [\![\mathrm{arrCon}(\uparrow(t,\mathcal{R}),\uparrow\mathcal{R})]\!]_{\mathcal{C}} \rightarrow [\![\mathrm{arrCon}(\uparrow(t',\mathcal{R}'),\uparrow\mathcal{R})]\!]_{\mathcal{C}}$ *in* $\mathcal{C}$

Moreover, initial models are given by constructing term models. Because the inverse of the facts presented above is shown for the initial models, completeness of the semantics is also proved.

3.5 Interpretation of Flage Expressions to Flage Calculus

Our semantics of Flage is completed by giving an interpretation of Flage expressions to Flage calculus. The example of databases illustrates our interpretation as follows.

Components of the system are modeled as in 3.1. We give a detailed account of interpretation for three important behaviors of the system.

- dm moves from the list DB field to the ordList DB field not only by immediate requests of users but also by the need to search for functions to manage unknown messages, for example, showlist. The interpretation of procedures in the latter case is as follows.
  1. When the message is sent, the state of the system in the meta-0 level is:
     ```
     { dm | data: ... field: [listDB] fldToEnter: [] } ( msg showlist from
     ... to dm )
     ```
     However because there are no rewrite rules which match this term in the current specifications (which means the message is unknown), no more transitions happen.
  2. On the other hand, there is a method for the corresponding metaprotocol for the message in the meta-1 level. Namely, there is a rewrite rule for the term which represents the state in the meta-1 level. Hence the following action happens.
     ```
     { dm | baseSpec: ... }
              ^^^
     ( msg send-msg(msg showlist)
                   from ... to dm )
     << listDB |
         baseSpec: [ ...,
                     [relatedFld,
                      ordListDB, ...]] >>
                      ^^^^^^^^^^
     => { dm |
           baseSpec:
     ```

```
            declareEnter( ...,
            ^^^^^^^^^^^^^^^^^^^

                      ordListDB ) }
                      ^^^^^^^^^^
  ( msg
    send-msg(msg showlist)
    from ... to dm )
  << listDB in base | ... >>
```

which means the declaration of entrance for the ordList DB field in order
to search a meta-0 level method for the message.

- The interpretation of procedures for **dm** to enter ordList DB is as follows:
  1. Declaration of entrance of **dm** into ordList DB. This declaration may
     happen in the meta-1 level as stated above, and may happen in the
     meta-0 level as follows.

```
{ dm |
  data: ... fields: [node]
  fldToEnter: [] }
             ^^
=>{ dm |
    data: ... fields: [node]
    fldToEnter: [ordListDB] }
               ^^^^^^^^^^^^
```

  2. Reference of the specification of ordList DB and execution of the pro-
     cedure of entrance in the meta-1 level. This happens as specification of
     meta-1 level.

```
{ dm |
  baseSpec: (spec ...) ... }
           ^^^^^^^^^^^
<< ordListDB |
   baseSpec: (spec ...) ... >>
 => { dm |
      baseSpec: modifySpec(spec ... )
               ^^^^^^^^^^^^^^^^^^^^^^^
      ... }
    << ordListDB |
       baseSpec: (spec ...) ... >>
       ~~~~~~~~~~~~~~~~~~~~~
       % Because the condition
       % "satisfySpec((spec of dm),
       % (spec of ordListDB)) = false"
       % is true.
 => { dm |
      baseSpec:
      enterFld(
      ^^^^^^^^^

        modifySpec(spec ... ),
        ^^^^^^^^^^^^^^^^^^^^^^^
```

```
        ordListDB) ... }
        ~~~~~~~~~~
   << ordListDB |
        baseSpec:
        addMember((spec ...),
        ~~~~~~~~~~~~~~~~~~~~~~

                 dm) ... >>
                 ~~~
```

Note that modification of the attribute **baseSpec** is reflected in the specifications of the meta-0 level by the reflection rule of rewriting. For example, a rewrite rule which is the interpretation of the method for the **showlist** message in the last state is added to the meta-0 level.

– When **dm** wanders among fields, it has functions to apply transformation functions to messages corresponding to data structures of arguments of the messages. The interpretation of the application are as follows.

1. An **add** message which has a hash list as an argument is sent. It cannot be handled in the meta-0 level, since the **add** method in the level can handle only ordinary lists.

   { dm | data: ... field: [listDB] fldToEnter: [] } (msg add(hl) from ... to dm)

2. On the other hand, there is a method for the corresponding metaprotocol for the message in the meta-1 level as the first example. Hence the following action happens.

   ```
   { dm | ... }
   ( msg send-msg(msg add(hl))
                          ^^
                from ... to dm )
   => { dm | ... }
      ( msg
          send-msg(msg
          add(listToOrdList(hl))
          ~~~~~~~~~~~~~~~~~~~~~~~
        from ... to dm )
   ```

   where **listToOrdList** is the transformation function.

3. At the same time the message in the meta-0 level changes and can be managed by **dm**.

   { dm | data: ... field: [listDB] fldToEnter: [] }
   (msg add(listToOrdList(hl)) from ... to dm)

4   Related Works

4.1   Reuse of Software

In object oriented programming, if an object cannot handle a message, the object can *delegate* it to other objects[8]. Delegation is useful for our purpose, but the range of its application is limited by the following reasons.

- If the destination of a forwarded message is at other node, the message must be sent and received between two nodes every time the object is required to handle it. Then, the message is often rejected by the state of the other node and the network. It is serious when the requirement to the object frequently happens.
- There can exist inconsistency between a forwarded message and the method of an object which receives it.

Another method is, like Telescript[4], to take an object(or its copy) which can handle the required message to one's node and use it for the message at the node from now on. The method provides a solution to the former problem of delegation but essentially cannot solve the latter problem.

On the other hand, our approach avoids both these problems because an evolutional agent can acquire several methods as its own definitions and redefine each method to resolve inconsistency occurring among them.

Some object oriented languages are incorporated with *reflection* that enables us to change structural and computational models of objects dynamically[10, 5]. Flage is based on Actor model[1] to express autonomous agents, and it is close to ABCL/R[15] in that an agent has and changes its own model dynamically. Open C++[2] and AL-1/D[12] are also concurrent languages with reflective programming facilities. In these approaches, the focus of study is on the dynamic management of the efficient use computational resources. In our approach, the focus is on adapting to changes of requirements and reuse of software components for them. The concept, *field*, plays a central role in our framework for reuse. For this reason, we call our language concept *Field Oriented Programming*.

4.2 Formal Semantics of Metalevel Architecture

[7] presents an algebraic specification of a reflective, functional programming language called Brown. This research makes clear an algebraic model of computational reflection, by dealing with metalevel notions of functional programming language, such as expressions and continuations.

However, this work stays only inside the framework of ordinary computational reflection of Brown. Therefore, it does not deal with dynamic modification of description. Moreover, since algebraic specifications is used only for description of the model, it does not treat reflection in algebraic specifications themselves.

On the other hand, our reflection model is concerned with dynamic modification of description and developed inside algebraic specifications themselves, by adopting rewriting logic as the base model of our work. Therefore our model exceeds beyond former models of reflection.

There are also some works attempting to give denotational semantics to reflective programming languages[3, 6, 13, 14]. Especially, [11] presents a continuation-based denotational semantics of reflective object-oriented language. It adopts reification and deification functions between semantic domains of metalevels. It also deals with structural reflection which is involved in dynamic modification of inheritance relations etc., though other works deal with only computational reflection. However, reification and deification functions are defined spreading over both of syntax and semantic domains, independently of the semantic mapping in this work. Hence the two domains are not separated strictly, which results in non-compositionality of the semantics like other works.

Moreover, most of former works is developed in the framework of higher-order functional languages. Therefore, they can hardly give perspective of automatic verification, which is possible in first-order algebraic languages.

On the other hand, our work succeeded in strict separation of syntax and semantic domains by realizing reification and deification functions in each domain. Moreover, since our work is developed in the framework of a first-order algebraic language, it is possible to verify abstract properties of descriptions automatically, using techniques of inductive theorem proving, such as inductionless induction.

5 Conclusion

Our main goal is to provide a framework for building software adaptive to changes of requirements. Such adaptability is essential in open networks. In the meanwhile, we can enjoy various application functions, which also have a great potential for software reuse, in networks. In this paper, we proposed new concepts, *Evolutional Agents* and *Field Oriented Programming*, as a bridge between the needs and the seeds. *Flage* is a framework for implementing architecture based on the concepts and has the following features.

- Fields are defined for custody and reuse of software components.
- Agents can go around to fields in networks, acquaint components by entering fields, and preserve the components after exiting them.
- Agents modifies themselves for resolving inconsistency between acquainted components by their meta-architecture.
- Field attributes are defined for reuse of adaptation methods.
- Inclusion relation facilitates field construction and modification.
- Agents control their evolutions themselves by their metalevel definitions, or by entering metalevel fields.

Moreover, Flage has formal semantics which is the basis for rigorous verification for practical use of agent evolution in software development.

We are developing a prototype version of interpreter of Flage. We also intend to develop a verification system and accumulate examples of Flage specifications, programs, and verification practice.

Acknowledgment

This work was performed under the management of Information-technology Promotion Agency, Japan(IPA) as a part of the Industrial Science and Technology

Frontier Program "New Models for Software Architectures" sponsored by NEDO (New Energy and Industrial technology Development Organization).

References

1. G. Agha. *ACTORS: A Model of Concurrent Computation in Distributed Systems.* MIT Press, 1986.
2. S. Chiba and T. Masuda. Designing and Extensive Distributed Language with Meta-Level. In *ECOOP'93*, pp.482–501, 1993.
3. O. Danvy and K. Malmkjær. Intentions and extensions in a reflective tower. In *Proc. of 1988 ACM Conference on Lisp and Functional Programming*, pp. 327–341, 1988.
4. A. Davis. The digital valet, or Jeeves goes online. In *EDUCOM Rev*, vol.29, no.3, pp.44–46, 1994.
5. J. Ferber. Computational Reflection in Class based Object Oriented Language. In *OOPSLA'89*, pp.317–326, 1989.
6. D. Friedman and M. Wand. Reification: Reflection without metaphysics. In *Proc. 1984 ACM Conference on Lisp and Functional Programming*, pp. 348–355, 1984.
7. M. Kurihara and A. Ohuchi. An algebraic specification and an object-oriented implementation of a reflective language. In A. Yonezawa and B. C. Smith, editors, *Reflection And Meta-Level Architecture, Proceedings of the International Workshop on New Models for Software Architecture*, pp. 137–142, 1992.
8. H. Lieberman. Using Prototypical Objects to Implement Shared Behavior in Object Oriented Systems. In *OOPSLA'86*, pp.214–223, 1986.
9. J. Meseguer. Rewriting as a unified model of concurrency. In *Proceedings of the CONCUR'90 Conference, Amsterdam, August 1990*, LNCS 458, pp. 384–400, 1990.
10. P. Maes. Concepts and Experiments in Computational Reflection. In *OOPSLA'87*, pp.147–155, 1987.
11. S. Nakajima. What makes a language reflective and how? In A. Yonezawa and B. C. Smith, editors, *Reflection And Meta-Level Architecture, Proceedings of the International Workshop on New Models for Software Architecture*, pp. 125–136, 1992.
12. H. Okamura and et al. Metalevel Decomposition in AL-1/D. In *Object Technologies for Advanced Software*, LNCS742, pp.110–127, 1993.
13. B. C. Smith. Reflection and semantics in lisp. In *Proc. POPL'84*, pp. 23–35, 1984.
14. M. Wand and D. Friedman. The mystery of the tower revealed: A nonreflective description of the reflective tower. In P. Maes and D. Nardi, editors, *Meta-Level Architectures and Reflection*, pp. 111–134. North-Holland, 1988.
15. T. Watanabe and A. Yonezawa. Reflection in an Object-Oriented Concurrent Language. In *OOPSLA'88*, pp.306–315, 1988.

Author Index

Baba, T. 38
Bahsoun, J.-P. 168
Banâtre, M. 219
Belhamissi, Y. 219
Bellissard, L. 290
Ben Atallah, S. 290
Boudinet, E. 148

Caromel, D. 125
Carrez, S. 187
Clark, K.L. 104
Commelin, E. 273

Darche, P. 273

Furuta, T. 38

Galmiche, D. 148
Garbinato, B. 238
Geib, J.-M. 83
Gransart, C. 83
Grenot, C. 83
Guerraoui, R. 238
Guidec, F. 18

Hamazaki, Y. 310
Honiden, S. 329
Hori, A. 1

Ishikawa, Y. 1
Issarny, V. 219
Itoh, J.-i. 205

Jacquemot, C. 187
Jensen, P.S. 187
Jézéquel, J.-M. 18

Kerbrat, A. 290

Konaka, H. 1
Kumeno, F. 329

Lea, R. 205

Maeda, M. 1
Mazouni, K. 238
McCabe, F.G. 104
Merle, P. 83
Merz, S. 168

Nishioka, T. 310

Ohsuga, A. 329
Otokawa, H. 310

Puaut, I. 219

Raverdy, P.-G. 273
Riveill, M. 290
Roudier, Y. 125
Routeau, J.-P. 219

Servières, C. 168
Shitomi, H. 257

Tahara, Y. 329
Takashio, K. 257
Taura, K. 59
Tokoro, M. 257
Tomokiyo, T. 1
Tsukamoto, M. 310

Yokote, Y. 205
Yonezawa, A. 59
Yoshinaga, T. 38

Springer-Verlag
and the Environment

W̲e at Springer-Verlag firmly believe that an international science publisher has a special obligation to the environment, and our corporate policies consistently reflect this conviction.

W̲e also expect our business partners – paper mills, printers, packaging manufacturers, etc. – to commit themselves to using environmentally friendly materials and production processes.

T̲he paper in this book is made from low- or no-chlorine pulp and is acid free, in conformance with international standards for paper permanency.

Lecture Notes in Computer Science

For information about Vols. 1–1034

please contact your bookseller or Springer-Verlag

Vol. 1035: S.Z. Li, D.P. Mital, E.K. Teoh, H. Wang (Eds.), Recent Developments in Computer Vision. Proceedings, 1995. XI, 604 pages. 1996.

Vol. 1036: G. Adorni, M. Zock (Eds.), Trends in Natural Language Generation - An Artificial Intelligence Perspective. Proceedings, 1993. IX, 382 pages. 1996. (Subseries LNAI).

Vol. 1037: M. Wooldridge, J.P. Müller, M. Tambe (Eds.), Intelligent Agents II. Proceedings, 1995. XVI, 437 pages. 1996. (Subseries LNAI).

Vol. 1038: W: Van de Velde, J.W. Perram (Eds.), Agents Breaking Away. Proceedings, 1996. XIV, 232 pages. 1996. (Subseries LNAI).

Vol. 1039: D. Gollmann (Ed.), Fast Software Encryption. Proceedings, 1996. X, 219 pages. 1996.

Vol. 1040: S. Wermter, E. Riloff, G. Scheler (Eds.), Connectionist, Statistical, and Symbolic Approaches to Learning for Natural Language Processing. IX, 468 pages. 1996. (Subseries LNAI).

Vol. 1041: J. Dongarra, K. Madsen, J. Waśniewski (Eds.), Applied Parallel Computing. Proceedings, 1995. XII, 562 pages. 1996.

Vol. 1042: G. Weiß, S. Sen (Eds.), Adaption and Learning in Multi-Agent Systems. Proceedings, 1995. X, 238 pages. 1996. (Subseries LNAI).

Vol. 1043: F. Moller, G. Birtwistle (Eds.), Logics for Concurrency. XI, 266 pages. 1996.

Vol. 1044: B. Plattner (Ed.), Broadband Communications. Proceedings, 1996. XIV, 359 pages. 1996.

Vol. 1045: B. Butscher, E. Moeller, H. Pusch (Eds.), Interactive Distributed Multimedia Systems and Services. Proceedings, 1996. XI, 333 pages. 1996.

Vol. 1046: C. Puech, R. Reischuk (Eds.), STACS 96. Proceedings, 1996. XII, 690 pages. 1996.

Vol. 1047: E. Hajnicz, Time Structures. IX, 244 pages. 1996. (Subseries LNAI).

Vol. 1048: M. Proietti (Ed.), Logic Program Syynthesis and Transformation. Proceedings, 1995. X, 267 pages. 1996.

Vol. 1049: K. Futatsugi, S. Matsuoka (Eds.), Object Technologies for Advanced Software. Proceedings, 1996. X, 309 pages. 1996.

Vol. 1050: R. Dyckhoff, H. Herre, P. Schroeder-Heister (Eds.), Extensions of Logic Programming. Proceedings, 1996. VII, 318 pages. 1996. (Subseries LNAI).

Vol. 1051: M.-C. Gaudel, J. Woodcock (Eds.), FME'96: Industrial Benefit and Advances in Formal Methods. Proceedings, 1996. XII, 704 pages. 1996.

Vol. 1052: D. Hutchison, H. Christiansen, G. Coulson, A. Danthine (Eds.), Teleservices and Multimedia Communications. Proceedings, 1995. XII, 277 pages. 1996.

Vol. 1053: P. Graf, Term Indexing. XVI, 284 pages. 1996. (Subseries LNAI).

Vol. 1054: A. Ferreira, P. Pardalos (Eds.), Solving Combinatorial Optimization Problems in Parallel. VII, 274 pages. 1996.

Vol. 1055: T. Margaria, B. Steffen (Eds.), Tools and Algorithms for the Construction and Analysis of Systems. Proceedings, 1996. XI, 435 pages. 1996.

Vol. 1056: A. Haddadi, Communication and Cooperation in Agent Systems. XIII, 148 pages. 1996. (Subseries LNAI).

Vol. 1057: P. Apers, M. Bouzeghoub, G. Gardarin (Eds.), Advances in Database Technology — EDBT '96. Proceedings, 1996. XII, 636 pages. 1996.

Vol. 1058: H. R. Nielson (Ed.), Programming Languages and Systems - ESOP '96. Proceedings, 1996. X, 405 pages. 1996.

Vol. 1059: H. Kirchner (Ed.), Trees in Algebra and Programming - CAAP '96. Proceedings, 1996. VIII, 331 pages. 1996.

Vol. 1060: T. Gyimóthy (Ed.), Compiler Construction. Proceedings, 1996. X, 355 pages. 1996.

Vol. 1061: P. Ciancarini, C. Hankin (Eds.), Coordination Languages and Models. Proceedings, 1996. XI, 443 pages. 1996.

Vol. 1062: E. Sanchez, M. Tomassini (Eds.), Towards Evolvable Hardware. IX, 265 pages. 1996.

Vol. 1063: J.-M. Alliot, E. Lutton, E. Ronald, M. Schoenauer, D. Snyers (Eds.), Artificial Evolution. Proceedings, 1995. XIII, 396 pages. 1996.

Vol. 1064: B. Buxton, R. Cipolla (Eds.), Computer Vision – ECCV '96. Volume I. Proceedings, 1996. XXI, 725 pages. 1996.

Vol. 1065: B. Buxton, R. Cipolla (Eds.), Computer Vision – ECCV '96. Volume II. Proceedings, 1996. XXI, 723 pages. 1996.

Vol. 1066: R. Alur, T.A. Henzinger, E.D. Sontag (Eds.), Hybrid Systems III. IX, 618 pages. 1996.

Vol. 1067: H. Liddell, A. Colbrook, B. Hertzberger, P. Sloot (Eds.), High-Performance Computing and Networking. Proceedings, 1996. XXV, 1040 pages. 1996.

Vol. 1068: T. Ito, R.H. Halstead, Jr., C. Queinnec (Eds.), Parallel Symbolic Languages and Systems. Proceedings, 1995. X, 363 pages. 1996.

Vol. 1069: J.W. Perram, J.-P. Müller (Eds.), Distributed Software Agents and Applications. Proceedings, 1994. VIII, 219 pages. 1996. (Subseries LNAI).

Vol. 1070: U. Maurer (Ed.), Advances in Cryptology – EUROCRYPT '96. Proceedings, 1996. XII, 417 pages. 1996.

Vol. 1071: P. Miglioli, U. Moscato, D. Mundici, M. Ornaghi (Eds.), Theorem Proving with Analytic Tableaux and Related Methods. Proceedings, 1996. X, 330 pages. 1996. (Subseries LNAI).

Vol. 1072: R. Kasturi, K. Tombre (Eds.), Graphics Recognition. Proceedings, 1995. X, 308 pages. 1996.

Vol. 1073: J. Cuny, H. Ehrig, G. Engels, G. Rozenberg (Eds.), Graph Grammars and Their Application to Computer Science. Proceedings, 1994. X, 565 pages. 1996.

Vol. 1074: G. Dowek, J. Heering, K. Meinke, B. Möller (Eds.), Higher-Order Algebra, Logic, and Term Rewriting. Proceedings, 1995. VII, 287 pages. 1996.

Vol. 1075: D. Hirschberg, G. Myers (Eds.), Combinatorial Pattern Matching. Proceedings, 1996. VIII, 392 pages. 1996.

Vol. 1076: N. Shadbolt, K. O'Hara, G. Schreiber (Eds.), Advances in Knowledge Acquisition. Proceedings, 1996. XII, 371 pages. 1996. (Subseries LNAI).

Vol. 1077: P. Brusilovsky, P. Kommers, N. Streitz (Eds.), Mulimedia, Hypermedia, and Virtual Reality. Proceedings, 1994. IX, 311 pages. 1996.

Vol. 1078: D.A. Lamb (Ed.), Studies of Software Design. Proceedings, 1993. VI, 188 pages. 1996.

Vol. 1079: Z.W. Raś, M. Michalewicz (Eds.), Foundations of Intelligent Systems. Proceedings, 1996. XI, 664 pages. 1996. (Subseries LNAI).

Vol. 1080: P. Constantopoulos, J. Mylopoulos, Y. Vassiliou (Eds.), Advanced Information Systems Engineering. Proceedings, 1996. XI, 582 pages. 1996.

Vol. 1081: G. McCalla (Ed.), Advances in Artificial Intelligence. Proceedings, 1996. XII, 459 pages. 1996. (Subseries LNAI).

Vol. 1082: N.R. Adam, B.K. Bhargava, M. Halem, Y. Yesha (Eds.), Digital Libraries. Proceedings, 1995. Approx. 310 pages. 1996.

Vol. 1083: K. Sparck Jones, J.R. Galliers, Evaluating Natural Language Processing Systems. XV, 228 pages. 1996. (Subseries LNAI).

Vol. 1084: W.H. Cunningham, S.T. McCormick, M. Queyranne (Eds.), Integer Programming and Combinatorial Optimization. Proceedings, 1996. X, 505 pages. 1996.

Vol. 1085: D.M. Gabbay, H.J. Ohlbach (Eds.), Practical Reasoning. Proceedings, 1996. XV, 721 pages. 1996. (Subseries LNAI).

Vol. 1086: C. Frasson, G. Gauthier, A. Lesgold (Eds.), Intelligent Tutoring Systems. Proceedings, 1996. XVII, 688 pages. 1996.

Vol. 1087: C. Zhang, D. Lukose (Eds.), Distributed Artificial Intelliegence. Proceedings, 1995. VIII, 232 pages. 1996. (Subseries LNAI).

Vol. 1088: A. Strohmeier (Ed.), Reliable Software Technologies – Ada-Europe '96. Proceedings, 1996. XI, 513 pages. 1996.

Vol. 1089: G. Ramalingam, Bounded Incremental Computation. XI, 190 pages. 1996.

Vol. 1090: J.-Y. Cai, C.K. Wong (Eds.), Computing and Combinatorics. Proceedings, 1996. X, 421 pages. 1996.

Vol. 1091: J. Billington, W. Reisig (Eds.), Application and Theory of Petri Nets 1996. Proceedings, 1996. VIII, 549 pages. 1996.

Vol. 1092: H. Kleine Büning (Ed.), Computer Science Logic. Proceedings, 1995. VIII, 487 pages. 1996.

Vol. 1093: L. Dorst, M. van Lambalgen, F. Voorbraak (Eds.), Reasoning with Uncertainty in Robotics. Proceedings, 1995. VIII, 387 pages. 1996. (Subseries LNAI).

Vol. 1094: R. Morrison, J. Kennedy (Eds.), Advances in Databases. Proceedings, 1996. XI, 234 pages. 1996.

Vol. 1095: W. McCune, R. Padmanabhan, Automated Deduction in Equational Logic and Cubic Curves. X, 231 pages. 1996. (Subseries LNAI).

Vol. 1096: T. Schäl, Workflow Management Systems for Process Organisations. XII, 200 pages. 1996.

Vol. 1097: R. Karlsson, A. Lingas (Eds.), Algorithm Theory – SWAT '96. Proceedings, 1996. IX, 453 pages. 1996.

Vol. 1098: P. Cointe (Ed.), ECOOP '96 – Object-Oriented Programming. Proceedings, 1996. XI, 502 pages. 1996.

Vol. 1099: F. Meyer auf der Heide, B. Monien (Eds.), Automata, Languages and Programming. Proceedings, 1996. XII, 681 pages. 1996.

Vol. 1101: M. Wirsing, M. Nivat (Eds.), Algebraic Methodology and Software Technology. Proceedings, 1996. XII, 641 pages. 1996.

Vol. 1102: R. Alur, T.A. Henzinger (Eds.), Computer Aided Verification. Proceedings, 1996. XII, 472 pages. 1996.

Vol. 1103: H. Ganzinger (Ed.), Rewriting Techniques and Applications. Proceedings, 1996. XI, 437 pages. 1996.

Vol. 1104: M.A. McRobbie, J.K. Slaney (Eds.), Automated Deduction – CADE-13. Proceedings, 1996. XV, 764 pages. 1996. (Subseries LNAI).

Vol. 1105: T.I. Ören, G.J. Klir (Eds.), Computer Aided Systems Theory – CAST '94. Proceedings, 1994. IX, 439 pages. 1996.

Vol. 1106: M. Jampel, E. Freuder, M. Maher (Eds.), Over-Constrained Systems. X, 309 pages. 1996.

Vol. 1107: J.-P. Briot, J.-M. Geib, A. Yonezawa (Eds.), Object-Based Parallel and Distributed Computation. Proceedings, 1995. X, 349 pages. 1996.

Vol. 1108: A. Díaz de Ilarraza Sánchez, I. Fernández de Castro (Eds.), Computer Aided Learning and Instruction. Proceedings, 1996. XIV, 480. 1996.

Vol. 1109: N. Koblitz (Ed.), Advances in Cryptology – Crypto '96. Proceedings, 1996. XII, 417 pages. 1996.

Vol. 1112: C. von der Malsburg, W. von Seelen, J.C. Vorbrüggen, B. Sendhoff (Eds.), Artificial Neural Networks – ICANN 96. Proceedings, 1996. XXV, 922 pages. 1996.